CULTURE AND ANOMIE

CHRISTOPHER HERBERT

CULTURE AND ANOMIE

ETHNOGRAPHIC IMAGINATION

IN THE NINETEENTH CENTURY

THE UNIVERSITY OF CHICAGO PRESS
Chicago & London

CHRISTOPHER HERBERT is professor of English at Northwestern University. He is the author of *Trollope and Comic Pleasure*, published by the University of Chicago Press.

The University of Chicago Press, Chicago 60637
The University of Chicago Press, Ltd., London
© 1991 by The University of Chicago
All rights reserved. Published 1991
Printed in the United States of America
00 99 98 97 96 95 94 93 92 91 5 4 3 2 1

ISBN 0-226-32738-8 (cl.)
ISBN 0-226-32739-6 (pbk.)

Library of Congress Cataloging-in-Publication Data
Herbert, Christopher, 1941–
    Culture and anomie : ethnographic imagination in the nineteenth
century / Christopher Herbert.
        p. cm.
    Includes bibliographical references and index.
    1. Culture.   2. Ethnology—History.   I. Title.
GN357.H47   1991
306—dc20   91-4366

For Bernadette, Sophie, and Stéphane: my tribe

CONTENTS

CONTENTS

ACKNOWLEDGMENTS

B efore having any idea of the shape this book would eventually take, I began research for it during a quarter's leave from Northwestern University in 1985; the manuscript came finally to completion during a leave in the academic year 1989–90, for which I have to thank the generosity of Dean Lawrence B. Dumas of Northwestern's College of Arts and Sciences. At every step of my work in these years, I have relied on the extraordinary resources of the Northwestern University Library. I am fortunate indeed to be employed by a university which has supported my scholarly activity in many ways, not least by providing me with a vigorous intellectual community within which to work. In between the two leaves aforementioned, I was the grateful beneficiary of an American Council of Learned Societies senior fellowship in 1987–88, without which my project might never have gotten effectively under way.

The investigations which led to this book carried me inexorably ever further from areas in which I felt relatively secure of my expertise and altered the bearings of my intellectual compass more than I could possibly have foreseen. As a result, I have depended even more than usual on help and moral support from willing friends and colleagues; it is a pleasure to name some of these people here.

My wife, Bernadette Fort, has always been ready to set aside her own work to read my lengthy chapters when they needed it, and her comments have been unfailingly valuable to me. In matters of scholarly argumentation as in other professional and domestic areas, I have come to trust her judgment implicitly. Steve Greenblatt and Michael Warner read some early versions of an introductory chapter, and each administered the judicious mix of learned critique, encouragement, and friendship that was just what I needed at that unsteady moment. My thanks to them both, and to another helpful reader of early material, Martin Mueller. Chapter 2 was very forgivingly read by two colleagues with specialists' knowledge of the literature of political economy, Bill Heyck and Cormac O'Grada. Both were more generous to my venture into this field than it deserved, but I shall never hold this critical laxness on their part against them. Sarah Maza read a revised chapter at a moment's notice almost as it was ready to go to press (and she almost boarding a plane for France) and did what she could to assuage last-minute authorial anxiety. Special thanks, finally, are due to the two readers of this manuscript for the University of Chicago Press, James R. Kincaid and George W. Stocking, Jr. As my lucky star would have it, my professional path has crossed Professor Kincaid's at more than one important juncture, always to my great advantage. His thoughtful comments have greatly assisted and stimulated me in the process of final revisions. It will be apparent to any reader how indebted I am to Professor Stocking's distinguished scholarship on various areas of the history of anthropology. It will be apparent to him, I hope, how indebted I am to his astringent but generous and constructive comments on my manuscript, which forced me to think through some fundamental methodological issues more rigorously than I had seen the need for. My book has been greatly improved by the contributions of all these readers; it is more than a legalistic formula to say at the same time that whatever errors of fact or failures of interpretive intelligence that remain are the author's exclusive property.

INTRODUCTION

SUPERSTITIONS
OF CULTURE

I attempt in this book to reconstruct several significant epi-sodes in the emergence of the "anthropological" idea of cul-ture in the nineteenth century. Besides the hope of rendering the record of modern intellectual history more lucid at various points, my aim in undertaking this project has been to make visible certain aspects of our own exploitation of the culture idea which usually go unrecognized, for reasons both of rhetorical expediency and of histor-ical amnesia. Accordingly, by strongly keying my reading of nine-teenth-century texts to twentieth-century points of reference, I risk being charged with anachronism or with arguing in a circle. Recon-struction of this kind can seem like a deconstruction and can take a toll of potentially severe embarrassment if the idea on which it centers has come to occupy in our minds, as the culture idea has, the status of a manifest truth unsullied by historical contingency, a principle which we can call to our aid in exposition or debate without needing to worry (for instance) about its provenance or its logical wholeness. Its originators may not turn out on close examination to be the ancestors we would have chosen for ourselves, and its explanatory power (to the extent that this is genuine to begin with) may turn out to have affini-ties with other modes of power which we would prefer to disavow. Yet the culture concept was produced for reasons which have left their imprint permanently upon it, and it is worth risking a price of embar-rassment to restore them to view, if only in hopes of becoming some-what less befuddled by our own vocabulary—or at least of opening the way to possibly more productive befuddlement of other kinds.

The belief that human life consists of the multifarious phenom-ena of a condition or a set of conditioning factors or processes called "culture" holds in fact a peculiarly ambiguous status in the discourse of our century. That it has become a ruling principle of thought, both within the specialized research discipline built upon it, that of anthro-pology,[1] and throughout a far wider field as well, needs no demonstra-tion. In various areas of current debate that are grounded in the principle that our categories of thought are, as the phrase goes, "cul-

1

turally constructed," it is called upon to exert ever more leverage.[2] Yet its implications are hard to formulate in coherent terms, and thoughtful specialists often complain that "the term culture has never been satisfactorily or fully defined" (Lemert 60). As Kroeber and Kluckhohn's anthology of quotations reveals, anthropological literature yields scores of rival definitions of its essential concept. One consequence of this very remarkable state of affairs is that the idea of culture can be cited to opposite purposes. In certain politically driven discourses built around it, feminist ones for instance, one describes structures of allegedly inequitable distribution of social resources as "culturally constructed" in order to deprive such structures of any natural, permanent, necessary, or transcendent character, and to proclaim their openness to immediate intervention aimed at reconstructing them on radically different principles. The "cultural" and the inauthentic prove in these discourses to be congruent categories throughout most human history. Yet such usage, a fairly recent growth, inverts a long tradition in which "culture" is understood to figure precisely as an overriding principle of authenticity which one invokes to protest against interference by powerful outsiders in other peoples' established social practices. Opposed to both of these rhetorically loaded usages is the supposedly value-neutral one of social science, in which "culture" refers simply to a mode of correlation among social phenomena. These ambiguities are signs that one draws upon the rhetorical potency of the concept of "culture" only at the risk of becoming snarled in problems of definition.

Consider, for example, recent contributions by Richard Rorty and Barbara Herrnstein Smith to the debate on "cultural relativism"—a debate still marked by the sense of urgency which has surrounded it at least since Ruth Benedict courted scandal by giving polemical form to this principle in *Patterns of Culture* (1934). In his essay "Solidarity or Objectivity?" Rorty, declaring that the objectivist account of truth "simply isn't working any more," addresses this predicament (which he suggests may itself ultimately be a response to the crisis caused by ethnographic awareness of primitive societies) by boldly proposing that we embrace "ethnocentrism," though one fully aware at every step of its own notorious philosophical circularities and ethical limitations, as a principle of mental operations (Rorty 4, 12, 15). This proposal does not amount to a theory of truth, and specifically not, as it might seem, a "relativistic" one, Rorty insists; it is merely a "pragmatic" expedient. Still, the crux of the essay lies in its move to escape the relativistic dilemma provoked in large measure by the ascendancy of the culture thesis in modern thought by installing culture itself, in however equivocal and philosophically hedged a form, as a ground of value. Rorty's obviously problematic maneuver is sharply criticized by Smith, a committed relativist, in *Contingencies of Value*. Her claim in effect is that by taking a more radical position one can deliver oneself from the philosophical discomfort which imprints itself so clearly upon Rorty's attempt to reconcile us, despite his own misgivings, to a creed of "ethnocentrism." Smith assigns the idea of culture a determining role in her own argument, yet she too invokes it in ambivalent terms. In order to refute the notion of inherent value, she offers a long hypothetical account of "the cultural re-production of value"—a process described by her in uncomplicated functionalist terms involving more logical difficulty than she allows for[3]—and she sets forth as a basic proposition that we ourselves are "formed" by "culture and cultural institutions" (B. H. Smith 47, 50–51). Yet the burden of her critique of Rorty is an attack on the supposition that any culture, or at least ours, is in reality coherent or permanent enough to sustain any ethnocentric positing of it as a ground of value. We and our culture, she declares, are essentially and inescapably "scrappy" (incoherent, prone to contention), and Rorty's evasion of relativism by appeal to an assumed cultural unity therefore cannot stand. Having so emphatically introduced the notion of a "culture" which performs "functions" and perpetuates norms of value, she then in effect denies that such an entity has any existence after all. This exchange can stand unresolved as an illustration of the extreme instability of the term "culture," upon which disputants commonly stake so much theoretical capital and which just as commonly involves them in logical difficulty.

It has seemed to me that unriddling this state of affairs even partially, and even if unriddling brings new riddles forward, would contribute to preserving modern speculations from the futility which too often seems built into them. Where does the culture thesis get its great influence upon our minds, why does it resist coherent definition, and why does it lead its partisans into self-contradiction?

One way to begin answering these questions is to sharpen our understanding of the culture idea as a historical artifact, hence a provisional thing loaded willy nilly with (among other things) ideological baggage and unconscious associations peculiar to particular sets of historical circumstances, rather than as a timeless truth.[4] To see this idea as one which was embroiled at its inception in the whole dense matrix of nineteenth-century experience—political, religious, erotic, artistic, philosophical—is to perceive it as having been as much a vehicle for preexisting passions, anxieties, and (sometimes sharply contradictory) habits of thought as it was a discovery. In any event, and this is the guiding principle of my book, no one discovered it. No missionary, colonial official, or ethnographer visiting a tribal community looked about one day and suddenly perceived the presence of "culture." Nor could any such event possibly have occurred, according to the theoretician of scientific knowledge Thomas S. Kuhn. "Discovering a new sort of phenomenon is necessarily a complex event," he declares. If observation of facts and the observer's presuppositions are interconnected, as they necessarily are, "then discovery is a process and must take time" (Kuhn 55). In his important book *Genesis and Development of a Scientific Fact*, Kuhn's precursor Ludwik Fleck had strikingly illustrated this principle with reference to the "discovery" of syphilis. "It was not so-called empirical observations that led to the construction and fixation of the idea [of syphilis]," he insists. "Instead, special factors of deep psychological and traditional significance greatly contributed to it" (Fleck 3). Important scientific research consists in a reorganization of sensibility which, causing empirical observation to occur, fixes itself in structures of emotionally charged symbolic imagery. I want to argue that the construction of the idea which itself undergirds all Fleck's arguments, the anthropological idea of culture—culture, representable as another kind of virulent infectious disease spread by its "carriers," as they are called—was just such a laborious and epistemologically problematic process as the one he evokes, involving just such factors.

No sign of this process is allowed to transpire on the surface of what is taken to be the official promulgation of the culture idea, the opening sentence of E. B. Tylor's *Primitive Culture* (1871). "Culture or Civilization, taken in its wide ethnographic sense," says Tylor, "is that complex whole which includes knowledge, belief, art, morals, law, custom, and any other capabilities and habits acquired by man as a member of society." The crux of this definition, the locus both of its radical modernity and (if this is not redundant) of its inescapable instability, lies in the phrase "complex whole," which at first glance seems precisely to banish all instability. That a people is to be defined at least in part (setting aside the racial component that Franz Boas effectively expelled from responsible anthropology in 1911) by its beliefs, morals, customs, and so forth is a commonplace; what gives it ethnographic significance—what enables it to generate a method of research, a set of directed assumptions, problems, and procedures—is the presumption that this array of disparate-seeming elements of social life composes a significant *whole*, each factor of which is in some sense a corollary of, consubstantial with, implied by, immanent in, all the others. Culture as such is not, therefore, a society's beliefs, customs, moral values, and so forth, added together: it is the wholeness that their coexistence somehow creates or makes manifest. The unifying principle of culture may be expressed in "functional," logical, semiological, or psychological terms, but under these various aspects the assumption of cultural wholeness has been taken for granted almost uniformly across a broad spectrum of anthropological and sociological theory.[5] For theorists of all persuasions, a cultural formation takes its meaning from its involvement in what Darwin, speaking not of culture but of nature, called an "inextricable web of affinities" (Darwin 415), and it is this presumption that renders the various elements of a way of life systematically *readable* just as the notion of organic unity in literary texts rendered them readable according to the norms of the discipline of "new criticism." The importance of Marcel Mauss's work, according to Lévi-Strauss, is thus that it is here for the first time that "the social . . . becomes a system, among whose parts connections, equivalences and interdependent aspects can be discovered" (*Introduction* 38). In studying cultures, said Mauss, stressing the axiom on which all else depends, "we are concerned with 'wholes,' with systems in their entirety" (*The Gift* 77). To speak of "culture" nowadays in any other sense is, I take it, to use the term in an attenuated and finally insidious way, perhaps as a mere rhetorical intensifier masquerading as a scientific category. Speculation on culture has emphasized the point by focusing specifically on the philosophical concept of the whole, which is to say, the proposition that a whole is not the sum of its parts but "a new entity" (Benedict 42; see also Durkheim, *Rules* 39).

Yet the paradigm which Lévi-Strauss identifies with Mauss is not a self-evident truth but a potentially contestable hypothesis. A determined agnostic could insist on seeing each human society as a bundle of more or less haphazardly coexisting institutions not logically derivable one from another, as indeed Smith's thesis of "scrappiness," which echoes Robert H. Lowie's notorious designation of culture as a mass of "shreds and patches" (*Primitive Society* 441), tends to do. Lowie echoes in turn, consciously or unconsciously, a notable passage from Mill's essay on Bentham (1840), a text rich in implications for the emergent doctrine of culture. British law before Bentham was in fact a mere "thing of shreds and patches," says Mill, a "jumble" of disconnected elements to which legal theorists, driven by vested interests and deploying fantastical methods of exegesis, had given a wholly specious air of "systematic form" (*Bentham* 78). Not to be guilty of this kind of wilful pseudointerpretation, ethnographers could just as well presume the interrelations of the social characteristics of a given people to be metonymic—metonymy being the figure of "chance" collocation, as Paul de Man says—rather than metaphoric, which is to say, governed by "necessity" (de Man 14). But such an approach, if rigorously held to (as Lowie himself did not do), would have one undesirable outcome: it would condemn the science of human society to an intellectually sterile activity of endlessly cataloguing data unable ever to cohere in a meaningful way. We would need, for example, to take Foucault's claim to be able to divine "the fundamental codes of a culture—those governing its language, its schemas of perception, its exchanges, its techniques, its values, the hierarchy of its practices" (*Order* xx) as hopelessly delusive, pre-Benthamite legal metaphysics in a new guise. This in fact is precisely Ruth Benedict's argument in favor of the culture concept: to deny the factor of cultural wholeness, she says, would be "to renounce the possibility of intelligent interpretation" (Benedict 43) and to bring about, in Durkheim's words, "the death of analysis" (Durkheim, *Elementary Forms* 172). The menace that the various elements of a people's way of life might *not* be so constituted as to sustain the activity of interpretation is brusquely set aside by a writer like Benedict, not on reasoned grounds but as an affront to intelligence. Does "culture" embody purely and simply the imperious will to interpretation? We need not put the case quite so baldly, perhaps, to make the point that the most convincing verification of the culture theory has always come in the form of especially brilliant ethnographic performances, and that the production of virtuoso technical discourse full of effects of subtlety, complexity, and elegance is the sole way of demonstrating that the theory has succeeded in its cardinal goal of setting aside the danger of a stoppage of "intelligent interpretation."

To describe anthropological discourse in this way, stressing its circularity and its overriding need for stylistic felicity, is neither to discredit it nor to distinguish it at last from any other system of interpretive discourse; it is simply to highlight the often-dissimulated rhetorical urgency of such writing, and to locate its origin in the problematics of the theory of the complex whole. We should illustrate the argument at this point with reference to a particular ethnographic text. One might single out for this purpose Clifford Geertz's essay "Person, Time, and Conduct in Bali," which claims to demonstrate the logical congruence of these three seemingly diverse sectors of Balinese experience, and, if rhetorical brilliance and interpretive ingenuity are capable of producing such a demonstration, surely does so. Or one might adduce Pierre Clastres's study of "the basic dimensions of [Guayaki Indian] culture," which distinguishes in one Guayaki institutional pattern after another the same symbolic imagery and the "same relational structure," giving to Guayaki social life an aspect of rigorous logical symmetry: "game is to the hunter what the wife is to the husband" (Clastres 114, 116, 120). Here is "intelligent interpretation" at its subtlest. But since I began by mentioning Ruth Benedict, possibly the most influential of all writers in crystallizing the discourse of culture, let us look briefly at her classic account of the Zuñi in *Patterns of Culture* [*PC*].

Public ceremony, religious organization, systems of sexual and marital relations, dance style, initiation practices, personal sensibility: all these aspects of Zuñi life and others besides are shown by Benedict to correspond to one another and to a single ruling principle, "the love of moderation to which [Zuñi] civilization is committed" (*PC* 87). Interpretation based on such a premise consists in representing the combination of various elements as nothing less than a syllogistic structure in which cultural formations are in effect logically entailed by one another. "Just as according to the Zuñi ideal a man sinks his activities in those of the group and claims no personal authority, so also he is never violent" is a typical formulation (*PC* 97). The richness of the ethnographic materials which Benedict unifies in this way makes her study deeply impressive as a demonstration of the reality of "culture." The seamless unity of the discourse—its elegant logical operations, its sustained and finely modulated prose style—vouches for the unity of the integrated cultural "configuration" it claims to represent. Yet this formidable text proves on reflection to be rife with methodological difficulties and to make the idea of culture seem ever more like a conundrum and a rhetorical pretext the more closely we examine it, ever less like a secured principle of analysis.

I pass over possible objections, though these are by no means beside the point here, that Benedict artfully manipulates or even distorts evidence to suit her thesis about the Zuñi.[6] A more telling issue for our purposes is that of how she ascribes to various Zuñi practices the particular values which, treating them as empirically observable facts, she then declares to be mutually consistent and consistent with the overarching interpretive principle of "moderation." According to the theory of culture which she champions, values are ascertainable only as functions of the wholes within which they come into being. This principle is the essence of "cultural relativism," which Benedict is famous for professing and which Dan Sperber calls "the most general and the most generally accepted theory in anthropology" (Sperber 8). Yet it can hardly be rigorously applied, for if it were, it would seem to rule out all possibility of valid ethnographic discovery and analysis. If, that is, a "culture" truly generates its own (even partially) closed system of significance, an outside observer can *never know—or at least never be sure of knowing—what anything means to a man or woman native to the society under study.* In other words, research based on the doctrine of culture both requires and prohibits the relativistic corollary, a key self-contradiction which has been noted by a series of writers.[7]

How then are we able to determine, say, that Zuñi fertility rites are properly to be classed as "unemotional" (*PC* 113), hence a sign of Zuñi moderateness, or that various Zuñi practices spring from an abhorrence of "individualism"? Nothing entitles us, once we adopt even a weak version of the culture doctrine, to presume that the behavioral cues which we deploy as signifiers of "emotion" bear the same relation to moral concepts of self-restraint and self-release for the Zuñi that they do for us; nor can we presume that "individualism" is a relevant or even an intelligible concept for inhabitants of another culture which in all probability does not even possess words to express such a concept. In order not to be paralyzed by these and analogous questions, cultural analysis has no option except to proceed by means of what by its own axioms it ought not to allow, a process of comparison with some point of reference external to the "culture" under study. Benedict's argument is in fact systematically comparative in form, though she masks the imposition of her own categories and standards of measurement upon her subjects by setting the "Apollonian" Zuñi off for purposes of analysis against the norms of what she construes as the exact antitype of Zuñi culture, that of the "Dionysian" plains Indians. Her exposition reveals its deep scheme of logic by hinging throughout on *negative* findings. "In the pueblos [as opposed to plains societies] . . . there is no courting of excess in any form, . . . no indulgence in the exercise of authority, or delight in any situation in which the individual stands alone" (*PC* 112). In such formulas, devoid as they are of positive descriptive content, all is absence, inversion, and difference: a tactic of interpretation that makes clear above all else the interpreter's difficulty in defining in unequivocal terms the object of her study. The powerful flow of the discourse cannot be missed; but the Zuñi themselves, negative mirrorings of a set of foreign images, an absence of this quality or that, seem ever more insubstantial and indeterminate. Pueblo culture seems to melt into an analytical mirage directly as the result of striving to intellectualize it. Benedict tries by what seems to be an almost unconscious reflex to overcome this difficulty and to give her analysis a positive and not just a negative character by speaking of Zuñi cultural trends as though they embodied a motivated, deliberate program of opposition to antithetical trends—an implication which she tries to make plausible by repeatedly stressing the physical proximity of the Zuñi to their wild plains neighbors. But even as she does so she disavows her own maneuver with evident embarrassment. In describing cultural processes, she says defensively, "we inevitably use animistic forms of expression" which suggest that a culture is endowed with "choice and purpose," but the truth is that this impression is due merely "to the difficulty in our language forms" (*PC* 43) and has no objective basis. The Zuñi do not really organize their lives as they do out of opposition to individualism and excess: putting it this way is merely a figure of speech, an artifact of the analytical method. No concrete link exists between the "Apollonian" and "Dionysian" culture-modes. But if this is so, no empirical information whatever would seem to be conveyed by the statement that a culture does *not* display this or that potential feature.

Given that Benedict's chosen point of reference is by necessity an essentially arbitrary one, it need hardly be added that a very different set of descriptive terms from the ones she employs would emerge if we compared the Zuñi to, say, Trappist monks or university professors rather than Apaches. A society that indulges in ritual drug use, glorifies the scalping of enemies, and routinely tortures individuals who disturb their neighbors by possessing excessively strong personalities would by these other standards scarcely seem to represent the principles of all-pervading moderation and "mildness" (*PC* 97) which Benedict attributes to the Zuñi. These principles, again, are highly problematical artifacts of comparative analysis, in other words, not substantive properties of Zuñi existence. Nor, finally, are Benedict's pseudosyllogistic equations of culture traits with one another at all self-evident. A society devoted to suppressing "excess" might just as plausibly, or even more plausibly, take on an authoritarian rather than an antiauthoritarian cast, for instance; nor is there a logical necessity correlating anti-individualism with revulsion from violence. One concludes that Benedict's assertion that Zuñi "culture" comprises a logically or stylistically unified whole remains, for all the imaginative power and rhetorical felicity which her interpretation displays, an unproved assertion open to doubt at every point. Nor is it easy to see how *any such assertion* could ever rise above the plane of mere impressionism, or, by the same token, how the hypothesis of "culture" could ever defend itself by reference to empirical evidence against the charge that it is nothing at bottom but a methodological prejudice.

The difficulties of Benedict's text are those of the culture theory itself, and we can see now that they stem directly from the need to think of culture (in the sense of complex whole) as the composite of *relationships* existing among the phenomena of a given society. Values are the essential subject matter of cultural analysis, and values are by definition functions of economic interrelations. The "formality" of Zuñi fertility ritual (*PC* 113) is thus brought into significance, for example, by virtue of its contrastive relation to the "casual" (*PC* 68) character of Zuñi marriage. Such relationships enable one in principle to determine the values attached to various elements of their life by Zuñi themselves, and taken all together they are what constitute the supreme characteristic of a culture, its "complex wholeness." No amount of individual particles of observed data will suffice to represent a "culture" until one has a theory of their systematic interrelations. (A given institution such as "cannibalism," "totemism," or "suicide" may carry radically different values in different cultural environments.) This principle may appear self-evident, but it creates a galling dilemma for a rigorously empirical science of the kind that classical anthropology and sociology aspired to be, a science of "concrete, observable facts" (Radcliffe-Brown 2), for *relationships are not observable phenomena*. In some fashion they inhabit the empty space between observable phenomena, or, putting the problem in temporal rather than spatial terms, can be mentally constructed by the observer only after empirical observation has been done. They lie in the analytical region coextensive, according to Foucault, with modern human sciences: the one "in which visibility no longer plays a role" (*Order* 218: see also 138, 227, 229, etc.). To the extent that this is so, the entity that Tylor names "culture" takes on a distinctly hypothetical or conjectural character and reveals itself to be a thing the existence of which in space and time can never be demonstrated, only posited ahead of time as a device for organizing one's data. It is, this line of reflection again suggests, a fiction that exists to gratify a passion or an institutional demand for certain kinds of interpretive work.[8]

Tylor's innocuous-sounding definition points in this way to the kinds of epistemological issues engaged in more overt terms a couple of generations afterward in Saussurean linguistics, with its dominant hypothesis of a self-referential system "without positive terms," in which all is difference and relativity. Usually obscured in anthropological writing (as it is in Benedict's), this principle is very forcefully stated in E. E. Evans-Pritchard's classic study *The Nuer* (1940). Everything in social experience, declares Evans-Pritchard, consists of "relations, defined in terms of social situations, and relations between these relations" (*Nuer* 266). What flows from such a doctrine is the proposition that the analysis of culture, like that of language, is *devoid of positive terms*. No cultural entities are immune to "structural relativity" (*Nuer* 135). Hence, for example, "a man can be a member of a group and yet not a member of it," there being "always contradiction in the definition of a political group, for it is a group only in relation to other groups" (*Nuer* 137, 147). He does not say so, but since the number of groups definable in a society is infinite, analytical relativity must itself be infinite, and any definite sociological description must in consequence be wholly arbitrary. For Evans-Pritchard, writing well in the aftermath of Saussure, Ernst Mach, and Einstein, the vertiginous indeterminacy to which one is thus almost inescapably led by the logic of the culture concept seems not a fatal disablement to his science but rather the catalyst for developing at long last a sufficiently sophisticated theoretical apparatus for it.[9] One primary consequence of this train of thought, we should note, is Evans-Pritchard's explicit shift of operations from the zone of concrete ethnographic data to "the abstract plane of structural relations," where, he frankly proclaims, "theory" takes precedence over "facts" (*Nuer* 265, 261). For Victorian commentators, any such trend of implications was bound to arouse anxiety, and it by no means passed unnoticed by them. It was very fully probed, for example, by the most advanced anthropological theorist of his day, Herbert Spencer.

In *The Study of Sociology* (1872–73), Spencer declares that this new science is the most difficult of all, since, as he pointedly says, "the phenomena to be generalized are not of a directly-perceptible kind"

(72). He returns to this essential point in *The Principles of Sociology* (1876–96) and makes its import clearer. The lesson preached continually by Spencer is that the true subject matter of social science is not so-called concrete facts considered as entities unto themselves but, rather, "the relations of structures and reciprocities of functions" (*Principles* 1:424). "Among [the] many groups of phenomena [in a society] there is a *consensus*," he affirms; "and the highest achievement in Sociology is so to grasp the vast heterogeneous aggregate, as to see how the character of each group . . . is determined partly by its own antecedents and partly by the past and present actions of the rest upon it" (*Principles* 1:431)—a far more fully developed statement than Tylor's, obviously, of the culture idea. This goal of conceptualizing the "consensus" that unifies a society is rendered almost unattainable, Spencer prophetically argues, for two main reasons. First there is the Heisenberg Uncertainty Principle of sociology, the "difficulty . . . caused by the position occupied [by the observer], in respect to the phenomena to be generalized" (*Study of Sociology* 74): by virtue of being necessarily a product of a particular society and its distinctive mode of thought, the ethnographer will never be able to attain scientific objectivity in analyzing the elements of any society, whether his or her own or some alien one. Second, significant sociocultural phenomena—that is, the webs of interrelations that according to Spencer's, Evans-Pritchard's, and Benedict's foundational principle constitute social life—"cannot be manifest to perception, but can be discerned only by reason" (*Principles* 1:436). Sociology thus is hostage to the same logical predicament that affects all empirical study, Spencer declares. "In no case can the data of a science be stated before some knowledge of the science has been reached": but how can such knowledge be gained before the relevant data have been recognized? (*Principles* 1:424).

The epistemological anxiety implicit in Tylor, occluded in Benedict, and thus spelled out with almost reckless emphasis by Spencer—at heart, the anxiety that the culturalist hypothesis of the complex whole means the necessary engulfing of "facts" by "theory"—furnishes the key, or so one can plausibly infer, to the aggressively positivistic rhetoric that dominates the early period of modern social research, and later periods too. Like other writers on nineteenth-century English thought, Philip Abrams has emphasized the hegemony in this period of a Baconian insistence on "the direct observation of facts" in social inquiry, an insistence that in the case of an organization like the

Statistical Society of London led to rigorous and deliberate exclusion of theoretical speculation about social structure: "pure empiricism," meaning the fetishizing of "facts which can be stated numerically and arranged in tables," was the ideal aimed at in the 1830s and afterward (Abrams 7, 21, 14). In just this spirit, Beatrice Webb praises her mentor Charles Booth for his development of a paradigm of sociological investigation based on "microscopic" study of the "precise details" of actual social life, freed from any historical or developmental hypotheses (Webb, *My Apprenticeship* 234).[10] Spencer himself, for all his incipient skepticism, represents the leading nineteenth-century champion of the belief that a society is collectively "an entity," "a thing," and one governed by the same kinds of fixed laws that govern physical nature (*Principles* 1:435–36). His successor Durkheim echoes him in this (as in much else), insisting strongly on the need to recognize social phenomena as being "things," "facts of nature" (*Rules* 71) able to be directly observed and quantified—notably in the statistical tables extensively relied upon in his classic study of suicide. Like the Victorian statisticians, Durkheim deplores the intrusion of abstract philosophical speculation into objective sociology: "We must abandon generalities and enter into the detailed examination of facts," he militantly proclaims (*Rules* 160). "In order to be objective science must start from sense-perceptions and not from concepts that have been formed independently from it" (*Rules* 81). Tylor, Boas, and Malinowski, among others, all declare in the same tone of militancy this credo that modern social science must found itself unequivocally on what Malinowski calls "solid sociological facts" (*Scientific Theory* 19).

The excessive and, as it may often seem in retrospect, naïvely uncritical character of this positivistic rhetoric lets us guess that its real function was to repress the disturbing awareness that "fact" in the field of sociocultural research has a severely equivocal status, and that the main premise of the whole collective enterprise—the premise that it was founded on "concrete observable facts"—threatened at any moment to unravel before its practitioners' eyes into mere rhetorical procedures like the reliance on "animistic forms of expression." The unravelling occurs with special poignancy in the work of Malinowski, who, having long insisted on the need to base the theory of culture on organic needs and on the production of material resources to meet them, comes at last to acknowledge in effect that in the field of culture all is symbolic relations and that physical things as such have no existence (*Scientific Theory* 138). Even J. S. Mill, while explaining that the branch of "social philosophy" known as "political economy" deals specifically with material wealth, concedes the philosophical unsoundness of this principle, "since, when we are said to produce objects, we only produce utility" (*Principles* 1:57)—that is, a factor definable only in symbolic relations of transposition and exchange within a given social matrix. Such insights are fully consonant with the Tylorean doctrine of culture, which, to repeat the essential point, posits a metaphysical, immaterial substance, complex wholeness, that is *not commensurate with observed data* and can only be perceived (if at all) by a kind of extrasensory perception.

Lévi-Strauss registers this point with great precision in his eulogy of Mauss's discovery of the social as "a system": "for the first time," says Mauss's self-professed disciple, "an effort was made to transcend empirical observation and to reach deeper realities" (*Introduction* 38). The distinction between empirical and transcendent observation is not a speculative subtlety but a point of method bearing directly on modern anthropological work at all levels as it does on every field of inquiry indebted to the concept of culture. For example, it bears directly on the twentieth-century cult of ethnographic fieldwork and of the individual fieldworker's supposed faculty of empathetic intuition. The literature describing this faculty is full of transcendental overtones (see, for example, Lévi-Strauss, *Structural Anthropology* 373–74) and goes plainly to show that the subject matter of these inspired field-researchers is conceived to be not ordinary empirical fact but "deeper realities," relations "which cannot be manifest to perception": that is, something essentially occult. This suggestion is particularly emphasized in anthropological texts whenever the writer attempts to conceive social structures or principles of social cohesion as *agencies,* for the result—a potentially scandalous one for a would-be objective and empirical science—is a persistent invocation of the occult. Such a trend of what Benedict, uncomfortably aware of her own implication in it, calls "mystical phraseology" (*PC* 213), is again witnessed already, in especially vivid forms of imagery, in nineteenth-century texts.

Spencer, for example, very suggestively elaborates the proposition that "another agency" than physical influences is responsible for the cohesion which arises among members of a society. "Not in contact, they nevertheless affect one another through intervening spaces" by virtue of the agency of language, through which "impulses [are] . . . conveyed from part to part" in a society (Spencer, *Principles* 1:447–48). Here the relations which constitute society as a "complex whole" are expressed in imagery of quanta of communicable psychological energy. These "impulses" that magically transmit themselves "through intervening spaces" in the form of linguistic symbolism do not have unrestricted freedom of movement, but are governed by the cultural structures that Spencer, perceiving the unperceivable, claims to be present even among the most primitive savages. "Though one of these rude societies appears structureless," he says, setting the agenda for social theory for many decades afterwards, "yet its ideas and usages form a kind of invisible framework for it, serving rigorously to restrain certain classes of its actions" (*Principles* 2:322). On the next page, this fantastic imagery of invisible forces and frameworks—the figurative expression, I am arguing, of the inherently paradoxical nature of the Tylorean conception of culture—takes still more specific and more surprising form. The process in social evolution by which traditional customs gradually become codified into laws means that life in the present is in fact secretly dictated by past generations, says Spencer: "the political head becomes still more clearly an agent through whom the feelings of the dead control the actions of the living" (*Principles* 2:323). Life in society is in effect—almost in fact—pervaded by vampire-like spirits exercising their power over the living "by transmitting their natures, bodily and mental" (*Principles* 2:514). Such formulas, in which social relations again take the form of imagery of uncanny transmissions, have a provocative symmetry with Spencer's lengthy arguments that religion, and ultimately all of human culture, originates in the superstitious belief that the dead leave behind ghosts who demand propitiation. It has turned out (though Spencer does not make this rapprochement himself, needless to say) that the persecution of the living by predatory spirits is no primitive delusion after all, but a basis of scientific sociology! For Spencer, it is *ghosts* who inhabit the problematic empty spaces between observable phenomena and whose function it is to transmit the impulses that somehow constantly traverse them. We have here a perfect instance of Fleck's paradigm of superstitious "proto-ideas" evolving at length into scientific facts, one closely parallel, indeed, to his own account of how the original demon-theory of disease "haunted the birth of modern concepts of infection and forced itself upon research workers irrespective of all rational considerations" (Fleck 60).

The disjunction that emerges in Spencer's work between the idiom of rigorous scientific investigation and the "mystical phraseology" of uncanny forces is specifically addressed in the third volume of

The Principles of Sociology, where he treats this problem as a central one of the field. His reply to it is that the whole drift of modern scientific thought is to transform a universe of tangible realities (which now, most inconsistently, Spencer declares to be the universe believed in by primitives) into one of occult phenomena. Modern man "has thoughts about existences which he regards as usually intangible, inaudible, invisible; and yet which he regards as operative upon him" (*Principles* 3:159). Thus "each generation of physicists discovers in so-called 'brute matter,' powers which but a few years before, the most instructed physicists would have thought incredible." Thanks to this superstitious-seeming line of discovery in physics, "dead matter" turns out to be "everywhere alive," says Spencer, and a new awareness of occult indwelling forces "gives rather a spiritualistic [he ought to have said animistic] than a materialistic aspect to the Universe" (*Principles* 3:172–73). Sociology's contraband traffic in uncanny impulses and invisible frameworks detectable only "by reason" does not therefore impugn its modern and scientific character, as might be thought. Rather, it confirms it.[11]

Durkheim begins *The Rules of Sociological Method* (1895) with just the same high-risk maneuver, defending the new science of society against the charge of being materialistic by expressly aligning it with spiritualism, since it begins with the postulate that psychological phenomena cannot be derived from organic or material origins (*Rules* 32). The full significance of the equation of modern sociology with spiritualism (the pseudoscience of communicating with the dead) comes out in Durkheim's evocation of the occult influence that presides over his conceptual field as Evolution does over Spencer's, or, more pertinently, as "the common mind" does over J. C. Prichard's: the *conscience collective*. The mysteries of religion, he declares, are the expression of man's sense of being subject to "forces which transcend him and for which he consequently cannot account." These transcendent forces are not imaginary but real: they emanate from what Durkheim defines as a genuinely metaphysical entity, the social collectivity, which is wholly a mass of relations. "By aggregating together, by interpenetrating, by fusing together, individuals give birth to a being, psychical if you will, but one which constitutes a psychical individuality of a new kind," says Durkheim (*Rules* 128, 129). This disembodied collective psychical being surges fantastically into the history of scientific social theory as one more apotheosis of those patterns of relations in society that "cannot be manifest to perception." Durkheim insists, however, that the sociologist "is engaged in scientific work and is not a mystic," even though this work deals with phenomena defined by their "immateriality" and seemingly, as he makes a point of saying, "bereft of intrinsic reality" (*Rules* 159, 162, 120).

The persisting and sharply diverging themes of rhetoric which such examples illustrate tell us that the idea of culture has been in crisis from the moment it began to take distinct shape and that it has embarrassed as much as it has empowered its users. This embarrassed condition has been inescapable for the science which derives from it, based as it is on the study of concrete ethnographic particulars yet postulating a numinous reality (inhabited variously by "structural relations," "invisible frameworks," or collective psyches) that lies beyond perception. More recent theorists have been subject to the same anxiety-laden dilemmas. Benedict herself denounced in her first publication, choosing her term with care, the "superstition" that a culture amounted to "an organism functionally interrelated" (quoted Harris 401). Lévi-Strauss echoes her in warning decades later that anthropology "is too susceptible to those forms of thought which . . . we call superstition" and that it inherits from the founders of the culture concept a variety of "metaphysical phantoms" (*Scope of Anthropology* 7, 10). He tries to exorcise some of them in a 1952 essay, claiming in a convoluted argument to vindicate "the reality and the autonomy of the concept of culture" (*Structural Anthropology* 295) in the face of the awareness that what counts as a culture is determined in practice by the kind of investigations an anthropologist happens to have in mind. The truth is, he says, echoing Evans-Pritchard, that such a term as culture or social structure "has nothing to do with empirical reality but with models which are built up after it" (*Structural Anthropology* 278). In attempting to confront in this drastic way the predicament embedded in Tylor's originating sentence, Lévi-Strauss claims to dispel a host of perennial problems in anthropological theory; but since he does so by ostensibly giving up all purchase on the reality of "things," thus rendering his field of interpretation an hermetically closed artificial system, he risks making the whole enterprise of the study of culture seem narcissistic and arbitrary and producing just that interpretive sterility that the theory of culture was intended to forestall.[12]

Clifford Geertz, specifically protesting against Lévi-Strauss's attempt to create a "closed, abstract, formalistic science of thought," spells out in *The Interpretation of Cultures* [*IC*] an ethnographic definition of culture based on "thick description" of empirical reality and a patient process of "guessing at meanings" of cultural phenomena (*IC* 351, 20). We can instance this book as a final example, a particularly telling one, given its project of mediating with practical good sense the excesses of modern theoretical speculations, of the ineradicable difficulties associated with the theory of culture. Clearly ill at ease about the superstitious ambience which pervades his field, Geertz labors the point that his "semiotic" concept of culture as "webs of significance" involves no flight into a world of "abstracted entities," still less into arcane mysticism or what he calls "dark sciences" (*IC* 5, 17, 30). The study of culture is "a positive science like any other," he thus declares, for although the meanings encrypted in symbols are often enigmatic, "they are, in principle, as capable of being discovered through systematic investigation . . . as the atomic weight of hydrogen or the function of the adrenal glands" (*IC* 362–63). The vulnerable point in this set of claims—which represent a resurgence of the most extreme Victorian positivism—is as always the treacherous point of transition from "the particular, the circumstantial, the concrete" (*IC* 53) to the incommensurate level of "meaning," an ambiguous term which Geertz, though he invokes it continually and in a seemingly technical sense in *The Interpretation of Cultures*, avoids defining in a rigorous way.[13] What *are* meanings, where do they come from, how exactly do they become inscribed upon material objects or social practices? Geertz's evident distress at the difficulty of giving answers to such questions leads him at one point to refer recklessly to "meaning," the term on which his theory of culture and his very impressive work in ethnography depend, as an "elusive and ill-defined pseudoentity" (*IC* 29)—a metaphysical phantom, one might say. Given this designation of culture as a "web" of what turn out to be only pseudoentities, it should come as no surprise when Geertz almost violently contradicts his own unqualified assertion that cultural analysis can be as conclusive as positive science. Ethnographic studies, he cautions in another passage, are not "scientifically" verifiable, "and the attempt to invest them with the authority of physical experimentation is but methodological sleight of hand" (*IC* 23); they are "intrinsically incomplete" and produce "no conclusions to be reported" (*IC* 29). He goes so far as to assert that "the more deeply [cultural analysis] goes the less complete it is" (*IC* 29). One need not take this last declaration as a considered judgment to see how vividly it reflects the crisis-laden character of the mature culture doctrine.[14]

The theoretical difficulties which surface in Geertz are in fact ever more troublesome the more clearly one draws out the implications of the basic principle linking his ethnography to that of Benedict a half century before, and ultimately, I shall argue, to cultural analysis of far earlier date still: the principle of the *symbolic* character of the "complex whole," of the need to define it as residing in no material substance but in a ramified chain of signifiers binding into a single scheme of expression all the disparate features of the life of a society. In a later section of this book we can seek to trace in particular texts the emergence of the principle of the symbolic character of culture. What this process entailed was the increasing displacement of the biological model of physical *function* in the name of the philological and linguistic model according to which, as Foucault says, in a concise definition of the ethnographic culture concept, "man's behaviour appears as an attempt to say something; his slightest gestures . . . have a *meaning*; and everything he arranges around him by way of objects, rites, customs, discourse, all the traces he leaves behind him, constitute a coherent whole and a *system of signs*" (*Order* 357). To analyze this chain or system is first to be obliged to ponder the metaphysics of the fantastic transferences of (unconscious) metaphor, and then to bring to light the disconcerting possibility that all the interlinked signifiers of a given culture *signify nothing but one another*, in an eternal circular or labyrinthine traffic of "meaning" which never attains an authentic signified. (This, or so I guess, is the embedded allegory of Malinowski's attempt in *Argonauts of the Western Pacific* to grasp the cultural metaphysics governing the Trobriand *kula,* a vast circular path of exchange around which a stock of trinkets of no practical utility but charged with intense symbolic and affective values migrates forever, doomed to perpetual displacement.) Anthropologists try to intervene in this inconclusive traffic of metaphors by establishing hierarchies of significance in the cultures they interpret—treating moral values, religious belief, and kinship structures as fundamental, for instance; but these hierarchical arrangements are always subject to the charge of being impositions based on our own conventions of moral order, and of being unverifiable by experience. Having discovered a cryptic correspondence between, on the one hand, the conjoining of symmetry and asymmetry in Caduveo graphic design and, on the other, the tension between "asymmetrical" caste division and "symmetrical" moiety division in Caduveo society, Lévi-Strauss declares that the former "expresses" the latter (*Tristes tropiques* 195–97); but this is an unwarranted conclusion, even if one accepts his highly imaginative claim of a metaphoric relation between the two sets of phenomena. The hierarchy could just as easily be inverted, for social structure is fully as rich in symbolic content as is graphic art. Or each of the two phenomena could "express" some prior, still higher, deeper, or more fundamental—for at this level also, metaphor is both all-determining and indeterminate—principle of Caduveo thought; but how could one ever know when it had been identified? From what other principle might it not derive in turn? As Jacques Derrida says, "from the moment one puts in question the possibility of . . . a transcendental signified and recognizes that every signified is also in the position of a signifier, the distinction between signifier and signified and thus the notion of sign [and *à plus forte raison* of the system of signs called 'culture'] becomes problematic at its root" (quoted Culler 188). Under such conditions, analysis if rigorously pursued is bound to take the form of an infinite regress. Theorists of ethnography seem to have perceived this dilemma—that cultural "fact" is tainted with incurable indeterminacy—from an early date,[15] and to transcribe it in figures of occult relations.

It is apparent that the idea of culture issuing from Tylor's original definition is a wavering, self-contradicting thing, one which it behooves any scholar to approach with utmost caution. Its history since 1871, in any case, reveals strikingly the immense effort that has been required to maintain it by continually repairing or diverting attention from its defects. No wonder that a number of anthropological writers, rather than seeking, like Geertz, to mount necessarily perplexed defenses of the culture idea, have disavowed it, even though a modern anthropologist disbelieving in culture is something like a contradiction in terms. As early as 1920, Lowie, using language which we have seen to be endemic in this field of discourse, called for an end to "superstitious reverence" for the idea of culture as a complex self-integrated whole (*Primitive Society* 441). Having somewhat softened his stand in the intervening years, he pointed out in 1937 some "fairly obvious" grounds for limiting one's assent to this notion, which he identified with Boasian and Malinowskian functionalism in particular. Granted that "many of the cohering elements in the life of a people are not chance concomitants," says Lowie, "it has never been proved that *all* the traits are linked" (*History* 142–43).[16] He makes a point of endorsing the definition of ethnography as "the study of so many integrated wholes, the single cultures," but then, in the name of the ethnological study of culture as a global phenomenon, he broaches an

issue more threatening than he seems to realize for the defining concept of his discipline, and one closely related to the issues raised by
Benedict's analysis of the Zuñi. "In defiance of the dogma that any one
culture forms a closed system, we must insist that such a culture is
invariably an artificial unit segregated for purposes of expediency"
(*History* 235). In other words, what is a whole to begin with, and how
can its existence be shown? Whatever we decide to call a whole is in
fact just a fragment detached more or less arbitrarily from some more
broadly encompassing system of relations. In the same spirit, A. R.
Radcliffe-Brown indicts the notion of culture as a "fantastic reification
of abstractions." "We do not observe a 'culture,'" he says, "since that
word denotes, not any concrete reality, but an abstraction, and as it is
commonly used a vague abstraction" (Radcliffe-Brown 10, 2). Edward
Sapir, cautioning similarly about the danger of making "historical or
psychological actualities out of merely conceptual abstractions"
(quoted Lowie, *History* 160), speaks of the idea of culture as nothing
but a "statistical fiction" (quoted Kroeber and Kluckhohn 247–48).
Outbursts of skepticism such as these underline the main point of this
chapter: that the fundamentally equivocal nature of the doctrine of
culture, which claims to ground itself in minute observed detail yet
moves in a realm of pseudoentities where "no positive terms" are to be
found, but only "a relation in which visibility no longer plays a role"
(Foucault, *Order* 218), and where analysis tends if rigorously pursued
to take the form of infinite regress, is almost its chief characteristic.

■

If the concept of culture, on which so much hinges nowadays, is after
all infested with logical incoherence, the question of its historical
origins takes on particular interest and even urgency. Where did so
problematic, so self-defeating a concept, one vulnerable to so many
"fairly obvious" objections, one which leads in practice to such dubious scientific results—where did such a concept originate, and in obedience to what influences? Boas attributes certain anthropological errors to "the modern insistence of recognizing a structural unity of
concomitant phenomena" (*Mind* 130), and no doubt the culture concept expresses this compulsive habit of modern thought, of which
deconstruction is the equally compulsive inverse form. But it arises
also from more historically and sociologically specific factors, and has
always marked a locus of emotion and of controversy. Marc Augé interprets twentieth-century "culturalism" in this spirit as an emanation

of antistate philosophy and as a vehicle for nostalgic idealizations of "solidary, communal and egalitarian" communities (*Anthropological Circle* 103). Yet the doctrine of culture, in its nineteenth-century context at least, does not allow a narrowly ideological interpretation: its political valences have been highly unstable (like everything else about it). The early history of this doctrine suggests, rather, that ideas once having reached a certain stage of consolidation and having absorbed a certain amount of "cultural" energy no longer may be controllable by their users and may take on a wayward, opportunistic life of their own.

In setting out to examine this early history, I may seem about to recapitulate Raymond Williams's *Culture and Society 1780–1950* [*CS*], which first set forth the problem of the genesis of the idea of culture as a crucial one for modern intellectual history. I can perhaps best explain the method of argument of the present book by a comparison with Williams's, toward which it stands somewhat ambiguously in the double relation of a supplement and a critique.

Two of his axioms I adopt unreservedly: that "it is from the [early nineteenth century] on . . . that the idea of Culture enters decisively into English social thinking" and that the modern sociological sense of the term "depends . . . on the literary tradition" (*CS* 59, 233). According to Williams, the idea of culture appears on the scene as the central element of a long, closely knit English tradition of social criticism directed against the disintegrating and debasing effects of industrialization. Starting with Burke, what writers began calling "culture" was an ideal of harmonious personal and collective perfectibility, "a body of values superior to the ordinary progress of society," "the true standard of excellence for a people" (*CS* 84, 34). Gradually this conception was joined (at an unspecified period and for unspecified reasons) to what Tylor would call culture "in its wide ethnographic sense," the idea of a whole way of life used as the basis of "a general intellectual method" (*CS* 233). As it brings into view and expertly articulates an important train of discourse, Williams's study endows the idea of culture both with seemingly unassailable historical coherence and with all the moral and philosophical prestige of the noble lineage of writers who figure in this treatment as its first enunciators: Burke, Cobbett, Wordsworth, Coleridge, Carlyle, Newman, Ruskin, Arnold, T. S. Eliot, among others. *Culture and Society* makes "culture" into a touchstone of value, almost into a sacred word, and in the process helps us to understand, perhaps, the persistence of its influence in various fields of debate ever after.

None of the philosophical difficulties which appear to be permanently bound up in the modern idea of culture, none of the chronic ambivalence which surrounds it, enter into Williams's redaction of its history. Certainly it would have been hard to reconcile such themes with the rhetorical privilege bestowed upon "culture" in *Culture and Society*. Their exclusion from Williams's argument is manifest in his treatment of the shift from the older sense of "culture" as a superior body of values to the newer, sociological or ethnographic sense. The "emphasis on 'a whole way of life'" which characterizes modern social anthropology, he declares, "is continuous from Coleridge and Carlyle, but what was a personal assertion of value has become a general intellectual method" (*CS* 233). In its imagery of continuity and expansion, which represents the modern culture-concept as the seemingly unproblematic outgrowth and affirmation of a rich literary tradition, this phrase, the blandness of which is a deliberate rhetoric, elides altogether the fact that the old assertion of value and the modern intellectual method are in large measure sharply antagonistic modes, and it elides in the same movement all the incoherence which this shift from one meaning to another implants in our own usage of the equivocal word "culture." In fact, the new idea of culture, an expressly relativistic one, appears in writers like Malinowski and Ruth Benedict, and throughout modern anthropological literature, precisely as an instrument of attack on idealizing and totalizing Victorian moral discourse: far from being smoothly continuous with the notion of asserting a body of national values superior to actually prevailing ones, it stands for the principle that the holistic interpretive study of societies begins with the uncompromising rejection of any a priori "standard of excellence."

In what follows, therefore, I diverge from Williams's version of the story by leaving almost entirely to one side the development of the idealized sense of the word "culture." I concentrate instead on the emergence of a way of thinking which leads more directly to the "general intellectual method" of the modern analysis of cultures, but which in the nineteenth century had not yet undergone its somewhat illogical attachment to the word itself—in fact, had not yet been clearly formulated in propositional terms. I argue that this complex of ideas, along with its immediately attendant difficulties, particularly

INTRODUCTION

those raised by the evacuation or relativizing of moral value implicit in the notion of the complex whole, form a traceable presence in English writing long before Williams or other historians have allowed.[17] The determining of dates of appearance of this or that line of thought is always subordinate in my account, however, to the goal of discovering in relatively early texts signs of what I will call (taking my cue from some of the writers to be studied in this book) the primitive logic of the culture idea itself, a logic often studiously obscured in the rhetoric of sophisticated cultural theorists of a later day. What I seek to define is nothing so coherent and conscious of itself as a tradition, and it is not affiliated with a body of eloquent philosophical discourse, as Williams's version of "culture" is. It appears intermittently, often in marginal or trivial-seeming texts, always in troubled, contradictory relations to its own stated principles: its rhetorical sign is not assured statement, so to say, but inarticulacy and evasiveness. To find out this movement of thinking, if it is there to begin with, will mean departing in some measure from the usual methods of intellectual history, since it requires a historian to deal not with explicit lines of argument but with largely inexplicit ones, with ideas which may shape their texts in significant ways and yet never appear in plain view by coalescing in formal statements. Like an astronomer tracking an invisible planet by studying deflections in the orbits of visible ones, an analyst of nineteenth-century texts often is forced to make out the presence of the culture idea (always a site of disturbance in the intellectual cosmos) through oblique reasoning focused on pieces of anomalous evidence. From the point of view of traditional historical scholarship, such a method of analysis may well seem disreputable and will always be open to the charge of wilful anachronism, of reading modern notions highhandedly into old texts.

I do not make light of such dangers, but the price of shying away from them is resigning ourselves to knowing nothing of the prehistory of ideas, of remaining unaware of their determining incipient phases of development and of their linkage to elements of mental life, elements including irrational unconscious associations, lying deeper than the stratum of articulate intellectual statement. Therefore I take as my point of departure Fleck's proposition that scientific theories have a kind of larval phase in which they exist as "proto-ideas" or "pre-ideas," often of a thoroughly superstitious character, embodied not in logical discourse but in emotionally loaded metaphors. The only way to assess this argument or to apply it to a particular problem of intellectual history is by way of a concerted literary analysis of texts, analysis keyed intensively to the recurrences of constellations of figurative language, and by the same token keenly wary of the falsification of data which occurs whenever one abstracts an idea for purposes of analysis from the expressive form it takes in a given text. This method, the one which I try to employ here, in effect treats all texts as if they were poems. The practical consequences of carrying on intellectual history by insisting in this way upon the indivisibility of literary and scientific or philosophical expression are significant, as we shall see. The premise of such a method is that research must become frankly *interpretive,* must work by unravelling implications, and must be candid in basing its findings on conjectures. Historians schooled in traditional styles of research are bound to find such an approach unsatisfactory. Yet it is able to defend itself energetically against the charge of having a loose, unscientific standard of proof; on the contrary, it claims to study texts with heightened rigor and precision.

The hazards and limitations of the method which I am describing are sufficiently plain. Its tactic of trying to recuperate thought processes of earlier periods by focusing closely on the problems of deciphering individual texts, presuming as it does that these problems are likely to be difficult enough to require a reader's utmost attention, carries with it a relative reticence with regard to such projects as marking out chains of influence among writers and ideas or constructing taxonomies of schools of thought. As I have said, it concedes its dependence on interpretive guesswork and makes only provisional claims of proof. In compensation for its liabilities, however, it offers distinctive potential benefits, of what could be called both positive and negative kinds. On the positive side, it tends to generate provocatively refigured historical narratives and to make possible a sharpened sense of intimate contact with the functioning of an earlier mentality. On the negative, it may help to open up to thoughtful reappraisal the methods by which the history of ideas has usually been conducted and on which its strong claim of factual objectivity has grounded itself.

There is no need, this late in the game, to rehearse the arguments by which recent theory claims to demonstrate the fictionality of historical reconstructions, the necessarily interpretive and conjectural character of even the most innocent-seeming particle of information in a historical text (not to mention its large structures of plot), the way conventions of documentation, mnemonic devices, and calculations of probabilities silently are transmuted into facts for purposes of historiographical rhetoric. There *is* a need to respond to the near-illegibility which now characterizes much of this rhetoric for a growing number of readers. "The specific attraction of evolutionary social theories was that they offered a way of reformulating the essential unity of mankind, while avoiding the current objections to the older theories of a human nature everywhere essentially the same" (Burrow 98): from the disenchanted viewpoint which is the heritage of contemporary trends in theory, such a sentence—a fine example of the kind of analysis which intellectual history is constituted to perform—truly seems to be "a fantastic reification of abstractions" almost preposterously remote from any conceivable particular data.[18] In its overdetermined imagery of influence and causality operating upon wholly abstract entities, this pseudonarrative seems reducible without much loss of content to an allegorical assertion that history (that is, concatenations of real events in the world, not only the literary structures produced by historical writers) is a logical sequence of causes and effects.

The presumption that history is logically coherent and intelligible, and therefore subject to extensive operations of summary and synthesis without serious distortion, is exemplified vividly in Raymond Williams's history of the culture idea. All in his representation is testimony to coherence, logical connection. Each writer studied is shown by means of a few quotations to hold a precisely definable doctrine of culture which then is linked unambiguously in an historical step-by-step chain with each other writer's. If the idea of culture or its evolution presents any intractable difficulties of understanding or documentation, they are wholly subsumed in Williams's confident, masterfully lucid explanatory prose. This prose yields so much understanding and brings into play so rich a body of literary materials that it may be perverse for a reader to feel mounting skepticism precisely in proportion to Williams's success in making sense of the texts he describes. But the whole course of analytic literary studies over the past fifty years or so, from Empson and New Criticism to deconstruction, teaches one to anticipate that significant literary expression is bound to be an affair of paradoxes, dense textures of implication, logical disjunctions and circularities, ambiguities and illegibilities which only the most intensive interpretive labor can suffice to master even partially; and for one used to this anticipation, schematic intellectual history arouses an uncontrollable reflex of disbelief.

If the book which follows is strong, then, in its emphasis on logical and rhetorical incoherences within and among texts and correspondingly weak in its mapping of "influences," it is not only because of the special incoherence that is bound to infect all attempts to exploit the unstable concept of culture, but more generally because I presume that ideas circulate and reproduce themselves within an historical period very diffusely and in a plethora of self-contradicting forms.[19] This is true especially in ideas' early stages, when they appear only in their original chrysalis of metaphor, and especially when they draw upon widely ramified and affectively loaded themes of what Fleck calls the "thought style" of an age. The image of a chain of verified interconnections along which an idea is transmitted makes a striking figure of the intellectual historian's will to explanatory mastery, but perhaps only a dubious one of the real dynamics of thinking. At all events, my predominant goal in the following chapters is to examine how characteristic idea-patterns seem to have condensed themselves into the logic of particular texts, not to construct an exhaustive narrative of transmission or to try to identify definite points of origin. I do not claim exemption from the dilemmas of method which I have laid at the door of traditional histories of ideas. My book, too, creates its data out of a set of presuppositions in order to cite this data in support of the presuppositions; it treats abstractions as if they were real things; it constructs its own imagery of would-be intellectual mastery. Such are the conditions of the game of scholarly enterprise. And I do not propose a radical new paradigm for the practice of the history of ideas, although my arguments in the chapters to come are likely to seem more than unorthodox enough to some readers. I am simply trying to find a way to a style of history of ideas which can remain plausible or at least legible once one has become sensitized to the equivocal status of "so-called empirical observations" and of systems of explanation of all kinds. If it be said that I offer a method unable to provide a rigorous self-justification, I can only reply that the lesson of much contemporary theory is that this state of theoretical disablement has become our inescapable one for the time being, and that we had better get used to it.

What I have said implies a certain effect of arbitrariness in my choice of texts for study and a certain disjunctiveness from one chapter to another. Yet my book has an organizational rationale which I had best spell out briefly. Most importantly, despite situating its themes in modern thought by making frequent reference to anthropological literature, what follows is *not* a history of the discipline of nineteenth-century anthropology, most of which, as Burrow rightly says, is preoccupied with the theory of evolutionary social development and thus has only marginal relevance to the development of the ethnographic concept of cultural wholeness. Therefore I give only incidental treatment to writers such as Tylor, McLennan, Spencer, Robertson Smith, or Frazer, all of whom have frequently been surveyed, in any case, by historians of anthropological thought.[20] The bulk of my examples comes from British writing, in the hope of capturing in this way something of the common sensibility running through them and substantially inflecting, if I am right, the notion of culture which they develop. Were I attempting a full genealogical history of the culture concept, attention would need to be given to such precursory figures from other nations as Montesquieu, Vico, Herder, and Comte (not to mention Herodotus, Ibn Khaldun, and many others); this, again, is a ground which has been well surveyed in scholarly literature, and which I have felt justified, if only for this reason, in bypassing here.

Chapter 1 presents the broad thesis of this book: that a fixation on the dangerous power and potentially boundless scope of human desire was fundamental to the construction of distinctive nineteenth-century metaphors of social organization. Chapter 2 traces these metaphors in selected texts of political economy, a field given priority in my account both for its precociousness in developing central themes of culturalist thinking (and for very deeply exploring the dilemmas which go along with those themes) and because its importance in serving as a catalyst for the development of modern sociocultural imagination has been widely neglected, for what seem to me finally to be reasons of ideological prejudice. Chapter 3 investigates a body of early-nineteenth-century missionary ethnography, to show some of the historic origins of what appears to be the essential link between the culture theory and the doctrine of risky personal observation. Chapter 4 extends this theme by studying Henry Mayhew's *London Labour and the London Poor* as the preeminent nineteenth-century instance of full-scale ethnographic research on the modern model—and as a sustained encounter with the almost insuperable contradictions which this model entails. Chapter 5 centers on a single novel of Anthony Trollope as a way of articulating the conflict between broadly diffused norms of Victorian sensibility and the new trend of culturalist thinking. In a brief concluding chapter, I sum up my results and comment on some of the methodological issues which the inquiry has raised.

CHAPTER ONE
_____

FROM ORIGINAL SIN
TO ANOMIE

T he holistic or ethnographic idea of culture takes ever clearer shape in nineteenth-century writing, and then decisively in Durkheim, as a theory of the dominance of the symbolic in human experience (a process to be traced more fully in a subsequent chapter). Yet the culture idea is never a unitary thing but always a protean one encompassing several interwound elements: the proposition that the customs and values of a society form a totality, "an inextricable web of affinities"; the postulate of cultural relativism; the notion of an occult or unconscious force exerted by the collectivity past and present upon individuals. Each of these constituent principles, to which still others cohere, gives rise to varying interpretations. Consequently the modern culture idea—if it can properly be named in the singular at all—has no more a determinable origin than it has a single moment of emergence, but coalesces, rather, at various points and in significantly different versions along numerous lines of thought. Yet the coalescence is decisively conditioned—such at least is the argument of this book—by one powerful and, in nineteenth-century Britain, seemingly almost ubiquitous influence: the myth of a state of ungoverned human desire. The doctrine of culture can be said to take form as a scientific rebuttal of this myth, but it has never succeeded in dispelling it, for it is invoked in various extreme forms in theoretical and polemical writing, and in colloquial parlance as well, to this day. Indeed, despite their antagonistic logical relationship, one can think of the ideas of culture and of free desire as two reciprocal, complementary elements of a single pattern of discourse, albeit a conflict-laden and necessarily unstable one. Trying to decipher this pattern seems a promising strategy for uncovering the forces of emotion that have endowed the "superstition" of culture with the status of a scientific axiom and that have obscured, as an essential part of this operation, their own role in it.

This analysis is sure to be a problematic one, given the way that the culture concept reacts back upon any attempt to interpret its history. What we may construe as logical discordances between ideas and conquests of the weaker by the stronger prove from the viewpoint of cultural analysis to be refigurings of constant themes in which rules of formal reasoning count for little. The attempt to explain on such a basis how intellectual models of human society change will be as hard as it is for Kuhn to explain how shifts of paradigms can occur in physical science or for Foucault to address the problem of the displacement of one period *episteme* by another. Nietzsche frames the terms of this now widely felt predicament in his essay "On Truth and Falsity in Their Ultramoral Sense." Our every word and concept is purely metaphorical, he declares, and "what passes for truth in every age" is nothing in reality but a "mobile army of metaphors, metonyms, and anthropomorphisms: in short a sum of human relations which become poetically and rhetorically intensified, metamorphosed, adorned, and after long usage seem to a nation fixed, canonic and binding" ("Truth and Falsity" 180). In order to account for intellectual history on this premise, one must suppose that metaphors have a powerful inward dynamic of their own. Trying to glimpse this dynamic is the theme of the present chapter.

Victorian Ambivalence

The desire-world invented and inhabited by the Victorians and immediately preceding generations encompassed sharply contradictory trends.

On the one hand, Victorian middle-class sensibility until at least 1870 or so defined itself largely through its fixation on the dangers of desire and through its at least nominal adherence to a code of "earnestness" and self-denial. Scarcely any man or woman could have failed to be aware that these were the official norms of the society of the day. The immediate origins of this trend lie in the great Evangelical revival of the late eighteenth century, and more particularly in the teaching of the founders of the Methodist movement, John Wesley and George Whitefield. My argument in what follows may be surprising for how far it seeks to spin out the ramifications of this movement into areas of discourse seemingly remote from it. It is therefore worth noting that a well-positioned and skeptically inclined nineteenth-century observer like Robert Southey considered Wesley to have been the presiding figure of one of "the great moral and intellectual revolutions" of history (*Life of Wesley* 1:2), a revolution which, it seemed apparent to him, had profoundly altered thinking across a far wider field than that of Methodism narrowly defined. In what sense could Wesleyanism, with its often fantastical theology and its overriding moral urgency, be seen to have generated an *intellectual* revolution? In venturing some answers to this question, I both take Southey's proposition about Wesley's far-reaching influence for granted and offer evidence to support it. I need it to be understood, however, that I invoke Wesley's name and quote his sermons in an argument about the formation of modern social thinking more as an expository shortcut than as a substantive argument about specific lines of influence (which I have no special interest here in trying to identify). His writings provide a conveniently tangible and definite point of reference for modes of sensibility broadly diffused throughout the period with which we are concerned.

At all events, it is probably Wesley's sermons that are decisive in crystallizing for modern awareness the compulsive imagery which we shall track in various discursive realms throughout this study: imagery of desire expanding at least potentially without check and in a mysterious way assaulting, throwing into radical uncertainty, the operation of symbolism in human life. "Every man born into the world," says Wesley, "now bears the image of the devil, in pride and self-will; the image of the beast, in sensual appetites and desires" (*Sermons* 2:230–31). Such language emphatically identifies overflowing natural passions with figurative representations: according to Wesley, man is a slave to imagery which is inscribed upon him and which he is bound to reflect. In a strange way, he is both wholly uncontrolled and at the same time wholly determined by symbolic mirrorings. Such symbolism is not culturally produced, but is inherent in fallen human nature. Wesley's name for this provocatively ambiguous state is original sin, and the aim of all his evangelizing is to arouse the keenest possible revulsion from the "natural" and yet perverse, denaturing heritage of the human species.[1]

Wesley undoubtedly forms one of the fountainheads of that late-eighteenth and early-nineteenth-century development described as an epistemic mutation by Foucault: the wholesale invasion of a field of symbolic "representation" by ideas of "great hidden forces" (Foucault, *Order* 251), primitive energies prior and alien to *and implicitly destructive of* symbolic order. This upheaval is the one portrayed in Wesley's contemporary Sade, who stands "on the threshold of modern culture," as Foucault memorably puts it, in his depiction of "the obscure and repeated violence of desire battering at the limits of representation" (*Order* 210). Wesley and Sade employ drastically opposed rhetorical registers, but at the heart of each (and then, as we shall see, of the social discourse of the ensuing two centuries) is the notion of "the lawless infinity of desire" (Foucault, *Order* 362).

Wesley's disavowal of the natural on the plane of moral value, linked as it is to the pregnant hint that man is unique in creation by being fundamentally a creature of figurative imagery, led in unforeseen directions. It issued ultimately in that disavowal of the natural which forms the leading axiom of modern anthropological thinking ("there is no human nature, only human history"). What flowed more directly from the Wesleyan mythology of sin was a widely influential moral theory which made a fetish of self-control, discipline, work, "purity," resignation, self-abnegation. Max Weber's analysis of how this theory and the spirit of early capitalist culture interlocked in a systematic denial of "the spontaneous expression of undisciplined impulses" (Weber 167) is abundantly borne out in the annals of Victorian society. The success of the Wesleyan moral dispensation in early nineteenth-century Britain—a dispensation whose influence extended, it bears repeating, far beyond Methodism itself—had to do with the need of the modern industrial system for a population trained to high levels of discipline;[2] among other things, it had to do also with the still-vivid trauma of the French Revolution—easy to conceive as an outbreak of "the lawless infinity of desire"—and with the fears of a repetition of the events of 1789 which were aroused throughout the century by eruptions of anarchic-seeming political forces in Britain and in its overseas territories. But these fears were themselves outgrowths in large measure of a system of moral discourse based above all on the injunction to suppress dangerously volatile personal urges, a discourse sometimes powerful enough to override all other cultural imperatives. The widespread public approval of Governor Eyre's pitiless flouting of laws in putting down the 1865 Jamaican rebellion (condemned though it was by Mill and others), for instance, needs to be understood as the expression of a broad, deeply internalized dread of ungoverned desires. Suppressing rebellious "primitives" like Eyre's Jamaicans, numbers of whom were summarily hanged, took on much of its character of necessity and righteousness by giving objectified allegorical form to the spiritual drama of the suppression of unruly drives which ordinary Victorians strove to enact in their own daily lives and which (being human beings) they longed to portray in vivid figurative representations. On one fairly obvious level of morbid cultural symbolism, in other words, the Jamaicans and many others—all the victims of the spectacularly theatricalized public hangings at Tyburn, which long constituted "the most popular mass spectacle in England" (R. Hughes 31)—were made to play the role of sacrificial scapegoats for the characteristic moral anxieties of Evangelical culture: to take "the image of the beast" upon themselves. The carnivalesque effervescence released at public hangings suggests the force of the anxieties to which they ministered by the process of in effect reimposing the regime of symbolic imagery upon anarchic desire.

The same configuration of metaphors stamps itself upon the Victorians' popular fiction, where the necessity of policing and stringently subduing "undisciplined impulses" was no less insistently represented than at Tyburn. The characteristic normative gesture of Victorian fiction is that of renunciation, of wilfully purging one's self of desire—or at least of refusing to act on desires that resist being purged. Maggie Tulliver, the heroine of George Eliot's *Mill on the Floss* (1860), epitomizes this gesture and defines precisely the distinctive structure of sensibility which Wesleyan piety leads to when she admits to feeling "that, by forsaking the simple rule of renunciation, she was throwing herself under the seductive guidance of illimitable wants" (*Mill* 284). This polarity of strict renunciation and "illimitable" libido with scarcely any intermediate term between the two means that extreme self-violence may be the necessary cost of personal moral hygiene. "I will take / This yearning self of mine and strangle it," declares, for example, Fedalma, the heroine of Eliot's narrative poem of 1868 *The Spanish Gypsy* (163). Her imagery is closely coincident with that of the hanging of disruptive Jamaicans three years before by order of Governor Eyre—an equivalence which may even involve a direct association of ideas, considering that Eliot's tale centers on a rebellion by a despised dark-skinned tribe against European authorities, and that its climactic scene is in fact a public hanging. Later generations of readers may no longer be conscious of any reference to so macabre an image as the gallows in the sentimentalized abstract phrase "self-sacrifice," but Victorians undoubtedly were. Subduing egoism required no less drastic an act than the implicitly suicidal one of strangling one's "yearning self," given the Victorian idea of desire as an almost overwhelmingly powerful, subtle, and dangerous force—as in fact the Freudian id.

Yet the annihilating of desire in nineteenth-century fiction often—nearly always—is inflected with the same obvious ambivalence that pervades the euphoria of public executions. Can desire be harshly put down without mutilating personality? Scarcely a significant work of the age fails to press this question upon its readers. The activation of so much cultural machinery for idealizing the suppression of desire is enough to tell us in any event that desire was a powerful, unsubdued presence in Victorian society and that the Victorian war on it was after all a troubled and equivocal one. The machinery itself, as Foucault argues with reference to the medical analysis of "sexuality" at the end of the century, tends by its contradictory logic to irritate and inflame the very desires that it nominally strives to suppress (*History of Sexuality* 48, 71). Symbolic gestures of suppression seem to call up more cultural energy than they themselves are able to capture; the surplus is absorbed into imagery of desire.

This principle implicates Methodism itself, which on the level of moral and political ideology preached quietism, the acceptance of the social status quo, and the idealization of labor and discipline. As it had been for Wesley, the presiding nightmare of this movement lay in the spectacle of desire breaking free of instituted controls and manifesting its inherently "illimitable" character.[3] Yet it is a paradox often noted that Methodism, which aimed at the iron control of human drives, was wildly emotionalistic in its ritual observances and made of religion, as Southey wrote, "a thing of sensation and passion, craving perpetually for . . . stimulants" (quoted Thompson 369). Faced with this perverse-seeming doubleness of sensibility, E. P. Thompson stresses "the *intermittent character* of Wesleyan emotionalism," arguing that Sabbath excesses served as a safety valve for pent-up emotions and thus helped ensure obedience to external discipline the other six days of the week (Thompson 368). Herbert Spencer, looking more broadly at modern religious culture, turns Thompson's formulation inside out, but highlights just the same contradiction in his portrait of the contemporary scene in *The Study of Sociology* [*SS*] (1873). Victorian life, he declares, institutionalizes "two coexisting religions—the religion of enmity and the religion of amity" (*SS* 178). "The nobility of self-sacrifice, set forth in Scripture-lessons and dwelt on in sermons, is made conspicuous every seventh day" (*SS* 179), while the rest of the week is ruled by exactly the opposite code, one that, as we may say, gives the id free rein, glorifying unrestricted aggression, egoism, vengefulness. At first glance, Spencer remarks (shrewdly exploring the question of cultural incoherence that has lately become central to anthropological and sociological theory), "it might be thought impossible that men should continue through life holding two doctrines which are mutually destructive" and that thus organizes social life into a system of "glaring incongruities" (*SS* 180, 388). It is as though Ruth Benedict had discovered a society both "Apollonian" and "Dionysian" at once. Like Thompson, Spencer explains the paradox by claiming that the two Victorian "religions" are sharply segregated from one another, one being for Sunday, the other for Monday through Saturday. Yet the segregation could never have been so absolute as this (for one thing, didactic popular fiction, one of the chief Victorian institutions, had the express function of carrying Sunday lessons through the rest of the week). The intense cultivation of desire and the vigilant repression of it cannot merely have alternated as disjunctive phases in nineteenth-century life, but must have been inseparably locked together in a culture that in fact fostered desire as powerfully as it did puritanical repression, and must have generated as a result no small quotient of tension and ambivalence.

The Theory of Social Control

I begin by stressing the "glaring incongruities" of the nineteenth-century text of desire in order to help understand one facet of contemporary interest in the "primitive," but, first of all, to make it easier to understand the construction of what emerged as a leading paradigm of modern social thought: the one which conceives society or culture not, say, as an expression of immanent natural, divine, or semiological order, but as an artificial restraint imposed by necessity upon volatile, uncontrollably self-multiplying individual impulses and desires which in a state of unimpaired freedom, could any such state exist, would act without limit. This set of assumptions and figures of speech was woven everywhere throughout nineteenth-century social discourse, and it is still fundamental to common sense and social science.[4] Yet it is quite a dubious model after all, one which can scarcely be tested by empirical evidence, and increasingly it has an antiquated appearance.[5] How did it gain credence in the first place?

Evidently its claim to unquestioning belief was its consonance with the well-established propositions and resonant moral rhetoric of original-sin theology. In place of the myth of the Fall, secular social theory had only to set up the mystery of "instinct" to leave intact the core of the Wesleyan pattern, its familiar story of human nature as a bundle of unruly drives needing to be severely repressed. This is the story which is recited *sotto voce* even in the social theory of so progressive a libertarian as John Stuart Mill. The principal condition of social order, he declares, is a system of education of which "one main and incessant ingredient [is] *restraining discipline";* this is what instructs the individual to suppress "his personal impulses and aims" even in the face of "all temptation." Given the persistence of "natural causes of evil," says Mill, "whenever and in proportion as the strictness of the restraining discipline [is] relaxed, the natural tendency of mankind to anarchy [reasserts] itself" (*Bentham* 121–22). This is the Wesleyan idiom in full flower.[6] Such a theory served practical domestic and international purposes, tending to legitimize, for example, politically driven attempts to "civilize" wild savages in other countries, including London's East End, by imposing upon them the ever-expanding structures of authority and restraint which writers like Mayhew, Mill, and, especially, Spencer bitterly decried. These practices, which we can think of as the extension to nineteenth-century society at large of the Methodist system of highly organized surveillance and discipline,[7] seemed to reflect confirmation back upon the theory in turn. At the same time, the discourse of social control reinforced itself by association with a system of the kinds of "naturalizing metaphors" that scientific ideas rely upon, according to Mary Douglas, to acquire the force of recognized certainties (*How Institutions Think* 52–53).

The primary metaphor which one unpacks from the theory of social control depends on the supposedly manifest and natural distinction between mankind and the animals.[8] Animals according to this idea are driven at every moment by blind instinctual cravings which humans, as the very expression and proof of their humanity, can and must learn to govern: hence the reification of the drives that man learns to restrain as the "animalistic" part of his nature. Not only are human beings figuratively *like* animals in some respects, not only do they "bear the image of the beast, in sensual appetites and desires," they actually *are* "animal" in part, and "civilization in every one of its aspects is a struggle against the animal instincts" (Mill, *Principles* 1:446). Nineteenth-century writers use this ideologically saturated language, its metaphorical character altogether submerged, freely and in distinctive structures of rhetoric, especially in disparaging reference to "primitive" peoples; as the work of Werner Stark attests, it still can command a measure of scientific as well as colloquial currency today.[9]

The theory of social restraint brought into play at the same time another complex of naturalizing metaphors closely related to the theme of "animal instincts," those represented by images of surging forces contained or redirected ("channelled") by physical objects. These increasingly became the metaphors of choice in expositions of sophisticated, unsensationalistic social-control theory. Tylor thus highlights the conjunction of sociological theory and metaphors of physics in a series of passages at the beginning of *Primitive Culture*, portraying it as the device upon which the emerging discipline of cultural anthropology will depend. "Rudimentary as the science of culture still is," he says, "the symptoms are becoming very strong that even what seem its most spontaneous and motiveless phenomena will, nevertheless, be shown to come within the range of distinct cause and effect as certainly as the facts of mechanics" (*Primitive Culture* 1:18). Tylor does not pursue in specific terms the equation of social phenomena with "the facts of mechanics," but other nineteenth-century writers do, notably Comte (who calls his science "social physics"), Spencer, and then Freud, whose imagery of forces repressed in one place surging up hydraulically in another is basic to our model of the mind. But no social theorist of the time leans more heavily than Walter Bagehot on figures of speech drawn from what he self-reflexively speaks of as "our physical science, which is becoming the dominant culture of thousands, and which is beginning to permeate our common literature to an extent which few watch enough" (*English Constitution* 254). The anthropological speculations of Bagehot's 1876 work *Physics and Politics*, as the title indicates, are consistently couched in the prestigious terminology of forces and interfering solid masses, movement and inertia. Exactly prefiguring the phraseology of Freud and Werner Stark, Bagehot thus says of riots that they "have always been said to bring out a secret and suppressed side of human nature; and we see now that they [are] the outbreak of inherited passions long repressed by fixed custom, but starting into life as soon as that repression [is] . . . removed" (*Physics and Politics* 540). The plausibility as technical discourse of this highly figurative language, which sets forth the theory of social control in its most unequivocal form, is among other things the sign of the authority of the science of force and matter that it covertly invokes.

These two arrays of metaphor, of animality and of physical mechanics, function therefore in nineteenth-century writing to mediate and to mystify the problematic operation of transposing fantasies of

original sin into secular social doctrine. Given the very equivocal origins of this program of figurative imagery, scientific hypothesis, and
moral ideology, it is unsurprising that it was never free, despite its
tremendous successes, of internal tension. The fruit of this tension was
the development of which I try in the rest of this book to glean signs
from nineteenth-century texts: the polemically charged shift from the
social-control model toward a symbolically oriented theory of "culture" in which society is configured in a new metaphorical guise as "an
inextricable web of affinities" and as an enigmatic object of interpretation.

The chronology of this movement is only approximately specifiable, and one can perhaps only guess at the logical sequences which
produce it—if indeed logic has at last a determining role to play in a
shift of thinking which involves such deep currents of period feeling
and period fantasy. I have found no text which can serve as a Rosetta
Stone for decoding this shift. What I have found is an abundance of
texts in different domains in which the two themes of free desire and
of culture as "complex whole" enter into intense, always deeply problematic competition, out of which neither one emerges unmodified.
But authors are rarely able to stage this process in a philosophically
coherent fashion. Typically the two ideas come together in the form of
sharp, unreconciled juxtapositions which give the texts in question a
more or less wildly unresolved, irrational character; extreme self-contradiction, we shall see, is their commonest feature. The suggestion is
that finally there may be no way to derive the second concept logically
from the first, and that what these texts document is one of those
epistemic or paradigmatic shifts between radically discontinuous
structures which form the watershed episodes, and the most enigmatic
ones, of intellectual history.

It is possible to construct a plausible general narrative along the
following lines. The pessimism of original-sin theology is contradicted
by the evident fact that members of human societies live together
ordinarily not in a state of barbaric disorder but of orderly coopera-
tion. It is the theological intervention, in other words, that brings the
fact of social order into view *as a problem,* and thrusts it indeed into the
foreground of social theory and of a great deal of early modern ethnography. To explain this discrepancy of theory and data, one postulates a commanding role for social agencies of control, as Hobbes
classically does in *Leviathan* (1651). But no number of social agencies
can make a convincing counterweight to instinctual desire once Evan-

gelical theory has constructed its idea of the latter as "illimitable" and of human nature as "altogether corrupt in every power and faculty" (Wesley, *Sermons* 2:286). One is driven therefore by the pressure of Evangelical thinking to try to conceive some comprehensive, in a sense *absolute*, power to account for the orderliness of social life in the face of "the natural tendency of mankind to anarchy." From this impulse, we can guess, there emerges first the sacralizing of human society itself, as in Carlyle's claim that social union possesses "ever something mystical and borrowing of the Godlike" (*Sartor Resartus* 209), and then what may be just the secularized version of this doctrine, the hypothesis of a "complex wholeness" immanent in collective life and giving unity and regularity to all its varied phenomena. Attempting to justify such a model, early sociological theorists posit a natural instinct for adherence to cultural forms—the very antithesis of the instinct for anarchy.[10] But the suspect notion of instinct fairly soon drops out of this line of thinking, too; social order in the culture hypothesis is henceforth treated no longer as a problem to be explained, but as a manifest fact to be taken for granted and described in its various particular configurations. If this hypothesis has "ever something mystical" about it even in its most sophisticated versions, this may be nothing but the indelible trace of its origin in the doctrine of a divine curse upon the human race.

The above schema is more a heuristic myth than a description of a sequence of real events, yet it helps to explain why the first major essay of evolutionary cultural anthropology in Britain should have been a work like Sir Henry Maine's *Ancient Law* (1861), which focuses single-mindedly on institutions of external control as the bases of social life. According to Maine's theory, the original form of Indo-European society was that of the "family" governed by the principle of absolute patriarchal authority, a form which evolved by stages into society of a more modern type based on the institution of binding legal contracts between individuals. In both "status" and "contract" societies, social life is conceived by Maine as a system of *governance*, of imposed law. This theory both appealed to the Wesleyan sensibility, which attained its historical high water mark at about this moment, and also, for the reasons guessed at above, was bound to seem insufficient. From the point of departure of a text like *Ancient Law*, a crucial move toward the ethnographic culture concept occurs therefore when the theory of social control comes to frame itself chiefly not in terms of external agencies of enforcement (patriarchs, sovereigns, laws) but of internalized, unconscious controls which one does not so much obey as simply exhibit—a move rendering the concept of "control," like that of "freedom," philosophically ambiguous ever after. This broad thesis has its classic modern formulation in Freud's *Civilization and its Discontents* (1930), where it coexists, after all, with ideas of anarchic animal instinct close to Wesley's own, but its philosophical antecedents reach well back into the eighteenth and nineteenth centuries. The tradition of liberal political economy, in particular, was closely wed to ideas of rigorous psychological determinism[11] which must have taken much of their philosophical urgency precisely from the theoretical issues injected into modern thinking by Wesleyan arguments. Spencer makes apparent the confluence of this tradition with modern ethnological theory in his study of the coercive nature of culture in volume 2 (1879) of *The Principles of Sociology*.

The collective feeling of the community, Spencer declares, is to some extent spontaneously created by its members, but "is to a much larger extent the opinion imposed on them or prescribed for them." Not only the ideas and codified values but even the "emotional nature" of the members of a given society is "a product of all ancestral activities," says Spencer, as are all their "special desires," which simply grow out of and in fact (as Spencer's analysis allows us to see, though it does not make the point explicit) are merely symbolic representations of the usages of the past.[12] Here is the radical solution to the problem of original sin, viewed sociologically: emotions and desires are not autonomous forces which precede society and which are describable in terms of limitlessness and animality, but are merely established customs, radically human, radically limited, best describable in terms of symbolic replication. "From these inherited customs," Spencer concludes, "there is no escape" (*Principles* 2:321). Thus human desire by its very nature is keyed to the constitutive principles of a society and acts not to disrupt but, inescapably, to express and to reinforce them. Spencer's starkly deterministic language on this theme is often echoed in subsequent literature. Cultural forms, says Durkheim sixteen years later, have as their leading property "a compelling and coercive power by virtue of which, whether he wishes it or not, they impose themselves upon [the individual]." As believers in individual autonomy, "we are the victims of an illusion which leads us to believe we have ourselves produced what has been imposed upon us externally" by formal education and subtler forms of influence (Durkheim, *Rules* 51, 53). Several decades later still, by which time the culture concept has been fully articulated, Ludwik Fleck applies Spencer's principle to the field of conceptual thought. "The individual within the collective is never, or hardly ever, conscious of the prevailing thought style, which almost always exerts an absolutely compulsive force upon his thinking and with which it is not possible to be at variance," he says (Fleck 41). From a creature tending always to anarchy, inherently refractory to social life, man has become in nearly every aspect of his being a hostage to society, not merely enslaved but deprived of any knowledge of his own fate.

This turn of thought marks the inauguration of the distinctive *episteme* of modern social science and carries the gravest possible implications for absolutist theologies. Yet it remains in the above formulations a theory of absolute control, specifically of mind control, which bears after all a weird resemblance to Evangelical conceptions. That it develops in a fairly direct way from the problematic of original sin, and can even be seen as an attempt to salvage the essential structure of Wesleyan argument, is the conclusion to which one may be led by analysis of some of its characteristic patterns of rhetoric. Considered as fantasy, the principle of the inescapable subjection of the individual to the thought-world of his or her society can be seen to project on the plane of theory the ideal scheme of Evangelical moral discipline, and to realize in effect that sweeping renunciation of individual will and desire which that discipline strove to achieve.

In his analysis of the dynamics of "puritanism" in Victorian society, Matthew Arnold nicely highlights this convergence. The puritan's goal, driven as he is by anxieties about the fundamental flaws of human nature, says Arnold, is to construct "a network of prescriptions to enwrap his whole life, to govern every moment of it, every impulse, every action" (*Culture and Anarchy* 131). Arnold might have glossed this statement with reference to any number of Wesley's sermons. "The will of God is the supreme, unalterable rule for every intelligent creature," says Wesley in one passage, for example; "equally binding every angel in heaven, and every man upon earth. . . . But if the will of God be our one rule of action in everything, great and small, it follows . . . that we are not to do our own will in anything." Divine law is in effect, he stresses, "not at some times or in some things only, but at all times and in all things" (*Sermons* 2:285–86). The theory of culture as social control mechanism (the theory which survives, if a little ambiguously, in the writing of Clifford Geertz) disavows puritan moral coerciveness in the name of "cultural relativism," yet it closely replicates this absolute, fantastically detailed network of prescriptions, from which not the slightest respite is possible. Even the most trivial-seeming human gestures are governed by law, whether God's law or the law of "inherited customs."

This principle stands forth plainly in early passages of the work from which this discussion, like modern anthropological theory itself, took its departure, Tylor's *Primitive Culture,* where so much rhetorical stress is laid upon promoting "the general study of human life as a branch of natural science"—as a study from which religious values have been wholly evacuated, in other words. As we saw, Tylor predicts that even what appear to be the "most spontaneous and motiveless phenomena" of social life will prove to be subject to laws as definite as those of mechanics; what is disparagingly called "the popular notion of free human will" will be exploded. "The tendency of modern enquiry," says Tylor, "is more and more towards the conclusion that if law is anywhere, it is everywhere" (*PC* 1:2, 18, 3, 24). Such a conclusion (the one necessarily implied by the theory of culture as complex whole) is decisively reached long afterward in Malinowski's argument that every human function without exception, "even such activities as breathing, the work of internal secretions, digestion, and circulation," are enmeshed in the system of "norms, customs, traditions, and rules" which constitutes "culture" (*Scientific Theory* 68). This line of argument shifts a doctrine like Wesley's wholly off center by the substitution of sociological law for divine will, yet the impression of a cryptotheological structure within the Tylorian tendency of "modern inquiry," the impression in this discourse of authoritarian restraint being summarily imposed upon the tiniest atom of individual freedom, and also of the seizure of power by a caste of lawgivers (here, the anthropological theorists themselves), is unmistakable. The conclusion to which these juxtapositions of texts point is that the emergence of the scientific doctrine of culture may best be described not as a process of dispassionate investigation of evidence or as what it believed itself to be, an emancipation from Victorian prejudice, but rather as a complex and sometimes insidious reconfiguring of moral and religious ideas, in fact of a whole sensibility, at a historical point of crisis.[13]

It is a sign of this underground continuity of opposed-seeming trends of reasoning that early objections to modern social science by defenders of the "illusion" of free human will lately have resurfaced in their own new guise among anthropologists concerned that the traditional concepts and research methods of their discipline constitute in some sense an authoritarian system and a menace, in particular, to their special objects of study, the members of vulnerable primitive societies.[14] Even in a work that strives as hard to overcome Eurocentric prejudice and to demystify the self-serving European image of primitive people as does Malinowski's *Argonauts of the Western Pacific,* the denial of personal individuality and freedom that his study entails can be viewed as carrying an irreducible quotient of aggression. Malinowski emphasizes that the focus of his ethnographic research falls wholly upon "stereotyped manners of thinking and feeling," though this is merely, he assures us, a matter of the technical procedure of his discipline. "As sociologists, we are not interested in what A or B may feel *qua* individuals, . . . we are interested only in what they feel and think *qua* members of a given community" (*Argonauts* 23). The imposition of this principle of insignificance upon individual informants is not at all a morally neutral one, however. It is as tendentious and contestable as is the use of animal subjects for laboratory experiments. Moreover, the truth of the "natives'" own communal lives, according to the doctrine of the science of culture, is an invisible, occult one to which they themselves have no access. "The natives obey the forces and commands of the tribal code, but they do not comprehend them" (*Argonauts* 11): almost by definition, only the learned European ethnographer can do that. He expressly seizes for himself the role of lawgiver. "Ethnology," he declares in praise of his newly consolidated and self-aware science of culture, using what by now is both a familiar and evidently a loaded and equivocal phraseology, "has introduced law and order into what seemed chaotic and freakish" (*Argonauts* 9). Long afterward, Lévi-Strauss praises in almost the same language the achievements of modern cultural analysis: "what had been merely a huge and disordered scene [of seemingly heterogeneous customs] became organized in grammatical terms involving a coercive charter for all conceivable ways of [organizing human societies]," he declares (*The Scope of Anthropology* 32).

It is hard to think that writers using such language could be wholly oblivious to the suggestion of a deep-running equivalence between the reign of conceptual "law and order" instituted by the "coercive charter" of theoretical anthropology on the one hand, and the rigorous puritan law of conduct on the other. Whether they are oblivious to it or not, such equivalence is not merely a hypothetical thing, but an oft-enacted historical reality. It is manifest in the way in which the pioneering missionary ethnographers acted also, impelled by imperative religious duty, as the bringers of European discipline and European concepts of legality to "chaotic and freakish" primitive peoples: compelling Tahitians, for instance, to rebuild their previously scattered, irregular villages on strict geometrical grids of streets (Ellis 2:82), to adopt Christian laws regulating sex and marriage, to abolish traditional licentious pastimes, or, on another plane, to collaborate in what one is surprised to discover is implicitly an act of cross-cultural violence, "the reducing to writing, and a regular grammatical system," of their rich oral traditions (Ellis 1:449).[15] To misquote Tylor's original premise, if European law is anywhere, it must be absolutely everywhere. Imposing the theory of culture as an instrument of analysis and imposing all-pervasive systems of practical control go hand in hand.[16]

Yet to represent the theory of culture purely as an adjunct or expression of an impulse of domination would be seriously incomplete. We shall see more fully in subsequent chapters that it often was employed in precisely the opposite manner. To learn to think of an alien society as a seamless web of institutions with its own inherent "law and order" is at least potentially to confer on it an integrity not legitimately to be violated by outside interventions. As deployed by a writer like Ruth Benedict, the culture theory formed one the most lethal instruments of dissidence from Victorian thinking. One of its chief effects was after all to abolish the legend of the aberrant, crazily passionate primitive (a main theoretical prop for colonial usurpations), and indeed, to nullify ultimately the very conception of naturally unlimited desire. But this figure was too deeply ingrained in modern social discourse to die away. Having been exorcised by the growing ascendancy of the culture concept from our image of primitive society and psychology, it was resituated in our own society and our own psychology, and endowed in honor of this transposition with a new scientific name. We shall trace this ultimate move at the conclusion of the present chapter.

Boundless Desire, Freedom, and "Restlessness"

To some extent the longevity of the myth of a state of uncontrolled desire stems from its ability to carry both negative and positive value. For a society as imbued with fetishized principles of discipline as respectable Victorian society was, the notion of freely acting, unconfined desire was bound to arouse anxiety or even (in connection, say, with representations of "the dangerous classes") panic. But it was bound also to form a perennial ideal, in which guise it went and still goes by the name "freedom." Throughout the nineteenth century, the ideology of freedom acted as one of the main catalysts to philosophical investigation of "culture." It was not itself free, but reproduced the dominant polarity of external control and instinctive desire given in Wesleyan polemics, only with the positive and negative charges reversed between the two poles. Hence the curious interchangeability of texts representing opposite sides of the debate on freedom. Consider, for example, Mill's *On Liberty* [*OL*] (1859) and Arnold's response to the political turmoil preceding the Reform Bill of 1867, *Culture and Anarchy* [*CA*] (1869).

Mill founds his argument on the presumption of a necessary antagonism between "individual liberty" and what he calls "the tyranny of the prevailing opinion and feeling" (*OL* 4), and he is straightforward in asserting his central definition, which Arnold later echoes, ironically, verbatim: "liberty consists in doing what one desires," in "doing as we like" in opposition to "the despotism of custom," which by its nature is hostile to the life of desire (*OL* 97, 12, 70). According to Mill, the puritanical and authoritarian-spirited society of middle-class England has fostered a "general atmosphere of mental slavery" (*OL* 33) which deprives individuals even of the *inclination* to desire. His countrymen have so internalized conventional habits of thought and particularly the injunction "to desire nothing strongly" (*OL* 69) as actually to have become "incapable of any strong wishes or native pleasures" (*OL* 61). In its pessimistic assessment of contemporary society, *On Liberty* thus defines "desire" as almost necessarily transgressive; one only desires strongly that which is forbidden.

Arnold stresses just as strongly the severe governance of individual desire which forms the great cultural theme of Victorian society, but gives a very different appraisal of the late-nineteenth-century scene. The dominant influence in Britain for two centuries has been, he declares, that of "Hebraic" puritan repression, aimed especially at governing "the body and its desires" (*CA* 131). But side by side with this encasing system has grown its antithesis, the phenomenon with which Arnold is especially concerned: the fetishistic worship of "the free action of individuals," and "that passion for doing as one likes" that dominates modern social life (*CA* 74, 102). Far from being extinguished by the reign of puritanical discipline, freedom has become sacrosanct and has gone out of control. "The moment it is plainly put before us that a man is asserting his personal liberty, we are half disarmed," Arnold complains, "because we are believers in liberty," because we are infused with what he calls, in a phrase precisely germane to the themes of this study, the modern "hatred of all limits to the unrestrained swing of the individual personality" (*CA* 78, 49). All of Arnold's treatise is directed against the supposed tendency in modern life toward "giving unchecked range . . . to [one's] mere personal action" and toward "allowing no limits or government to this" (*CA* 183). The urbane and ironical stylistic surface of Arnold's book, not to mention its generally negative tone with regard to Protestant moralism, could cause one not to recognize how closely it allies itself with the rhetorical schema of, say, Wesley's sermons.

It is thus the cult of unlimited freedom of desire, says Arnold, that leads directly to the distinctive phenomena of modern politics: "tumult and disorder, multitudinous processions in the streets of our crowded towns, multitudinous meetings in their public places and parks," and other similarly frightening disorders (*CA* 97). "Culture" in its "Hellenistic" form, the form especially eulogized by Arnold, is defined antithetically, as the process of cultivation that preserves order by moderating potential outbreaks of anarchic desire such as these. He does not put it in just these terms, but it is clear that the sovereign benefit of "turning a stream of fresh and free thought upon our stock notions and habits" (*CA* 6) and of occupying ourselves in the study of the finest writing of the past is that in this way we achieve detachment from our own desires, and thereby reduce their power to rule us. It may seem paradoxical that the cure for an epidemic of amoral freedom could be the prescription of thought enabled "to play freely and disinterestedly" (*CA* 197) upon life, but this ideal, since it decrees a position of noncommitment to particular political causes, means emancipation from what Arnold most detests, "fanaticism," and indeed, from any compelling personal desires. In place of the violent manacling of desires by "Hebraic" moralism, which evidently has only served to exacerbate them, Arnold proposes humanistic self-cultivation as a means of sapping the dangerous energy of desire from within.

Arnold has immediate polemical purposes in mind, but in his sensationalistic evocations of modern civil disorder, his essential goal is to renovate the mobile army of metaphors which since the upsurge of Wesleyan piety had, as he says, been the dominant force in British culture. He seeks in effect to find new empirical coordinates, a new set of suitably lurid imagery, for the fantasy of illimitable desire, and thus to reinvest it with its original rhetorical and ideological power. He

identifies the loss of influence of such thinking in modern Britain with
the rise of a reckless, anarchic cult of personal freedom and with the
frightening effects to which it supposedly gives rise in contemporary
politics. The truth, indeed, is that the polarity of external control and
potentially unlimited desire, the polarity which both Mill and Arnold
for their opposite polemical purposes sought to reinstitute, had long
been the site of a subtle but highly significant mutation which tended
to rob it of its force—and to imply a fundamentally new idea of the
nature of social experience. Its sign was the appearance in nineteenth-
century discourse of a very characteristic, ever-more-influential stream
of imagery which was a kind of Wesleyan hybrid: one in which the idea
of desire subject to "no limits or government" is indeed central, but
only in a sharply attenuated or decayed form. It presents a post-
Wesleyan idea of desire in its original form as "boundless" only in the
sense of incomplete, incoherent, nonsensical, and thus as prone to
such volatility as to be wholly ineffectual until inscribed with the organizing principles of culture. We can observe this newly inflected
imagery in a series of texts from the first half of the century.

One such text would be Wordsworth's "Ode to Duty" (1804). The
speaker of the poem invokes a youth spent "loving freedom" and trust-
ing to the guidance of a natural, spontaneous moral sense, but leading
at last to a special kind of disorientation summed up in the key cou-
plet: "Me this unchartered freedom tires; / I feel the weight of chance
desires." As Wordsworth does not need to state directly, this nominally
autobiographical text has a broader referential context as a fable of
the predicament of the whole emergent movement of "Romanticism,"
which based itself, in direct opposition to Wesleyanism (not that the
two contemporaneous movements were without points of affinity), on
the glorification of freedom and of natural spontaneity, yet also on a
strict "coercive charter" of moral principle. As the Shelleys' scandalous
self-emancipation from contemporary sexual morality would soon dramatize, freedom in these circumstances is necessarily equivocal, indeed doubly so. It is equivocal, first (though Wordsworth veils this
aspect of his theme), because Romantic "unchartered freedom" is
likely to be hard to distinguish from obedience to a highly standardized cultural code—much the one expounded, with much bookish
affectation, by Marianne Dashwood in *Sense and Sensibility* at just this
time. Is "unchartered freedom" anything but a delusive figure of
speech? Perhaps the attaining of genuine freedom requires more drastic measures than Wordsworth's poem or Jane Austen's novel are pre-

pared to envision. In any case, because this ideal conflicts with the equally compelling one of "duty," it is bound to yield a state full of unease and anxiety, and to be endangered by what Wordsworth's poem calls "vain temptations" from which only a strict code of principle can "set [one] free." The "Ode to Duty" thus concludes on the paradox that bondage to law is liberty from excessive freedom and its necessary concomitant, "chance desires." It is above all the fatiguing haphazardness of desire placed under the aegis of "freedom," its amorphous, random, disorganizing character, that Wordsworth highlights in this poem.

This theme is elaborated in a contemporary text of a different type altogether, one tracing more clearly the implications of the idea of free desire for a theory of culture: Dr. Jean Itard's commentary on his work with Victor, the famous "wild boy" of Aveyron. Itard's 1801 report on "The First Developments of the Young Savage of Aveyron," translated into English in 1802 and supplemented by his second report in 1807, belongs to a substantial eighteenth- and nineteenth-century literature on "savage" or feral people enacting the symbolic drama of suddenly entering "civilized" society—the inverse, in other words, of that enacted by ethnographers going out to inject themselves into alien social worlds.[17] Even the best-documented instances of such material are ambiguously fictionalistic, and Itard's redaction of the wild-boy story in the form of a scientific inquiry has its own inherent fictive or mythic structure, the central figure of which is that often hypothesized but forever unobservable being, man utterly devoid of culture. The development by Itard of a training program to teach Victor to speak and to function in society was rich with practical applications in such areas as deaf-mute education, but fundamentally—as Victor himself seems to have discovered, to his infinite resentment—it was designed as an experiment to investigate scientifically the dynamics of the relation between individual human nature and society. More particularly, Itard's reports narrate a parable of the sociocultural basis of desire.

Victor seemed to have performed in the most unequivocal and literal way the estranging act which Wordsworth attempts far more cautiously, that of stepping outside the control-system of society so as to attain something like genuine emancipation from conventionality. He intermittently takes on in Itard's account the character of a freedom-worshipping Romantic idealist filled with an "empassioned taste for the liberty of the fields" (Itard 99). Yet Itard invokes a literary myth

of instinctive love of unbounded liberty and nature only to subject it
to a withering critique after all. The results of Victor's simulacrum of
natural freedom are not empowerment and expansion of potentiality,
but the reverse: a devastating collapse of all his faculties, or perhaps
rather, a failure of these faculties ever to become operative in the first
place. Itard's characteristic imagery is a concentration of the figures
of aimless, restless fluctuation that mark Wordsworth's poem and that
turn out to pervade the field of nineteenth-century social discourse as
one of the most telling signals of an imminent reorganization of sensibility. The imbecilic and speechless Victor at first was "a disgusting,
slovenly boy," says Itard, "affected with spasmodic, and frequently with
convulsive motions, continually [rocking back and forth] like some of
the animals in the menagerie." He would veer unpredictably "from a
state of profound melancholy, to bursts of the most immoderate laugh-
ter," and his efforts to focus on any activity were short-circuited by his
"wild impetuosity" and by what Itard calls in an especially noteworthy
phrase the "meaningless mobility" of all his psychic life (Itard 96, 98,
145, 148). Here is the very image of freedom as the reign of "chance
desires."

Itard discovers that his ward's devotion to the state of asocial freedom has involved not just a massive intellectual disablement, but,
more surprisingly, at least if we consider this text from the perspective
of Evangelical moral theory, a radical disablement of desire. Apart
from Victor's longing to escape and his "insatiable rapacity" for food
(Itard 173), his desire-world is largely a blank. His mad gluttony is the
sign that in almost every other area his capacity for desire has deteriorated drastically. His mercurial shifts of mood are thus not evidence of
emancipated vitality, but are part and parcel of the torpid, amorphous,
somnambulistic state, the "dull apathy" and "lethargy" (Itard 102,
168), in which he seemed to Itard to be imprisoned. Especially significant, since discussions of human "desire" commonly take sexual appetite as their main referent, was Victor's display of one symptom universal among victims of extreme cultural deprivation (Zingg 270; Malson
48), disablement of the sex drive. Itard dwells with a deep philosophic
intent on this aspect of the boy's predicament. According to him,
Victor was caught in a cruel dilemma, being erotically oblivious to
women, whom he was evidently incapable of recognizing as objects of
his sex drive, and being preyed on at the same time by overwhelming
sexual needs. His puberty was thus an "explosion" causing him to be
"consumed by desires of an extreme violence" that he had no notion

of how to gratify and that led to convulsive frenzies in the course of which—the most graphic possible imagery not of exploding but of imploding desire—blood burst copiously from his nose and ears (Itard 175–177). "This continuity of violent yet unsatisfied desires," says Itard, in a phrase that resonates in the double context both of Evangelical psychology and of later social science and psychoanalysis, "has led to a habitual state of restless suffering and anxiety" (Itard 177).

The lesson of this scientific fable is spelled out with great distinctness: it is that in order for desire to exist in any coherent, active, and potentially satisfiable form, it must embed itself in a fully social matrix, which is to say, become directed toward objects conventionally defined and symbolically coded as desirable by human society. In the therapeutic context of the case of Victor, this meant constructing virtually out of nothing the boy's missing faculty of symbolic apprehension. Itard's attempts to penetrate Victor's apathy by awakening desire through direct sensory stimulation (hot baths, massages, spicy foods) thus gave way to laborious programs focused on initiating him into "the symbols of thought": for example, exercises designed to teach him to conceptualize "the link between objects and their signs" (Itard 156, 162). Desire operates not directly upon objects, Itard came to realize, but only upon systems of symbolic linkages. For Itard, any notion of regaining an original plentitude of desire by the shedding of social constraints (like any notion of unsocialized man as a monster of "animal" passion) is a delusion, and the only possible result of such a process would be a pathetically disabled derelict like this wild boy.

Equally delusive, he declares, pointedly setting his medical case history in the context of anthropological theory, is the idea that various "wandering tribes" exhibit man in a state of nature, for "in the savage horde the most vagabond, as well as in the most civilized nations of Europe, man is only what he is made to be" (Itard 91). Could he exist in "a pure state of nature," declares Itard, *Homo sapiens* could only be a formless, forlorn nonentity suspended in a sub-animalistic "state of vacuity and barbarism" in which he would be "deprived of the characteristic faculties of his species" and limited to the satisfaction of a small range of rudimentary physical needs (Itard 138). He would be, "without the aid of civilization, one of the most feeble . . . of animals" (Itard 91). It is this overriding stress on *feebleness* and incapacity that marks the divergence of Itard's analysis from the theory of social control. The special form of imagery which such feebleness takes in his discussion is that of erratically centrifugal impulses shooting out uncontrollably into amorphous and dimensionless (because socially vacant) space. In other words, Itard conceived that he had discovered that the "natural" condition of anarchic, unsatisfiable desire—called original sin in Christian theology—was indeed an observable reality, but also that this condition and the opposite-seeming one of numbed, perpetually "restless" apathy and inertia were simply the two aspects of a single state, as interchangeable in theory as in fact they were in Victor's vertiginous succession of moods. The agency by which this disabling condition is cured is membership in human collectivity. Culture is not a system of controls imposed upon desire, but rather, says Jean Itard, ultimately a system *of* desire.[18]

If we look for signs of the above complex of themes in the field of early British anthropology, the first material to be checked is the "ethnology" of Wordsworth's and Itard's contemporary James Cowles Prichard, called by Tylor (*Britannica* 108) the founder of modern anthropology—the title usually bestowed on Tylor himself. We seem at first to find no such signs. Prichard's *Researches into the Physical History of Mankind* expressly disavows speculation on such matters as how culture exerts its mysterious influence upon populations (2:3–4), limiting itself instead to gathering factual information on the ancient migrations of peoples. In Prichard's substantial writings on abnormal psychology, however, we find once again a strong concern, so typical—almost definitive—of the Evangelical streak of the nineteenth-century mentality, with phenomena of aberrant desire.[19] His *Treatise on Insanity and Other Disorders Affecting the Mind* (1835) makes it possible to guess at an important unspoken link between this side of his work and the ethnological side.

Prichard was the discoverer and analyst of the condition that he named "moral insanity," which he defined as mental disease characterized by no intellectual disablement or delusions, but simply by "a *moral perversion,* or a disorder of the feelings, affections, and habits of the individual" (*Treatise* 7). This condition amounts very precisely to a collapse of what we may call the *cultural* structure of the individual, and is definable, though Prichard does not highlight this point, only by reference to the moral, affective, and behavioral norms of a surrounding community. An idea of "culture" in the sense of the whole normal ensemble of "feelings, affections, and habits" is the hypothesis to which one is led by the recognition of a certain sort of disorder, in other words. Prichard hesitates to assign a specific cause for this pathology, which he declares to be the most widespread of modern mental disturbances, but he significantly stresses, in addition to organic factors, such others as the "want of moral discipline" in contemporary education (*Treatise* 172) and, more broadly, a general breakdown of traditional customs, habits, sentiments, opinions, religious convictions (*Treatise* 191–92)—precisely the arguments made by Durkheim many years later to explain the same condition, as we shall see. Derangement of individual personality is to this extent read by Prichard as signifying pathological disturbances in the institutional structure of society at large.

The theme of the absence of a securely delimiting cultural pattern calls up in Prichard's text the same distinctive imagery of centrifugal, unconstrained, and as a result haphazard or "chance" desires that presides over Wordsworth's poem and over Itard's account of Victor. The sufferer from "moral insanity," says Prichard, "follows the bent of his inclinations; he is continually engaging in new pursuits, and soon relinquishing them without any other inducement than mere caprice and fickleness" (*Treatise* 13). In defining this complex of symptoms, Prichard seems to be reaching back into the literature of early Romanticism to quote, no doubt unconsciously, Rousseau's eulogies of his ideal state of *paresse*, idleness, in book 12 of his *Confessions* ("I love to busy myself about trifles, to begin a hundred things and not finish one of them, to come and go as my fancy bids me, to change my plan every moment, . . . to fritter away the whole day inconsequentially and incoherently, and to follow nothing but the whim of the moment" [591–92]). Rousseau momentarily evokes this state of volatile fleeting impulses as one of blessed freedom, but his autobiography focuses with ever more anguished intensity upon his sensation of being so disunified, so much a prey to incoherent desires, that experience perpetually escapes him untasted. This seems to be Prichard's underlying thesis: that desire liberated from its cultural script is insane not so much because it violates prohibitions as because it contradicts itself. Unlike strongly moralized accounts such as Wesley's or Freud's, Prichard does not treat overflowing desires as "animalistic," base, or aggressive by nature; nor is it their *force* that he stresses; what he emphasizes is what Wordsworth and Itard do, their amorphousness and consequent impotence. In the terms of the psychology which can be seen emerging from this series of texts, the function of culture is not to restrain bestial drives, but to consolidate and articulate energies that become garbled and wholly ineffectual when left to find their own track by themselves. By its uncontrollable fragmentation and multiplication of objects, modern desire, desire, that is, conditioned by the post-Rousseauistic cult of personal freedom from conventionality, *dooms itself to frustration*: such is the theme that arises ever more clearly from Prichard's long catalogue of case histories of men and women "desirous of undertaking every thing, and capable of applying themselves to nothing," "extravagant and mobile in the utmost degree in their opinions and sentiments"; subject to "evanescent and unconnected emotions," "wild desires," "morbid excitement, wildness and irregularity of conduct" (*Treatise* 17, 7, 14, 43). The "continually repeated acts of extravagance" (*Treatise* 7) that mark the conduct of these unfortunates are evidently the signals not of the release of powerful bottled-up passions, but of an agonized longing for experience that forever eludes them.

What we see in the three texts just mentioned (and in others to be studied in later chapters), then, is a progressive deterioration of the mythology of anarchic natural desire. We can perhaps only guess at its causes. Presumably the hyperbolic myth of original sin was increasingly found not only to be too heavily freighted with the will to power and control of those who professed it (the despotic Wesley, for instance), but also, as I have said, to be ever harder to square with empirical reality—especially when the ethnographic record of "savage" societies proved to lend only equivocal support, even when compiled by Methodist missionaries whose writ was to produce allegories of natural depravity (see chapter 3). The three texts just sampled indicate, too, that the failure of the original-sin model was inseparable from still embryonic conceptions of society not wholly in thrall to the theory of social control.

The clearest sign of the appearance of such a new conception is the persistent collapsing together in nineteenth-century writing of the two antithetical terms, freedom and control. The result of this oxymoronic trope is the effective nullification of each opposed term. Indeed, the opposition of freedom and social limitation so often collapses in upon itself in theoretical writing of the period that we are concerned with that one is led to conclude that "freedom" commonly functions in this discourse simply as a polemical intensifier, a fetish (as Arnold calls it), a positive cue that has now been severed from any practical referent or definite logical content.[20] One declares whatever social arrangements one advocates to be "freedom," even if these arrangements include strong principles of discipline and control. Whatever ideological overtones of its own may be read into this formula, it offered an escape from the impasse of Wesleyan antinomies and opened the way to a more sophisticated, an at least nominally value-neutral, ethnographic social science.

This maneuver takes place even in so rhetorically militant a text as *On Liberty*. Mill's advocacy of freedom and its near synonym, desire, and his sharp divorce of these terms from their opposite ones, society and custom, is after all far less radical than it seems. Thus he proposes at one point that "the free development of individuality" does not after all imply the negation of custom and social bonds, far less an upsurge of "tumult and disorder," but rather is an essential element of "civilization, instruction, education, culture" (*OL* 56). A man's "desires and impulses . . . are the expression of his own nature," he says elsewhere, adding the significant qualification "as it has been developed and modified by his own culture" (*OL* 60). In both phrases, Mill seems to use the word "culture" in an ambiguous sense suspended precisely at the point of transition from the older meaning of "the growth and tending of human faculties" (R. Williams, *Marxism* 1) to the incipient modern "ethnographic" meaning of the term. What underlies the lexical shift is the implication that liberty and social discipline, desire and control, are not the absolute antinomies that they appear to be in other passages of *On Liberty*. Other social scientists of the late nineteenth century invoke the same principle. It occupies a prominent position in the argument of Herbert Spencer, an even more extreme libertarian than Mill himself (Spencer, *Principles* 3:124, for example), and it is emphatically restated by his ungrateful disciple Durkheim: "it so happens that liberty itself is the product of regulation," declares the latter in 1893 (*Division of Labor* 320).

Arnold himself invokes the same pivotal paradox. "The only perfect freedom is, as our religion says, a service," he declares (*CA* 182). To grasp what he means by such a formula is to see how he, too, like Mill, arrives by way of revising Wesleyan antinomies at the threshold of a modern theory of culture. George W. Stocking, Jr. is right to argue that in its stress on internal, ideational factors, Arnold's idea of "culture," though clearly designed to carry a lot of ideological and political baggage, is in some ways closer to the anthropological sense of the term than is Tylor's own use of it (Stocking, *Race, Culture, and Evolution* 89). The argument could be considerably extended, for much of Arnold's thought in *Culture and Anarchy* moves strongly in the direction of later anthropological theory. The Arnoldian phrase corresponding most closely to what an anthropologist means by "culture" is

55

"right reason," that body of thought which supposedly emanates from the collectivity as a whole and which has as its chief function, Arnold thinks (clinging to his conceptual ground in the theory of social control), the setting of limits to "the aberrations of individual eccentricity" (*CA* 123). Right reason is "the nation in its collective and corporate character controlling . . . the free swing of this or that one of its members in the name of the higher reason of all of them" (*CA* 81). The submersion of the individual in "the common reason of society" has for Arnold a genuinely metaphysical significance, for it is what makes possible "the growth and predominance of our humanity proper, as distinguished from our animality" (*CA* 123, 47). In all this, he links the Wesleyan idea that fallen man bears "the image of the beast" to the propositional ground of modern cultural anthropology, in which humanness is radically a social attribute. "Man is human only because he is socialised," says Durkheim, for instance (*Selected Writings* 232), echoing Itard and framing a phrase that appears in a thousand subsequent variations in anthropological literature.[21]

The crucial aspect of "right reason" is that it is wholly produced by society and has no transcendental point of reference. From this point, it is only a short step (one that Arnold avoids taking, at great cost to the cogency of his argument) to proclaiming the relativistic doctrine that each society must then have its own "right reason," and that the values produced by one have no claim on any other. Yet quasi-religious ideas of transcendence are part and parcel of Arnold's scheme after all, as Catherine Gallagher's discussion of *Culture and Anarchy* emphasizes (*Industrial Reformation* 233–37). Arnoldian "culture" means a set of absolute values with which our "best self" is in touch. It is common therefore to regard Arnold's idea of "culture," which is said to be merely a name for the author's own preferred ideology, as the antitype of the relativistic, value-neutral "culture" of modern social science. The curious thing, given this ideologized reading of *Culture and Anarchy,* is that Arnold allows the table of superior values which he supposedly is advocating to go altogether unspecified. What does he mean when he speaks in maddeningly general terms (maddening for a reader who seeks to extract from this text a set of practical values) of the struggle to attain "perfection"? The answer is that "culture" means for Arnold, at bottom, something close to what it means for latter-day ethnographic theory: it refers not to any particular norms but to the unity, the complex wholeness, of *all* a society's constituent norms. It is a formal principle vacant of specific content, as far as Arnold's treatise tells us. The paradoxical, almost ineffable perfection which he urges his readers to seek to attain is, to use one of his key terms, a "totality" able to encompass ideals as radically opposed as those of "Hebraism" and "Hellenism" or those of the violently clashing interests of the three social classes. "What," he asks in an especially noteworthy phrase, "if we tried to rise above the idea of class to the idea of the whole community, . . . and to find our centre of light and authority there?" (*CA* 94). In place of promoting any specific moral program (excepting the condemnation of anarchy, which in his view overthrows the very possibility of value), Arnold simply preaches the sibylline doctrine of the existence of "the whole community" above all its seemingly contradictory particular elements, and thus the identity of "culture, and the harmonious perfection of our whole being, and what we call totality" (*CA* 21). It is precisely because Arnold imagines that the ideal thought-world of his society, were one able philosophically to grasp it in its "totality," forms a perfect, an almost mystical immanent unity that he focuses his outrage upon fetishism, fanaticism, mechanism, "class spirit": his lexicon of names for seizing wilfully upon this or that value out of context and promoting it at the expense of the complex integrated whole of *all* our values. We are free to object to this Arnoldian idea of "culture" on the grounds that it invests "the whole community" with a metaphysical, transcendent character, but not, finally, to contrast it with ethnographic "culture" in this regard; it is metaphysical in the very way that all theories of the "complex whole" are and no more dependent than they upon what Benedict, referring to anthropological literature, called "mystical phraseology."

The closeness of Arnold's thinking to modern culturalism stands out with particular clarity in his treatment of religion, which he defines as primarily a vehicle of membership in a certain collectivity and of participation in "the main current of national life" (*CA* 23). Given this secularized, sociological view of religion, we can make out a significant double meaning in Arnold's declaration of what he names as his fundamental principle: that "the framework of society . . . is sacred" (*CA* 202–3). The compacted logic of his phrase is spelled out a couple of decades later in Robertson Smith's meditation on primitive religion in one of the founding texts of modern anthropology, *The Religion of the Semites*. "Ultimately the only thing that is sacred [in early religion] is the common tribal life," says Robertson Smith (289). The sacred is merely another name for the collective. This principle is then taken over and greatly extended by Durkheim. "It is inter-social factors which have given birth to the religious sentiment," says Durkheim. If an individual "enters into relationship with the gods, it is not personally, but as a member of a society." The conclusion to which this thesis leads is that divine beings are "collective states objectified; they are society itself" (*Selected Writings* 220, 237). What we revere as divine and conceptualize as transcendent force is in fact the mysterious necessity by which we are fused with collective patterns of thinking, feeling, and behaving; and as we have seen, the collectivity in Durkheim, for all his emphatic empiricism, is expressly a metaphysical entity. In this sense one can truly say that "the framework of society . . . is sacred." Arnold's idea of "culture" as the immanent unity of society thus opens a door upon modern anthropological theory (and upon its series of unresolvable conundrums) even as it dramatizes its own origins in Wesleyan anxieties over the prospect of anarchically overflowing desire. Of all nineteenth-century texts, the Rosetta Stone for deciphering the emergence of the culture concept in its "wide ethnographic sense" may be *Culture and Anarchy*, after all.

The ever more equivocal status of the category called "freedom"— for one thing, its entanglement in a matrix of imagery of "restless," "extravagant and mobile," ultimately aimless and ineffectual desire— can seem to call for the taking of ever riskier and more drastic measures, or at least the manufacture of ever more hyperbolic metaphors, in order to attain the state of authentic freedom which is the goal of so much modern striving. Numbers of later writers have taken this path, striking aggressively anti-Victorian postures as a matter of course; but, in their attempt to exorcise once for all the specter of original sin, they often simply muster for new engagements the mobile army of nineteenth-century rhetorical devices. Such tactics generally involve resurrecting the antinomy of potentially boundless desire and of control which it has been the special historical mission of the concept of culture, in its attempt to bring all social phenomena within the scope of interpretation, to seek to abolish. But these figures have been instrumental to all Western endeavors to ponder social life over the last couple of centuries, and they continue to surface in something like their classic form. Liberation psychology as developed by writers like Herbert Marcuse and Norman O. Brown thus professes the ideal of "polymorphous perversity," a hypothetical condition of freely playing, presocial, unorganized forces of libido which realizes from afar Marianne Dashwood's creed of a spontaneity that "should know no moderation" and should reject "every commonplace notion of decorum" (*Sense and Sensibility* 56, 58). Evoking the state of ideal commonality which he calls "antistructure" or "communitas," the anthropologist Victor Turner, applying Western patterns of metaphor directly to African ritual, dwells in the same way on the possibility of euphoric release from social restraints. This movement as he invokes it "transgresses or dissolves the norms that govern structured and institutionalized relationships and is accompanied by experiences of unprecedented potency" which signal the liberation of "instinctual energies" (V. Turner 128). But it is of special interest here, given the attempt of the present book to write intellectual history informed by trends of current literary theory, that similar rhetoric, at once innovative and regressive in its imagery of what Allan Bloom speaks of as the modern "longing for the unlimited, the unconstrained" (Bloom 100), has found an important outlet in contemporary literary theory.

Writers in this tradition pursue the project not only of attacking false uniformitarian authority and "structure" but of transgressing the basic norms which hitherto have governed the institution of reading itself: norms easily figured as limitations imposed upon potentially free creative energy. From such a premise, critics reinvent the mythic theme of human boundlessness. This is the thrust of Roland Barthes's claim that a "writerly" literary text has no determinate limits of meaning, as allegedly held by the traditional decorum of interpretation, but consists instead of endlessly multiplying potentialities of meaning, "a triumphant plural, unimpoverished by any constraint of representation" (*S/Z* 5). It is as "multitudinous" as the civil disorders that haunted Matthew Arnold's nightmares. This suppositious text in all its polymorphous perversity becomes in Barthes's view "a galaxy of signifiers," a sudden opening-out of nearly boundless space, rather than a confining, arbitrarily imposed "structure of signifieds" (*S/Z* 5). Barthes attempts in this way to reconcile the semiological idea of culture—which takes highly structured form in his positing of a fixed series of "codes" of fictional representation—with its historical antecedent and catalyst, the drama of boundaries and boundlessness. The important point here is that he conjures a semiological realm which, as he says, "removes all limits to the freedom of reading" (quoted Culler 70) not as a disinterested academic theorist, if there is any such thing, but as an evangelist, to promote a mobilizing of desire and of its practical expression, a newly active and perilous method of reading. To follow this method is "to enter," he says, "into the limitless process of equivalences" (*S/Z* 40), a process describable as "free play" and as closely identifiable with (promiscuous, scandalous) erotic pleasure; to decline to follow it is "to return to the closure of Western discourse" (*S/Z* 7), the despotism of limitation and custom which, as Mill and Nietzsche claimed, sabotages desire. Rather than effecting a radical emancipation from "Western discourse," however, Barthes rehearses a line of rhetoric with a long history, part of which we are engaged in tracing—according to a method consonant in important ways with Barthes's own.[22]

The literary-critical mythology of limitlessness takes on another profile in the writing of Leo Bersani, who treats "established social order" as synonymous with political "authoritarianism" (Bersani 56) and invokes in drastically polarized terms the dualism of confining society and anarchic individuality which much modern inquiry has sought to dismantle on the grounds not only of its intellectual crudeness but also of its sinister political valences. He would concur in Pierre Bourdieu's assumption that cultural representation can only be seen as a process of "symbolic violence" aimed at securing vested interests (Bourdieu, "The Market of Symbolic Goods" 24). Thus the paramount function of society in Bersani's model is "to stifle the diversification and the originality of desire" (Bersani 41). The phrase echoes Mill and contains a pointed hint of its ultimate affinity to the doctrine of "original sin" as Wesley formulated it—only portrayed now from the inverted standpoint of, let us say, Satanic propaganda. Modern thought seems once more to have described a gigantic arc to return, counterclockwise as it were, to its point of departure. From this rediscovered perspective, the way to rejuvenate desire seems to lie in "going beyond the limits of a . . . socially defined . . . self" so as to recapture the human birthright—"radical psychic mobility" and what this author calls "the intensities of a body left to itself" (Bersani ix, x, 100). In this way, literary criticism can claim to open the way to "a liberating participation in the dissolving of fixed identities" (Bersani 29). This rhetoric of unlimited, which is to say, unorganized desire calls up the monitory ghost of Victor of Aveyron, a sacrifice to exactly this disarticulation of identity and this entrance into a state of what Itard called "meaningless mobility" and which he, like Wordsworth and Prichard, saw as the extreme opposite of liberation. Reasserting the paradigmatic opposition of ideas of free polymorphous desire on the one hand and of culturally-constructed boundaries on the other, Bersani's rhetoric at the same time reconstructs the theory on which totalitarian ideologies such as John Wesley's have long depended.

The Vicissitudes of the Passionate Primitive

Anthropological theory in its mature forms disavows the myth of boundless desire, but one of the paramount functions of anthropology in its early modern stage was in effect to validate scientifically this very myth and thus the theory of social control with which it has always been inseparably connected. This it did by claiming to locate this hypothetical state empirically in contemporary "savage" societies and, on a more speculative basis, in Europeans' own primitive past. The assumption was that social control was effectively nonexistent in preliterate tribal societies, and that as a result desire manifested itself there in an atmosphere of what one nineteenth-century commentator termed "brutal uncontrolled freedom" (Lovett 1:161). To furnish a context for detailed consideration of a set of relevant documents in chapter 3, we can take an overview here of the career of this nineteenth-century imagery of primitive society.

J. C. Prichard rehearses the commonplace of the day, hinting at the filiation between his anthropological and psychological interests, in declaring that "in a barbarous state of society the passions are under no restraint," and indeed "are in perpetual and violent agitation" (*Treatise* 175). Primitives seem to live in a permanent state of moral insanity, in other words. They are devoted helplessly to "the excess of the passions," says Harriet Martineau three years later (Martineau 69). This overdetermined legend had a long career. No less august an authority than Durkheim himself repeats it as late as 1902–3: "We know," he says, "of the intractability of primitive passions, their inability to restrain themselves, their natural tendency to excess" (*Moral Education* 133). In between, the cliché was repeated habitually, in fact compulsively, by writers operating within or on the frontiers of ethnography. Francis Galton thus refers in characteristic language to the "wild, untameable restlessness" that is "innate with savages" (quoted Stocking, *Victorian Anthropology* 95), Spencer discourses at length on the "explosive, chaotic, incalculable behaviour" of primitives, the result of their "uncontrolled following of immediate desires" (*Principles* 1:71, 63), and Bagehot declares that savages, having "no tutored habits," are "at the mercy of every impulse and blown by every passion" (*Physics and Politics* 439). In nineteenth-century evolutionary anthropology, one form of this mythic complex which bore an especially strong rhetorical charge was the thesis, identified with John McLennan and others, that among the earliest groups of human beings, "more or less promiscuous intercourse between the sexes . . . prevailed" (McLennan, *Primitive Marriage* 66). Ethnography backs up this presumption, he reports, by furnishing "examples of general promiscuity" among living primitive peoples (*Primitive Marriage* 70; see also 72n). The primary cultural institution, that of marriage, is represented by McLennan as a set of determinate boundaries (and moral significances) imposed upon desires that in the natural or primitive state are fluid, amorphous, limitless—and morally "depraved" (*Primitive Marriage* 12).

Such themes, driven as they are by deep currents of sensibility stemming more or less directly from the Wesleyan movement, are pervasive in the ethnographic literature of the first two thirds of the nineteenth century but find perhaps their fullest expression in the writings of the school of "degenerationist" anthropology. The doctrine of this long-lived school was that existing primitive societies, far from exhibiting the original state of mankind out of which "civilized" society evolved, are in fact degraded vestiges of originally higher civilizations founded under divine auspices. In the works of Richard Whatley, archbishop of Dublin and the best-known publicist of degenerationist thought, this argument, which was taken to rest on Biblical authority, serves as the vehicle for the crudest possible racism and cultural boasting,[23] but in those of Whatley's disciple W. Cooke Taylor, it leads unexpectedly to some of the most interesting cultural speculations of the first half of the nineteenth century.

The crux of Taylor's argument in *The Natural History of Society* [*NHS*] (1840) is the assertion that "civilization is natural to man" (*NHS* 1:19), which is to say that human faculties seem to presuppose life within society and to require it for their fullest development. If we substitute "culture" for "civilization" in Taylor's formula, and thus efface the invidious distinction between the latter and "barbarism," or tribal society, we find in this work the radical argument of Geertz and others, the argument which traces its roots back to the Enlightenment, was acted out experimentally by Itard, and given specifically Victorian form by Matthew Arnold, that *Homo sapiens* is wholly a creature of the social state, even to some degree in his physical constitution. Taylor thus collapses altogether the distinction between society and the "natural." His ideological presuppositions are as remote as possible from Itard's, yet in *The Natural History of Society* he often seems almost to be quoting from the two reports on the savage of Aveyron. "Man is formed in body and endowed in spirit for a social . . . life," he says, for example; deprived of such a life, he would be "the most helpless of all living things" (*NHS* 1:308, 98). This argument sharply contradicts the picture of man as naturally or originally a bundle of dangerous antisocial lusts needing to be held in check by agencies of control. Taylor accordingly denies the thesis of an aboriginal state of "promiscuous intercourse between the sexes" (a thesis which we thus see to have been current long before it was argued by McLennan in 1865) on the grounds of the same analogy with animals that Darwin later develops in *The Descent of Man,* and states that "domestic union [is] natural and necessary to man" (*NHS* 1:35). Biblical anthropology tends here, almost despite itself, to discountenance the idea of brutish, uncivilized "savagery." One finds surprisingly in degenerationist doctrine the germs of a theory of primitive society not wholly in thrall to the framing of negative judgment and to the phobic dread of "bestial" human propensities.

Nevertheless, the core of Taylor's treatise is a moral critique of primitives which takes the characteristic form of a meditation on the phenomena of boundlessness and restraint. At the center of the demonstration is the iconic Victorian image of "the uneducated savage, who has never been trained to check any impulse or control any passion" (*NHS* 1:270). Thus "among barbarians passions rage without the check or control which is always imposed by civilization"; they are licentious, addicted to gambling and to every other vice, and are afflicted with what Taylor describes as an "anarchical and selfish restlessness" (*NHS* 2:128)—this last term being, as we have seen, a central one in the nineteenth-century theoretical lexicon—that renders their social life chronically disordered and precarious.

For Taylor, depraved desire is thus natural in the sense that it occurs spontaneously and must always be strictly repressed by social means, yet at the same time it is "unnatural" in the sense that the social state, the state of established restraints, is man's proper and original one. This crucial paradox, and the charge of anxiety that it releases, are reflected in a remarkable excursus on cannibalism, which Taylor considers not as a social institution but rather as "a depraved and unnatural appetite"—yet one that automatically, by a kind of natural link with human instinct, gains control of a person the moment the circumstances are right. He cites the case of a European who indulged in cannibalism following a shipwreck and whose thoughts of this practice ever after were marked by "desire strangely mixed with loathing" (*NHS* 1:127). In explanation of such strange phenomena, Taylor offers the line of reasoning that has become a standard feature of twentieth-century theories of culture. Unlike animals, which are born with definite systems of instinctually programmed behavior patterns, man, Taylor postulates, is inherently indefinite and flexible, polymorphous, able potentially to assume a great variety of characters. He gives to this indeterminacy principle the special nineteenth-century twist that reveals in another aspect the persistent linkage of scientific speculation in this period to Wesleyan trends of thought. "When therefore [man] once yields to corrupting influences," says Taylor, "there are no limits to his degradation" (*NHS* 1:305). In short, boundlessness, conceived expressly in the idiom of boundless depravity called original sin, is the native characteristic of man, at once his great source of power and his constant peril. It is the reason why he is so prone to perverse extravagance and yet also, paradoxically, longs for limitation. "Hardly any restraint is so irksome to man . . . as to be left to his own discretion," says Taylor (*NHS* 2:166), drawing the same lesson that Wordsworth did in the "Ode to Duty." Again paradoxically, though man has so deep-rooted a tendency toward unbridled desire, this state appears in Taylor's anthropology not as a natural or original human state, but as a pathological departure, as "moral insanity."

Not only in the area of the carnal passions, the area of principal anxiety for Victorian moralists, but also in social, intellectual, and linguistic areas, Taylor detects evidence of the same natural/unnatural tendency, showing as he does so the same obsessive concern with uncontrollable processes of multiplication and expansion that runs through later theorists as ideologically remote from one another as, say, Arnold and Barthes. For example, he gives a strong stress to the supposedly fluctuating, unsteady state of savage languages, which thus evince the same morbid want of fixed limits that their bodily desires do. "All barbarous languages err both in excess and defect: by a very extravagant use of suffixes and affixes they multiply . . . synonyms to an almost incredible and very perplexing extent, while the number of objects for which they have names is very limited" (*NHS* 1:27). Primitive language seems attacked by a kind of cancer that spreads as uncontrollably as do certain perverse desires, causing linguistic entities to proliferate fantastically of their own accord, opening truly onto "a galaxy of signifiers" liberated from their referents. In this evocation of a kind of hemorrhage of symbolic order itself, we see a deep-running period fantasy stamping itself on ethnographic data in an especially aggressive way.

The degenerationist school is mainly known nowadays (if at all) as the object of E. B. Tylor's refutation in the evolutionary anthropology of *Primitive Culture,* but there is no necessary conflict between the two. Surprisingly perhaps, Taylor's *Natural History of Society* is in fact strongly committed to an evolutionary, progressive hypothesis. The chief component of the idea of civilization, says Taylor, is "the idea of progress, development, amelioration, or extension" (*NHS* 1:5), and he formulates the same distinction later made by Bagehot and others between societies in progressive advance and lower ones fixed in "permanent uniformity" (*NHS* 1:2). "Civilization is progressive, and barbarism stationary," he declares (*NHS* 1:5). Yet this does not mean that the "lower races" are permanently fixed and incapable of attaining civilization. "The very fact of the Indians having become degraded is a clear proof that their intellect is not stationary" (*NHS* 1:270). An anomaly runs throughout this argument and throughout a wider field of discourse as well, for on the one hand, "civilization" is identified here in the conventional way with a system of fixed restraints upon human drives, and is identified almost in the same breath with fluidity and progressive, expansive movement as against the stultifying fixity of "savage" society. It was apparently in large part in order to resolve the dilemma posed by this highly unstable configuration of ideas that nineteenth-century writers initiated a long campaign to refute the myth of unbridled primitive desire, and indeed, to replace it with something like its very opposite. This crucial paradigm shift reconstructed the field of anthropological inquiry and led inescapably in the direction of the concept of culture.

The revisionist view presented itself as a mere case of perfected observation of data. In E. B. Tylor's popularizing work *Anthropology* (1881), for instance, he directly addresses the issue. "Explorers of wild countries, not finding the machinery of police they are accustomed to at home, have sometimes rashly concluded that the savages lived unrestrained at their own free will." This, however, "is a mistake, for life in the uncivilized world is fettered at every turn by chains of custom" (*Anthropology* 409). John Lubbock had said the same thing in almost the same words (Lubbock 303), as would Frazer: the savage, he states, far from being "the freest of mankind," is in reality a slave to "the chain of custom" (*Golden Bough* 1:217). So also would McLennan himself, the theorist of "primitive promiscuity." It is wholly an error to imagine that savages are animalistic and anarchic, he declares in the posthumous *Studies in Ancient History* (1896), for in fact they are intensely religious and live "under the constant pressure of a rigid body of customary law"

(32). As early as 1861, Maine, too, had described the "rigidity" of primitive law, which, he declared, "chained down" most societies of the world (quoted Evans-Pritchard, *History* 84–85). Franz Boas in the twentieth century was still refuting the hardy nineteenth-century legend that primitives, being "unrestrained," show "a lack of control of emotions"; the truth is that among these peoples, "passions are just as much controlled as ours, only in different directions." Indeed, the more primitive a people, says Boas, unwittingly quoting Arnold's description of the puritan ethos in England, the more "it is bound by customs regulating the conduct of daily life in all its details" (*Mind of Primitive Man* 131, 133, 234). As for the technical theory of primitive promiscuity, it, too, proved hard to eradicate, so deep a grip does it have on the European imagination. Darwin and other writers labored to refute it, and as late as 1927, Malinowski still felt it necessary to declare that "even in the most licentious cultures nothing like 'promiscuity' exists or could ever have existed." In all societies, he declares, we find "a system of cultural taboos which limit considerably the working of the sexual impulse" (*Sex and Repression* 195, 197). The point has been worth making again and again. "Sex cannot safely be left without restraints," says G. P. Murdock. "All known societies, consequently, have sought to bring its expression under control by surrounding it with restrictions" (Murdock 4).[24] Such rebuttals as these dispute McLennan's data while taking for granted, we should be sure to notice, the basic figuration of fluid desire bottled up under pressure, thanks to society, within definite limits.

What we see, then, is a broad reversal of assumptions in which "savage" society is transformed from a void of institutional control where desire is rampant to a spectacle of controls exerted systematically upon the smallest details of daily life. The dynamics of this doctrinal sea-change of the mid- to late-nineteenth century are not necessarily easy to decipher, but we will be wasting our time if we seek to trace it to some new accession of empirical knowledge when it bears witness, in fact, to that kind of reorganization of fundamental interpretive categories and their associated emotional values which causes a familiar body of knowledge suddenly to appear in a new light—to open to scientists, as Kuhn says, "a different world" (*Structure of Scientific Revolutions* 111). The reformed view of savages only makes historical sense if we see it as intimately associated with the unravelling of orthodox moral ideas which took place in and about the depression-stricken eighteen-seventies, centering on that subversive attack on

Victorian principles of discipline and Victorian "machinery of police" which animates the writings of Mill, Spencer, Samuel Butler, Hardy, and others. As discipline increasingly took on negative connotations in late-Victorian discourse, becoming identified with hypocrisy, philistinism, sadism, exploitation, and prejudice, it became a natural operation now to discover it in its most oppressive forms in primitive society, just as the previous generation of sensibility steeped in Evangelical thinking had constructed its own didactic image of primitives as figures of crazily uncontrolled passion. In contrast to the ethic of emancipated critical thought newly ascendent among European intellectuals, tribal societies (like the unenlightened sectors of English society itself) were now disparagingly seen as "fettered," "bound," "chained down" by mindless conventionality. This reading of the new perspective on primitives is made crystal clear by the urbane, liberal-minded Bagehot, who explains to his late-century public that savages' exorbitant devotion to custom and discipline, their oppression by the stultifying "cake of custom," is precisely the reason for their (manifest) inferiority to progressive, developing European societies. The new current of thought was in some regards consciously anti-Victorian, but ended by reasserting Victorian ideas of cultural superiority after all, making primitives, who were in no position to protest, and who by virtue of their remoteness and obscurity were uniquely available for such operations, once again play their traditional role as the scapegoats of European self-perceptions.

We can catch an especially clear glimpse of the above-described paradigm shift at what amounts to the exact moment of its occurrence in volume 1 (1876) of Spencer's *Principles of Sociology*. On the one hand, Spencer very emphatically rehearses the traditional discourse on primitive savages: they are figures of wild uncontrolled passion and their lives are most often a pandemonium of violent anarchy. "Generally . . . among uncivilized peoples, as among animals, instincts and impulses are the sole incentives and deterrents"; as a result, "horrors beyond our imaginations of possibility are committed by primitive men" (*Principles* 1:735, 265). Spencer strongly asserts the truth of the theory of sexual promiscuity and the reign of "unrestrained sexual instincts" in "the primitive unregulated state" (*Principles* 1:657, 645). These passages from the pen of one of the most militant freethinkers of his time say a lot about the linkage of Victorian evolutionary theory to its never-acknowledged substratum of original-sin theology. They read indeed like direct quotations from the long anthropological passages of Wesley's treatise "The Doctrine of Original Sin," which asserts that in primitive ages "all manner of vice . . . reigned . . . without control," and that contemporary savages such as the Indians of Georgia, whom the author professed to know from personal experience in that colony, were all of them sadistic monsters, not to mention "gluttons, drunkards, thieves, dissemblers, liars" (Wesley, *Works* 9:200, 212). But the rehearsal of these notions also marks a crucial point of tension for Spencer, whose sociology is tied inseparably to his radical critique of Victorian agencies of surveillance and discipline, and who makes individual freedom his cardinal value. It seems to confirm the above thesis about the political origins of theories of savagery, therefore, that Spencer regularly contradicts his own (which is to say, Wesley's) arguments. The anarchic savage, he asserts, is purely a fiction after all, particularly in reference to his supposed sexual promiscuity. "I do not think the evidence shows that promiscuity ever existed in an unqualified form," he declares. Ethnographic evidence requires us to infer "that even in prehistoric times, promiscuity was checked by the establishment of individual connexions." Generally speaking, even "among the lowest savages," he tells us, life is governed by "a considerable amount of ceremonial regulation" (*Principles* 1:632, 635; 2:4). Later he quotes with approval Lubbock's dictum that "the savage is nowhere free," but, rather, lives a life strictly "regulated by a complicated and often most inconvenient set of customs (as forcible as laws), of quaint prohibitions and privileges" (*Principles* 2:322). From being the exemplar of anarchic freedom, primitive man is troped within a single text into the reverse, the exemplary case of abject subservience to law.

Here again, however, a strategically introduced idea seems to have generated unforeseen consequences. The thesis of custom-shackled savagery could be given, as it was, a wholly different twist, with genuinely revolutionary consequences this time. Thus a later generation of writers including Boas and Malinowski turns the revised myth of savagery inside-out, using it as the basis of a determined rehabilitation of the (twofold) Victorian image of technologically underdeveloped people. To demonstrate that primitives are bound by severe rules of conduct is in this interpretive light to normalize them, and thus in principle to dispel the repugnance and dread that the alien always arouses, and that Victorian culture, with its acute fixation on vice and uncleanness, emphasized to a morbid degree. The most significant outgrowth of this altered perspective from the disciplinary point of view is the newly formalized theory of "participant observation" in ethnography, which amounts first and foremost, perhaps, to the affirmation on the ethnographer's part that his objects of study are not so morally degenerate and otherwise repellent that a respectable European academic should be squeamish about living physically among them. It constitutes a warrant of acceptance (even though for Malinowski, the theory's first professional practitioner, acceptance was far easier to postulate in the abstract than to act on in the field).

Fully as much as the original fantasy of savage life, in any case, this rehabilitation, which one can think of as the paramount achievement of the culture concept, was a tendentious one charged with political motives and emotions, notably a (usually veiled) revulsion from Victorian bigotry, ethnocentrism, and cultural aggression, and from the devastation of native societies that these combined influences had brought about. Whatever truth it may contain, it was a fabrication which had little to do with the disinterested operations of that make-believe activity called pure empirical science. Reconfiguring savages in anthropological literature as possessors of culture and thus "control" of passional drives was at heart an Oedipal act of repudiation of one's own Victorian forefathers and of the cultural scapegoating they practiced habitually. We have touched already on the irony that modern ethnography could only express the redeemed, normalized image of primitives through an imposition of scientific "law and order" that seems (in its compulsion to master the smallest details of primitive life) to reinstate the Victorian ideology of unrelenting discipline that it claims to overthrow. Spencer was right: the cultural past is a conspiracy of ghosts from which we have scarcely any way to extricate ourselves.

Durkheim's Fable of Modern Desire

The decay of the Evangelical mentality in Britain after midcentury thus made the idea of boundless human desire seem ever more like the fantasy it was and implied the need to organize sociological thinking around new categories and new methods of research. It is a sign of the essential role which it has played in modern social discourse that it was at this point in its career given a new lease on life and a more elaborate philosophical exposition than it had ever before received. Its new champion was a writer with no evident ties to Evangelical Protestantism and whose broad intellectual principles would be anathema to any variety of Christian belief, but whose arguments sometimes show an intriguing continuity with Evangelical ones: Emile Durkheim.

Like Spencer, whom he often disparages rather than acknowledging his important debt to him, Durkheim in *The Division of Labor in Society* [*DLS*] (1893) argues that social differentiation is the process by which advanced society arises from primitive forms, and that this process leads to increased rather than decreased social solidarity. However, in the contemporary world, the reverse result seems to have occurred, and Durkheim's discussion of this fact involves him in theoretical difficulties. In his effort to banish moralistic preconceptions from sociology, he stresses two years later in *The Rules of Sociological Method* that any trait widely generalized in a society and in similar societies is by definition "normal" and not "pathological." Thus criminality, for instance, is a normal and essentially healthy feature of our society, and one that it would be impossible to eliminate without causing the most harmful consequences (*Rules* 97–99). But in *The Division of Labor* and other works, he defines a contemporary state that is apparently both general *and* pathological.[25] Modern morality, he says, "is in the throes of an appalling crisis." "Our beliefs have been disturbed. Tradition has lost its sway. Individual judgement has thrown off the yoke of the collective judgement" (*DLS* 339). He bestows on this condition of inoperative norms the technical name that has stood ever since for one of the fundamental concepts of modern social analysis: the name *anomie.*

In subsequent sociological interpretations, this term has taken on various meanings. In Robert K. Merton's influential account, it refers to a discrepancy between accepted social norms of success and the institutional means which a society offers for the attainment of such norms. But in its original form, the term refers very distinctly to a social state in which norms have ceased to act effectively in their role of restraining influences. Durkheim's explication of modern-day anomie is not wholly consistent, but one strand of his thinking on anomic disorder *is*: his steady linking of this issue to the problematic nature of "freedom" and specifically to the concept of boundlessness. The modern predicament, according to him, is specifically an epidemic of boundlessness. For instance, the erratic, uncontrolled nature of modern economic life can be traced, he argues, to the vast dispersion of consumer markets. Consequently the producer of goods "can no longer keep the whole market within his purview, not even mentally.

He can no longer figure out to himself its limits, since it is, so to speak, unlimited" (*DLS* 305). The same principle holds in even more pronounced fashion in the area of individual will and desire. "Our ambitions are boundless," says Durkheim, seeming here to refer to the human race at large, "and are consequently only moderated when they are mutually held in check by one another" (*DLS* 318). This is just what fails to occur in the modern setting. "[The] liberation of desires has been made worse by the . . . development of industry and the almost infinite extension of the market" (Durkheim, *Suicide* 255), but economic change is just one of an array of contributing factors. The idea of desires *intrinsically without limits,* thus always volatile and dangerous, recurs throughout Durkheim's writings; and at this point in our argument it cannot be surprising that behind it one persistently traces the outline of original-sin theology. "Nothing appears in man's organic nor in his psychological constitution which sets a limit" to his longings for comfort and luxury, he declares. "Human activity naturally aspires beyond assignable limits and sets itself unattainable goals"; it is "an insatiable and bottomless abyss" (*Suicide* 247–48). Where does Durkheim find grounds for these assertions? It can only be in the complex of metaphysical ideas summed up in Wesley's claim that "sensual appetites . . . have . . . the dominion over [man]" by virtue of "the entire depravation of the whole human nature" (*Sermons* 2:219, 222).

Both writers accordingly stress one principle that has had a long and influential career in modern discourse: the principle that, in Durkheim's words, "unlimited desires are insatiable by definition" and have an intensely addictive character of increasing tolerance levels such that "the more one has, the more one wants, since satisfactions received only stimulate instead of filling needs" (*Suicide* 247, 248). Wesley himself was perhaps the original analyst of this pathological state, which with the advent of the problem of mass alcoholism in the nineteenth century and the calamity of heroin and cocaine epidemics in the twentieth has become one of our principal categories of interpretation. "Who would expend anything in gratifying . . . desires," asks Wesley, "if he considered, that to gratify them is to increase them? Nothing can be more certain than this: daily experience shows, the more they are indulged, they increase the more" (*Sermons* 2:321). All worldly pleasures are found to be "flat and insipid" when no longer novel, he remarks elsewhere, but "the same desire will remain still. The inbred thirst remains fixed in the soul; nay, the more it is indulged, the more it increases, and incites us to follow after another, and yet another object; although we leave every one with an abortive hope, and a deluded expectation" (*Sermons* 2:220–21). This is precisely the state described by Freud in nearly the same words (with specific reference now to erotic desire) under the name "psychanesthesia."[26] "Nothing gives satisfaction," echoes Durkheim, "and all this agitation is uninterruptedly maintained without appeasement" (*Suicide* 253). "Desires will tend naturally to keep outstripping their goals," he says in *Socialism,* so that even those who achieve all they currently desire will "continue to be plagued by the same restlessness that torments them today." "Needs are limitless" (*Selected Writings* 177). The "continuity of violent yet unsatisfied desires" which Itard diagnosed in Victor turns out not to be a pathological aberration, but the general modern condition.

This insistent Durkheimian thesis and its consequences for sociology are most elaborately developed in *Moral Education* [*ME*], originally a lecture series of 1902–3. Durkheim lays great stress in this work on one essential principle of the emerging culture concept, the absolute consubstantiality of the individual and his or her society. "It is outside us and envelops us, but it is also in us and is everywhere an aspect of our nature. We are fused with it" (*ME* 71). The result of this postulate is that the idea of inherently unlimited desires is able to underwrite a specific sociohistorical analysis in which limitlessness appears not after all as "natural," still less as a trait peculiar to tribal societies, but now as a distinguishing element of modern thought and experience. It is rooted, for one thing, in the glorifying of social mobility in the ideology of democratic capitalism, according to Durkheim. "Because, in principle, all vocations are available to everybody, the drive to get ahead is more readily stimulated and inflamed beyond all measure to the point of knowing almost no limits" (*ME* 49). As he stresses in many passages, this tendency is sponsored by concerted agencies of propaganda which operate under the banners of the sacrosanct concepts of individualism and freedom and which are calculated, he says, to arouse "an impatience with all restraint and limitation, the desire to encourage unrestrained and infinite appetite" (*ME* 36). It is this "malady of infinite aspiration" (*ME* 40) and its accompanying breakdown of social discipline that Durkheim names as the keynotes of nineteenth-century European history.

His solution to the form of "moral insanity" that he calls anomie is not, like Merton's, the provision of effective instruments for satisfying socially legitimate aspirations, but rather, the empowering of authoritative public moral and educational institutions to set norms that will as their primary function impose limits upon what people desire. This will entail no infringement on a state of original or natural freedom, for "man, in fact, is made for life in a determinate, limited environment" (*ME* 48), which is to say, a social environment. Durkheim rests this axiom not, as W. Cooke Taylor did long before, on Scriptural authority, but on what he presents as empirical evidence that people freed from a constraining sense of limits at once suffer acute, even suicidal distress. Boundless desire, that morbid ideal that since the late eighteenth century has repeatedly masqueraded as "freedom" in polemical writing, is thus a cruel hoax. "A need, a desire freed of all restraints, and all rules, no longer geared to some determinate objective and, through this same connection, limited and contained, can be nothing but a source of constant anguish for the person experiencing it. What gratification, indeed, can such a desire yield, since by definition it is incapable of being satisfied?" (*ME* 39–40). "In sum, the theories that celebrate the beneficence of unrestricted liberties are apologies for a diseased state" (*ME* 54). Their true result is not expanded and enhanced freedom but anomie, which means lapsing into the very condition which Evangelical theologians called original sin: bondage to one's own unfocused, unbounded appetites. We should not be misled by the different technical and rhetorical idioms in which nineteenth-century Evangelicals and modern social theorists have elaborated this principle or by the tenuousness of any chain of direct transmission of ideas which might be constructed between, say, John Wesley and Durkheim; the congruent metaphorical structures of their texts tell us plainly that they are participants in a single movement of thought. This movement is nothing other than the great "moral and intellectual revolution" of modern times which Southey identified primarily with the influence of Wesley himself.

From the point of view of scientific sociology, the diagnostic phenomenon of the state of unappeasable cravings and its accompanying "dejection and pessimism" (*ME* 68) is a rising curve of suicide rates. Its predominant metaphor in Durkheim, as in numerous other writers noticed in this chapter, is imagery of that state known almost technically by now as "restlessness": erratic, irregular, redundant, uncontrollably self-contradicting motion. This is what we see, Durkheim asserts, both in savages and in children: "a mind endlessly moving, a veritable kaleidoscope that changes from one moment to the next" (*ME* 134); "a state of nervous agitation, of contagious feverishness" (*ME* 152).

Anomic individuals, in their "state of endless instability," are "subject to momentary impulses, to the disposition of the moment, to whatever notion is in mind at the moment" (*ME* 27), to "the most contradictory inclinations, the most antithetical whims" (*ME* 44–45). In other words, to what Wordsworth called "chance desires" and what Bersani long afterwards would glorify as "radical psychic mobility."

In his effort to portray individual moral and psychological states as integral to their social milieu, Durkheim protests against "some hoary habits of thinking, which oppose society and the individual as two contrary and antagonistic categories" (*ME* 67). Yet his own argument about the need to construct walls of moral restraints around individual appetites seems to depend on just this paradigm after all, and thus to resurrect a long tradition of discourse. "Morality is . . . like so many molds with limiting boundaries, into which we must pour our behavior" (*ME* 26). "Moral rules are genuine forces, which confront our desires and needs, our appetites of all sorts, when they promise to become immoderate" (*ME* 41). But if desire itself emerges from social origins, how can morality decide when this point has been reached? And does it make sense, after all, to speak scientifically of boundless desires? How can there be such a thing as a desire that is infinite, without a definite object? Durkheim asserts the reality of this dubious category on the strength of a complex of supremely prestigious traditional metaphors. The concept of anomie as a state of unconstrained, pathologically "restless," unsatisfiable desire represents the furthest possible thing, in other words, from a scientific "discovery." Rather, it represents the codification of a set of moral concepts and of naturalizing metaphors that had been fully developed in many complex ramifications throughout the preceding century and, having long held a central position in European social discourse, were indispensable to the invention of "culture." It would be hard, indeed, to think of another concept that more convincingly illustrates Fleck's claim that scientific theories do not arise from "so-called empirical observations" but rather are always crystallizations of broadly based "thought styles." "The true creator of a new idea is not an individual but the thought collective," he states (Fleck 123). The materials surveyed in this chapter demonstrate that the idea of anomic desire was a collective and a long-drawn-out production, and a concatenation of audacious rhetorical devices, if ever there was one.

CHAPTER TWO

DESIRE, WEALTH, AND VALUE: ANOMIC THEMES IN POLITICAL ECONOMY

O ne of the minor enigmas of modern intellectual history has been the apparent lapse of "anthropological" writing, particularly that strand of it based on theories of evolutionary stages in the development of civilization, in the first half of the nineteenth century.[1] George W. Stocking, Jr.'s *Victorian Anthropology* goes a long way toward filling in the record of the missing half-century, but if we focus less on evolutionary theories of civilization than on the problem of the emergence of the ethnographic concept of culture, the impression of a hiatus in anthropological inquiry persists. J. C. Prichard, whose "ethnology" forms the dominant line of anthropological thought in this period, explicitly disavows, as we noted, any inquiry into the nature and causes of cultural diversity, and by the same token displays no awareness of cultural unity as a phenomenon worthy of speculation or analysis. Enlightenment probings into the philosophical theory of culture per se—the theory that could provide the rationale for detailed ethnographic analysis of particular societies—seem not to have been pursued by anthropologists in the first half of the nineteenth century.

They were pursued by writers in other fields, notably in one which played a fundamental but largely unrecognized role in crystallizing the modern idea of culture and thus in defining a dimension of modern consciousness itself: political economy.[2] The great upsurge of this discipline coincides significantly with the period of recession of speculative energy in anthropology, and just as significantly slackens with the emergence of the latter as a reconstituted science of culture in and around the eighteen-sixties. Walter Bagehot reports in his essay on Ricardo in *Economic Studies* [*ES*] (1880) that political economy "was . . . the favourite subject in England from about 1810 to about 1840," but since then has lost its great prestige (*ES* 154). Various hypotheses have been offered to explain the decline of the rage for political economy.[3] The truth may be that the decisive factor in this decline was the increasing usurpation after midcentury of some of the economists' most philosophically resonant themes by other branches of social science, notably sociology and, as it was defined in 1878, that "artificial assemblage of heterogeneous inquiries known by the name of anthropology" (quoted Abrams 192). The signature of the close original affinity between the two spheres of study, in any case, is the great frequency with which early economists' arguments run off into "the scientific study of savage tribes," the vogue of which, as Bagehot twice remarks, "is so peculiar a feature of the present world" (*ES* 57; see also 166). We shall see that these arguments develop essential themes of scientific theories of culture, including the theme of the anxious awareness that scientific logic in this field may never be able, try as it may, to free itself from a swarm of "metaphysical phantoms." As early economic theorists pursue these subjects, they inscribe themselves in the history of the mentality of their age by their preoccupation with the idea of anomic desire. This idea surges insistently, and not always in a logically intelligible way, into their work, yielding glimpses of the deeper stratum of subjectivity which political economy both draws upon and, as a condition of its status as a technical discourse, strives with all the rhetorical means at its command to suppress from view.

The issue of anomie does not play the same role in the economic work of John Stuart Mill, whose *Principles of Political Economy* (1848) defined the field for Victorian readers, that it does in that of the three writers to be considered in the present chapter. This absence is no surprise, given Mill's conviction that the capacity for desire of modern British people had atrophied almost beyond recall. His political economy plays out nonetheless the traditional allegorical drama of desire and limitation, ramified now into an intricate configuration of reasoning and of abstract-seeming technical vocabulary that may conceal the inner structure of his thought. On the one hand, his theme is wealth, the "universal object of human desire" (as he calls it on his first page) and thus to some extent a metaphor for desire itself; yet Mill thrusts well into the realm of sophisticated cultural theory by demonstrating at length both that the "desire of accumulation," which according to his theory provides all the motive power for the capitalist machine, is not constant but radically variable from one society to another, and that what people seem in fact to crave is not wealth itself, but rather the panoply of symbolism which represents it (*Principles* 1:1, 198–212). "A polity having grown up [in England] which made wealth the real source of political influence, its acquisition was invested with a fictitious value, independent of its intrinsic utility"; and "so strong is the association between personal consequence and the signs of wealth, that the . . . desire for the appearance of a large expenditure has the force of a passion among large classes of a nation which derives less pleasure than perhaps any other in the world from what it spends" (*Principles* 1:211). What Mill describes, in other words, is not a "violence of desire battering at the limits of representation" (Foucault), but rather, desire conceived as wholly penetrated by and predicated upon representation. This passionate desire for signs, for the metaphorical imagery of wealth, is subject, however, to the harsh limiting principle defined in what Mill claims to be "the most important proposition in political economy" (*Principles* 1:214): the law of diminishing returns on marginal agricultural land.

As population expands with national prosperity and ever greater supplies of food are needed, ever more land must be put into cultivation (or previously cultivated land must be farmed more intensively, which amounts to the same thing). This supplementary land being necessarily of declining quality, ever greater amounts of expenditure are required to produce a given amount of food. Food costs are therefore bound to rise and to sabotage the prosperity that had made the expansion of agriculture necessary to begin with. That this law grounds economic science in a fundamental principle of limitation upon human desire, rendering desire in effect self-contradictory and necessarily a source of grief and frustration,[4] is plainly underscored in Mill's language. "Land differs from the other elements of production, labor and capital, in not being susceptible of indefinite increase. Its extent is limited, and the extent of the more productive kinds of it more limited still. . . . This limited quantity of land, and limited productiveness of it, are the real limits to the increase of production" (*Principles* 1:213). Showing his awareness of the dependence of this argument on its central figure of speech, he pauses to reflect on just this question. "The limitation to production from the properties of the soil, is not like the obstacle opposed by a wall, which stands immovable in one particular spot, and offers no hindrance to motion short of stopping it entirely," he remarks. "We may rather compare it to a highly elastic and extensible band" (*Principles* 1:214). Just as material wealth itself is displaced by signs and by a system of "fictitious value" in the life of society, so the analytical science of wealth can only proceed, it seems, by spinning a web of (morally loaded) metaphors which, generating arrays of metametaphors, themselves turn out to be the subjects of technical exegesis.

In more than one respect, political economy might seem impossible to reconcile with the idea of culture. For one thing, it is based not on the hypothesis of social solidarity but on that of strife and competition, for, as Mill says, "only through the principle of competition has political economy any pretension to the character of a science" (*Principles* 1:286). Economists accordingly take it as a rule of procedure, Mill stipulates, to exclude from consideration any causes of "economic" phenomena other than competition—causes based in particular on customary usages, the very material upon which a science of culture builds (*Principles* 1:526). To rephrase the same point, political economy can be said to confine itself to the study of quantifiable material entities and the causal processes that operate upon them, to the neglect of all the immaterial phenomena, patterns of symbolic meaning and of moral and affective values, which form the order of "culture." "The laws and conditions of the production of wealth, partake of the character of physical truths," says Mill at one point, emphatically banishing from his science the dimension of cultural relativity (*Principles* 1:241; see also 1:60–61). Yet political economy was so constituted as never to be able to stay within the bounds of such a restrictive formula.

Mill himself contradicts it in a memorable early passage which dissolves altogether the border between economics and what came to be called cultural anthropology. "In so far as the causes [of the economical condition of nations] are moral or psychological, dependent on institutions and social relations or on the principles of human nature, their investigation belongs not to physical, but to moral and social science, and is the object of what is called Political Economy" (*Principles* 1:26). The main expression of this speculative and philosophical impulse within political economy, and indeed the preeminent achievement of this science, was the development of a new paradigm of analysis in which all social productions—all "commodities" at least—are endowed with the peculiar property of standing for all others, and thus of creating a social field which in a very distinct way embodies "an inextricable web of affinities." This field proves to consist not in physical things at all, but *wholly in abstract relations*. Woolens, silk, cutlery, sugar, timber, corn: on the theory of political economy, "any one of them," says Mill, "may be taken as a representative of all the rest" (*Principles* 1:524; see also 2:2). Political economy comes into being to this degree as nothing other than the science of symbolic representation in society, which is to say, of culture. This train of thought is logically continuous with the problem of desire and limitation, but in fact the problem of desire tends in Mill's economics to recede from view (this is the basis of his dispute with Malthus, as we shall see), and it is not farfetched to read the development of the conception of society as a matrix of symbolic forms as a means of mastering that panicky anxiety with regard to desire that forms so frequent and so keen a motive in nineteenth-century sensibility. The disruptive force of desire is made to evaporate, on the level of rhetoric at least, as it is diffused throughout the galaxy of signifiers which political economy opens to view.

What this move generates as its necessary byproduct, however, is the sense of indeterminacy and cognitive instability that comes with the loss of faith in the transcendental signified—the sense which in the field of cultural theory crystallizes in the principle of "relativism." Mill's habitual rhetorical mode calls for asserting categorical solutions to the various conceptual difficulties of political economy. But again and again the *Principles of Political Economy* goes out of its way to emphasize problems which at least potentially do not lend themselves to resolution. Hence, for example, Mill's exploration of the riddle of the relation of "value" to another relation, the ratio of supply and demand. In order for the idea of a ratio here to make sense, he reasons, we need to construe "demand" as meaning the *quantity* of a commodity which is demanded (a significant logical maneuver to which we shall return). "But . . . the quantity demanded is not a fixed quantity, even at the same time and place; it varies according to the value. . . . But it was before laid down, that the value depends on the demand. From this contradiction how shall we extricate ourselves? How solve the paradox, of two things, each depending on the other?" Mill identifies here precisely the paradox inherent in the hypothesis of culture, as we have seen: if no phenomenon in society can be defined except relativistically, as a set of internal and external relations without positive terms, logical indeterminacy insinuates itself into every act of analysis. The very notions of internal and external collapse ambiguously into one another in this context. That Mill does propose what he calls a solution to this problem of seemingly uncontrollable referential circularity is less significant than his stress on the issue itself, an example, as he says, of the kinds of dilemmas in political economy that "obscurely haunt every inquirer into the subject" (*Principles* 1:533; see also 1:34, 38, 523.). There is no need to dwell on Mill's invocation here of that figure of ghostly haunting which virtually defines, as we have seen at some length, the anthropological imagination in the act of reflecting upon itself.

Striving as he does to establish political economy on the solid footing of an autonomous scientific project, Mill does all he can to efface the linkage between the development of economic science and the cultural problem of desire. That such a link existed from the first is evident, however, in the works of other classic economists, starting with Adam Smith himself.

Adam Smith and the Natural System of Society

Any attempt at a full account of the evolution of nineteenth-century social thought in Britain needs to stress the originating influence of Adam Smith. *The Wealth of Nations* (1776) lays the groundwork for a theory of culture by proposing a model of society as an integral, quasi-natural system the one essential function of which is the maintenance, through a network of specific institutions, of its own equilibrium. This it achieves, he argues, through coordinated agencies of exchange and through what these presuppose, agencies of the construction of *value*, both of which principles are so deeply implicated in human desire as almost to be its prerequisites. But his exposition of these themes is haunted from the outset by the aura of ambiguity which surrounds his notion of "system."

In a long, odd-seeming passage in *The Theory of Moral Sentiments* [*TMS*] (1759), he argues that an estheticized "love of system" (*TMS* 185) forms one of the ruling compulsions of the human psyche. When public-spirited citizens propose schemes for social reform, for example, they may declare and actually imagine that they are motivated by concerns for human welfare, whereas in fact they are merely infatuated with the entrancing appearance of order and rationality in their own proposals. Similarly, when we glorify in our imaginations (and long to share in) the luxurious lives of the great, it is not really, though it may seem to be, the personal enjoyment afforded by luxury that we admire and crave, for "we naturally confound it in our imagination with the order, the regular and harmonious movement of the system . . . by means of which it is produced" (*TMS* 183). These comic illustrations of Smith's hint plainly at the epistemological problems we may encounter in trying to distinguish systems existing in the real world from the fictions of orderly systems which we generate all unconsciously under the influence of our own ardent aesthetic impulses. Specifically, they forecast the equivocal nature of modern theories of culture, which seem unable to do more than dogmatically impose upon the phenomenal chaos of an observed society the groundless presumption that all its many features constitute a "complex whole." Smith's argument that our thinking at every level is motivated by a compulsive "love of system" implies that social theory will necessarily be estranged from social reality itself. How can it escape simply imposing the structure of its own desires upon the world it surveys?[5]

This issue is sharply highlighted in Smith's brilliant essay "The History of Astronomy" [Astron], which presents in effect a theoretical prolegomena to his subsequent work of cultural and economic analysis—masking its potentially devastating implications for every branch of social science by its apparent reference to physical science only. In this essay, Smith uses the term "system" to refer specifically to constructs of philosophical ideas, and strikes a distinctly modern note in refusing to identify these constructs with properties of reality itself. By definition, a system in this sense expresses relationships among ideas only, says Smith: its claim to give knowledge of outward reality is necessarily specious. In the last paragraph of the essay, he gives this theme the fullest possible emphasis. The flawless correspondence of Newtonian astronomy, which he has just surveyed, with all observed facts of nature tends to make one attribute to this mesmerizing theory more reality than even the most fully verified ideas ever can possess, says Smith. "Even we, while we have been endeavouring to represent all philosophical systems as mere inventions of the imagination, to connect together the otherwise disjointed and discordant phaenomena of nature, have insensibly been drawn in, to make use of language expressing the connecting principles of this one, as if they were the real chains which Nature makes use of to bind together her several operations" (Astron 105). Smith evidently presumes that "real chains" connecting phenomena do exist, but they seem to lie beyond any conceivable description and analysis. The "imaginary machines" of scientific systems (Astron 66) are thus not just moot, but false. What we call the organization of outward reality expresses our own profoundly delusive psychic craving, and *nothing more.*

Except in the passages that I have cited, Smith does not belabor this issue in "The History of Astronomy," but it seems implicit in others where he shows how the system-hypothesis has led various scientific theorists to posit the presence in nature of occult forces and substances. What he articulates here is the fundamental logic of the imagery that is endemic, as we saw, in modern sociological theory: Smith lets us see that when an "imaginary" construct—that is to say, any system—emerges in the guise of a real fact of nature, it is bound to assume a ghostly or magical character. This is the sort of entity brought into being, says Adam Smith, in Descartes' account of the movement of an iron object when placed near a magnetic one: "we imagine certain invisible effluvia to circulate around one of them, and . . . to impel the other . . . to move towards it" (Astron 42). In the same fashion, the brilliance of Newton's identification of gravity as "the connecting principle which joined together the movements of the Planets" (Astron 98) seduces Smith into speaking of gravity as though it were actually a physical force, a new kind of "invisible effluvium" emanating from objects and instantaneously exerting force upon others vast distances away; it is only with difficulty that he chastely reminds himself and us that gravity is after all just another fictionalized relationship emanating not from material objects at all but from the sole origin of all relations, the human mind.[6]

Smith thus performs upon the ratiocinative method of physical science exactly the same deconstructive analysis that E. B. Tylor and then Frazer, in some of the key texts of early anthropological theory, perform upon primitive belief in "imitative" and "contagious" magic. According to their exposé of the "false and barren" principles of "savage" thought (Frazer 1:222), magic expresses "the tendency of the uneducated mind to give an outward material reality to its own inward processes," and thus to imagine between mentally associated objects a "real connexion" (Tylor, *Researches* 111, 101) which links them together by a "secret sympathy" or "a kind of invisible ether" (Frazer 1:54). One may wonder: does the anthropological assault on primitive superstition spring at last from a troubled consciousness that the scientific investigation of culture is by its nature in thrall to magical reasoning of its own?

This question is to some degree authorized by the equivalence drawn in Adam Smith's work between the uncanny forces of Newtonian science and the forces ascribed, in similar arrays of imagery, to systems of "culture" in anthropological theory. However, when he passes from the historical analysis of physical science to the practice of his own social science, he is stricken with amnesia as to his own philosophical principles, and portrays "imaginary machines" of his own manufacture as empirically observable realities.

Amnesia intervenes specifically at the point of linkage between "The History of Astronomy" and *The Theory of Moral Sentiments,* two works which could hardly be more dissimilar in subject matter, but which share the same dominating theme of *making connections.* Philosophy generally is defined by Adam Smith as the work of tying together into unified systems things that appear separate. It is, he says in language which Tylor and Frazer echo in their very different context later on, "the science of the connecting principles of nature," of "the invisible chains which bind together . . . disjointed objects" (Astron 45). Ultimately, the philosopher seeks "one great connecting principle . . . sufficient to bind together all the discordant phaenomena that occur in a whole species of things" (Astron 66). Philosophically problematic as it is, this ambition is by no means treated as valueless by Adam Smith, who, for instance, eulogizes the "very sublime doctrines" of the Stoics as inspirational expressions of the radical human impulse to see things in the world as interconnected. "All, even the smallest of the co-existent parts of the universe, are exactly fitted to one another [in Stoic thought], and all contribute to compose one immense and connected system" (*TMS* 289). This formula (repeated almost verbatim by Lévi-Strauss two centuries later in his account of Mauss's pioneering theory of culture) defines the program that presides over *The Theory of Moral Sentiments,* where the particular sphere of system-building inquiry is that not of physical nature but of human society. Smith never states the problem to which this great work in its entirety in fact addresses itself: the problem of the binding "invisible chains" of society. According to what logic does a society cohere? To interpret the book as a response to this unspoken question is to recognize it as one of the urtexts of modern cultural theory and of what we can call more broadly the anthropological imagination.

The cornerstone of Smith's answer is the principle of *custom,* which functions in social experience, he argues, just as the principle of habitual association does in Humean epistemology.[7] "When two objects have frequently been seen together, the imagination acquires a habit of passing easily from one to the other," says Smith at the outset of his chapter on custom. As in the regular patterns of physical nature, which we think of as necessary and call causation, so too in the perception of social phenomena: even in the absence of any logically necessary conjunction, when things are habitually associated by custom, "we feel an impropriety in their separation." It is at this point that *value* enters the social universe (and Smith's universe of theory) and that social practices become invested with powerful charges of emotion— become sanctified, in fact. Moral value is attached, Adam Smith observes, to all customary things, down to the most insignificant details of etiquette and costume, simply because they are customary: "we feel a meanness or awkwardness in the absence even of a haunch button" (*TMS* 194). Value seems identical, according to this formulation, to the emotion provoked by customary things. Whatever is habitually associated in social life is felt to be necessarily so, and to infringe this association is felt to be blameworthy. From this mental reflex arises in effect the invisible magnetic fluid that holds a society together.

Smith boldly spells out the relativistic implications of his principle, even though his argument on this score sometimes contradicts itself. "There is, perhaps, no form of external objects, how absurd and fantastical soever, to which custom will not reconcile us," he declares, for example (*TMS* 200). No less boldly, he tries to identify the agency through which the automatic annexing of value to customary practices occurs. Frazer, Boas, and other anthropologists who follow much later in Smith's theoretical footsteps simply presume the transition from *is* to *ought*—in other words, the establishment of a culture—to occur as an unfathomable human reflex.[8] Smith offers a more particularized theory. For all his warnings about the fallacy of confusing necessarily fictional philosophical systems with real connections in nature, he proposes in *The Theory of Moral Sentiments* to account for the sacrosanct character of custom with reference to a specific psychological mechanism, the drive that he calls "sympathy": a propensity to identify with other people, and a longing to have them identify with us. This is precisely the instinctual force which Freud almost two centuries later calls Eros and to which he ascribes all social cohesion (*Civilization and Its Discontents* 69). "Fellow-feeling" (*TMS* 10) thus emerges for Smith as the "great connecting principle" of his system, the logical equivalent of gravity for Newton. On another plane, it forms also the active binding agency of collective life. Customs are given sacred status because they are instrumental to our instinctive longing to lead the same life as those around us. "It is thus that man, who can subsist only in society, was fitted by nature to that situation for which he was made" (*TMS* 85).

We have seen how persistently post-Tylorean theories of culture betray their inherent vein of "superstition" in tropes of uncanny or metaphysical forces. The prototypical form of the culture idea developed in *The Theory of Moral Sentiments* already is embroiled deeply in superstitious reasoning, according to the argument of "The History of Astronomy"; so it is significant that this book gives a prominent role to imagery prefiguring the motifs of gothic necromancy that loom large in subsequent generations of popular fiction. Sympathy as Smith explains it takes the form of a magical power of metempsychosis which causes us, for instance, to participate directly in the sufferings of a victim on the rack. "By the imagination we place ourselves in his situation, we conceive ourselves enduring all the same torments, we enter as it were into his body, and become in some measure the same person with him" (*TMS* 9). This fantastic displacement of identity is no mere figure of speech, Smith insists, but a true physical, or metaphysical, phenomenon. "Persons of delicate fibres and a weak constitution of body complain, that in looking on the sores and ulcers which are exposed by beggars in the streets, they are apt to feel an itching or uneasy sensation in the correspondent part of their own bodies" (*TMS* 10). We seem for a moment, in this sober philosophical treatise, to step into the world of Poe. Our grief for the dead arises from "our putting ourselves in their situation, and from our lodging, if I may be allowed to say so, our own living souls in their inanimated bodies" (*TMS* 13); when this uncanny sympathetic transfer fixes upon a murder victim, "the very ashes of the dead seem to be disturbed" by the desire of vengeance, and we call into a kind of being "the ghosts which, superstition imagines, rise from their graves to demand vengeance" (*TMS* 71). Such are the effects of the culture-creating faculty of "sympathy." Most ghostly and most significant of all the occult apparitions in Smith's world, however, is that of his most original conception, "the impartial spectator," the symbolic representative of all the norms of one's society, conceived as "the man within the breast" (*TMS* 130) to whom one perpetually and as it were instinctively refers one's conduct. Freud long afterward names this psychic element the superego, which he defines as civilization's means of subduing the individual's instinct for aggression "by setting up an agency within him to watch over it" (*Civilization and Its Discontents* 71). As we shall see, the sympathetic bond by which one is tied to this noumenal *Doppelgänger* carries into Smith's argument implications of potentially acute disturbances.

All this explicit and slightly veiled imagery of "metaphysical phantoms" is keyed in the final analysis to the epistemological problem that according to Smith haunts all "systems," but it serves more immediately to dramatize the irresistible power of the influence generated by the sympathetic instinct. In all social circumstances, Smith argues, each person "passionately desires a more complete sympathy" with those about him, and with the impartial spectator as well (*TMS* 22). This is more than a boundless desire, it is a desire for boundlessness itself, for a complete emancipation from the boundaries of the individual ego.[9] Its effect, however, is precisely the reverse of anomie, for it subjects the individual to the strenuous perpetual discipline of governing his or her conduct so as to achieve the approval and sympathy of others and of the impartial spectator—toning down the expression of strong emotions, for example, to a level that can be sympathetically identified with by an onlooker (*TMS* 22–23). The ideal man of this system, like that of the system of Smith's much-admired Stoics, is the one who has "completely subdued all his private, partial, and selfish passions" (*TMS* 290), and it is the very nature of the social bond to suppress disorganizing desire. At what seems to be its historical moment of inception, the philosophical and scientific idea of culture is thus identical with a puritanical moral ideology that exalts the denial of individual desire by the collectivity—though the prescriptive nature of this argument, its willed imposition of "connections," is figured (as Smith's account of scientific theorizing would predict) as a discovery of natural law.

There is obviously something anomalous in this system. The citizens of Smith's theoretical society are driven by a passionate desire to achieve the gratifications of sympathy, yet this desire has as its goal the nullification of desire itself and the subordination of ego to the bland, detached, spectral gaze of the impartial spectator. The purely logical incongruity in this set of propositions is less significant perhaps than the ways in which Smith's analysis sets before us, all unwittingly, the image of a distinctly modern condition, the one mapped long afterwards by writers like Freud, Proust, and René Girard, in which all experience has become weirdly oblique and equivocal, and in which potentially extreme forms of self-division prevail. *The Theory of Moral Sentiments* suggests that the dawning awareness of "culture" and the appearance of these modern forms of disturbed sensibility are cognate phenomena, and sheds a great deal of light on their interconnections.

For one thing, the sympathetic impulse is after all perpetually at odds with unsubdued egoism, and always, Smith concedes, again anticipating Freud, falls short (*TMS* 21; see *Civilization and Its Discontents* 88). From the inescapable failure of sympathy come the psychopathologies of everyday life which Smith copiously annotates. Their context is that of a perpetual and profound dislocation of selfhood. Our fate as human beings, which is to say, as social beings, is according to Smith's account to live our passions not immediately but vicariously, or as it were symbolically, and even at a second remove of vicariousness, from the point of view of that purely hypothetical construct, the impartial observer. All of a man's experience is reflexivity and impersonation: "he almost identifies himself with, he almost becomes himself that impartial spectator, and scarce even feels but as that great arbiter of his conduct directs him to feel" (*TMS* 147). Under a *régime* of autosurveillance such as this, introspection can only take the aspect of a drastic fragmentation. "When I endeavour to examine my own conduct, . . . it is evident that, in all such cases, I divide myself, as it were, into two persons; and that I, the examiner and judge, represent a different character from that other I, the person whose conduct is examined into and judged of" (*TMS* 113). Fusion with the collectivity entails a fission or decomposition of personal identity, which Smith represents as existing in a permanent state of crisis and as inevitably suffering the mutilation and harsh curtailment of individual instinctual life diagnosed by Freud. This process reaches extreme form—the conclusive correspondence between Smith's theory and Freud's—in the bad conscience undergone by a man who knows that he has infringed his society's rules. "By sympathizing with the hatred and abhorrence which other men must entertain for him [or would if they were aware, as the impartial spectator infallibly is, of his bad actions], he becomes in some measure the object of his own hatred and abhorrence" (*TMS* 84). Masochism, Smith in effect tells us, is the characteristic syndrome of civilized life.[10]

Desire itself, even before it is altogether usurped by the passionless influence of "the man within the breast," tends necessarily to decompose into vicariousness, according to Adam Smith. One of the most striking passages of *The Theory of Moral Sentiments* explains that "it is chiefly from regard to . . . the sentiments of mankind, that we pursue riches and avoid poverty" (*TMS* 50). Craving for all the carnal gratifications afforded by wealth and ease only appears to be the motive for our love of riches: rather, what drives us to pursue worldly greatness is the intensified sensation of sympathy that the great receive from others, the sensation of seeing our own image reflected back to us in the mirror of others' eyes. Narcissism is the other profile of the masochistic character of collective life. Thus to be rich is above all to be "the object of the observation and fellow-feeling of every body about [one]" (*TMS* 51). "It is not ease or pleasure, but always honour, of one kind of another, though frequently an honour very ill understood, that the ambitious man really pursues" (*TMS* 65). The comic symptom of this state of affairs is the huge prestige and social power vested in the most absurdly trivial symbols of wealth and greatness, such as the way a man "holds up his head or disposes of his arms while he walks through a room" (*TMS* 55). At another level, Smith's analysis gives the reader a premonitory pang of deprivation at seeing tangible realities, "ease and pleasure," evaporate as objects of desire, to be replaced by nothing more substantial than a play of symbolic gestures and sympathetic refractions. It is the same pang that is undergone in a mode of unbearable anguish, and brought to full self-consciousness, by Charles Swann in his passion for Odette de Crécy a century and a half later.

The sympathy-hypothesis of *The Theory of Moral Sentiments* is open to the obvious objection of being at best a pseudoexplanation which simply postulates the existence of a psychological impulse toward the various human phenomena put forth for analysis. Equally dubious is Smith's claim that the craving for sympathy, having been planted by "Nature" in the human breast, represents "the unalterable principles of human nature" (*TMS* 128). No critical system informed by modern anthropology could entertain such a theory, even if "Nature" were divested of all anthropomorphic quality. But these difficulties in reading *The Theory of Moral Sentiments* largely disappear if we regard it not as the philosophical speculation that it professes to be, but as what it really is: a searching ethnography of one variety of modern European culture at a specific historical period. Its object is not after all to isolate universal principles of human nature (Smith makes no attempt to show that the principles in question are in fact valid for any society other than his own) but to decipher according to a startlingly original method of analysis the often unconscious and "frequently . . . very ill understood" values held conventionally by men and women in this particular culture, and to interpret a broad inventory of social materials as symbolically expressing these values. At its core, this is a theory not of psychological laws but of a system of cultural representations.

In order to provoke this discovery, Smith's strategy is insistently to document customs and attitudes which are bound to appear wholly self-evident to his readers. "Such is our aversion for all the appetites which take their origin from the body: all strong expressions of them are loathsome and disagreeable" (*TMS* 28). "The expression of anger towards any body present [at a social gathering], if it exceeds a bare intimation that we are sensible of his ill usage, is regarded not only as an insult to that particular person, but as a rudeness to the whole company" (*TMS* 35). It is a curious method indeed that so carefully specifies the values attached to social symbolism which has been chosen for analysis precisely because the reader can be counted upon to take it for granted. The result is a heavily emphasized effect of defamiliarization that reveals habitual and thus natural-seeming social phenomena as philosophical riddles to be unravelled through a process of concerted interpretive analysis. Customary gestures and judgments, it turns out, possess an involved logic that we perpetually express in the most elliptical terms *without being aware that we are doing so.* Smith's demonstration hints that our unconsciousness of the train of thought submerged in our own customs may be the crucial aspect of the coercive power which they exercise upon us.

Customary practices and ideas are thus what Durkheim calls representations: such is the semiological principle brought forth ever more clearly in *The Theory of Moral Sentiments.* They express cultural themes—that of "sympathy" above all—in symbolic form. To explicate this process, Smith develops the thesis that determines much of the course of subsequent social theory: that a society's customs cannot be made intelligible if interpreted piecemeal—from which point of view they seem more nonsensical the longer we study them—but must be taken all together, as a "complex whole." Lacking a theoretical vocabulary for describing the systematic aspect of social experience other than that of individual psychology, he frames the hypothesis of the all-pervading sympathetic instinct, but it would be a mistake to put too narrow a construction upon this argument, which in a sense merely uses "sympathy" as a name for the principle that each item within a given social sphere coincides or is cognate with all the others and thus symbolizes the unity of the whole system. The assertion that Adam Smith "not only lacked the concept of social structure, but . . . it was . . . obvious to him . . . that there are *only* individuals" (Manicas 42) needs much qualification therefore if it is not to obscure his most profound intuition. The predominating European cultural theme of "sympathy" is immanent, Smith argues in great detail, in customs of grief, in clothing fashions, in the quest for riches, in the modesty affected in society by upstarts (*TMS* 41), in the fact that a book rendered boring by repeated rereading acquires new interest when we read it aloud to someone else (*TMS* 14). Smith shows these and a hundred other apparently disparate phenomena all to be expressions of a single system of inexplicit meaning which the ethnologist can decipher through the application of techniques of ingenious close reading: every particle of the culture under study is logically coordinate with every other particle and performs an essentially expressive function. What results from this set of assumptions is a work that strikingly anticipates, say, Benedict's *Patterns of Culture*, with its portrayals of a series of societies each of which is found on analysis to possess a distinctive "configuration" determined by this or that ruling psychological principle. It would be stretching the point only slightly to think of "sympathy" as nothing more than Smith's term for that occult system of relations designated "culture" by later anthropological theorists.

■

In many respects, *The Wealth of Nations* [*WN*] seems to depart sharply from the protoethnographic thinking of *The Theory of Moral Sentiments,* and to be alien to what theorists today generally mean by cultural study—that is, the study of institutions as expressions of unconscious collective themes. The analysis of abstract principles of finance and commercial exchange almost entirely excludes consideration of the system of moral ideas and customary behavior which, as the earlier work showed, constitutes the life of a nation by giving expression to such unifying values as "sympathy." Smith confines his interest in *The Wealth of Nations* largely to a category of social mechanisms governed not, it seems, by norms of meaning but by what he takes to be uniform natural law. Thus he insists on the need to base economic theory and practice on moral values (for instance, he denounces social policies that fail to provide for the welfare of the poor laborer, whose right to the fruit of his own labor is "sacred and inviolable" [*WN* 1:136]), but never factors into his argument the culturally relative character of such values or shows them exercising any significant influence upon economic behavior. Market phenomena like the movement of capital or the determination of prices and wage levels are construed for the purposes of scientific economics just as Mill will construe them later on, as operating automatically, in accordance with principles as foreign to cultural values as are those which govern physical nature. These principles act upon institutions but are not institutions themselves; they are patterns of nature and express nothing but a kind of mechanical necessity. Even so, we find ourselves enmeshed in the theory of culture—and catch a glimpse of the underlying linkage between *The Theory of Moral Sentiments* and *The Wealth of Nations*—from the moment that Smith introduces the concept of economic "value," a subject, he warns us, inherently enigmatic and "in some degree obscure," and likely to remain so even after his best attempts to clarify it (*WN* 1:33). So large does this concept and all the problems which it engenders loom in subsequent economic literature, Mill reports, that political economy is defined by many as being nothing other than "the Science of Values" (Mill, *Principles* 1:519).

Smith's evident intent in pondering this subject is to set economic science upon a maximally solid conceptual base by establishing "value" as an empirical constant which inheres in material reality itself, or at least originates in physical action, or at the very least—for his argument is hard to pin down—can be measured in physical terms. Economic value, he declares, is a function of, or is actually created by, the human labor expended in the production of commodities. "What is bought with money or with goods is purchased by labour, as much as what we acquire by the toil of our own body. That money or those goods indeed save us this toil. They contain the value of a certain quantity of labour which we exchange" (*WN* 1:34). "Labour, therefore, . . . is the only universal, as well as the only accurate measure of value" (*WN* 1:41). Value is no speculative abstraction; it is a tangible reality which we can feel in the abrasion of "toil and trouble" (*WN* 1:34) upon our own physical bodies. Given the need to sustain life and thus labor with biologically determined amounts of food, corn (wheat) figures in Smith's system as the absolute commodity, the yardstick enabling comparative computations of "real value" to be made over long stretches of time: "the nature of things has stamped upon corn a real value"—I give here the provocative reading of the first edition—"which no human institution can alter" (*WN* 2:21n). Value thus is not, as *The Theory of Moral Sentiments* endeavored to show, generated by human institutions, but is precisely that which is immune to their influence. It determines them, rather than vice versa. By the same token, prices of commodities may fluctuate, yet each commodity, Smith affirms, has its "natural price, to which the prices of all commodities are continually gravitating" (*WN* 1:65). In practice, this price may be equivalent, as Smith's exegetes say, to the purely statistical entity which post-Marshallian economics calls long-term prices, but the (mystifying) force of the term "natural" is crucial, as is the noteworthy equation with the force of gravity. Smith wants us to think of price as controlled by a real, quasi-physical force: "value."[11] In all this, and in Smith's move into political economy itself, it seems possible to see an attempt to reinstitute the solidly tangible realities that in various ways had tended to evaporate under the analytic strategies of both the works of his which we have just considered. At the same time, the appearance of the gravitational metaphor in this context strikes a ringingly equivocal note, given the use of gravity in "The History of Astronomy" as the preeminent instance of the fallacy of taking scientific fictions as though they truly represented what no human can never perceive, the "real chains" of nature. Flying in the face of his own injunctions in this essay, Smith insistently uses the compromised term "real" in *The Wealth of Nations*—in such phrases as "real price" and "real value," for example—for making allegedly scientific discriminations among various classes of phenomena.

In other words, the earlier claim that the organization of reality is inexpressible in mental systems is here aggressively suppressed—so aggressively, indeed, as almost to ensure the reverse effect of highlighting the possibility that economic "value" may in truth be merely a symbolic construct, a rhetorical figure with no necessary link to substantial reality at all. If this were so, economics could scarcely keep itself safely separate in the long run from the kind of cultural theory elaborated in *The Theory of Moral Sentiments,* where values are wholly determined by custom and where scarcely any margin exists for the intrusion of unsymbolized realities in social life. And indeed, despite Smith's repeated declarations that the labor theory makes value a definite and absolute thing, one needs to emphasize at the outset that the labor theory identifies it as a human artifact after all. Unlike utility or scarcity theories of value, which define value merely as a property found by mankind in natural things, and which Smith rejects, the labor theory implicitly sees value as a potentiality conceived first in the human brain, then transferred symbolically to matter through bodily labor of one sort or another. The transfer takes a particular form which we meet in various contexts in *The Wealth of Nations:* that of building form into, or impressing it upon, nature—just what a philosopher or scientist does, in Smith's account, in imposing a "system" of hypotheses upon the phenomenal chaos of reality.

This mode of action is represented by Adam Smith in what I take to be an allegorical tableau in the midst of his long early discussion of the history of money. The nominal theme of the discussion is that money is nothing more than a convenient instrument of commerce, a mere cultural signifier, and that money price is not to be confused with what is philosophically prior to it and free of its equivocal and ambiguous character, the "real value" of commodities. He explains then that mints, like certain other analogous institutions, are "meant to ascertain, by means of a public stamp, the quantity and uniform goodness" of the metal in coins:

> The first public stamps of this kind that were affixed to the current metals, seem in many cases to have been intended to ascertain, what it was both most difficult and most important to ascertain, the goodness or fineness of the metal, and to have resembled the sterling mark which is at present affixed to plate and bars of silver, or the Spanish mark which is sometimes affixed to ingots of gold, and which being struck only upon one side of the piece, and not covering the whole surface, ascertains the fineness, but not the weight of the metal. Abraham weighs to Ephron the four hundred shekels of silver which he had agreed to pay for the field of Machpelah. . . . They are said however to be the current money of the merchant, and yet are received by weight and not by tale. . . .
>
> The inconveniency and difficulty of weighing . . . metals with exactness gave occasion to the institution of coins, of which the stamp, covering entirely both sides of the piece and sometimes the edges too, was supposed to ascertain not only the fineness, but the weight of the metal. (*WN* 1:29–30)

These stamping techniques (as to which he offers much further information) evidently exercise a hold on Smith's imagination which runs counter to the doctrine of the purely practical character and thus the philosophical insignificance of money. The reason seems to be the vividness with which they figure what Smith intuitively understands to be nothing less than the original act of human culture, the inscribing of symbolic form, and thus *value*, upon the raw materials of nature. His theme here, to give it its technical name in anthropology, seems to be the fundamental human institution which later theorists call *taboo*, the designating of certain things and people as sacred, hence dangerous and contaminating. The classic etymology of the Polynesian word (first introduced in English in 1784) derives it from *ta*, to mark, and *pu*, an adverb of intensity; it therefore means in its root sense "marked thoroughly," with reference perhaps to the practice of marking sacred places and people with symbolic insignia to alert the unwary (Shortland, *Traditions and Superstitions* 81).[12] The supreme taboo of modern commercial society is undoubtedly the one attached to gold, the most sacred and valuable, thus the most intensely dangerous of all substances (and, as Freud reminds us, one closely associated, like taboo things in primitive cultures, with ideas of filth). What Smith portrays in such detail in the passage cited above is precisely the process of "marking thoroughly" by which the taboo thing is invested with its full magical—in other words, symbolic and affective—power. The allegorical import of the minting scene is that value inheres not in things but only in significant markings, in "representations." It is an occult power exerted by human institutions, something injected into the world not originally by bodily "toil and trouble," but by a collective process of symbolizing inscription. Smith never mentions, but scarcely needs to, the psychological correlative of the marking of gold and silver and other things: the way things once figuratively and literally stamped as valuable acquire the power to arouse maddening human desire.

That this activity of sacralizing symbolic transference is after all the crucial dimension of the labor theory of value is highlighted when Smith surprisingly concedes the uselessness of the theory for the very function it was supposedly devised to perform, namely, making possible scientifically accurate cross-measurements of value (the value of the same manufactured product at different historical periods or in different countries, for example). Such measurements are in fact impossible, Smith explains, since "labor" cannot meaningfully be quantified without incorporating in one's computation all the social and subjective factors which render certain forms of work more laden than others with "hardship" (in modern jargon, "disutility") and that govern the "ingenuity exercised" in a given piece of work (*WN* 1:35–36). Physical labor and its supposedly direct byproduct, value, turn out after all to be inextricably bound up in cultural norms, and to be deeply problematic. Mark Blaug has asserted on the basis of the seeming incompleteness of Smith's argument that he had, in fact, "no theory of value whatever" and actually meant to contradict the labor theory (Blaug 40, 41; see also 54). This may be a perverse reading, but it points to the susceptibility of Smith's exposition of value to being read, as it were, against the grain, and yielding anomalous conclusions.

The theme which we have teased from Smith's discussion of minting takes more distinct form elsewhere: for instance, in his analysis of the meaning of the terms "necessities" and "luxuries," the one passage in *The Wealth of Nations* that makes direct reference to the principle of cultural relativism expounded at length in *The Theory of Moral Sentiments*. By the former term, he declares, "I understand, not only the commodities which are indispensably necessary for the support of life, but whatever the custom of the country renders it indecent for creditable people, even of the lowest order, to be without." According to this relativistic calculus based on what he terms "established rules of decency," therefore, leather shoes are inscribed with the mark of a necessity of life even for the very poor of both sexes in England, but only for men in Scotland, and for neither sex in France (*WN* 2:399–400). Again, symbolic marking and cultural relativism take precedence over "the real chains of nature," at least for the purposes of a science of society.[13]

The truth is that the purely customary and symbolic, which is to say cultural, dimension of value is implicit from the first in a theory that bases itself, as Smith's strongly does, on the principle of *exchange*. He gives this concept philosophical weight at the outset by identifying it (in a familiar trope) with primordial instinct, or, as he puts it, "a certain propensity in human nature . . . to truck, barter, and exchange one thing for another," which, if not actually one of "the original principles of human nature," represents, he very strikingly speculates, "the necessary consequence of the faculties of reason and speech" (*WN* 1:17). To be human is to long to exchange, and, on a more practical plane, "every man . . . lives by exchanging" (*WN* 1:26). Most of the argument of this treatise on political economy necessarily does unfold on the practical plane, but the philosophical aspect of the idea of exchange keeps claiming attention, especially since it sets up a powerful reverberation with the themes of *The Theory of Moral Sentiments*. A reader of the earlier work is bound to see the alleged instinct of commercial exchange as just a special instance of the principle of "sympathy," the passion for changing places with others: exchanging goods, in this reading, would symbolically enact the more basic longing to exchange identities. What is more, if the commercial propensity is conceived as "the necessary consequence of the faculties of reason and speech," it almost explicitly becomes the vehicle not for exchanging material goods as such, but for trafficking in symbolically encoded information inscribed somehow upon objects—which is to say, in *meaning*. This is strikingly corroborated by Smith's statement in his

Lectures on Justice, Police, Revenue and Arms that the "real foundation" of the exchange-instinct "is that principle to persuade which so much prevails in human nature" (quoted Myers, *The Soul of Modern Economic Man* 113). Exchanging commodities is at heart a rhetorical and linguistic transaction, according to Adam Smith.

Thus he discloses a view of economic value as not, after all, a quantifiable coefficient of sheer labor (whether commanded or embodied), but as something quite different, a metaphysical substance produced in and through the cultural act of exchange. This means that value does not inhere in objects of commerce at all, but purely in *the institutionalized system of relations which enables exchange to occur.* Rather than a fixed index, it is necessarily constituted in any transaction as a ratio, and manifests itself only in an actual or potential moment of transposition, the epiphanic moment when, say, goods pass in one direction as money passes in the other and when the social bond is itself symbolically enacted. *The Wealth of Nations* closely anticipates in these respects the philosophical theory of exchange propounded by Georg Simmel—writing in 1907 among other things specifically to refute labor theories of value. Exchange, "the purest and most concentrated form of all human interactions," is nothing less, says Simmel, than "the economic realization of the relativity of things" (Simmel 43, 69). Relativity expresses itself in the specific form of economic exchange, he argues, as *sacrifice;* value itself is therefore by its nature "the issue of a process of sacrifice" (Simmel 48), of painfully surrendering something to get something else which one desires more. This is close to Smith's insistence on anchoring the concept of value in the painful wear and tear of labor, of sacrificing our ease, as he says, to acquire wealth, but Simmel carries the argument a step further. Paradoxical as it may sound, we set values on objects according to the sacrifice required to obtain them, he asserts. *"Economic value as such does not inhere in an object in its isolated self-existence, but comes to an object only through the expenditure of another object which is given for it"* (Simmel 54). Value in other words refers purely to desire, and desire itself is fundamentally a function of the exchange-system. "It is always the relation of desires to one another, realized in exchange, which turns their objects into economic values" (Simmel 62). Simmel's model opens directly upon the issue of the way cultural systems perform their primordial task of inscribing significance upon raw natural materials, or, as he puts it, "so attack the given that as many quanta as possible ascend from the realm of reality to the realm of value as well" (Simmel 47). His theory of exchange argues at heart that the production of the human world of experience comes about solely through the agency of a cultural system: without the institutionalized system of economic exchange, which amounts to a means of seeing things symbolically as standing for or in relation to other things, human beings would in effect be vacant of desires and their world would as a result be an amorphous, undifferentiated void. These are just the implications that lie at a slightly deeper level in *The Wealth of Nations*, as Simmel was undoubtedly aware.

Simmel was not the first to understand that Smith's idea of value made it, in spite of his own somewhat misleading language, a matter of social forms and an expression of "the relativity of things," for Mill had in fact elaborated these very themes. He effaces the role of desire, but he dwells almost obsessively on the differential and relativistic character of "value," as though grasping the potential of this doctrine, if it were once fully understood, to produce a fundamental reorganization of thought and sensibility. "Value is a relative term," he declares, for example. "The value of a commodity is not a name for an inherent and substantive quality of the thing itself. . . . The value of one thing must always be understood relatively to some other thing, or to things in general" (*Principles* 1:549; see also 1:523, 553, 557, 573; 2:100).

Once such a schema is established, value can never again be conceptualized and fetishized as a positive term, but only taken as a contingent and indeterminate one, subject to potentially endless interpretation; and desire by the same token can no longer signify a direct psychological grappling of individuals onto tangible realities but only a phenomenon of a system of symbolic relations. Value always depends on one's point of vantage and is impossible to grasp except as a conventionalized fiction of a particular social system—which is to say that *it becomes identical after all to its price in money*. Simmel says just this, in fact. "If value is, as it were, the offspring of price," he declares, then it follows that "value and price are equivalent in every individual case" (Simmel 59). There is no way to pry value apart from the symbolic medium which represents it in a given culture. It has no other existence. Adam Smith's theory of value thus leads at last, once its implications are spelled out by interpreters like Mill and Simmel, to something like Joan Robinson's sweeping demystification of "value" as obscurantist metaphysics. "Logically," she declares, "it is a mere rigmarole of words." In ascribing it to objects we obscure its true nature, for "value is a relationship between people." Used in any other sense, it is "just a word" (Robinson 37, 32, 46). This argument about "value" brings us back full circle to the deconstructive turn of "The History of Astronomy" and to the stress on cultural bonding of *The Theory of Moral Sentiments.*

The surprising movement toward such a conclusion is marked in *The Wealth of Nations* by a viral spread of ambiguity among Smith's key terms. At first he posits a distinction between "value in use" and "what may be called . . . relative or exchangeable value," two factors wholly unrelated to one another, as the diamond-and-water paradox indicates (*WN* 1:32). As we saw, he proceeds to identify as "real" value that which is imparted to goods directly by the "toil and trouble" of human labor, and to identify "relative or exchangeable value" as value *tout court,* leaving "value in use" out of the picture for purposes of economic science. But he increasingly emphasizes, to confusing effect, the term "relative." "Equal quantities of labour, at all times and places, may be said to be of equal value to the labourer" (*WN* 1:37), he declares, but this tautological-sounding formula is far from setting a fixed valuation on labor, as he promptly reminds us. "Though equal quantities of labour are always of equal value to the labourer, yet to the person who employs him they appear sometimes to be of greater and sometimes of smaller value" (*WN* 1:37). How then can we predicate "real value" on the labor standard? The result of this ambiguity is that on the next page, "real" price and value, as opposed to "nominal," seem to be identified after all with "value in use" in order to keep them safely apart from the relativistic sphere of economics. And having made at length the theoretical distinction between "real" and merely "nominal" or money value, Smith, looking ahead to Simmel's treatment of the same problem, acknowledges that "at the same time and place, . . . money is the exact measure of the real exchangeable value of all commodities" (*WN* 1:42). But the phrase "real exchangeable value" collapses together the two contrary categories of Smith's theory. It apparently has turned out that "real," determinate value is only a hypothetical device for making certain comparisons across time and space—the very instance of a philosophical construct with no grounding in natural reality. Worse yet, as mentioned already, this one is inherently unusable to begin with, given the incommensurability of the subjective factors that enter into the measurement of labor. Smith stops on the brink of the conclusion to which his disorienting argument tends: that money, the most arbitrary of signifiers, is not only "the exact measure" of "real" value, but *is* "real" value itself, if that term has any meaning at all.

Hence, to conclude this theme for now, Smith's striking discussion of the relations between the two precious metals (*WN* 1:45–46). Silver is designated the official standard, but law prescribes the exchange rate obtaining between it and gold. Opening a philosophical conundrum that may seem trivial (Blaug 54) but that in fact bristles with significance for his whole argument, Smith wonders whether under these circumstances the arbitrary distinction of standard and nonstandard is "little more than a nominal distinction," as it would seem. But since accounts are conventionally expressed in pounds sterling rather than in gold guineas, any shift in the regulated exchange rate—exchange asserting itself again as the dominating problem of Smith's work—has the result that "this distinction becomes, or at least seems to become, something more than nominal again." The nub of the passage is precisely here, in the equivocation between being and seeming that necessarily arises in a phenomenon of exchange. Since in such a case all the accounts noted in terms of silver would still be payable exactly as before if paid in silver, but would involve a change in the amount of gold that would be required, "silver would appear to be more invariable in its value than gold." Silver "would appear to measure the value of gold, and gold would not appear to measure the value of silver"—but only because of the customary practice of writing down accounts in silver. To someone holding "one of Mr. Drummond's notes for five-and-twenty or fifty [gold] guineas," exactly the reverse effect would occur in case of a shift in the exchange rate: gold rather than silver would seem revealed as the invariable, fixed "standard or measure of value." Smith uses this odd speculative detour in order to crystallize ideas that run implicitly throughout his work and pull it in the direction of a full-blown theory of culture: the stress on how conceptual categories are dictated by social sign-systems, and especially on the radically, incurably indeterminate nature of all such categories within a system where meaning is generated exclusively in relations of exchange. The passage seems to take us at one stride into the analytical idiom of the structuralist anthropology of such a work as Evans-Pritchards's *The Nuer* (1940), where structural formulations assume their own vertiginously paradoxical forms: "A man is a member of his tribe in its relations to other tribes, but he is not a member of his tribe in the relation of his segment of it to other segments of the same kind" (*Nuer* 137). This is just the mode of sophisticated ethnographic awareness which is adumbrated in Adam Smith's ever more perplexed account of economic "value."

What this account presupposes at every step is the principle that undergirds in a different way *The Theory of Moral Sentiments:* that a society forms above all an integral, self-sustaining, self-regulating *system*. The primary difference between the two works is that social coherence appears in the *Theory* as a matrix of fixed symbolic correspondences, while in *The Wealth of Nations* Smith attempts to conceptualize the dynamic and productive character of society—an aspect which manifests itself, he saw, both on the plane of material manufactures and in the metaphysical dimension where the generation of "value" occurs. In the famous analysis of the day-laborer's wool coat that opens *The Wealth of Nations* (1:15–16), what is stressed is the sheer vastness and intricacy of the modern productive mechanism. To bring into being even so banal an object as this requires the interlocking functions of so widely ramified a network of individuals and institutions that the mind can scarcely apprehend it. Thus from the beginning, Smith conceives of society (as he conceives of value) in the particular aspect of a conceptual problem, and as an entity with the peculiar ability somehow to be immanent, as a vast, mysterious whole, in every social production, in material commodities as well as in the customs and psychological structures which had formed the data of the *Theory*. The laborer's coat is a symbolic palimpsest of a gigantic organization largely unconscious of its own existence and needing an interpretive intervention in order to emerge in intelligible form: of "culture."

The problematic character of social life for Smith is made ever clearer as he moves from discussion of the system of physical production of goods to that of the mysterious financial phenomena associated with modern society. Here we enter a noumenal realm where all realities—the prices of goods, the levels of wages, and so on—are "economic," that is, functions of an ensemble of relationships wholly dispersed in time and space, and where the same question that was central to *The Theory of Moral Sentiments* emerges again with a new set of referents: How does a society hold itself together? We return here to our point of departure, for the answer to this question can only come, according to Adam Smith, in the form of a theory of desire.

In the *Theory*, as we saw, desire was in chains, under the unblinking surveillance of the impartial spectator and the impulse of "sympathy"; this presumption indeed is what allows Smith to construct the static social model which emerges in that work. Desire forms a far more potent presence and a more challenging speculative problem in *The Wealth of Nations*. The primordial organic need, much emphasized by Smith, is the need for food; once satisfied, this need gives way in modern society to a set of other compelling drives. His discussion of them bears strongly, though in a register of extreme optimism, the mark of Scottish puritanism and its loathing of waste and—a central Smithian term of opprobrium—"prodigality." He speaks of "the passion for present enjoyment" and thus the impulse to spend as "sometimes violent and very difficult to be restrained" but yet as a pathological aberration (*WN* 1:362). The values that he professes, those of frugality, saving, and work, he portrays as natural in most men and as tending to the benefit of society. Yet this thesis contains certain incoherencies, and to some degree it is precisely in its incoherence that it serves as a springboard for social discourse of the two centuries that follow.

Smith identifies, above the level of physiological necessity, two fundamental drives, which turn out in practice to be much the same. The first, the propensity to "exchange one thing for another," is subordinate in his account to the second, which he considers to be the mastering drive of all men: "the natural effort of every individual to better his own condition" (*WN* 2:49).[14] This "desire of bettering our condition" is, he says, "a desire which . . . comes with us from the womb, and never leaves us till we go into the grave" (*WN* 1:362–63). The proposition that compulsive desire lies at the base of social life goes back at least to Hobbes, and in fact Smith's formula is essentially a quotation of the account in *Leviathan* of "a general inclination of all mankind, a perpetual and restless desire of power after power, that ceaseth only in death" (Hobbes 80).[15] For Hobbes, founding a way of life upon a desire that never can be assuaged "till we go into the grave" leads to potentially anarchic social conflict. Sharply revising this scheme, Smith argues that the driving desire of self-betterment fosters the division of labor and leads, not to anarchy, but to prosperity and to order in society. The compulsion to better one's condition furnishes the dynamic principle of social life, generating the energy required to sustain the desideratum of social welfare, a perpetually expanding system of commerce and manufacture. At the same time, this compulsion acts to maintain a "natural" state of equilibrium, rushing capital, for instance, into any enterprise where profit margins are abnormally high, and through competition, adjusting these margins so as to restore prices to their natural "center of repose and continuance" (*WN* 1:65). The impulse of self-betterment thus works without interruption, "like the unknown principle of animal life," to sustain "the natural progress of things toward improvement" (*WN* 1:364). By enacting this set of postulates, *The Wealth of Nations* attempts to nullify the issue of anarchic individual desire and thus to lay the foundation for a coherent social science.

Significant ambiguities cluster around Smith's identification of unrestrained expansion and progress with repose and equilibrium, and at other points in his argument as well. For one thing, the desire for personal advantage seems largely futile in an economic system of which it is a basic law that all outlays of capital or labor bring equivalent returns. "Every individual is continually exerting himself to find out the most advantageous employment for whatever capital he can command" (*WN* 1:475). To what end, if "the whole of the advantages and disadvantages of the different employments of . . . stock [capital] must . . . be either perfectly equal or continually tending to equality"? (*WN* 1:111).[16] More significantly, what exactly are the ends sought and achieved by Smith's hypothetical economic man, perpetually occupied as he is in calculating his investment decisions? Clothing this issue in the would-be unambiguous metaphors of physical mechanics, Herbert Spencer later tells us that "as political economists have pointed out," business choices are directed to "that which offers the least resistance to the gratification of the totality of desires" (*Principles* 3:354). But it is not clear in *The Wealth of Nations* what kind of gratification, if any, the dominant desire of *Homo economicus* can lead to. He is depicted as a figure preyed upon by perpetual anxiety and uncertainty, stemming possibly, as we have said, from the awareness that one economic choice is by natural law as good as another. In any case, the capitalist's desire as hypothesized by Smith is by its nature boundless and permanent, anomic, incapable of gratification, a will o' the wisp which forever recedes before us "till we go into the grave." It is just that "futility of an endless pursuit" that Durkheim diagnoses as the special torment of the capitalistic environment (*Suicide* 256), or that "continuity of violent yet unsatisfied desire" that Jean Itard diagnoses in the wild boy of Aveyron.

What would bettering one's "condition" exactly consist in? Smith is significantly obscure on this point. It expressly does not consist in enlarging one's abilities to indulge in "the passion for present enjoyment," since by Smith's reckoning any self-indulgent expense, any departure from strict frugality, necessarily impairs one's condition. Seen from another point of view—one very strongly insisted upon by Hobbes, for example—the desire of improving one's "condition" only has meaning if it implies doing so at others' expense: such a principle indeed would be just one more "economic realization of the relativity of things." All of Smith's stress on the relational nature of phenomena within a social system goes to remind us that improving one's condition by acquiring wealth in a capitalistic environment can only mean rising *relative to others*. One's sympathy with the rich whom one wishes to emulate has as its necessary converse side one's repudiation of sympathy with the equals whom one wishes to leave behind. Smith's rhetorical strategy obliges him to obscure as much as possible what Hobbes emphasizes, the competitive and predatory aspect of the economic system that he describes: contenders in the capitalist economy are accordingly represented as playing a game against abstract market forces, not against their fellow citizens, and not for antisocial motives. All the mystifying force of Smith's science of wealth thus converges upon aggressive and exclusionary economic motives, which appear in the guise of socially benign influences which cause "a general plenty [to diffuse] itself through all the different ranks of the society" (*WN* 1:15). This doctrine entails problems of its own, since in enriching one's self, one seems compelled by a structural irony to enrich one's neighbors at the same time, and to this extent to be forever at cross purposes with one's craving not just to be rich, but to be richer and more powerful than they. Smith's analysis suggests that a strain of frustration and anger seems bound to compromise even the successful capitalist's prosperity, though this point is of course never explicitly raised.

These hints of inherent contradictions and of at least potentially pathological strains in the capitalist body politic come to the surface in various passages where the unrestrained desire of egoistic self-betterment is seen not as maintaining social equilibrium at all, but as taking malignant forms and flying out of control. These passages destabilize Smith's economic gospel by suggesting that rather than that steady, regular desire for self-betterment which expresses itself in frugality, hard work, and deferral of gratification, what prosperity tends automatically to develop is a complex of highly volatile, inflamed, unsatisfiable desires. This is the theme, for instance, of the famous passage in which Smith ascribes the decay of feudal aristocratic power to the development of trade in luxury goods, which for the first time enabled the rich to squander their income on the sort of personal gratification found in "trinkets and baubles" such as diamond shoe-buckles (*WN* 1:437). Here the submerged complex of sociopsychological motives for "bettering one's condition" surges abruptly and disruptively into view, even as it provides the clearest statement in Adam Smith's work of the idea that desire is itself a cultural production and flows irresistibly toward whatever symbolic objects the culture may "mark" as desirable, even if this means ruining rather than bettering one's "condition."

Smith tries to deflect the impact of this discussion on his general argument by (highhandedly) assigning such perverse tastes only to the rich, as well as by a puritanical moral analysis in which luxury and aesthetic pleasure are marked as inherently culpable. When the availability of luxury goods enables a rich man to spend his wealth purely on himself, says Smith, introducing a strain of discourse destined, as we have seen, to become familiar in later social theory, "he frequently has no bounds to his expence, because he frequently has no bounds to his vanity, or to his affection for his own person" (*WN* 1:440). The strength of this tendency to pathologically boundless acquisitive desire is shown by the fact that "in commercial countries, . . . riches, in spite of the most violent regulations of law to prevent their dissipation, very seldom remain long in the same family" (*WN* 1:440). This factor of desire seems to multiply itself according to the same exponential ratios with which the division of labor multiplies production—and indeed, what are these in Smith's analysis but two manifestations of the same principle? It generates in turn its characteristic phenomena in the economic field proper. Thus the price of rare luxury goods "may rise to any degree of extravagance, and seems not to be limited by any certain boundary" (*WN* 1:242). Price in such instances of breached or nonexistent boundaries takes on the special anomic character proper to economic phenomena, flying wildly apart from any intelligible norms of "real value."

As an earlier passage on much the same theme makes clear (*WN* 1:182–83), such tendencies are normal rather than exceptional in modern society. As agriculture improves and food becomes abundant, population increases and the division of labor occurs; this process then fuels "a demand for every sort of material which human invention can employ, either usefully or ornamentally, in building, dress, equipage, or household furniture" (*WN* 1:183). As these culturally-indexed desires move into ascendancy, they reveal their cardinal characteristic of boundlessness. "The desire of food is limited in every man by the narrow capacity of the human stomach," says Smith; "but the desire of the conveniencies and ornaments of building, dress, equipage, and household furniture, seems to have no limit or certain boundary." Thus in the normal course of things, "what is over and above satisfying the limited desire, is given for the amusement of those desires which cannot be satisfied, but seem to be altogether boundless" (*WN* 1:183). The resonance of this theme for later social discourse is registered with particular clarity in the almost verbatim echoing of Smith's language in Durkheim's analysis of anomie, that morbid condition marked by "unrestrained and infinite appetite," of subjection to "a desire freed of all restraints" and for just this reason "incapable of being satisfied" (*Moral Education* 36, 40).

That a system founded on unsatisfiable desire is able to function in an organized way is evidence of nothing less than providential design: these are the terms in which Smith seems to forecast the notion that each human culture possesses its own immanent principle of justification. Like many a latter-day theorist, he is drawn by this notion to postulate the action of unseen powers, however rudely such a postulate may clash with the requirements of scientific analysis. The "political body" like the physical one is kept healthy, he thus asserts, by "some unknown principle of preservation" enacted by "the wisdom of nature" (*WN* 2:194, 195). The unknown principle is invoked in the book's most famous passage of all, where Smith reveals his essential logic in almost shockingly explicit terms by declaring that the capitalist, seeking "only his own gain," is "led by an invisible hand to promote an end which was no part of his intention" (*WN* 1:477). This amazing apparition, in effect a sociological variant of the "invisible effluvium" of Descartes' theory of magnetism (and the classic instance of the reign of "metaphysical phantoms" in modern social theory), is not to be dismissed as merely a casual figure of speech, for Smith's argument, driven as it is by the principle of boundless desire, carries him almost inescapably to postulate metaphysical—that is, "natural"—forces presiding over man's social existence. These forces create and somehow maintain the cohesiveness of the community in the face of the disorganizing influence of anomic, indeterminate desire: they represent the ultimately unfathomable "chains" which bind into unity "the otherwise disjointed and discordant phaenomena of nature." They exercise coercive power over individuals, and their distinctive feature is that those subject to them are wholly unconscious of their operation. In these crucial respects, the occult *régime* described by Adam Smith makes a good functional equivalent of what anthropologists since about 1871 have called "culture." Whether in the somewhat mechanistic form it takes in classic political economy or in symbolically oriented anthropological theory, it stands ultimately for the determination to assert that human society possesses an inherent principle of order, hence of moral legitimacy. Ideal economic life thus corresponds to what Smith calls, in a noteworthy phrase redolent of the language of a text like Wordsworth"s "Ode to Duty," "the natural system of perfect liberty" (*WN* 2:121)—perfect liberty being necessarily, according to Smith's argument, a *system*. We recall here one more time that it is his own doctrine that "systems" do not exist in nature, but only in human imaginations. The metaphysical phantom hovering over his vision of society turns out to be what it always is in such cases: the reflected silhouette of the social theorist himself.

Malthus

In the writings of Thomas Robert Malthus, who for the first two decades of the nineteenth century was not only a famous population theorist but also the most eminent living economist (Winch 7), Adam Smith's political economy is strongly affirmed and extended—and subjected at the same time to some fundamental revisions.

The implicitly biological basis of economic theory in *The Wealth of Nations* becomes explicit in Malthus's *Essay on the Principle of Population* [*EP*].[17] Like Smith, Malthus places his work under the sign of the absolute reality of tangible matter and of the determinism that arises from physical laws: hence his scorn for the kind of disembodied dialectical theorizing indulged in by Godwin and leading, says Malthus, to "puerile" fantasies of perfectibility (*EP* 86). His great dissent from Adam Smith centers on the supposition that "the wisdom of nature" has designed for human habitation an environment in a state of equilibrium and continually expanding prosperity, that need only be set free from wilful interference in order to function smoothly. Malthus portrays the scheme of physical and biological nature as drastically self-contradictory, as far as human welfare is concerned. "Through the animal and vegetable kingdoms, nature has scattered the seeds of life abroad with the most profuse and liberal hand. She has been comparatively sparing in the room, and the nourishment necessary to rear them" (*EP* 9). Hence the tragic predicament that population tends by natural law to outrun subsistence, and that as a result, human life can never be free of "misery and vice." Dissonance and not concordance is Malthus's predominant metaphor.

Smith's idea that the primordial human drives are to exchange goods and to better one's position drops out of Malthus, one can infer, because these alleged drives operate at too great a remove from physical reality: they lead to the fallacy of which Godwin is Malthus's chief representative, that of "[considering] man too much in the light of a being merely intellectual" (*EP* 89). Malthus declares instead that human life is dominated overwhelmingly by "bodily cravings." The rational decision-making agent of classical economics, like the virtuously self-abnegating heroes and heroines of romance, seems from the Malthusian point of view largely imaginary. "The cravings of hunger, the love of liquor, the desire of possessing a beautiful woman," are forces that readily overwhelm human reason, he declares (*EP* 90). Uncontrollable desire is the human trait par excellence. In later editions of the *Essay* Malthus firmly states the proposition that he everywhere implies in the first: that "after the desire of food, the most powerful and general of our desires is the passion between the sexes" (*EP*6 3:468). All his stress on the imperious force of human sexuality dramatizes the affinity of Malthus's thought with that of his elder contemporary John Wesley. Yet he adds immediately that his phrase about sexual passion needs to be taken "in an enlarged sense." The enlargement proves to be crucial to his theory, and to mark its sharp divergence from Wesleyan evangelism.

From the beginning, the idea of desire is surrounded in Malthus, as it was in Adam Smith, by that metaphorical imagery of boundless, uncontrolled expansion that runs throughout modern discourse. The opening two paragraphs of the *Essay on Population* are a torrent of such imagery. Recent times have been marked, says Malthus, by amazing intellectual advances, by "the increasing diffusion of general knowledge from the extension of the art of printing," by an "ardent and unshackled spirit of inquiry," and especially by the "blazing comet" of the French Revolution, which in seeking to free the human mind, he says later, "has burst . . . the restraining bond of all society" (*EP* 97). Utopian philosophers like Godwin and Condorcet stand for an optimistic belief in the possibility of attaining "illimitable, and hitherto unconceived improvement," for example through scientific breeding aimed at prolonging human longevity "beyond any assignable limits" (*EP* 61, 85). Such notions, according to Malthus, amount to a species of philosophical anomie, of boundless desires—more strictly speaking, desires for boundlessness—that necessarily will be frustrated. It is in fact "the height of absurdity to assert, that . . . progress [can be] unlimited or indefinite." Some amount of organic improvement through eugenic measures is indeed attainable, but "an improvement really unlimited" is beyond possibility. In all such speculations, "a careful distinction should be made, between an unlimited progress, and a progress where the limit is merely undefined" (*EP* 61, 62). *Limitation,* it is fair to say, is the cardinal principle of Malthus's thought at the outset of his career. Human experience is set within boundaries, and ideas of escaping these boundaries are folly, he insists.

Yet in the most influential passage of all his work, he appears to turn his own principle inside-out by showing population, the index of "the passion between the sexes," increasing potentially by uncontrollable geometrical ratios, food production increasing at the same time only by arithmetical ratios. After a thousand years, presuming no external checks upon population, the difference between the two series of figures "would be almost incalculable" (*EP* 13): humanity would in a sense have achieved boundlessness after all, with catastrophic results. We are reminded of Adam Smith's beginning his own treatise with a closely analogous (but optimistic) mathematical demonstration of the almost limitless multiplication of industrial productivity through the division of labor (*WN* 1:8–9): both writers' theories root themselves in the compelling theme of transcending natural limits on human productions. The important factor here is that while population may in Malthus's system hypothetically expand to incalculable dimensions, the drive which generates it cannot.

Malthus in fact is at great pains, for reasons which are not immediately clear, to deny the boundlessness of desire. Bodily cravings, particularly sexual desire, are immensely powerful, but fixed and permanent. "The passion between the sexes . . . will remain nearly in its present state" forever, he asserts as one of his central postulates (*EP* 8). This drive "has appeared in every age to be so nearly the same, that it may always be considered, in algebraic language, as a given quantity" (*EP* 48). In the first instance a denial of Godwin's prediction that sexual passion will wither away in an ideal society, it also declares that it is not prone to drastic expansion, either. The rule of the fixed quantum of sexual desire would hold even in the utopia of perfect freedom hypothesized by Godwin, according to Malthus (who here prefigures arguments made later in the nineteenth century by Darwin and other opponents of McLennan's theory of "primitive promiscuity"). Such freedom would not, says Malthus, "lead to a promiscuous intercourse," but rather to the forming of more or less durable couples—that is, to society (*EP* 67). Recasting this line of thought in anthropological terms in later editions, Malthus significantly complicates his original position. Rather than being "a fixed quantity" after all, sexual desire is shown by ethnographic research, he declares, to be intensified (not suppressed) whenever cultural obstacles are set up against "very early and universal gratification"; by the same token, in countries "where every impulse may be almost immediately indulged, the passion sinks into mere animal desire, is soon weakened and almost extinguished by excess" (*EP*6 3:469). Malthus thus draws in this passage an emphatic theoretical distinction between "mere animal desire" and what he terms a page earlier "the passion between the sexes, taken in an extended sense." Before trying to spell out what is at stake in this distinction, we should note Malthus's apparent denial that freeing instinctual drives from social restraint results in the reign of "desires which cannot be satisfied, but seem to be altogether boundless" (A. Smith, *WN* 1:183). Desire freed from its established limits soon fails, says Malthus.

He seems at first glance to contradict himself when he considers in this context the already notorious ethnographic record of the recently rediscovered South Sea islanders, whose various societies are marked by a prevalence of "debauchery and promiscuous intercourse" (*EP*6 2:51). He does not explain the apparent inconsistency in his argument as carefully as he might, but it can be unraveled without too much difficulty. Speaking in particular of the aristocratic *Areoi* societies found by Captain Cook in Tahiti, he reports that "promiscuous intercourse and infanticide appear to be their fundamental laws" (*EP*6 2:50). Thus he interprets sexual promiscuity—by which he means extramarital and unprocreating sex—in Polynesia (as in modern Britain) as first and foremost an obligatory social institution, the function of which is to inhibit the growth of population. Rather than signifying a spontaneous overflowing of "mere animal desire," it is a system of "fundamental laws" invented to protect the body politic *from* the consequences of those "bodily cravings" that obey "laws inherent in the nature of man" (*EP* 70). If promiscuous intercourse depresses libido, it is easy to see (filling in the links of Malthus's thought) that it would be practiced, along with infanticide, in a country menaced with excess population.

If Malthus is sometimes reticent in drawing conclusions like the above, it is because this functionalist mode of analysis is morally so equivocal. He is quick to identify such practices as those of Tahiti as "vice," and, for example, to brand the Chinese practice of exposing newborn infants as "a custom that . . . violates the most natural principle of the human heart" (*EP* 25); even so, his argument is hard to purify of morally dangerous implications. The *Essay on Population* has always been regarded as the supremely scandalous work of modern social theory, a reaction to it that registers ultimately what might be called the inherent scandal of anthropology. It is well to underline that Malthus does not argue, as he is sometimes said to do, that the population curve dooms mankind to mass starvation. Focusing on the many customs devised by simple societies for dealing with overpopulation, he argues merely that in all societies, "checks" have been necessary to contain population, and that all these checks—including the least pernicious, "moral restraint"—have injected distress into human experience, and will necessarily continue to do so. This means that the frequently appalling devices that various societies have invented for the purpose of relieving the pressure of population on food supplies are in fact not only natural and reasonable, but imperatively necessary. They are in harmony with those "fixed laws of nature" which serve in Malthus's discourse as the ground of truth. His own admittedly brutal proposal that public aid to starving illegitimate children be cut off is just one such device which from the point of view of Christian morals is a crime, but which is sanctioned by "the invariable laws of nature" (*EP*6 3:519). He declares that in the administration of charity (as indeed in all things), the key to wisdom is "to check our natural propensities" (*EP*6 3:536), but he really means the reverse: that "nature" rules invalid certain fundamental moral norms of "civilization."

In other words, there opens up at the center of Malthus's *Essay* a vein of radical moral relativism, muffled though it is in thick coatings of moralistic language. One suspects that the horror which this book inspired in its first generations of readers arose less from objections to its precepts for public policy than from the sense that its deep logic tended to subvert accepted morality itself. Do not Christian morals fall at last into the category of the "vain and extravagant dreams of fancy" spun out by philosophers in blithe disregard of the compelling reality of the material world and its laws? Is it not equally "puerile," once we have grasped the population calculus, to disapprove, say, of infanticide and promiscuity in Tahiti as to imagine that eugenics will bestow immortality upon the human race?

The thrust of Malthusian population theory into theoretical anthropology, and the troubling moral relativism that this move implies, is demonstrated in Malthus's mordantly deconstructive analysis of the institution of marriage and of one of its key modern corollaries, the double standard in sexual morality (*EP* 72–73). At one point he declares, in a resonant phrase, that the advent of new statistical methods offers hope of achieving "a clearer insight into the internal structure of human society" (*EP6* 2:19). He seems to mean by this a correlation of social phenomena with their true causes; but his own explorations of inner social structures take a somewhat different form, that of reconstructing the original function and meaning of particular institutions. Seen in this perspective, marriage does not at all appear in the light of a divinely sanctioned sacrament, nor does it as its essential function express and foster love between man and woman; rather, like infanticide, it is specifically an invention contrived at first by some hard-pressed tribe of savages for coping with food shortages by "[making] every man provide for his own children" (*EP* 72). Understanding the strain imposed by shortages upon society reveals by the same token "a very natural origin of the superior disgrace which attends a breach of chastity in the woman, than in the man" (*EP* 73). This cultural imperative has originally nothing to do, Malthus conjectures, with awareness of the morally exquisite nature of female character. Rather, it signifies a bluntly practical solution to the problem of illegitimate children, a problem doubly severe since women generally are unable to support children by their own resources. Moreover, "the father of a child may not always be known, but the same uncertainty cannot easily exist with regard to the mother. Where, the evidence of the offence was most complete, and the inconvenience to the society at the same time the greatest, there, it was agreed, that the largest share of blame should fall" (*EP* 73). This primordial arrangement continues, despite being manifestly morally unsound. "That a woman should at present be almost driven from society, for an offence, which men commit nearly with impunity, seems to be undoubtedly a breach of natural justice." Yet the origin of the custom "appears to be natural, though not perhaps perfectly justifiable" (*EP* 73). Whether one reads this analysis from the vantage of an orthodox Christian moralist upholding the sanctity of female chastity, or from that of a rationalistic

critic of orthodoxy, one sees one's principles of value being dismantled before one's eyes.

Malthus ends by noting that the original logic of such a custom as
marriage or the double standard "is now lost in the new train of ideas
which the custom has since generated," for instance, the idea of "female delicacy" (*EP* 73). He leaves this observation in the form of a
tantalizingly sophisticated hint, but clearly has in mind an evolutionary cultural process causing practices to persist as "survivals" when
they no longer play their original social role, and to generate delusive
new rationales to justify their own continued existence.[18] Even so sacrosanct a value as "female delicacy" turns out to be a cultural misrep-
resentation of this kind. Malthus's population theory moves decisively
into the field of cultural theory, in other words, in this analysis of the
unconscious etiology of moral principles, which claim to refer directly
to nature but turn out to be merely sign-systems manufactured out of
other sign-systems according to the dictates of social expediency.
"Like the commodities in a market," he incautiously remarks in the
course of a discussion of ancient Greece, "those virtues will be produced in the greatest quantity, for which there is the greatest demand"
(*EP*6 2:60). No wonder that the Anglican clergyman who preached
such doctrines was widely perceived as an immoralist by his original
readers.

This obviously is a writer not afraid to involve himself in dangerous paradoxes, as we can see particularly in spelling out the theory of
desire that underlies his population theory and his closely associated
ventures into anthropology and political economy. It is well to recall
the denigration of all desires save the one of financial self-betterment
that pervades Malthus's master, Adam Smith. The various "wants and
fancies of mankind" tend strongly to lead in Smith to anomic "prodigality" and unproductive luxury. Malthus seems at least initially to
share this attitude, and in the area of sexual passion calls for "prudential restraint" as imperatively as Smith calls for "frugality" in financial
affairs. The fundamental human institutions are interpreted by
Malthus, accordingly, as mechanisms for repressing sexual desire (as
in the code of premarital chastity), for channelling it toward less dangerous objects (as in prostitution), or, as a last resort, for eliminating
its consequences (as in infanticide). Malthus's proto-Freudian thesis
that the central task of society is to master the libido is easy to see as
an attempt to set sexually phobic Christian morals upon an improved

scientific basis. The surprise of Malthus's account is that it turns out to make just the opposite argument, as Catherine Gallagher has emphasized. "Bodily cravings" are not vile and animalistic after all, nor could they be successfully repressed without inflicting grievous harm on society. Malthus's work hinges on the paradox that he writes as a champion of desire against its adversaries such as Godwin, even as he proclaims the potentially catastrophic results of mankind's reproductive impulse.

"Implicit obedience to the impulses of our natural passions would lead us into the wildest and most fatal extravagancies," says Malthus; "and yet we have the strongest reasons for believing that all these passions are so necessary to our being, that they could not be generally weakened or diminished, without injuring our happiness" (EP6 3:467). To elucidate the unexpectedly ambiguous concept of "natural" passion, Malthus moves again into the realm of theoretical anthropology, and his redaction of the image of mankind in its original state goes a long way to qualify the received notion of the human organism as driven by irresistible and innate "bodily cravings." For he insists strongly that man in the primitive state is driven by scarcely any cravings at all beyond a monotonous need for food—surely by nothing resembling an impulse to exchange goods or to improve his position. On the contrary, the main human traits in this (hypothetical) state, and the ones which Malthus evidently regards as the permanent ones of the human biological constitution, are sluggishness, listlessness, amorphousness, inertia. He seems in developing this theme to provide the whole text for Itard's scientific allegory of the Aveyron "savage" a few years later. "The original sin of man," he declares (hinting again at the fundamental relations of modern anthropological thought and evangelical theology), "is the torpor and corruption of the chaotic matter, in which he may be said to be born" (EP 124). Malthus, who lays such emphasis upon the intractable reality of the physical and upon the insubstantiality of mere mental conceptions, conceives that God has designed the world as "a process necessary to awaken inert, chaotic matter, into spirit" (EP 123). But he gives a surprising definition of divinely-inspired mind or spirit: it is inseparable from an ideal of pleasure. God's plan, Malthus declares, is to develop in men and women "a capacity of superior enjoyment" and thus to afford them "the most exquisite gratifications" (EP 124, 77). Refining, intensifying, and multiplying desire and pleasure is nothing less than the purpose of existence. The problem of desire in Malthus is not, as in Hobbes, that it is too powerful or unruly, despite a few potentially misleading statements to this effect. Rather, it is that man is naturally dull and slothful, that "natural" desire is so *feeble*. The salvation of mankind from "original sin" is achieved if at all through the sharpening of desire. This conviction comes to play a crucial role in Malthusian political economy, as we shall see in a moment.

It is bodily cravings, according to Malthus, which initially stimulate the savage to rise out of his native torpor and lead in the fulness of evolutionary time to poetry, philosophy, "social sympathy," and other rarefied pleasures (*EP* 125). Even at an advanced stage of cultural development, "mind" is never able to sustain itself in a vacuum: the original primacy of the body and of carnal desires is never overthrown, Malthus observes in a number of malicious passages which earned for him the contemporary reputation of being a defender of sexual immorality (see P. James 121–26). In actual experience, erotic pleasure is the keenest that human beings ever are able to experience (*EP* 76–77), and nothing could be more fatal to human destiny, says Malthus, than the Godwinian earthly paradise in which "sensual pleasures" (*EP* 76) wither away. Such a perverse paradise would be "either . . . a cold and cheerless blank, or a scene of savage and merciless ferocity" (*EP6* 3:470). He is vague as to the exact mechanisms by which "the mind [is] awakened into activity by the passions, and the wants of the body" (*EP* 131), and it is not spelled out how the rudimentary cravings of the savage are able in the first stage of evolution to arouse him from his primal listlessness. But it is possible to reconstruct at least the broad principles of this inexplicit argument.

The agency of the perfection of pleasure is society. Mill, thinking that he is speaking the doctrine of Malthus, declares in a phrase quoted once already that "civilization in every one of its aspects is a struggle against the animal instincts" (*Principles* 1:446)—reminding us again in passing of how thoroughly traditional, not to say regressive, Freud's portrayal of civilization and its discontents was. But Mill gives here a seriously incomplete view of Malthus's idea of civilization, as we can see in one of the most striking passages in the *Essay*, Malthus's refutation of Godwin's argument against erotic pleasure. "Strip the commerce of the sexes of all its attendant circumstances, and it would be generally despised," says Godwin. Alive to the theoretical implications of this claim, Malthus counters that the stripping operation envisaged by Godwin, far from revealing the true animal nature of erotic passion, would altogether misrepresent it and rob it of its vital elements. A man is drawn sexually to a woman by "the symmetry of person, the vivacity, the voluptuous softness of temper, the affectionate kindness of feelings, the imagination and the wit" that she possesses, not by "the mere distinction of her being a female." In other words, sexual experience is for Malthus thoroughly immersed in cultural values and dependent on an elaborate sign-system of cultural stimuli; it has next to nothing to do with some conjectural absolute physical sexuality—really a chimera so void of meaning that Malthus can scarcely find words to evoke it. "To strip sensual pleasures of all their adjuncts, in order to prove their inferiority, is to deprive a magnet of some of its most essential causes of attraction, and then to say that it is weak and inefficient" (*EP* 77–78). So-called "animal instincts" in men and women turn out therefore not to be antithetical to civilization, but chiefly to be emanations of it, and the commerce of the sexes turns out to be more than anything else a commerce of the socially significant symbolism inscribed upon cultural "adjuncts." Once again, as in Adam Smith, the positing of instinctual desire takes a distinct turn toward a semiological interpretation of culture.[19] This is why Malthus carefully speaks of sex "in an enlarged sense" and declares that when sensuality becomes promiscuous—that is, emancipated from its constitutive social symbolism—it "sinks into mere animal desire." As we now can see, this latter state does not represent for Malthus desire in its unleashed primal force, but rather an impoverished, degenerate impulse of greatly diminished power.

Far from being devoted to the repression of desire, it thus appears that society's function in the field of sex is to enhance it, to extend its domain and to render it ever more potent by grafting upon it arrays of keenly stimulating "adjuncts." Conversely, Malthus sees "the passion between the sexes" not as an alien force to be contained, but as nothing less than the fundamental, all-pervading principle of social organization: few of the plans that people set for their lives, he declares, again anticipating Freud, "are not connected in a considerable degree with the prospect of the gratification of this passion" (*EP6* 3:469).[20] One of the principal cultural techniques for building this complex of desire is the erection of barriers to free sexual gratification, says Malthus (*EP6* 3:470); in our society, this is particularly the task of the Christian religion, which, according to Malthus's subversive-sounding interpretation, inculcates without seeming to "those virtues which tend to fit us for a state of superior enjoyment" (*EP6* 3:474). Cultural impediments to desire sharpen desire. Hence in a society which strictly observed the Christian-Malthusian regime of premarital chastity and late marriage, "the passion, instead of being extinguished, as it now too frequently is, by early sensuality, would only be repressed for a time, that it might afterwards burn with a brighter, purer, and steadier flame" (*EP*6 3:476). Malthus partly means here that marriage partners would be free of the moral degradation and unhappiness that come from such expedients as visiting prostitutes, and thus would be more responsible and dutiful spouses; but he also distinctly means that his system would generate heightened sensual pleasures.

The line of thought that we have traced in the *Essay on Population* is in its essential points congruent with the one elaborated long afterwards by Bronislaw Malinowski in *A Scientific Theory of Culture* [*STC*]. The crux of this theory is that social life forms itself first and foremost as a system of responses to "the fact that man has a body subject to various organic needs" (*STC* 36). Thus "the theory of culture," says Malinowski, harking back to Malthus, "has to start from the organic needs of man" (*STC* 72). Yet despite "the essentially physiological basis of culture" (*STC* 79), Malinowski insists that cultural analysis must move almost at once to the plane of symbolism, for even the primary physiological activities of mankind are necessarily saturated with cultural implications and serve as vehicles of social values, of "norms, customs, traditions, and rules" (*STC* 68). Just as Malthus argued about sex, no bodily function is exempt from culture, and "symbolism . . . is the modification of the original organism which allows the transformation of a physiological drive into a cultural value" (*STC* 132). Malinowski accounts for this process in behaviorist terms, as the result of habitual association between the use of various cultural techniques and the satisfaction of bodily wants. These techniques and all their "adjuncts" or "attendant circumstances," to use Malthus's terms, "become, in a derived or secondary manner, objects of desire," says Malinowski (*STC* 138). Once again, the theory of culture highlights the trope of the stamping of meaning and desire upon raw materials of nature, a process that "we can define," Malinowski says, hinting at the linkage of his thought to the traditions of political economy, "by the term *value*, in the widest sense of the word" (*STC* 138). But once the world is thoroughly inscribed in this way with cultural values, physiological drives as such effectively cease to exist. The value-laden symbol becomes not just a repository of meaning but the origin of human drives, strongly reacting back upon the organism "as a catalyzer of human activities, as a stimulus which releases responses" (*STC* 153).

The final stress of this theory thus recalls Malthus anew by falling not on the allegedly repressive but on the dynamic, stimulating character of the "apparatus" of cultural symbolism, which as its primary function "allows [human beings] to develop new needs and . . . leads toward the creation of new drives and new desires" (*STC* 143).

■

To read Malthus through Malinowski's eyes enables us therefore to grasp the embryonic culture thesis that is central to the *Essay on Population*, but highlights at the same time the problem of reconciling the expansive, increasingly ramified libido with social order. Malthus has nothing specific to say in this text about how "bodily cravings"—what Victor Turner names in the conventional way "the . . . forces of disorder that inhere in man's mammalian constitution" (*Ritual Process* 93)—are able to operate so powerfully without leading to anarchy. For a fuller exposition of this point, we need to turn to Malthus's economic writings, and particularly to his *Principles of Political Economy* [*PPE*] (1820, 1836), which he describes as an attempt to analyze "the laws which regulate the movements of human society" (11).[21] The close interconnection of the two main strands of Malthus's work may not be obvious at first glance, for the overpopulation issue drops out of the *Principles* altogether, and population is mentioned in this work, indeed, only to minimize its impact upon economics (*PPE* 6:252). This is another sign that the population calculus may not after all be the crucial element of the *Essay*, but rather, just the original axiom from which flows a philosophical meditation on culture. The persistence of the same train of thought is signalled as early as the opening paragraph of the *Principles*. Here Malthus declares that the science of political economy is less akin to the abstractions of mathematics than to "the science of morals and politics," the "great general rules" of which are "founded upon the known passions and propensities of human nature" (*PPE* 5:5). Even more distinctly than in the *Essay*, his portrayal of the relation between passion and social regulation in this text is not one of antagonism and strife, but of complex complementarity in which each is discovered to be a function of the other.

The central concept in Malthus's political economy, as in his population theory, is "the desire to possess" (*PPE* 5:48), though here the desire is oriented not toward members of the opposite sex but toward market commodities. When made effective by the command of adequate means of purchasing, this desire manifests itself in the economy as "demand." It is Malthus's insistence upon the role of demand that most strikingly sets him apart from Ricardo and other economic theorists of his day, as has often been noted. (By the same token, Adam Smith's neglect of demand is one of the failings of his system.) Malthus stands in especially sharp contrast to Mill, who stresses in a somewhat equivocal way the role of "the desire to accumulate" on the production end of the economy, but systematically denies the theoretical significance of motives of consumption. His insistence on interpreting "demand" as merely a measure of the quantity of a commodity sought in a market (*Principles* 1:533) is a sign of this bias in his thinking: it is a way of summarily excluding the dynamics of desire from consideration. Indeed, it is one of Mill's fundamental doctrines that demand does not figure in economics as an independent variable, but is always exactly equivalent to supply (*Principles* 1:536). The privileged category in his system is clearly production, not consumption, and production itself he ties inseparably to the capitalist's capacity for "abstinence" (*Principles* 1:484). One can only guess at Mill's reasons for configuring economics in this fashion, but manifestly his model is one which in many respects meshes with the moral sentiment of evangelical culture.

There is in Malthus nothing like the instinct of exchange or (though it is once mentioned in passing) the dominating urge to "better one's position" hypothesized by Smith; indeed, Malthus's insistence upon the desire to possess and to *consume* directly contradicts the supposed exchange-instinct and at least potentially contradicts the self-betterment thesis as well. As in the *Essay on Population,* Malthus takes as his premise that the driving motive of human action—or, as it may be, inaction—is *jouissance.* Not every member of society is equally in quest of pleasure, and in fact, as he makes a point of noting, there is a potentially harmful tendency in modern culture to elevate saving and self-denial to the status of absolute virtues (*PPE* 6:345). As if in illustration of just this claim, Mill unqualifiedly endorses Adam Smith's praise of frugality and his dispraise of consumption (*Principles* 1:87, 92, 108). Yet the survival of a free-market economy, which is to say, an economy based on demand, depends, according to Malthus's heterodox theory, on the extremely vigorous operation of the "passion for consumption" (*PPE* 6:261). Again he appears before the public in the role of a champion of desire. He does not attempt to draw any explicit correlation between this thesis in the field of political

118

economy and his earlier claims that of all human desires apart from hunger, the sex drive is paramount. Yet his depiction of the capitalist market is a strikingly eroticized one, and would be consistent with the argument (were it part of his design to make such an argument) that sexual desire is the basis of all other more specialized desires and thus pervades all of life, just as the *Essay* claimed.

Despite the aggressive overtones of the verb "to possess," and despite the presumption of exclusive self-interest in classical economics, Malthus's model of the sexualized market transaction is not fundamentally that of rape but of shared pleasure. The coupling of buyer and seller, or, as Malthus prefers to present matters, of two exchangers, ideally consummates itself in the pleasure of each; moreover, it is fruitful, engendering in the process a new supply of commodities. "Every exchange must imply . . . a reciprocal desire in the party possessing the commodity wanted, for the commodity or the labour proposed to be exchanged for it" (*PPE* 5:42; see also 6:251). He thus conceives a market, which we can fairly take as a synecdoche of social organization at large, as a great network of desires, or rather, of desiring individuals in search of willing partners. This model seems quite as subject as the *Essay on Population* to Hazlitt's complaint that "Mr. Malthus's whole book rests on a malicious supposition, that all mankind . . . are like so many animals *in season*" (quoted P. James 121). Yet Malthus in his fixation on desire and pleasure is far from malicious, for the ideal result of any exchange according to his system would be "the happy one of both parties being better supplied and having more enjoyments." Economic activity is, or ought to be, what he describes as an "intercourse of mutual gratifications" (*PPE* 6:258).

Here as in the *Essay* and as in his momentous correspondence with Ricardo as well, Malthus stresses his practical and pragmatic bent and his stubbornly skeptical attitude toward abstract dialectics. Yet his focus in *Principles of Political Economy* falls not so much on practical illustration of the working of economic libido as on expounding its significance for certain theoretical problems of the new science which he played a large role in founding. Foremost among these is once again the problem of defining the concept that forms the key link between political economy and subsequent cultural theory: the concept of value.

Malthus approaches value as the foundational concept of political economy and yet, recalling Adam Smith on the same theme, as a nearly insoluble riddle, "a term open to . . . much controversy" (*PPE*

5:21). Well might he say so, given his five-year public and private controversy with his friend Ricardo on just this issue. The elusiveness of the term gives to the discipline a dizzyingly uncertain status. "It is not a little discreditable to a branch of knowledge which claims to be called a science," Malthus declares, "that the meaning of a term which is constantly met with in every work on political economy, and constantly heard in every conversation on the subject, should not yet be settled" (*PPE* 5:96)—a lament, only with the word "culture" in place of "value," which has often been heard among anthropologists, suggesting not only the analogous roles played by the two terms in their respective disciplines, but also their close intrinsic connection with one another.[22] For Malthus, defining "value" in analyzable, empirically significant terms means giving his new science a secure standing and a durable lease on life.

His point of reference for this project of definition is Adam Smith's labor theory of value, which had been extended and confirmed by Ricardo. Given the sanctification of work which forms such a dominant principle throughout evangelical culture, this issue is easy to recognize as one with ramifications extending well beyond problems of technical definition in political economy—which no doubt is why it held its intense fascination for economists of the day. It is commonly said that Malthus, having at first opposed the labor theory, became in the final (1836) edition of *Principles of Political Economy*, following the publication of his *The Measure of Value* (1823), a convert to it. The matter is more complicated than this, however. For one thing, he observes, as do many of Smith's later exegetes (Reisman 143, for example), that Smith confusingly speaks of the equivalence between labor and value in two very different senses, one of which he, Malthus, accepts with qualifications, the other of which he decisively rejects (*PPE* 5:70). The latter sense, the one embraced by Ricardo and denied by Malthus, presumes that value is a quantity directly equivalent to the quantity of labor actually expended in producing a given commodity. In the other sense, Malthus's eventual acceptance of which is seen by V. E. Smith to indicate a shift of emphasis away from the demand factor in value (V. E. Smith 216, 219), the value of a commodity is taken to be equivalent to the amount of labor that the commodity can command in exchange. It is important to notice that Malthus accepts this principle not, however, as an absolute but as a practical expedient, a heuristic device able not to define value ontologically but only "to approach as near to a standard measure [of value] . . . as the nature of the subject will admit" (*PPE* 5:78)—which is to say, not very near. The principle is still further qualified in a footnote (which is where many of Malthus's key formulations are to be found). "The labour which a commodity will command is *not* the *cause* of its value, but . . . the measure of it," he declares (*PPE* 5:70n). It is a device for calculating equivalences, not for explaining philosophically what value *is* or where it originates. In the same footnote he declares that "the labour worked up in a commodity is the principal *cause* of its value," but this unfortunately is the last we hear of such a doctrine. Whatever "principal cause" may in fact be intended to mean here, all Malthus's subsequent argument hinges upon the proposition that measurable relative value is a function not of labor but of desire. A commodity is valuable in proportion as potential consumers long to possess it. "Beauty is the lover's gift," says Mirabell to Millamant in *The Way of the World;* by the same token, value is bestowed erotically on things by human admirers, by desire rather than by "toil and trouble," according to the essential principle of Malthusian economics.

Desire is quantifiable for practical purposes in terms of the sacrifices required to purchase "desirable objects" (*PPE* 5:62). Malthus thus sums up his doctrine of value in these words: "It is . . . the value set upon commodities, it is the sacrifice . . . which people are willing to make in order to obtain them, that in the actual state of things may be said to be *almost the sole cause* of the existence of wealth; and this value is founded on the wants of mankind, and the adaptation of particular commodities to supply these wants, independently of the actual quantity of labour which these commodities may have cost in their collection or production" (*PPE* 5:244). Malthus in his most distinctive contribution to economic theory thus exactly prefigures Georg Simmel's stress on *sacrifice* as the key element of a philosophical theory of economic exchange. The technical term which he introduces to express this defining principle of value is "intensity of demand" (*PPE* 5:53), which he carefully distinguishes from the conventional notion in political economy of "extent" of demand (*PPE* 5:55, 57).[23] Only when demand is conceived as varying in intensity as well as in extent can we grasp its power to exert influence upon prices. It is important to note that for Malthus, intensity of demand is not simply an abstraction derived mathematically from statistics of supply in the market, but a real, pre-existing force. The proof of this, as he argues, is that in certain conditions of low prices (where it is possible to obtain intensely desired objects without much sacrifice), the actual state of demand may be hidden: "the whole intensity of demand will not show itself" under these conditions (*PPE* 5:53). Malthus stresses this issue in another telling footnote (*PPE* 5:54n), where he insists, in opposition to another authority, that potential demand, not just actualized demand, deserves the name "demand."

Value is not determined by the quantity of labor invested in a commodity, then; almost as importantly, it is not determined by the natural properties of objects. "The remuneration [that will be offered for commodities] will be regulated, not by the intrinsic qualities, or utility of the commodities produced, but the state of the demand for them, compared with the supply" (*PPE* 5:62–63). In every respect, *price and value are socially produced.* Malthus makes so much of this point because it is full of philosophical implications, though he does not explicitly develop them. His science deals with material things and the laws governing their movements—wealth being "everything which gratifies the wants of man by means of material objects" (*PPE* 5:41)— but by his overriding stress on demand and on "wants" he strongly shifts the ground of analysis to that of human consciousness and thus makes the economic process circular. We do not desire things that are valuable in themselves; rather, we desire things and create agencies to produce them because we have collectively imparted value to them. "You have quite overlooked the consideration of *value* as the prime power of industry and the grand stimulus to production," he remarks in his correspondence with Ricardo [*R*] (*R* 7:312).[24] This principle, which applies as strongly to Mill as to Ricardo, stands out with particular clarity when we seek to measure comparative values of unlike objects. "There is no other way of estimating the degree of wealth which the possession and enjoyment of them confer on the owner [note the characteristic stress on enjoyment], than by the estimation in which they are respectively held," declares Malthus (*PPE* 5:242).

From this point, Malthusian political economy tends irresistibly in the direction of an interpretive and always value-oriented theory of culture. The ultimate cause of his passionate objection to Ricardo's theory of value (later embraced by Mill) as a coefficient of the difficulty of production is that such a theory renders value a purely mechanical and quantitative entity rather than the ideational-affective one that intuitively he knew it to be. He clearly sees that his own perspective leads outside political economy narrowly defined. If "the giving a greater price for a commodity . . . necessarily implies a greater intensity of demand," then "the real question is, what are the causes which determine the increase or diminution of this intensity of demand [?]" (*PPE* 5:53). It is not the province of *Principles of Political Economy* to respond in depth to "the real question," which would entail close cultural analysis, but the broad approach which Malthus takes to this question here is continuous with his identification of sexual appeal with cultural "adjuncts": the esteem in which commodities are held, their power, that is, to gratify desire, depends upon their involvement as symbolic representations in a system of collective values. The principle is not so much argued by Malthus as it is simply taken for granted by him, as when he insists on referring abstract hypotheses about the dynamics of supply and demand to "the actual habits and tastes of the society" (*PPE* 6:259), a point which he often stresses in writing to Ricardo as well (*R* 6:132, 7:70, 7:122). The question of possible overproduction of commodities in a given society relative to its "passion for consumption" depends directly upon "what the structure and habits of such a society will permit to be profitably consumed" (*PPE* 6:261, 262). This "passion," to repeat, is for Malthus purely a social habit, the result of a historical process of development, not an instinctive longing for intrinsically desirable things. The development and material enrichment of a society thus both fosters and (in the usual circularity) depends upon that expansive growth of desire evoked in different terms, as we saw, in *The Essay on Population*. "One of the greatest benefits which foreign commerce confers, and the reason why it has always appeared an almost necessary ingredient in the progress of wealth, is, its tendency to inspire new wants, to form new tastes, and to furnish fresh motives for industry" (*PPE* 6:321). Wealth varies according to the sole factor of intensity (and variousness) of desire, and desire is given its form by collective experience.

What emerges in this way from Malthus's theory of demand is a central principle of what comes to be the anthropological or ethnographic theory of culture. The essence of his thinking lies in the idea of human desire understood as a social construct inscribing "value," which is to say, meaning, upon amorphous natural materials—and thereby creating the metanatural system (one field of which is the capitalistic economy) which is man's self-constructed habitat. This process is the ground of the passion for consumption, which Malthus appears to consider as essentially a passion for symbolizing, for stamping upon the world the pattern of human social life. Attaching desire and its symbolic mark, price, to material things is thus the specifically economic response to "the original sin of man": "the torpor and corruption of the chaotic matter, in which he may be said to be born" (*EP* 124). *Homo economicus* in Malthus's system reveals himself ever more plainly as *Homo significans,* the maker, and also the enjoyer, of value and meaning amid a deadening chaos of matter.

This thesis will emerge more clearly if we step back to view the controversy over "value" in political economy in its wider historical bearings. I suggested at the outset of this chapter that the foundational discovery of economics was the concept that all the products of human action within a society are linked with all the others in an abstract network of correspondences, each item standing in a relation of equivalence to each other and being in fact convertible into it— each item being to this extent, indeed, a constituent element of each other one. The vehicle or medium of convertibility is "value." In effect the economists posited that each commodity symbolically represents all the others inhabiting the same social system in an indefinitely expansible series of binary relations. The philosophical significance of this representational system was partly obscured because the technical character of the science caused its practitioners to emphasize the element of physical exchange in market transactions and thus to consider the value relations among commodities in the aspect of sheer quantity: one shirt is worth how many loaves of bread? But it is because they were at least dimly aware of further implications of their essential doctrine, or so we can infer, that for several generations they invested so much energy in the controversy over the nature, origin, and mode of measurement of "value."

Malthus grasped more lucidly than his contemporaries prior to Mill that the propositional system of political economy implied abjuring any idea of fixed natural values in favor of an all-pervading principle of relativity or what he calls by one of the key terms in his theoretical lexicon: "proportionality." He means that the significance of any item in the economic system is only calculable as a series of ratios expressing its relations to other items; supply, notably, needs always to be seen in its binary relation to demand. He says characteristically in a letter to Ricardo, for instance, "it is not merely the proportion of commodities to each other but their proportion to the wants and tastes of mankind that determines prices" (*R* 6:132). "All the great results in political economy . . . depend," he declares elsewhere, putting his principle in broadest terms, upon *proportions"* (*PPE* 6:300). To this comment he appends a striking footnote which underlines the centrality of this idea in all his thought. "It is not, however, in political

economy alone that so much depends upon proportions, but throughout the whole range of nature and art." Clearly he feels that he has
struck on a momentous discovery, one which potentially could unify
diverse fields of research. He illustrates the principle, full as it is of
subversively modern hermeneutic implications, again and again, insisting, as Mill was to do later on, that things do not possess value in
themselves, but only in reference to the position they occupy in the
whole system of valued things in a particular society. This is "the doctrine of proportions," the doctrine, as Malthus strikingly puts it, that
value "depends upon the relation of parts, rather than on any positive
rule" (*PPE* 6:326).[25]

Even Malthus yielded to some extent to the impulse to see "value"
as a homogenous real substance parcelled out among commodities
and measurable by a fixed standard. It was Ricardo who at last firmly
grasped the futility of the quest for a fixed quantitative measure of
value. "The fact really is," he says in a letter to Malthus, summing up
their long, inconclusive debate on this subject, "that no accurate measure of absolute value can be found. . . . We have both failed" (*R* 9:346,
352). There is in economics no transcendent or privileged signifier
able to occupy any position outside the wholly metaphorical and relativistic field of "value." Writing to James Mill, Ricardo fleshes out this
conclusion into a kind of Heisenberg Uncertainty Principle of economic value: "I . . . am more confirmed than ever that strictly speaking
there is not in nature any correct measure of value nor can any ingenuity suggest one, for what constitutes a correct measure for some
things is a reason why it cannot be a correct one for others" (*R* 9:387;
see also 9:361). His disciple J. R. McCulloch agrees, writing to him that
the conundrum of value is "quite insoluble" and belongs to the "transcendental part of Pol Economy" (*R* 9:369).[26]

Having been drawn by the logic of the hypothesis of value into this
transcendental impasse, scientists of society were positioned to take
the decisive next step of breaking free of quantification and to speculate that not only were items of material wealth symbolically concomitants of one another, but so also were all the other nonmaterial phenomena of culture, including artistic forms, table manners, moral
values, rituals. At least on the plane of analysis, such phenomena
could prove to be derivable from or exchangeable for one another.
This next step was in fact taken not by the economists but by linguists,
and in particular by Ferdinand de Saussure, who in his *Course in General Linguistics* [*CGL*] lays out as early as 1906–11 the whole proposi-

tional structure of modern cultural analysis, and in terms that leave little doubt as to its direct affiliation with political economy. "Semiology" is of course the name he proposes for an inclusive new science that would proceed "by studying rites, customs, etc. as signs" (*CGL* 17), as forming part of an integral and self-referential system of meanings conventionally represented. "Here as in political economy we are confronted," says Saussure, "with the notion of *value;* both sciences are concerned with *a system for equating things of different orders*—labor and wages in one and a signified and signifier in the other" (*CGL* 79). The central chapter of the book is devoted to the attempt to define what Saussure calls "linguistic value." Value is wholly relative: it expresses the fact that in language all entities exist only as negatives of other entities. Seeming to quote directly Malthus's principle that value "depends upon the relation of parts, rather than on any positive rule," Saussure declares as the grand dogma of his linguistics that language is a system of binary oppositions *"without positive terms,"* in which "the value of each term results solely from the simultaneous presence of the others" (*CGL* 120, 114). "Even outside language all values are apparently governed by the same paradoxical principle," says Saussure (*CGL* 115), echoing Malthus's insight that it is "not . . . in political economy alone that so much depends upon proportions, but throughout the whole range of nature and art." The specific equation with the idea of value in political economy is then spelled out. Just as one exchanges money for bread, so one exchanges things for other things within the sign-system of language. "In the same way a word can be exchanged for something dissimilar, an idea" (*CGL* 115). Without pausing to inquire into the trustworthiness of this analogy, we can simply note the evidence that the genesis of structural linguistics and of the methods of cultural understanding that flow from it is to a large extent based on the paradigms of classical economics, and especially, perhaps (except that it is scarcely possible to identify exact origins when one is studying a movement of thought so widely ramified), on Malthus's perception that the essential function of the economy is not so much to allow the accumulation of material wealth as to create a fully articulated system of "value," of meaning, for human beings to inhabit.

In its concept of the relational nature of all symbolic meaning, which is to say, all social phenomena, Malthus's theory thus crystallizes the implication that we found originally in Adam Smith and illustrated more than once with reference to Evans-Pritchard's *The Nuer.*

CHAPTER TWO

The central principle of the method of analysis practiced by all these writers is, in Evans-Pritchard's phrase, that "each unit [in any cultural system] can only be defined in terms of the whole system" (*Nuer* 262)—in terms, we may say, of "the doctrine of proportions." Annexing Saussure and Evans-Pritchard to Malthus in this way highlights the fact that what drops out of Saussure's system is precisely what for Malthus was the all-important generator of value, desire. But we need finally to observe that in exalting desire as he does, Malthus renders it problematic in a way that strikes in quite a threatening fashion at the certainties of classical political economy. Other theorists were able largely to ignore the factor of demand, and to concentrate instead on the "supply side" and on the dynamics of production, because they took it as axiomatic that supply created its own demand, and that the two functions were necessarily equal to one another, like action and reaction in classical mechanics. Overproduction was a theoretical impossibility. This sacrosanct principle, known formally as Say's Law, is in fact valid only with regard to the relatively insignificant factor of "extent" of demand, according to Malthus. True, any supply of a commodity will be able to find a corresponding demand once its price falls low enough; but this principle fails to address the really vital issue of "intensity" of demand (*PPE* 5:52). Considered in this light, demand, as we have seen, is essentially independent of supply. Contrary to another postulate of classical economics, it is also at least partially independent of population growth (*PPE* 6:252). Thus demand is *not necessarily self-regulating* in such a way as to assure the overall equilibrium of the market. The point is significant—verges indeed on blasphemy—because it challenges the supposition that demand will automatically expand without limit to sustain the great desideratum of Adam Smith, an economy perpetually expanding. Taking issue with Smith's Durkheimian claim, to which Ricardo also subscribed, that the desire for luxuries has "no limit or certain boundary," Malthus specifically rejects the notion of "the *unlimited* desire of mankind to consume" (*PPE* 6:320).[27] As he had insisted with regard to the sex drive in the *Essay on Population,* the desire to consume is not infinitely extensible. He backs up this assertion by emphasizing the way in which contradictory motives in human character, notably "the love of indolence," work to set limits upon one another (*PPE* 6:337); and he concludes, in his most radical departure from orthodox doctrine, that desire or "demand" may under certain circumstances catastrophically fail.

What re-emerges at this crucial juncture of Malthusian economics is the image of primitive man as depicted in the *Essay*, a listless, torpid organism largely vacant of desire and thus incapable of significant, or signifying, activity. The economic symptom of his presence is the dislocation produced by the coexistence of an excessive drive to produce (and thus to save) and an insufficient drive to consume. It is Malthus's belief in the possibility that "intensity of demand" could fall to dangerously low levels that motivates his persistent dissent from Adam Smith's and Ricardo's dogma—itself an index of emergent Evangelical sensibility—that saving is always desirable, and that the frugal, abstemious man is always a public benefactor (*PPE* 6:260). In another of his dangerous deviations from economic gospel, he characteristically declares that "the final object in saving" is not amassing capital for investment and profit, but rather, "expenditure and enjoyment" (*PPE* 6:319–20), and that this object needs to be fostered, not discouraged, in order for a market to prosper. Directly contradicting Adam Smith's condemnations of luxurious expense (and giving a foretaste of the scandalous economics of Georges Bataille's 1933 essay "The Notion of Expenditure"), he portrays such expense as a strong force in building a diversified modern society liberated from the old division of rich and poor. "A taste for material objects, however frivolous, almost always requires for its gratification the accumulation of capital, and the existence of a much greater number of manufacturers, merchants, wholesale dealers, and retail dealers. The face of society is thus wholly changed" (*PPE* 5:35). Social life, having constructed certain patterns of desire, is itself reconstructed by them in turn. But a natural drag of inertia weighs upon this process at every point, rendering desire, as Itard had discovered in the case of Victor, exasperatingly hard to generate. Against the axiom that human desire is inherently expansive (thus always dangerous), Malthus declares in a letter to Ricardo that it is an error "to think that the wants and tastes of mankind are always ready for the supply" when the fact is that "few things are more difficult, than to inspire new tastes and wants, particularly out of old materials" (*R* 7:122; see also 7:70)). It follows that the economy could well suffer the calamity that Say's Law declares an impossibility, that of a "general glut" of commodities which would lead to collapsing prices and widespread impoverishment (*PPE* 6:257–59).[28]

In insisting prophetically on the reality of this danger, Malthus can be seen to come in his political economy to much the same scenario of disaster that opened the *Essay on Population,* with the rampant over-production of commodities now taking the place of the overpopulation of human beings. This version of the Malthusian disaster results from an entropic decline of desire, the roots of which seem to lie in that cultural complex of values in which frugality and productivity are idealized while expenditure and enjoyment are condemned. In its ultimate theoretical speculation, this text thus invokes anew the abiding nightmare of boundless desire, but in a version now turned exactly inside-out. Instead of there being no upper limit to desire, Malthus imagines that there is no lower limit, that desire can wither away almost to nothing, just as it was said to do in Godwin's utopia. Thus the market becomes flooded with goods for which there is no longer an adequate "intensity of demand"—goods, as we may say, from which value-bearing symbolism has leaked away.[29] This imagery of a listless, torpid population submerged in valueless commodities is at bottom a vision of "mind" sinking back into primal "matter"—a vision that was to be depicted in appallingly graphic form in the work of Henry Mayhew, as we shall see.

Bagehot

This chapter portrays political economy, preoccupied as it originally was with deciphering the connection between desire and value, as one field of discourse where essential themes of the modern theory of culture first took shape. We can track some of the same themes later in the nineteenth century in the writings of Walter Bagehot, the long-time editor of the *Economist,* where the nexus of economics and cultural anthropology is more distinctly marked than ever before, and where the rootedness of both lines of thought in a certain (unstable) mythology of desire is again made manifest. More a synthesizer of emerging ideas than an original theorist in his own right, Bagehot for this reason offers an especially valuable exhibit of late-century trends of thought.

Bagehot's *Economic Studies* [*ES*] (1880), like, for instance, *Lombard Street* (1873), testifies among other things to the hegemony achieved at this point in the century by the paradigm of society as a "complex whole." Economics for Bagehot is above all the explication of networks of intermeshed, mutually sustaining institutions: private ownership of land, laws of contract enforced by government, money, the banking system (and the general trust that enables it to work), and so forth, each of which he studies in detail with the goal of showing how it supports all the others. Material wealth is just one factor in an array of social phenomena which are "economic" in the essential sense of being interreactive throughout an entire system of institutions. The concept of "institution" is inexorably widened in the course of Bagehot's analysis, and it is this more than anything else that gives his work its significance for the emerging concept of culture. But the explicit sign of this orientation in his commentary on political economy is the way that it tends, like Malthus's and Mill's (and to a lesser extent Adam Smith's), to fly off at every turn, sometimes quite unexpectedly, into anthropology.

Bagehot found much to dissent from in Malthus's population theory, but he singled out his anthropology for praise: "there is much in his discussion of the savage society, which is still worth reading, and which was much before his time" (*ES* 139). He undertakes anthropological researches of his own nominally in order to illustrate the lack in primitive societies of the kinds of constituent institutions that enable the market economy to operate in advanced societies like modern Britain—for example, "the commercial spirit," which, far from being innate, in fact is a mental structure peculiar to particular historical circumstances and unheard of in many nations (*ES* 80). This line of analysis, in which non-Western society is defined primarily as an *absence* of various "civilized" structures, would seem to rule out awareness of culture "in the wide ethnographic sense." Yet there are signs in Bagehot of a significant if almost involuntary counterargument in this respect. Rather than treating the world of non-European cultures as negligible, he in fact makes it one of the main points of his critique of political economy that its principles apply to one type of society only, but not to others, which are organized, he declares, in radically different fashions and by implication can only be made intelligible through modes of analysis grounded in their different cultural principles (*ES* 17). In other words, what emerges here long before Ruth Benedict's attack on the tendency "[to] identify our local normalities with the inevitable necessities of existence" (Benedict 251) is a stress on the sheer variety and singularity of human societies, and thus, the impulse, fundamental to the discourse of anthropology, to expose the fallacy of supposing our own customary ideas and social arrangements to be "natural."[30] Having shown that in the traditional society of India the principle of the free movement of labor would be an "alien" and "incomprehensible" notion, Bagehot declares that "in this case as in many others, what seems in later times the most natural organisation is really the one most difficult to create, and it does not arise till after many organisations which seem to our notions more complex have preceded it and perished" (*ES* 29–30). "We now see . . . that what we have been used to call 'natural' is not the first but the second nature of men" (*ES* 66). This sophisticated denaturalizing of modern bourgeois social values in *Economic Studies* does not seemingly have for Bagehot any of the implications that the same critique has for dissident writers like Roland Barthes or Benedict; at least on the level of overt rhetoric it coincides with an evolutionist theory stressing the gradual improvement of human society and thus the superiority of modern societies over primitive ones. But undercutting the pretensions of our own ideas and social arrangements to be grounded in the "natural" is a move rife with dangerous implications, some of which come forth plainly elsewhere in Bagehot's writing. They suggest ever more strongly that the development of the idea of culture in the late nineteenth century was as much as anything else a vehicle for a profound disaffection from Victorian orthodoxies—so profound that it could govern the thinking even of a man like Bagehot, who represented himself as a spokesman for the Victorian establishment.

The same ambiguity affects his development of another theme much elaborated subsequently by Benedict, that of the "intense disposition in the human mind . . . to hate what is unusual and strange in other people" (*ES* 33). The essential idea of his anthropology in *Economic Studies* and in other works is that primitive society, in thrall to the hatred of uncustomary things, imposes stifling restraints upon personal thought and action, thus prohibiting progress.[31] In early times there reigned "a coercive sense of ingrained usage, which kept men from thinking what they had not before thought, and from doing what they had not before done; a vague horror that something . . . might happen if they did so; a close religion which filled the air with deities who were known by inherited tradition, and who hated uninherited ways" (*ES* 27–28). This stress on the binding power of primitive custom and on the occult nature of the collective mind looks ahead to the "coercion" theory of culture of Durkheim and others, and it clearly reflects the revised conception of primitives characteristic of the later decades of the nineteenth century (see chapter 1). For Bagehot, enlightened modern institutions, in contrast to primitive ones, have as their primary characteristic the facilitating of free activity. Parliament, for instance, is portrayed as a great machine for fostering the free, competitive exchange of ideas; the cabinet form of government ensures the immediate responsiveness of the state to currents of popular feeling. In the economic field proper, Bagehot lays all his stress upon the ability of the system of capitalistic institutions to bring about "the free circulation" of labor and of capital, which are enabled to move with mercurial swiftness to any point in the vastly diversified economy where enhanced returns are to be had. Had he been given to the organic metaphors of his contemporary Spencer, he would have described the capitalistic economy as a body in a state of nervous hypersensitivity, instantly transmitting impulses from the slightest stimuli and triggering appropriate physiological responses. Thus he expounds the operations of the national "speculative fund" of capital "to remind ourselves how mobile this sort of money is, and how it runs from country to country like beads of quicksilver" (*ES* 70). The implication of a pathological quality in so highly stimulated a nervous system comes strongly to the surface elsewhere in Bagehot's writing, as we shall see. It is worth noting, too, how his imagery registers the transformation of money—a tangible thing able to be stamped and weighed—into a kind of occult energy moving through society, instantly transmissible over great distances. But what we need to emphasize for now is how distinctly Bagehot conceives these features of the market as phenomena of the underlying force which money in the last analysis merely symbolizes: *desire*.

Political Economy, he declares in the classical idiom of the discipline, is simply the scientific study of "the effects of the desire to be rich," a "passion" upon which modern nations depend for their power and prestige (*ES* 80). Bagehot follows Malthus (without crediting him) in explicitly defining value and thus wealth as representations of desire, and goes beyond him in rejecting either form of the labor theory of value. The effect of this move is to situate value wholly within the field of mental and sociological variables, and decisively to expel from this field the "natural" absolutes which earlier generations of economists had striven to identify. "The quantity of labour which a thing will purchase depends on the degree in which it is desired by labourers," he declares, contradicting Adam Smith (*ES* 122). He analyzes the economic behavior of individuals in the same terms. Saving, for instance, arises from the confluence of several different currents of desire: from "the craving to have some stock of money laid against the unknown future," from "the desire to provide for the next generation," and lastly, "the desire to be rich" (*ES* 171–72). Yet by this point in the evolution of social thought, the conceptual problem involved in describing collective phenomena merely as aggregates of the phenomena of individual psychology is coming disturbingly into view.

Durkheim was to announce in his manifesto of fifteen years later that "sociology is not a corollary of psychology" (*Rules* 127) and must sever all ties with it. Bagehot's impulse to do just this causes the concept of desire in his economics to take on something of the same equivocal quality that money does—and in fact lands the entire science of culture in the ambiguous position from which it has never since been able to extricate itself. Thus he stresses repeatedly that *H. economicus* is not to be confused with any real man, full as real men are of variegated noneconomic desires. The human being whose psychology and conduct are analyzed by political economy is, he makes plain, merely a theoretical construct invented for the convenience of economists; their theories consequently "are only true," as Mill declares, echoing the views on scientific hypotheses put forward by Adam Smith in "The History of Astronomy," "*in the abstract*" (*Some Unsettled Questions* 144–45). "The abstract man of this science is engrossed with one desire only—the desire of possessing wealth," explains Bagehot (*ES* 74), closely following here Mill's treatment of the same theme.[32] Economics according to this theoretical schema is nothing other than the science of boundless desire. Yet the man who exhibits this condition *does not exist:* he is another occult entity like the ancestral ghosts of Spencer's theory, a precipitate of the logic by which the idea of culture treats individuals as projections of disembodied collective states which can only be figured in metaphorical models, never directly perceived. In his awareness of this principle, Bagehot thus gives another sign of the movement of economic thought away from Adam Smith's identification of economics with "laws of nature" and with material reality: economics as Bagehot understands it is sharply divorced from "nature" even in its invocation of the force of desire. Not that he despairs in principle of learning about the organization of desire in flesh-and-blood people. He expressly posits desire not as a given but as an enigma ripe for scientific study: "why men want so many things is a great subject fit for inquiry," he says (*ES* 81), echoing Malthus's remark that "the real question" underlying political economy is that of the institutionalization of desire (*PPE* 5:53). Bagehot thus situates political economy at the threshold of a broader "science of society" (*ES* 74) able to address the "great subject" of how human desires in all their bewildering multiplicity come into being. This new science is to be the one named by Tylor nine years before, if never actually practiced by him: that of culture "in its wide ethnographic sense."[33] But Bagehot's insistence that the economists' economic man is purely an abstract model gives a premonition of the problematic status that has always surrounded the accomplishments of modern social science.[34] Rigorously empirical as it may strive to be, can such a mode of inquiry ever furnish objective knowledge about social life—especially that of societies radically unlike our own—or is it forever locked within its own self-constructed world of abstract heuristic entities?

Bagehot seemingly stresses the fictive nature of economic man in order to make possible a dispassionate and scientifically objective inspection of him, but the very maneuver by which he was invented enmeshes this figure in subjectivity and in discourse, which is to say, charges him with emotional and ideological values. This being supposed to be "engrossed with one desire only," ceaselessly pursuing wealth and void of all other drives, is framed in fact in the image of a maniacal grotesque not unlike the obsessive monsters who populate late-eighteenth and nineteenth-century fiction, enslaved to greed, sexual lust, sadism, social ambition, revenge, or some other tyrannical drive. The hypothetical actors of political economy are homologous with themes of literary imagination, in other words: masquerading as purely technical devices, they pick up broad trends of "thought style" and carry a veiled but real expressive charge. Specifically, they give one more expression to the myth of the state of pathologically boundless desire. Bagehot's economic man is never limited in his craving for wealth by any countervailing impulses, and this craving is by definition perpetually unappeased and unappeasable. He seeks not just wealth, but infinite wealth; he will never have enough however much he gets. Bagehot may at first seem unaware of the disturbing syndrome embodied in this economic fiction—just the one that Durkheim calls anomie and identifies, with much stress on the specific factor of insatiable profit motives, as the distinctive strain of modern social life—but we shall see that he is not always so unaware of it as he appears to be. It transpires in *Physics and Politics* that modern life in Bagehot's eyes is in fact ruled by the principle of anomic desire.

In the meantime, the essential feature of his treatment of this theme in the economic realm and of the human image it generates is his attitude of studied scientific neutrality, which is to say, amorality. All possible value implications of a ceaseless, rapacious quest for riches are summarily evacuated from the discourse that Bagehot calls "political economy." Whether the longing for wealth be deserving of praise or blame "is," he makes a point of saying, "to the economist immaterial" (*ES* 81). Bagehot reaches the same conclusion on this score as Adam Smith, but by means of a more radical maneuver than Smith's—more radical because it proposes (in a deceptively bland-seeming rhetorical mode) a shift of the ground of value itself. *The Wealth of Nations* evades moral condemnation of greed by portraying this motive as a providential device for the promotion of general well-being: the capitalist system by this device is invested with positive moral value. Bagehot, scarcely pausing to invoke classical doctrine on this point, constructs political economy as a sphere in which moral values are irrelevant and meaningless since human drives and actions here are only hypothetical abstractions, not substantial reality. That this nullifying of moral values in the name of scientific methodology amounts to a provocative attack on Victorian habits of relentless moral interpretation could not have escaped any contemporary reader: this again is not a purely technical move, in other words, but one charged with cultural reverberations, and one closely affiliated with the many other lines of subversive free thought that were undermining Victorian principles in the late nineteenth century.[35]

Bagehot's thesis is but a step removed from the Nietzschean one, promulgated at about the same time, that truth is a mobile army of figures of speech, and that *all* moral discourse, given its origin in personal and cultural drives, is purely a mode of rhetoric and devoid of positive force. Raising in 1886 "the problem of morality itself," Nietzsche evokes the prospect of being "rid of this nightmare" of the belief in Good in Itself, of being able to "sail away right *over* morality," as an exhilarating freedom (*Beyond Good and Evil* 104, 2, 34). His goal in nullifying moral values is to proceed to the "transvaluation of all value" on behalf of a new, more creative, more "life-enhancing" morality, and here, of course, he parts company with a theorist of political economy like Bagehot, who in conjuring up a world emptied of moral reference claims merely to be defining the ground rules of a certain form of abstract inquiry. But if we accept Nietzsche's teaching that the exercises of abstract speculation are bound to have a basis in covert motives, we are compelled to guess at the purport of this theoretical invention of a world which so closely resembles our own except for its emptiness of moral significance. Thomas Common, an early translator of Nietzsche, turns the accusation that Nietzsche denied all morality back specifically upon the gospel of political economy, which, he says, "not only implicitly disregards morals, but on many occasions boldly and explicitly professes to have nothing to do with them" (Common ix). He means to say that the modern science of wealth not just hypothetically but in a practical and concerted way deconstructs moral values. Furthermore, Bagehot's declaration that the figure of the capitalist wholly devoted to amassing wealth is just a theoretical fiction is not quite ingenuous. In *The English Constitution* he declares that as a matter of actual fact the Anglo-Saxon "is always trying to make money; he reckons everything in coin; he bows down before a great heap, and sneers as he passes a little heap." Mill states just as pungently that unbounded economic desire is no fiction. For Englishmen in general, he asserts, no other interest exists "to divide the dominion over them with the one propensity which is the passion of those who have no other, and the satisfaction of which comprises all that they imagine of success in life—the desire of growing richer, and getting on in the world" (*Principles* 1:125–26). The economic monster has tangible reality after all. Yet even here, "whether this feeling be right or wrong, it is useless to discuss," says Bagehot, since it is largely involuntary (*EC* 124).

This axiom of late-classical political economy is cognate historically with the basic tenet of scientific ethnography: that the study even of customs and values that we find abhorrent must be conducted in an atmosphere of strict impartiality, from which moral valuation (or at least moral disapproval) has been expunged. Bagehot identified this abolishing of value judgment as nothing less than the key principle of the thought-world of his era. "The great maxim of modern thought," he says, "is not only the toleration of everything, but the examination of everything" (*EC* 191). It is precisely this attitude of universal toleration as the basis of analytical examination that defines the scientific status of modern cultural anthropology, and that marks the significant difference between a missionary observer of primitive life such as the Polynesianist William Ellis and, say, Frazer. Frazer is not more of a scientist than Ellis because he studied the empirical data of primitive culture more intensively than did Ellis—the reverse is arguably the case—but because he adopts toward the phenomena under study, however wildly macabre, a dispassionate and interpretive attitude, whereas Ellis, faced with various shocking practices among the peoples he visited, calls them abominable and devotes much of his text to describing his own active, keenly judgmental intervention in these peoples' lives. Juxtaposing the two figures makes the point once again that the modern view of culture is impelled by polemical and adversarial motives (for all its professed disinterestedness) and that it brings into play first and foremost a rhetoric of disavowal of Victorian sensibility. Frazer may not be the Antichrist, but he definitely is the anti-Ellis, a calculating opponent of the Evangelical mentality that formed the chief cultural norms of nineteenth-century Britain.

The strain of quasi-nihilistic modernism which runs at an almost subliminal level in *Economic Studies* takes more pronounced form in *The English Constitution* (1867), where Bagehot, moving out from his conceptual base in political economy, elaborates key elements of an anthropological theory of culture. The problem to which he increasingly devotes himself is that of the shared mentality of groups. "A great popular assembly [like Parliament] has a corporate character," he remarks at one point: "it has its own privileges, prejudices, and notions," and is by its nature impenetrable by outsiders (*EC* 201). Stressing this principle of the radical discontinuity of one collectivity from another, Bagehot quite fully anticipates Evans-Pritchard's thesis that "a man sees himself as a member of a group only in opposition to other groups" (*Nuer* 137): nothing is more characteristically human, he says, than the irrational impulse to exclude as alien anyone perceived as belonging to some other group. This impulse is fully manifest in members of Parliament (who are said to regard governmental department heads as untrustworthy aliens), but Bagehot associates it most particularly with "semi-barbarous people," a category meant to include much of the lower-class population of Victorian England. Such people are marked, he reports, by "diffused distrust and indiscriminate suspicion" toward all outsiders; they are "rooted to the places where they were born, think the thoughts of those places, can endure no other thoughts." A foreign country or even the next parish marks "a definite beginning of new maxims, new thoughts, new ways; the immemorial boundary mark begins in feeling a strange world," a world where "they have other laws, another aristocracy, another life" (*EC* 258–59). What this striking passage implies is that human beings urgently need a sense of *boundedness,* of definite limits, and that they create it collectively by classing other groups as alien and by reinforcing this principle of classification by feeling an invincible, quasi-instinctive repugnance for all ways other than their own.[36] The symbolic "mark" or taboo impressed upon nature by human culture is here seen in its quintessential form as the "immemorial boundary mark" delimiting one's native territory in reference to the "strange world" of aliens which abuts one's own world on all sides.

The analysis of modern Britain in *The English Constitution* focuses on the delusiveness of the "popular theory" of the significance of social agencies. What enables these agencies to function is precisely this characteristic, according to Bagehot. To understand the workings of the country truly it is necessary to penetrate beneath all officially defined rationales so as to reach their basis in those national patterns of thought and feeling and "imaginative sentiments" (*EC* 53) that have formed themselves over centuries of collective life and that cause us "instinctively, without argument, almost without consciousness" (*EC* 258) to adhere to a certain body of inherited custom which both enacts and at the same time utterly mystifies "the secret pervading disposition of society" (*EC* 67). As in the main stream of subsequent theory (and as Adam Smith had done in *The Theory of Moral Sentiments*), Bagehot thus ascribes the coercive, absolute force of national thought-patterns to their *unconscious* operation. Social life becomes in this model a display of implicit obedience to tendencies concealed from our apprehension—a sharp epistemic shift from the figure of desire bottled up within imposed boundaries to one of more insidious and pervasive influences in which the line separating individuality from the social milieu becomes ever more ambiguous. In Britain, the central principle of what Benedict was to call the "unconscious canons of choice that develop within [each] culture" (Benedict 44) is the principle of "deference."

So profound is the irrational British habit of wanting to be governed by one's "betters," Bagehot argues, that the ten-pound householders enfranchised in 1832 continued to elect to Parliament rich men who enacted taxes wholly for their own benefit and against the interests of their constituency (*EC* 6). The same perverse principle operates among the upper strata of the middle classes, whose declared ideology may proclaim their own superiority over the titled and untitled gentry, but whose "secret sentiment" (*EC* 19), secret even to themselves, is the worship of rank. In this hypothesis of an essentially masochistic cultural and political unconscious, what disintegrates altogether is the political economists' assumption of the primacy of rational maximizing of self-interest. Accounting for the maintenance of such a system, in which normalcy and stability have so clear an aspect of the pathological, becomes evidently an analytical problem.

Bagehot attempts to resolve it by identifying as the chief practical element of the British system its deployment of "what we may call the *theatrical show* of society" (*EC* 268) to surround the upper classes with that aura of transcendent value which the whole mentality of the culture unites in conferring upon them. It is this imaginative vision of their betters, the product of a concerted system of propagandistic rhetoric, and not the "machinery of police," that effectively ensures the lower classes' submissiveness and docility.

Bagehot couches his analysis of this phenomenon in the figures of occult forces which are native to the discourse of modern anthropology. Thus the institution of the monarchy is sustained chiefly by the "mystic reverence" which it arouses and which culminates in the "mystic enchantment" with which a king is surrounded in the eyes of his subjects (*EC* 53, 115). This reverential attitude is excited by "that which is mystic in its claims; that which is occult in its mode of action" as well as "brilliant to the eye" (*EC* 57). There is a slight but significant ambiguity in Bagehot's text as to the exact referent of "that which is occult in its mode of action," and there is every reason to think that he is referring here as much to the generative process of "the secret pervading disposition of society" (*EC* 67) as to the special doctrine of the British monarchy. The vehicles by which this superstitious doctrine is made operative are what Bagehot calls "symbols," visible images of the natural superiority of an elite social caste, images from which there radiates an irresistible mesmerizing and subjugating fluid just as the binding force of gravity radiates from heavenly bodies in Newton's physics. Pierre Bourdieu's concept of the "symbolic violence" of dominant social classes is fully expounded in this text of Bagehot's, in other words. The nimbus of the supernatural which surrounds the British upper classes is of course nothing but a vulgar mystification, but the process which generates it in Bagehot's account does have a magical aspect of its own. His analysis hints that any cultural system will possess an occult character by virtue of its ultimate rootedness in symbols, magical entities which are themselves and other things all at once, fantastically overleaping space and time and impressing their influence upon our unconscious thoughts in ways we can scarcely comprehend.

What emerges most distinctly from *The English Constitution* is finally an estranging idea of culture as an autonomous coercive force which has indeed the power to generate semblances of legitimate moral values, but which ultimately manifests a gigantic system of exploitation, pathology, and class power (one which Bagehot himself endorses as a bulwark against potential anarchy), a system indifferent to human welfare and without moral authenticity. Bagehot's analysis of culture strikingly resembles in this regard Mill's portrayal of the realm of "nature" two years earlier in *Three Essays on Religion* (1874), and it is continuous with the quasi-nihilism of his own insistence that the model of the world constructed by political economy is void of moral reference. This vein of thinking has as its key stylistic sign in Bagehot's writing his habitual identification of cultural principles with physical forces. The social analyses governed by this trope open not onto a realm of human value but onto a naturalistic one of mechanical laws which relentlessly follow morally nonsensical imperatives. "You may place power in weak hands at a revolution," he declares, for instance, "but you cannot keep it in weak hands: it runs out of them into strong ones" (*EC* 252). Bagehot is obsessed especially with the danger of social disorder that is inherent analogically in certain laws of physics. "A deferential community in which the bulk of the people are ignorant is . . . in a state of what is called in mechanics unstable equilibrium. If the equilibrium is once disturbed, there is no tendency to return to it, but rather to depart from it" (*EC* 271). Such a phrase points us back to our main theme by bearing witness once again to the linkage of nineteenth-century social speculation to the dread of the release of illimitable forces. This complex of metaphors operates tenaciously in Bagehot's writing even as he elaborates its historical successor, a conception of culture as a fabric of symbolic expressiveness.

The former theme is fully rendered in Bagehot's most potent speculative work, *Physics and Politics* [*PP*] (1876), where his earlier political and economic analysis reveals its implicit logic by developing into full-scale anthropological theory. He refers several times to Tylor's *Primitive Culture* (which had appeared in 1871), and may well have thought of this book as an attempt to unriddle certain issues inherent in Tylor's definition of "culture."

By "politics" Bagehot means essentially "social life"; "physics" carries several distinct but convergent meanings. It refers in its first sense to the modern explosion of "physical knowledge," which according to Bagehot has had a profound impact upon the social sciences (*PP* 427), yielding, for one thing, a new awareness of the vast antiquity of human existence, and making possible new explorations of the problem that especially preoccupied this writer: that of "national character." That members of any society are joined by deep mental affinities is, he says, is "the greatest commonplace in the world," but understanding this phenomenon in scientific terms represents a paramount issue for modern research (*PP* 428). Thus Bagehot, though he by no means abandons the idea of the evolutionary progress of civilization which had dominated Victorian anthropology until this point, heralds in *Physics and Politics* the advent of a new anthropology based at last on a fully articulated theory of culture focused on the complementary principles of the uniqueness and the coherence of human societies.

To some degree the scientific claims of this approach are delusive from the outset, in that the phenomenon to be accounted for is simply taken for granted, not demonstrated in a rigorous or even a casual fashion. Glossing over this difficulty, Bagehot explains that an adequate theory of "national character" will need to unfold along two axes: the diachronic, involving the factors controlling "how much a man is apt to be like his ancestors" (*PP* 428), and the synchronic, involving how much he resembles his own contemporaries. How is it that people in the same society live the same life, and continue to reduplicate this life for generation after generation? Bagehot's attempt to answer this riddle turns upon the second sense of the term "physics," the sense referring specifically to the cluster of human instincts and physiological processes which he postulates to account for cultural uniformities. The principles of social life and social evolution ultimately reside, according to him, in the structure of the human nervous system. Determined as he is to go beyond vacuous speculation, Bagehot prefigures the main imperative of anthropological theory up to the present day by seeking to establish his study upon tangible, observable realities. Yet he finds himself enacting the same predicament that one cultural theorist after another has since enacted: that of discovering that the transition from tangible data to phenomena of culture per se involves a transition from "physics" to the metaphysical.

Taking the existence of "national character" to be an evident reality, Bagehot inquires into the causes of its formation, and follows the political economists in postulating a fundamental human instinct akin to the supposed instincts of exchange or accumulation, of bettering one's position, of sexual reproduction: that of *being like other people*. His thesis harks back plainly, in fact, to the principle of "sympathy" as described in *The Theory of Moral Sentiments*. The basis of the social bond is thus found in "the innate tendency of the human mind to become like what is around it," he declares, in "the propensity of man to imitate what is before him," which constitutes "one of the strongest parts of his nature" (*PP* 452, 494). He then sets forth a key proposition of the culture concept—a proposition found, as we noted, in his earlier writings as well—by stressing more forcefully than any other writer had so far the *unconsciousness* and the fundamental irrationality of the imitative instinct, and he very suggestively focuses on linguistic "style" as the essence of what is imitated. As he does so, the rhetoric of magical transmission creeps insidiously into this sector of his argument as it had into other sectors. Rather than inventing an expressive style of their own, "most men catch the words that are in the air, and the rhythm which comes to them they do not know from whence; an unconscious imitation determines their words, and makes them say what of themselves they would never have thought of saying" (*PP* 449). They appear to operate under a kind of hypnosis which prevents them from being cognizant of their own fundamental ideas and from knowing that all their capacity of thought and expressivity is just their obedience to laws of style, to modes, that is, of textual reproduction:

> We must not think that this imitation is voluntary, or even conscious. On the contrary, it has its seat mainly in very obscure parts of the mind, whose notions, so far from having been consciously produced, are hardly felt to exist; so far from being conceived beforehand, are not even felt at the time. (*PP* 494)

In expounding this doctrine, Bagehot makes a point of divorcing himself from the utilitarian notions which pervade nineteenth-century evolutionary anthropology, Tylor's in particular. In the formation of the various national characters, he declares, "usefulness has had no share"; the process is always an irrational "accident" originating in the influence of this or that prominent person whose style, being widely imitated, becomes the style of the age (*PP* 452). In its insistent stress on irrationality and unconsciousness and in its disavowal of any idea of "usefulness" in social productions, Bagehot's theory of culture carries out—from the unexpected position of a spokesman for the Victorian political establishment—about as systematic and lethal a deconstructing of Victorian habits of thought as one could well imagine in 1876. It deconstructs most powerfully the leading Victorian premise of all, the assumption of moral significance. The bonding of men and women into collectivities is based in *Physics and Politics* upon the most powerful instinct, but one expressly emptied of moral intelligibility. By the very nature of our psychic constitution, we are incapable of determining our values and conduct through any aspiration to the Good; rather, like newborn ducklings being "imprinted" with the image of the first creature they see, we more or less blindly adopt the ways and ideas of those around us, being unaware even that we are doing so. It is no accident that each key respect in which Bagehot prefigures the ethnographic theory of culture amounts to a denial of orthodox contemporary ideas. As he himself acknowledges in stressing that the mechanisms he postulates are hidden in "the obscurest parts of our nature," he does not come to his conclusions by poring over any sort of empirical data. He evidently does so by taking as his guiding principle from the outset the (Nietzschean) impulse to cast off all the oppressive weight of contemporary pieties, utilitarian, moral, and religious. "Science" as expounded in this work seems not only consonant with this impulse and this rhetorical imperative but virtually identical to them. Scientific thought is that which confounds orthodox values. Read from the point of view of the sociology of knowledge, *Physics and Politics,* by imitating an ascendent rhetorical style of its own period, makes visible the cultural politics that seem to have been indispensable to the birth of the concept of culture itself.

Bagehot's skepticism makes a determined attack upon the very concept of rational belief. According to him, experience in any society is overwhelmingly constituted by "style," verbal style in particular, and it is our instinctive imitation of prevailing style that overwhelmingly dictates "belief." The world which we imagine ourselves to inhabit is for Bagehot, we may say, fundamentally a tissue of rhetorical patterns. In pursuing this line of thought, he again is close to his contemporary Nietzsche, who three years previously had issued his transvaluation of truth as nothing but "a mobile army of metaphors, metonymies, anthropomorphisms . . . which . . . after long usage seem to a nation fixed, canonic, and binding." We do not come to believe certain propositions to be true or untrue because of the force of evidence, because of logical reflection, still less through divine guidance, but simply, according to Bagehot, because we have "lived in an atmosphere of infectious belief, and [have] inhaled it." Whatever chimes stylistically with habitual patterns of expression seems true. "As to the imitative nature of credulity there can be no doubt" (*PP* 495, 494).[37] Even the shrewdest, most practical-minded European living for an extended period in the East will invariably come to believe or half-believe in witchcraft, says Bagehot: "in fact every idea vividly before us soon appears to us to be true" (*PP* 495). One can easily imagine Victorian readers stricken with vertigo at such a doctrine being preached by so respectable an authority as the editor of the *Economist:* we seem to have come by yet another route to that realm of political economy where moral values evaporate, except that here, objective truth itself has largely evaporated, and its place has been taken by "style" and by sociology. Is belief nothing after all but a matter of period fashion, and is it so that "all clear ideas are true" (*PP* 495)? In the midst of a long discourse demonstrating precisely this, Bagehot remarks in a subordinate clause, without the slightest elucidation, that "no maxim can be more unsound" (*PP* 495); but no reader of the day is likely to have been much reassured by so fleeting a gesture of orthodoxy. We are already, a half century ahead of time, in the destabilized world of Ludwik Fleck, where "we can . . . speak of a thought style which determines the formulation of every concept," exerting upon the individual "an absolutely compulsive force . . . with which it is not possible to be at variance," and where all ideas, even in so-called rigorously empirical branches of science, depend for their acceptance upon "special factors of deep psychological and traditional significance" (Fleck 3, 41, 9).

It is undoubtedly because his theory of social solidarity is thus so prone to self-deconstruction that Bagehot strives as hard as he does to anchor it in scientific fact, giving "physics" in the process yet another meaning. If people are like their contemporaries by virtue of the instinct of imitativeness, they are like their ancestors—and their descendants will in turn be like them—largely by virtue of the physical inheritance of acquired characteristics. Bagehot explains at length, with the help of extended quotation from physiology textbooks, that this process falls into two phases. First, the nervous system in humans is gradually modified by the repetition of responses to stimuli, such that the responses at last become automatic and involuntary. "All education," he states, is based on "this power which the nervous system possesses, of organizing conscious actions into more or less unconscious or reflex operations" (*PP* 429). In the second phase of the process, these modifications of the nervous system are transmitted to one's offspring, and "unconscious habit" (*PP* 433) is thereby instilled in ensuing generations. The Lamarckian idea of the inheritance of acquired characteristics is almost—though not quite[38]—a dead letter in cultural theory today, but Bagehot's use of it, like Freud's in *Moses and Monotheism,* serves to throw into relief the process taken for granted and variously interpreted by twentieth-century theorists: the process by which cultural norms are inscribed in individuals, are obeyed automatically, and govern in fact all our bodily as well as our mental life.

Nothing is more equivocal in Bagehot's own eyes than the status of this argument about culture from "physical knowledge." "I do not think that any who do not acquire—and it takes a hard effort to acquire—this notion of a transmitted nerve element will ever understand the 'connective tissue' of civilization," he says (*PP* 431–32). But he himself, for all his deployment of scientific references, acknowledges in the same breath the empirical shakiness of his theory. He admits that it rests on "a probability" only (*PP* 431), then goes further, speaking of it as a "mystery" that turns out to be as unverified by direct observation as was the propensity of imitation. "Our mind in some strange way acts on our nerves," he says, "and our nerves in some equally strange way store up the consequences; and somehow the result . . . goes down to our descendants" (*PP* 432). At every stage, the mechanisms of this process are almost entirely hidden from view and elude accurate description. Without quite saying so, Bagehot makes clear enough that the supposed physical basis of the process, rather than being the observable datum upon which theories may be constructed, is in fact a purely hypothetical device for giving credence to an argument which arises from other origins altogether.

Obscure as its physiological substratum may be, the social bond in Bagehot's theory manifests itself concretely in *custom*, the crystallized sociological form of the innate human hatred of variation. "National character is but a name for a collection of habits more or less universal," he declares (*PP* 504). Bagehot's theory again insists with unusual emphasis, we may say, on the boundary-building aspect of culture. "Man" as represented in this theory seems impelled above all by the natural compulsion to impose strict customary limits on all his experience, and on that of everybody else, too: he "might be described as a custom-making animal" (*PP* 531). But this argument takes on a perplexing twist from the moment that Bagehot, speaking now as the spokesman of the Victorian cult of progress and "civilization," inconsistently portrays the custom-making instinct as antithetical to the natural course of social life. In calling custom "binding [and] coercive" (*PP* 535), he does not simply mean, as Durkheim does in using the same phrase, necessary in the very constitution of society, but rather, tyrannical and oppressive. In Bagehot's famous phrase, there forms in primitive societies a "cake of custom" (*PP* 445) which represses liberty, individuality, originality, and social development. Progress requires freedom of thought and invention, and can only occur once the cake of custom has somehow been cracked, allowing "the principle of originality" to operate and thus releasing "the propensities to variation which are the principle of progress" (*PP* 468). Custom is not a human constant but a variable, in other words, less significant in enlightened and progressive modern societies than in primitive ones. Thus the fundamental human instinct of imitativeness and repetition, the instinct which was claimed actually to graft programmed behavior patterns upon the tissues of the nervous system, is suddenly overturned and replaced by its exact opposite. Now, instead of man's "propensity . . . to imitate what is before him," a trait anchored in "the most obstinate tendencies of human nature," Bagehot announces the existence of natural "propensities to variation" and speaks of "nature's perpetual tendency to change," a tendency only repressed with difficulty by the cake of custom (*PP* 494, 471, 468, 474). The logic of the cultural theory of *Physics and Politics* caves in around this contradiction, which can only be interpreted as a clash between two paradigms: one, modernistic and deconstructive; the other, an expression of received ideas of progress and of European cultural superiority. Bagehot's book exemplifies precisely that conflict between fixed habits of thought and new departures which it attempts to theorize.

The force impinging most powerfully and dangerously upon human society, according to Bagehot, who here reasserts the cluster of metaphors which define evangelical culture, is personal desire. In order to survive, a society takes as its primary task the suppression of potentially anarchic desires. In expounding this principle, Bagehot erects in the foreground of his book that mythological creature or rhetorical figment who played so important a role in Wesleyan theory and then long dominated Victorian cultural discourse, the passionate, uncontrollable savage. He declares it a known fact that primitive men of ancient times "were born to no tutored habits, no preservative bonds, and therefore they were at the mercy of every impulse and blown by every passion"; in this, they were like the modern savage, who "likes wild excitement and longs for stupefying repletion" (*PP* 439, 581). The crucial function of custom is to repress these forces of savage instinctual appetite: the imitative, custom-generating instinct seems in Bagehot's schema to serve fundamentally as a natural brake upon the unruly forces of libido. So far, his account is a sophisticated variant of the conventional one which flowed from the idealization of moral discipline in Victorian society. But Bagehot gives his version its modernistic slant by bringing into the open the subliminal anxieties which the conventional theory usually strives to conceal.

He proposes (in 1876) the theory that the primitive forces of the libido, rather than being subdued by the progress of civilization, are only forced down out of sight in the unconscious, where they retain their ancient potency and threaten at every moment to burst forth anew. Riots such as those that marked the French Revolution, he says, "have always been said to bring out a secret and suppressed side of human nature; and we now see that they were the outbreak of inherited passions long repressed by fixed custom, but starting into life as soon as that repression was . . . removed" (*PP* 540). In such a passage as this, especially when seen in the light of others in which Bagehot explores the concept of the unconscious, the transposing of the anthropological theory of "survivals," the theory particularly identified with E. B. Tylor, into the psychoanalytic theory of "repression" is explicitly performed. The heart of both theories is the idea of the covert persistence of ancient social and psychic structures into modern life, and both presume the subsequent development of structures antithetical to the original ones. This thesis causes the idea of historical progress to become severely ambiguous, as Bagehot himself observes in the later sections of *Physics and Politics*. It turns out that "order and civilization are . . . unstable even in progressive communities," he says, thanks to the tendency of men to return at the first opportunity to "their original savage nature" (*PP* 540). Bagehot's argument here bridges those of his great predecessor John Wesley and his great successor Freud, but it actually goes a step beyond either, for he declares the resurgence of primitive desires to occur not "even" but *especially* in "progressive communities," since the very effect of the liberating influence of free thought and free discussion—hitherto the panaceas of his system, as of Mill's—is to weaken the restraints which custom imposes upon repressed primitive urges. Bagehot puts this matter with startling directness. "As soon as discussion begins, the savage propensities of men break forth; even in modern communities, where those propensities . . . have been weakened by ages of culture and repressed by ages of obedience, as soon as a vital topic for discussion is well started the keenest and most violent passions break forth" (*PP* 560).

Bagehot focuses his sharpest attention not on riots and violent conflict after all, but on the dynamics of daily life. What he expressly diagnoses a generation before Durkheim does so is a general and acute modern state of anomic desires. These desires are boundless because they have no determinate goals, but this is not due to a failure of institutions to provide authoritative moral limits, as Durkheim was to argue; they are boundless *because they originate in sheer "physics" and thus are beyond the jurisdiction of cultural restraints.* They manifest themselves, that is to say, in an unappeasable, senseless urge to physical or quasi-physical action, in "the irritable activity, the 'wish to be doing something'" that Bagehot declares to be the mainspring of human history (*PP* 565). Since the conditions of modern European life put a premium on cautious reflection, complicated preparation, and self-restraint, the "wild passion for instant action" that Europeans inherit from their savage ancestors causes them perpetually to indulge in "excessive action" which is fatal to their own goals (*PP* 566, 567).

This blind "passion of activity" (*PP* 572) manifests itself in every field. One leading signal of the plight of "those who do not find in modern life any mode . . . of venting that energy" (*PP* 567) which lies in their overflowing instincts is a disordered sexual life. Modern people are preyed upon in the sexual realm, says Bagehot, by "a 'felt want,' as political economists would say, altogether greater than the 'real want'" (*PP* 571). In other words, sexual desire in modern people only seems to have erotic gratification as its object; in reality, it is yet another futile attempt to appease crazily anomic appetites with no real goal, no limits, and thus no possible means of satisfaction. The outward sign of this pathological state is the flourishing in London of the "vast evil" of prostitution (*PP* 571). Even in the rarefied realm of philosophical speculation, anomic boundlessness holds sway, suggesting a final identity of intellectual and sexual energy. "Every sort of philosophy has been systematized; and yet as most of these philosophies utterly contradict one another, most of them cannot be true. Unproved abstract principles without number have been eagerly caught up by sanguine men. . . . In a word, the superfluous energy of mankind has flowed over into philosophy" (*PP* 567, 568). Rather than being governed by a centripetal instinct of imitation, thought now seems to Bagehot to be governed by one of extravagant, centrifugal contradiction—though both theories have the same destructive impact upon any attempt to idealize rational belief.

The "same original vice" of "excessive energy" (*PP* 568), of laboring forever to gratify "a desire far in excess of what is needed" (*PP* 571), stamps itself no less deeply and with far greater practical consequences upon modern commerce. Here occurs Bagehot's most decisive rejection of the rational motive of self-betterment in the theory of political economy. Capitalists compete in the market, and often plunge to ruin, in obedience at bottom to instinctive energies with no conscious or rational purpose at all and no intelligible history beyond what is inferable from the description of them as the "original vice" of mankind—the habitual telltale phrase bearing witness once more to the inseparability of nineteenth-century social thought even in its most advanced and secularized forms from the paradigms of Evangelical homiletics. "In some degree, of course, this is caused by the wish to get rich; but in a considerable degree too by the mere love of activity. There is a greater propensity to action in such men than they have the means of gratifying" (*PP* 567). Bagehot does not spell out the point, but this dissolution of rational self-interest able theoretically to be condensed into a stable structure of "value" and its replacement by "mere love of activity" for its own sake makes the political economists' path to a science of social organization veer abruptly toward chaos. Economic literature since Adam Smith appeared to build a concept of culture as a means of defusing the menace of the idea of exorbitant desire; in Bagehot, the original menace, the "army of metaphors" basic to modern thinking, seems to break out anew to destabilize the whole theoretical edifice built to contain it in the course of the preceding century. In effect the "original vice" of the sociological imagination, long repressed by structures of scientific discourse, here surges back to the surface.

Bagehot has little encouragement to offer those who would seek "to cure an inherited excess of human nature" (*PP* 574). Having identified the system of free discussion as a main factor in the release of repressed desires, he inconsistently suggests that it may after all tend to mitigate their harmful consequences (*PP* 568–69). And he quotes Spencer's *Principles of Biology* to revive the Godwinian theory against which Malthus protested long before, the forecasting of a gradual evolutionary decline of the sex impulse and indeed of the whole range of human desires (*PP* 572–73, 590). With increasing intellectual activity, he theorizes, there will go a corresponding loss of libido, for, in obedience to the laws of physics, "there is only a certain *quantum* of power" in any individual (*PP* 574). *Physics and Politics* casts a utopian glow around the prospect of a wasting away of human desire.[39]

This final disconsolate turn of Bagehot's argument emphasizes the contradictory pattern which is central to the three writers surveyed in this chapter and which can be summed up as a simultaneous affirmation and denial of desire. For Adam Smith, desire is dangerously volatile and likely to take aberrant forms, yet represents the indispensable element of social welfare. Malthus almost scandalously champions the creativity of desire, yet sees desire both as prone to disastrous collapse and as the origin of the "misery and vice" with which human life is infested. Bagehot glorifies desire as the catalyst of social progress yet sees it as leading to a nightmare of anomie. A pattern which recurs so persistently over so long a span of social discourse is sure to be the signal of a deep cultural structure. What is revealed here would seem to be the inherently contradictory logic of a way of life based, as that of nineteenth-century Britain conspicuously was, on a fusion of the value-systems of capitalism and of puritanical Christianity. Classical political economy enacts this logic and strives to defuse its tensions—simply by making them explicit and by opening them up to supposedly disinterested scientific study, in the first instance. Its strong movement toward the formulation of a theory of culture based on the interlocking concepts of "value" and of integrated social systems apparently arises, in other words, from a state of urgent cultural instability, and bears witness to its origin in each new facet of the argument. Such, at least, has been the underlying thesis of this chapter.

Let us now approach the emergent culture idea from the perspective of a body not of theoretical but of ethnographic writing from the period which we have just traversed. The new element in this literature, and that which sets it so sharply apart from political economy that one could easily miss their close interconnection, is not the focus upon "primitive" society, for this, we have seen, forms a regular feature of early economics. It is the emergence of the interpreter's own subjectivity as a dominating factor in the science of society.

SAVAGERY, CULTURE, AND THE
SUBJECTIVITY OF FIELDWORK
IN EARLY POLYNESIAN ETHNOGRAPHY

F ormal anthropology in the first half of the nineteenth century was defined by the research project of Prichardian "ethnology" (the tracing of the prehistoric origins of peoples), and in its next major phase would be preoccupied with theories of the evolutionary development of civilization. Not until the twentieth century would it discover its vocation of closely scrutinizing particular societies from the point of view of the idea of culture in the "wide ethnographic sense"; nor would it institute until then the professional fieldwork procedures supposed to warrant the scientific authority of the reconstituted discipline. Here is the point of focus of the present chapter: the intimate historical and theoretical relationships by which the culture doctrine is linked to a particular fieldwork system and to the richly charged mystique of "participant observation."

The culture theory, which postulates that societies form configurations or complex wholes, not only lends authority to ethnographic fieldwork (providing it in effect with a significant and coherent object of study), it essentially presupposes it, and one can speculate that the theory was invented ex post facto to serve as the rationale for a certain method of intensely personalized, on-the-spot research. Malinowski comes close to suggesting as much in a notable passage in *A Scientific Theory of Culture*.[1] Field research in turn plays a key role in authenticating and preserving the theory, and is justly regarded as "the essential core of social anthropology" (Leach 1).[2] Culture per se is not empirically observable, as we have argued and as Malinowski became ever more fretfully aware in the later stages of his career; but fieldwork anchored in the hypothesis of culture can amass large enough quantities of detailed ethnographic data and can deploy about this data enough rhetoric of strict scientific procedure to screen its underlying conceptual problem from view. Once we follow Bagehot or Ruth Benedict in defining each "culture" as a discrete, self-contained whole, in any case, there can be no substitute for a system of concentrated fieldwork designed to generate something resembling an insider's view of it. Hence that development which James Clifford associates particularly with Malinowski, "the construction of a new public figure, the anthropologist as fieldworker" ("Ethnographic Self-Fashioning" 158)—a figure able to play a variety of important cultural roles, not all of which coincide with disinterested scientific inquiry.

Gaining insight into the nexus between the theory of culture and the institution of scientific fieldwork implies, as a first step, a critical analysis of the widely held assumption that both were the creations of philosophers and philosophical anthropologists, and that they emerged (allowing for inspired precursors like Vico and Herder) in the half-century following the publication of *Primitive Culture* in 1871.[3] The prestige of the discipline of scientific ethnography has owed much to this account of its origins, which endows the movement of thought presided over by such august academic figures as Tylor, Durkheim, Boas, and Malinowski with a fully respectable pedigree, depicting it in particular as the repudiation of a tradition of prejudice (and of evil practices) among earlier observers of primitive cultures. Malinowski rehearses a version of this account in *Argonauts of the Western Pacific* (1922), widely regarded as the founding text of modern ethnographic practice but less well recognized as founding at the same time the authorized myth of disciplinary history.

Malinowski places all his work under the aegis of "the final goal of which an Ethnographer should never lose sight. This goal is . . . to grasp the native's point of view, his relation to life, to realise *his* vision of *his* world" (*Argonauts* 25). The mission of ethnography thus defined can be fulfilled only through an act of almost violent self-effacement on its practitioners' part: one needs to divest oneself wholly of European values and prejudices in order to attain sympathetic understanding of one's exotic subjects. "To succeed in this feat," declares Malinowski's student Evans-Pritchard, "a man must be able to abandon himself without reserve" (*Social Anthropology* 82). One must subject oneself further to the rigors of extended fieldwork on the basis of "participant observation" so as to achieve intimate personal acquaintance with the self-contained world of the society one seeks to understand. Malinowski closely links this fieldwork code to condemnation of the missionaries and colonial administrators who, representing the European outlook at large, had heretofore visited primitive peoples only for the purpose of visiting European "civilization" upon them, and, blinded by their "elitist self-images" (Wagner 8), had been oblivious to the value of these cultures which they worked so effectively to destroy. Such people "were for the most part . . . full of the biassed and pre-judged opinions inevitable in the average practical man, whether administrator, missionary, or trader; yet so strongly repulsive to a mind striving after the objective, scientific view of things" (*Argonauts* 5–6). Repulsion focuses especially on the sinister activities of the missionaries, who, Malinowski says elsewhere, "destroy the natives' joy in life; they destroy their psychological *raison d'être*" (*Diary* 41).[4] E. B. Tylor showed much the same aversion to missionaries, who were, he declared, "so occupied in hating and despising the beliefs of the heathen" (*PC* 1:420) that they always misrepresented primitive life.

The ethnographic creed set forth in *Argonauts of the Western Pacific* had an exhilarating appeal, largely, no doubt, because it cast professional fieldworkers in so flattering a light as "scientific specialists" (*Argonauts* xv) and as campaigners against "Victorian" bigotry, complacency, ignorance, and hypocrisy, especially in their more distinctly Evangelical forms. The establishment of the theory of culture and of its corresponding research method is in any case emphatically portrayed in this not-disinterested mythic narrative as *a moral liberation* as well as a perfecting of scientific technique. Malinowski's text thus confirms much other evidence that the emergence of "objective" modern anthropology and of the culture theory on which it rests can scarcely be understood in isolation from the broadly diversified literary and artistic movement through which the nauseated rejection of Victorian prejudice expressed itself in the late nineteenth and early twentieth centuries. Anthropology has not "disturbed the general intellectual peace" merely as a byproduct of the data which it has innocently assembled (Geertz, "Distinguished Lecture" 264), but was impelled by the will to disturbance and self-emancipation from the outset. Samuel Butler's alter ego Ernest Pontifex, Ibsen's Nora, Faulkner's Charles-Etienne Bon, and Malinowski's "I" as ideal fieldworker all perform the same radical act of disavowing the "strongly repulsive" conventionalities of contemporary life. Readers of scientific ethnographies are meant to reduplicate this act in their turn by embracing what one theorist of fieldwork calls, in phraseology often met with in the literature, the promise "of being liberated from the parochial truths of one culture" (T. R. Williams 61).[5] To this extent, the theory of culture has always carried strong political and moral valences quite at odds with its professed scientific objectivity and disinterestedness.

Some of these valences are already detectable in a text which in the remarkably early year of 1838 explored the interconnection of the vocation of fieldwork and the still uncodified idea of culture: Harriet Martineau's *How to Observe: Morals and Manners* [*HO*], perhaps the first full-scale treatise on the theory and practice of ethnographic observation.[6] Martineau analyzes various aspects of what she calls "the science of morals" or "the science of society," and which she identifies both as the least fully articulated and as the most difficult "of all the sciences which have yet opened upon men." But nowhere does she lay greater stress than on the baneful effect of "prejudice" and on the necessary mental and emotional state of the observer for avoiding this disabling condition (*HO* 14–15, 45, 46, 189–90). Her appeal is to the great faculty of "sympathy." Like Malinowski long afterward, she lays down as her cardinal rule that "the observer must have sympathy [with the people under observation], and his sympathy must be untrammelled and unreserved" (*HO* 45). A close reader of this program will soon see the issues it raises. First, there is the issue of the good faith of such precepts: are we really to enter into sympathy with many of the cruel customs of other peoples, which Martineau frequently instances? She seeks to elude this issue by postulating, in flat contradiction to her assertion elsewhere that no limits can be placed on human diversity and especially (*HO* 29) that a universal moral sense is a delusion, that in fact universal moral agreement binds cultures together. "Charity is everywhere. The human heart is always tender, always touched by visible suffering" (*HO* 181; see 30–32). A difficulty of a different order is that "sympathy" is postulated as negative capability, an emotional attitude of unlimited receptivity—but at the same time as something very different, a positive interpretive method. This in fact is one of the main features of Martineau's book: her insistence that scientific or, as she often says, "philosophical" observation of foreign societies is not at all a matter of mere emotional responsiveness (a potentially disruptive factor) any more than it is one of amassing random collections of data (an inherently futile activity: *HO* 16) or of simply quizzing natives about the logic of values of their society (which they themselves, she declares, do not recognize, for they are "unconscious" of them: *HO* 165). Ethnography instead is a specific technique of observation and classification, must be focused on specific problems and be in no way "hap-hazard," and is by its nature a work of *interpretation* (*HO* 13, 21). All observation is to be put "to interpretive uses" (*HO* 14–15), and if an ethnographer lacks theoretical "principles" around which to organize observations, "he cannot determine their bearings, or be secure of putting a right interpretation upon them" (*HO* 23). Or, putting the issue most clearly: "unless a traveller interprets by his sympathies what he sees, he cannot but misunderstand the greater part of that which comes under his observation" (*HO* 46). Sympathy is evidently the vital principle of the deciphering of visible phenomena to reach the logic of "what is fixed and essential in a people" (*HO* 20), but it seems antithetical, in fact, to the process of technical analysis which Martineau wants to posit as the basis of a "science of morals." In a passage which articulates the principles of fieldwork subjectivity in precisely the language in which they will frequently be invoked by twentieth-century writers, she makes clear that the prized attitude of "sympathy" can in fact only be defined as a kind of psychological emptying, a voluntary creation of a vacuum into which the ideas and affective forces of a foreign people can rush. "If the observer goes with a free mind and an open heart, not full of notions and feelings of his own, but ready to resign himself to those of the people he visits; if he commits himself to his sympathies, and makes himself one with those about him, he cannot but presently discover and appreciate what interests them most" (*HO* 189–90). The ideal observer is one "with no bias of his own" (*HO* 193). Sympathy here is vacancy and a state of radical personal displacement; the ethnographer is definable only as a nonentity. What then can be the role of the interpretive "principles" necessary to pierce cultural unconsciousness?

Not only was the Malinowskian origin myth of anthropology open to doubt (as it is the main purpose of this chapter to show), but the charter of the modern ethnographer was, as Martineau's redaction of it already made apparent, a more complicated and ambiguous one than Malinowski's rhetoric allowed to be seen. It even appears to have had its potentially sinister side. One incident which helped to make this clear, indeed, was the publication in 1967 of his own fieldwork journal, *A Diary in the Strict Sense of the Term,* which scandalized readers by revealing that the wise, infinitely benevolent ethnographer of *Argonauts* was in fact full of unadmitted antipathy for his Trobriand subjects, whom he repeatedly names to himself "niggers" and "savages." "*Exterminate the brutes,*" he exclaims at one point (*Diary* 69), quoting Conrad's Kurtz. The enlightened scientist portrayed in *Argonauts* suddenly seemed an imposter; the legitimacy of the whole enterprise of empathetic ethnographic study which Malinowski's work had fostered seemed compromised.[7] To the extent that fieldwork empathy served in fact as a vehicle and a screen for the very different motive of social disaffection, one could have expected that ethnography would be full of this sort of ambivalence and that the project of discovering and portraying "the native's point of view" could lend itself, as a number of writers have recently claimed that it does, to insidious forms of exploitation.[8] Can the submersion in a tribal mentality by a sophisticated Western academic ever be anything but a self-serving pretense?

Without attempting fully to answer this question, one can guess that in constructing a mythic history of their discipline in which missionaries and colonial officials figure as the arch-Victorians and the arch-nemeses of culture, modern anthropologists obey an impulse to exorcise or at least to distract attention from whatever may be dubious in their own activities. They fictionalize their predecessors and rivals in "the field" (both senses) in order to reinforce their deeply equivocal fictional image of themselves as both scrupulously "objective" professionals and as bearers of a gospel of liberation—as missionaries, in fact. The complementary fictions of the bigoted missionary and the enlightened modern ethnographer are by no means travesties at all points. But if we twitch aside the shroud of obloquy in which the literature of pre-professional modern ethnography by missionaries and others has long been enveloped, we discover, first, that this literature is often so impressive as science as to overthrow entirely the notion that the rigorous, methodologically sophisticated study of primitive society began with the establishment of the twentieth-century vocation of fieldwork by "scientific specialists." One discovers too that rather than mystifying (as it is alleged to do) the moral and epistemological predicament of the European observer in primitive society, this literature enacts it—enacts, that is, the conflictual interplay of prejudice and ethnographic experience—with an anguished frankness that throws strong light on the academic complacencies of a later era. It reveals the secret, suppressed by later writers with their own vested interests to attend to, not only that the ethnographic and relativistic doctrine of culture was not invented out of thin air by a high-minded caste of disinterested professional researchers, but that such a doctrine bears from its inception the mark of almost fatal self-contradiction.

Let us pursue these themes with reference to a body of writings which for the most part we shall need to retrieve from near oblivion: the early ethnography of the South Pacific. I single out this region somewhat arbitrarily in order to define a fairly cohesive and manage-

156

CHAPTER THREE

able group of texts for study. But Polynesia and adjacent areas (notably Fiji) do have special claims on our interest. For one thing, they exercised from the time of their rediscovery in the last third of the eighteenth century an especially powerful influence upon the European imagination and served as a theater for elaborating key themes of European thought, as Bernard Smith has shown in *European Vision and the South Pacific 1768–1850*. He stresses Cook's and other voyages of the late eighteenth century, treating the published accounts of these voyages as the records of a prolonged dispute between "noble" and "ignoble" theories of savagery, and as exemplifying the rise of scientific "empirical" methods of observation. There is nothing epistemologically or morally dubious about this last privileged category in Smith's account, which broadly matches what I have called the mythic history of anthropology. But if one seeks to apply such terms of analysis to the ethnographic literature on this region in its next phase, that of the first sustained study of Polynesian life by European visitors, the difficulties of taking so unsuspicious a view of what Fleck terms "so-called empirical observations" come to the surface and point the need for a much more complicated account than Smith provides.

We shall consult to this end a series of remarkable texts, the most notable of these being the following: John Martin's rendering of William Mariner's involuntary four-year residence in Tonga, *An Account of the Natives of the Tonga Islands* [*NTI*] (1816); William Ellis's *Polynesian Researches* [*PR*] (1829); John Williams's *Narrative of Missionary Enterprises* [*NME*] (1837); William Brown's *New Zealand and its Aborigines* (1845); Edward Shortland's two books on New Zealand of 1851 and 1854; Thomas Williams's *Fiji and the Fijians* [*FF*] (1858); James Calvert's *Missionary Labours Among the Cannibals* (1858); and George Turner's *Nineteen Years in Polynesia* (1861). Some of these works, especially those of Mariner, Ellis, and Thomas Williams, are documents of almost inestimable value, for they represent our primary eyewitness accounts of traditional life in various South Pacific groups before its rapid—in some cases, almost instantaneous—liquidation by such intimately intertwined European influences as firearms, infectious diseases, and Christianity. More to our purpose, these books act out behind a screen of sectarian rhetoric a concerted and also (given among other things their ideological commitments) an extravagantly risky experiment with modern modes of thought. Without fully realizing it themselves, or at least not at first, their authors were engaged collectively in a project amounting to the invention of a new subjectivity, the basis of which appears to be an impulse to experience a state of radical instability of value—or even the instability of selfhood itself.

Paradoxes of Intimacy

Few among this generation of Polynesianists could claim a disinterested academic perspective on their subject matter, and especially not Ellis, John or Thomas Williams, Calvert, or Turner, who all were dedicated Protestant missionaries, and whose ethnography was enlisted totally, if we take its rhetoric at face value, in the service of expounding their own beliefs and justifying their own proselytizing activities. Shortland, like Sir George Grey, another eminent early student of Maori culture, was a colonial administrator, and William Brown was a newspaper proprietor in New Zealand writing expressly to promote emigration; they, too, present themselves in the first instance as wholehearted partisans of European thought and social arrangements. It seems inevitable that such versions of the culture idea as appear in the writings of such men will be deeply inscribed with dominating ideology, and that the value of this work as science is bound to be severely compromised as a result. Governing prejudice was manifest especially in the case of the missionaries; already in the heyday of their activity in the South Pacific, they were exposed to the criticism that their conviction of moral and cultural superiority rendered them worthless, or worse, as observers of primitive society.[9] Shortland prefaces *Traditions and Superstitions of the New Zealanders,* for example, by declaring that the missionaries' religious bigotry and their deliberate policy of working "to extirpate the original memorials of the natives" has prevented them from gaining accurate knowledge of aboriginal life (v–vi). In support of this indictment he might have pointed to the megalomaniac self-portrayal of the famous missionary John Williams presiding over the methodical suppression of the ancient traditions of the Samoan islands of Savaii and Upolu, personally dictating which customs might be allowed to continue at least temporarily, and which must be legally banned at once (*NME* 443). Ethnocentrism and cultural vandalism reach here their apparent apogee. Yet the ardent championship of British Christianity, British capitalism, and the British work ethic which unites all these writers expressed itself in the anomalous-seeming maneuver of a radical estrangement from home, and this fact alone should alert us to the possibility of a more perplexed dynamic of thought than appears on the surface of their works. If the "distinctive ethnographic subjectivity" consists, as Clifford and others have said, in the almost impossibly problematic state of being both submerged in and detached from an exotic cultural milieu ("Ethnographic Self-Fashioning" 141), the missionaries and their secular colleagues strikingly exhibit just this state with regard to their culture of origin. According to Lévi-Strauss, ethnographic work by its deepest logic expresses hostility toward the ethnographer's own society; it is always an act of repudiation of and of atonement for one's origins (*Tristes tropiques* 383–84). Even in the texts under study here, this principle—which runs against the grain of any uncomplicated equation of ethnography and the will to power—seems partly confirmed.

As a matter of fact, the motive of atonement for origins takes emphatic doctrinal shape in reference to the missionaries, who began their campaign in the South Pacific with the landing of a first contingent in Tahiti in 1797. They saw themselves as saving souls, as working to lessen the sum of human suffering, and as engaging in direct personal combat with Satan. Very likely they also were guilty, as their critics charged, of longing for personal glory and of seeking to use their activities in foreign lands to enhance the influence of the Evangelical party in church politics (see Ellis 1:140–41). But they were impelled by a further motive which gave their enterprise a quasi-scientific character from the outset and which ties it closely to the main theme of the present study. This was their need to portray the countries selected for evangelism as sites of almost unqualified moral depravity.

This need reflects, first, a set of practical and political imperatives. The missionaries' design of imposing their own religious system upon "heathens" and of dismantling native life wherever it failed to square with their brand of European values was by no means immune to potential challenge, as was attested by a series of colonial governors' orders and acts of Parliament designed to protect the South Sea islanders from outside interference.[10] In order to justify their aggressive incursions into native societies, missionaries needed therefore to be able to appeal to a discourse which endowed them with incontestable moral authority over indigenous populations. So it was a principal function of this discourse, which they made it their business to produce, to people the South Seas with the very beings that had, for expediency's sake, to be found there: depraved, brutish savages.[11] Intervention in the lives of such people was not only permissible, it was an urgent duty.

But the Evangelicals' invasion of Polynesia had a scientific, or perhaps one had best say a pseudoscientific, rationale as well, though it was never so fully articulated as was their mission of suppressing moral evil; and it is in this connection that the idea of atonement for origins stamps itself powerfully upon early experiments in ethnography. Among their other roles, these missionaries were attempting to gather authenticated empirical proof of the proposition that unredeemed human nature is a horrifying mass of lust and wickedness.[12] To gauge what was at stake in this attempt, we should recall that according to John Wesley, the belief that "every man born into the world now bears . . . the image of the beast, in sensual appetites and desires" forms nothing less than the cardinal principle of Christian religion; not to believe it is to be a "heathen," he declares (*Sermons* 2:230–31, 223). In the pioneering ethnographic literature which missionary writers produced, the linkage between modern social theory and the doctrine of original sin (the linkage discussed above in other connections from a more hypothetical point of view) is as a result very plainly set forth.

As expounded in contemporary Evangelical discourse, this doctrine must always have had a farfetched, hyperbolic, rhetorically precarious quality in view of the evidence of human nature provided by ordinary decorous British society. Wesley's contemporary, the skeptic Hume, had pointed to the difficulty, declaring that the state of nature, a condition of unrestrained "war, violence and injustice," amounted to "a mere philosophical fiction" (*Treatise* 493). So it was in substantial part to demonstrate its factual existence and thus shore up the institutional edifice built upon it that missionaries undertook their perilous voyages to what in the early nineteenth century were almost unthinkably remote lands. Here, as they conceived, it would be possible to observe humanity in something like its unimproved state and in this way to document the truth of their theory of human nature. The depravity of "savages" was thus the hypothesis for which they needed to find confirmatory data, and, not surprisingly, did, in what proved to be almost unhoped-for abundance. William Ellis spells out the logic of this discovery in one remarkable passage where he notes that among Tahitian converts to Christianity, personally acquainted as they were with the wickedness that ran rampant in their society before the arrival of the missionaries, "we never met with one who doubted the natural depravity, or innate tendency to evil, in the human heart." Ellis tells us that this fact is "important . . . as an evidence of the universality of the depravity of man" and thus as "one of the strongest modern evidences . . . of the unequivocal origin of Christianity" (*PR* 2:314–15). Thomas Williams strikes the same theme, asserting in would-be scientific language of his own that in Fiji "the theory of those who teach the innate perfectibility of man . . . has had a thorough test, resulting in most signal failure" and bringing out unambiguously "that innate depravity which [the Fijian] shares in common with other men" (*FF* 103, 97).

Polynesian depravity expressed itself for British observers in such customs as cannibalism and systematic infanticide, but especially in the natives' promiscuous, glaringly dramatized sexual life and in their proneness to outbreaks of sadistic violence. Even after Christianization, declares the missionary J. M. Orsmond, "Tahiti is a vortex of iniquity, the Sodom of the Pacific" (Davies 358). Like other missionary ethnographers, Ellis fills his account with startling tableaux of Tahitian vices: for instance, his censorious description of the institution of public stills, where the islanders would occupy themselves "for several days together, drinking the spirit as it issued from the still, sinking into a state of indescribable wretchedness, and often practising the most ferocious barbarities" (*PR* 1:230–31). Similar passages include treatments of the debaucheries indulged in by the aristocratic *Areoi* societies (*PR* 1:311ff.) or those associated with the public breadfruit-ovens (*PR* 1:356), of the "savage infatuation" characteristic of Tahitian funerals, which often, we are told, ended in murderous violence (*PR* 1:528), or of the unspeakable "abominations," fertility rituals which Ellis declines to particularize, practiced at festivals of the god Oro (*PR* 2:359). Focusing their attention on such themes, nineteenth-century observers portrayed the Polynesian savage in the conventional imagery that has played so important a role in the social thought of the last two centuries: that of the figure of boundless, exorbitant, uncontrollable desires. That which in the idiom of Prichardian psychology was called "moral insanity," and in that of Durkheimian sociology was to be called anomie, was what most of the writers surveyed in this chapter called in Wesleyan parlance "the principle of evil," original sin.

The missionaries' standard image of the Polynesian is thus in outline a wholly prefabricated one, a piling-up of monotonous rhetorical formulas which clearly exert a strong determining influence upon all their so-called empirical observation. These formulas are especially profuse in Ellis, who frequently proclaims that the natives in their unconverted state were guided by nothing but "the unbridled influence of their passions" (*PR* 1:37). At the public stills, it was "their unbridled passions," he tells us in the stereotypical way, that impelled them on their ferocious rampages (*PR* 1:231). The *Areoi* society gave institutional form "to the indolent habits and depraved uncontrolled passions of the people" (*PR* 1:328); Christianity, on the other hand, contradicted at every moment their deeply ingrained "impatience of control" and their addiction to "unrestrained indulgence and excess" (*PR* 1:472, 2:359). John Williams has much of the same kind to say about the natives' hostility to "the restraints which Christianity imposed upon them"; the Gospel alone, he declares, "can subdue the fierce passions of our nature" (*NME* 129, 533). In primitive society, says John Martin in his preface to Mariner's *Account,* "the passions of man are more openly and strongly developed" than in our own, "and his actions, generally speaking, under much less restraint" (Martin 1:xiv–xv). The same language runs through Thomas Williams as well. During Fijian victory celebrations, he says, "the ordinary social restrictions are destroyed," and the consequence is "the unbridled and indiscriminate indulgence of every evil lust and passion." The Fijian's mind in general is "defiled by unchecked appetite," as, for instance, in the case of one "monster" king famous even among Fijians as an insatiable devourer of human flesh. Not surprisingly, many Fijian gods, he reports, "had a monster origin, and wear a monster shape" (*FF* 42, 103, 181, 184). Prior to the arrival of missionaries, states James Calvert, "every evil passion had grown up [in Fiji] unchecked." "The savage of Fiji broke beyond the common limits of rapine and bloodshed" (*Missionary Labours* 225). This brief set of quotations should be enough to show that the trope of absent boundaries to desire and the idea of "savages" as vessels of unchecked carnal passions form the governing and catalyzing principles of this whole project of ethnographic research, just as the hypothesis of an insatiable drive to self-aggrandizement forms that of classical economics.

This theory of primitive life as the realm of all-pervading anomie is of course the very antithesis of the culture idea as summed up, for instance, in Lévi-Strauss's declaration that "the customs of a community, taken as a whole, always have a particular style and are reducible to systems" (*Tristes tropiques* 178). Scarcely any room remains for the idea of anarchically centrifugal individual passions—and certainly not as a widespread, typical feature—once we have adopted the model of society as a logically organized, stylistically consistent ensemble of customs and other institutions. Thus the early Polynesianists set out for themselves a self-contradictory task. If only to give credence to their theological and practical arguments, they were impelled to undertake a project of richly detailed scientific ethnography; they were at the same time committed to a thesis of anarchic primitive passions which in effect rendered cultural particularities null and void, and ought to have precluded any significant awareness of the idea of culture in "its wide ethnographic sense." This contradiction chiefly expresses itself in their writings not as uncertainty about principles of research, however, but as a seemingly unresolvable moral and emotional predicament.

To understand it, one needs to stress, as these writers do themselves, the overwhelmingly existential character of this phase of the history of ethnographic theory and practice. Unlike subsequent armchair anthropologists like Tylor, McLennan, Frazer, and Mauss, and unlike the philosophical economists whom we have just considered, the writers featured in this chapter took as their chief premise the active personal implication of the observer in the process of observation. Their intimations of the idea of culture all presuppose this principle, as we shall see. It meant exposing not just their theories but their bodies to extreme danger—John Williams, like other missionaries of this period in Polynesia, was at last murdered and eaten by his intended converts—and it meant exposing themselves, too, to psychological traumas of such severity that the mind could almost be unhinged by them.[13] Everything one knows of the Evangelical mentality goes indeed to suggest that the enactment of traumatic drama formed at some level the very raison d'être of the missionary project. Given this mentality, it is hardly surprising (to come back to our point of departure) to find that these writers gain their special purchase on the doctrine of culture by exploring the problematics of the fieldwork vocation itself. In their ethnographic writing, they testify very fully to an awareness that they were engaged not only in spreading the gospel, but in unfolding a new technique of scientific study—one that made at best an uneasy fit with their mission as evangelizers. The most surprising revelation which this literature gives us, in any case, is that the modern creed of self-reflective ethnographic fieldwork was largely its authors' own invention.[14]

The image of John Williams as the doggedly prejudiced annihilator of Polynesian culture is thus strangely inconsistent with the methodological code which he sets forth in the preface to *Missionary Enterprises*. In order to convey full understanding of such remote societies as those he seeks to evoke, it is necessary, he states, for a writer to go beyond "mere outlines and sketches," and to report them in ample and painstakingly exact detail (*NME* vii). One may fail to recognize at first glance the originality and significance of this principle, which, we should recall, was preached by Malinowski nearly a century later as a new departure in anthropology and in fact as the foundational principle of scientific ethnography. The observer's task, he declares, is to record the "*imponderabilia of actual life and of typical behaviour,*" which "have to be collected through minute, detailed observations, in the form of some sort of ethnographic diary, made possible by close contact with native life" (Malinowski, *Argonauts* 20, 24). If we unpack it a bit, we can see that this methodology of the "exhaustive survey of detailed examples" (*Argonauts* 17) springs from the implicit principle that *meaning and value are all-pervasive in culture*, lodging themselves somehow even in the most trivial- and opaque-seeming materials of quotidian life and becoming apparent only at the cost of exhaustive study and interpretation. Thus it is that the formalized idea of culture emerges in twentieth-century ethnography as a gloss on the Malinowskian research method, "culture" being defined in effect as that which can only be perceived by personal immersion in an alien society and can only be represented by a notation of the seemingly insignificant so detailed as to constitute a new mode of awareness (and of prose style). From the first, the culture thesis seems to crystallize in this fashion around the solitary figure of the ethnographer executing a program of painstakingly detailed investigation, filing data in the approved way.

This theory of fieldwork is scarcely what one would expect from a militant missionary like John Williams, whose mind is supposed to be made up concerning the significance of native institutions before he so much as wades ashore for his first look at his subjects. Savage life by his doctrine is a phantasmagoria of unlimited desires. Williams, however, carries himself along another doctrinal line by expanding boldly on his own philosophically charged fieldwork principle, stressing, for one thing, the importance of his rule of reporting native statements to him in strict verbatim quotation, "in the phraseology and under the figurative garb in which they were expressed" (*NME* viii). This rule, again unpacked, can mean only one thing: that cultural meanings are to a significant degree untranslatable, expressible only in the semiological system in which they originate. Ethnographic research based on such a premise is arduously demanding, Williams declares, and makes it incumbent upon the explorer of primitive life to undergo the most rigorous preparatory training. The goal is partly to acquire technical expertise, but just as importantly—here Williams enters upon treacherous ground—to undergo a kind of deep acculturation leading to intuitive sympathetic understanding of the phenomena he observes. Armed with "intimate knowledge of the habits of thought and modes of communication" of the natives, and having trained himself to keep "a minute record" of all the "interviews and events" which he will report, the missionary ethnographer will be able to produce documentation of great accuracy, says Williams (*NME* viii). He especially emphasizes the supreme importance of conducting fieldwork on the basis of fluency in native languages. "The greater portion of the Author's life," he says, excusing any stylistic roughness there may be in his text, "has been devoted either to active labour, or to the study of uncultivated dialects, the idiom, abruptness, and construction of which are more familiar to him than the words and phrases . . . of his native tongue" (*NME* x–xi).

Long before Boas and Malinowski revolutionized anthropology by codifying these very principles, John Williams thus lays out the whole modern program of ethnographic research based on the unique efficacy of total cultural immersion, on verbatim quotation of informants, and on linguistic competence as the sine qua non of fieldwork.[15] He evidently presumes that the heroic discipline which he prescribes for fieldworkers will have no unintended side-effects, that one can acquire with impunity that extreme degree of intimate sympathy enabling one "to grasp the native's point of view, his relation to life, to realize *his* vision of *his* world," and that one can carry cultural immersion so far as actually to become more fluent in native speech than in one's own language without incurring any inward change in the process.

Other Polynesianists of Williams's day speak with the same fervor of the vocation of scientific fieldwork and echo and amplify his rigorous, risk-laden prescriptions for ethnographic study. William Brown begins his book on New Zealand, for instance, by emphasizing the need for acquiring knowledge of "the minutest shades of the national character" (Brown 2) if one hopes to interact successfully with primitive peoples. Edward Shortland, having denounced the disabling prej-

SAVAGERY, CULTURE, AND FIELDWORK

udices of the missionaries, declares that the only means of learning about the lives of primitives is "by residing among them on terms of intimacy" (*Traditions and Superstitions* vii), and prefigures Malinowski by loading his work with native chants and proverbs quoted verbatim—sometimes untranslated when (as often occurs) the text is too indecent for British eyes. "We have always done all our work on the spot in the native language," says James Calvert, emphasizing the inadequacy of communicating with natives through interpreters ("Preface" xvii). Even George Turner, usually a shallow ethnographer and one who frequently voices his contempt for Polynesian ways, declares that insight into the organization of a culture like the indigenous one of Samoa necessarily presupposes being to some extent submerged within it. "It is not until you have landed, lived among the people, and for years closely inspected their movements, that you can form a correct opinion of the exact state of affairs," he says (*Nineteen Years* 279), implying that the organizing principles of a society are not the explicit, formal institutions the rules of which may be extracted by relatively unproblematic observation and correlated at one's ease back home, but are expressed so cryptically in daily life that discovering them requires an experience of years of intimate familiarity. The overriding theme of all these writers, in other words, is that knowledge in this domain can only be *experiential* and necessarily involves a profound personal investment and exposure. "The anthropologist cannot simply 'learn' the new culture," says Roy Wagner long afterwards, "but must rather 'take it on' so as to experience a transformation of his own world" (*Invention of Culture* 9). This peculiarly modern impulse of self-displacement—an integral function of the culture theory—evidently shows up at an early date in ethnographic literature.

It should be clear that the fieldwork principles so precociously developed by nineteenth-century writers were, as much as Martineau's, rife with contradiction and ambivalence. For one thing, the early study of South Pacific culture was inseparably linked to a broad and deliberate campaign to dismantle it, and thus implied continually that even the most innocent-seeming ethnographic observation was by its nature a destructive act of violence. In many texts of the period, the point is plainly made: observation and understanding are merely preliminaries to the imposition of tangible power upon the natives; and "intimacy" is treachery. William Brown thus calls for learning "the minutest shades of the national character" of the New Zealanders in order to serve the practical end of devising an effective "system of treatment" of the often obstreperous natives by colonists (*New Zealand* 2). Similarly, James Calvert's profession of the need to carry out all fieldwork in the local language, which I quoted in truncated form above, goes on to explain this technique as necessary if one wishes "to implant right views and make proper impressions in the minds of the natives" ("Preface" xvii). The paradox in which all this literature is involved, in other words, is that it calls for the minute, sympathetic study, at the cost of arduous training, of social phenomena defined from the outset as worthless and marked out for the speediest possible forcible elimination. John Williams catches the paradox memorably in an admiring reference to "the peculiar and intricate character of some of the ancient usages which we were anxious to see abolished" (*NME* 138). The ambivalence inherent in such a phrase and pervasive in ethnographic discourse of the period is spelled out with unusual fulness and poignancy by the doyen of early Polynesianists, William Ellis.

Ellis's hostility to traditional culture in the Society Islands is emphatic. In his role as Christian missionary, he makes no scruple of saying, his sole task was to convert the natives and utterly to reform their pathological condition of life. It would be easy by selective quotation to make him appear as the consummate example of the bigoted missionary antagonistic to every ideal of enlightened modern anthropology. More than once he declines to record native legends on the grounds that they are "too absurd to be recorded" (*PR* 1:179), and he does not conceal his boundless contempt for native superstition. "The system of idolatry . . . presents a most affecting exhibition of imbecility, absurdity, and degradation" (*PR* 2:219), he declares, and the gods it worships are "monsters of iniquity" (*PR* 2:190). He reports often and with great satisfaction on the successes of the missionaries' assault on native culture, and of their replacement of the traditional carefree, pleasure-loving Tahitian temperament by a serious, anxiety-ridden Evangelical one. Virtually all the traditional games of the islands have been abolished through missionary influence, he proudly reports: "we cannot but rejoice that they have ceased with that system of barbarism and cruelty with which they were associated, and by which they were supported" (*PR* 1:293). The crux of all this discourse is Ellis's insistence not just on the desirability of introducing true religious beliefs and of abolishing cruelty and immorality, but on systematically stamping out *every element* of traditional life, however innocuous or trivial it may seem. His goal, he says, is to achieve a "new order of things" through a radical "transformation of society" (*PR* 2:129, 130) and of the native psyche itself. To the end of this transvaluation of all Tahitian values, architectural styles are to be altered; villages are to be constructed on geometrical grids, instead of following natural contours of landscape in the traditional fashion; European clothing and new hair-styles are to be instituted as emblems of respectability (*PR* 2:71, 82, 115–17, 125). The natives' adoption of new styles of headwear, he blandly reports, will "[tend] perhaps ultimately to alter their physical structure" (*PR* 2:131). One thinks immediately of Lévi-Strauss's indictment of writing as the chief instrument of organized tyranny (*Tristes tropiques* 296–300) in following Ellis's extended account of how the Tahitians were first taught to read and of the immense significance of the introduction of printed Christian materials among them. The first step, he says, in a previously quoted phrase full of implications of covert violence, is "the reducing to writing, and a regular grammatical system," of "uncultivated and oral languages" (*PR* 1:449). Obviously there is a close correlation on the metaphorical and practical planes alike between this activity and that of "reducing" the wild Tahitian libido by imposing a system of restraint upon it (indeed the very idea of "oral languages" in this context carries perhaps a hint of puritanical dread of bodily orifices themselves and of the brutish desires fixated upon them). Finding the Tahitians' all-important instruction in reading to be hindered by the native habit of rote learning, Ellis obliges them to adopt another pedagogical method and to alter to this extent their traditional manner of thought—an episode which epitomizes vividly the use of writing as a means of reordering the mind itself and putting it in thrall to new institutions (*PR* 1:493).

In other words, cultural study as such—disinterested cultural study—seems for an observer like Ellis to be ruled out beyond recall by what he unequivocally takes to be the divine authority of his own religion and his own "civilized" society. Logically, any interest on his part in the specific details of Tahitian culture for their own sakes is almost prohibited, for it is all, root and branch, absurd, contemptible, and disgusting at best. In fact, it is all an expression of diabolical evil, and not in a merely metaphorical sense of that phrase. In the words of the official history of the London Missionary Society, Tahiti prior to its conversion was "the very seat of Satan, the centre and the home of the foulest vices that can degrade humanity" (Lovett 1:147). The depraved native religion, Ellis says repeatedly, suffuses and regulates every detail of traditional Polynesian culture; even so innocent a subject as techniques of canoe-building is thoroughly implicated in a system of abhorrent evil. (For one thing, the launching of Tahitian canoes was marked traditionally by human sacrifices.) In view of this set of assumptions, it can only appear an astounding contradiction that the two large and scholarly volumes of Ellis's *Polynesian Researches* offer a cornucopia of detailed ethnographic information regarding Tahitian crafts (notably canoe-building [*PR* 1:163–82]), religion, art, architecture, games, domestic customs, and so forth. This enthralling text is our authoritative source for knowledge of early culture in the Society Islands. It reflects a mind that has observed this culture not just with abhorrence but with fascinated intensity. Nor is the prescribed rhetoric of condemnation in Ellis as uniform as it ought to be. He regularly denounces the "brutal licentiousness and moral degradation" of the Tahitians and the inhabitants of neighboring islands (*PR* 2:25), but he also, as though despite his own professed program, breaks out often in praise of such things as the "beautiful, figurative, and impassioned eloquence" of the Tahitians, "and above all, the copiousness, variety, precision, and purity of their language, with their extensive use of numbers" (*PR* 2:19). No reader could be so obtuse as to miss the contradiction of finding so much elevated culture, beauty, intelligence, and "purity" in a system declared to be brutally degraded, ruled by anomic excess, and, indeed, under the direct ministration of the devil.

Ellis bears witness to his ambiguously divided motives no later than his preface. Christian missionaries are not social scientists in search of "accurate information," he sternly tells his readers here, but rather are dedicated to counteracting "delusive and sanguinary idolatries," which are responsible for "moral debasement and attendant misery" (*PR* 1:v). Barely a page later, a very different note is struck. Since all the "usages of antiquity" have now, thanks to missionary influence, been overthrown in the Society Islands, Ellis says, there is a danger that all memory of the ancient system will very soon be lost, unless "a variety of facts, connected with the former state of the Inhabitants, can be secured" at once, while reliable informants are still alive. Thus one motive of his book, he says, is "to furnish, as far as possible, an authentic record of these [ancient usages], and thus preserve them from oblivion" (*PR* 1:vi–vii). The anomaly could scarcely be starker: how can a Christian missionary justify laboring to preserve in minute detail the memory of a satanically inspired system of degradation and evil? Is not oblivion its proper fate? Ellis seems almost to say that this system which it was the mission of his adult life to annihilate possessed value. The suggestion is more than confirmed in the following paragraph, where he praises Polynesian polytheism for the "truly remarkable" greatness of imagination which it exhibits. "The Polynesian system will not suffer by comparison with any systems which have prevailed among the most polished and celebrated nations of ancient or modern times," he says (*PR* 1:vii), full of evident admiration for this structure of satanic delusion.

The contradiction at the heart of Ellis's project is significant enough, one would think, to have paralyzed him altogether.[16] He carries out his momentous work of ethnography only by allowing it to stand wholly unreconciled. To the not insignificant extent that *Polynesian Researches* contributed to bringing into focus the relativistic modern idea of culture, it stamps in this way upon that still embryonic idea the conceptually equivocal character which it has possessed ever since. It enters modern awareness, this text suggests, not as an achieved resolution of problems but as itself a virtually unresolvable problem, a site of impossibly contradictory loyalties and "schizoidal epistemologies" (Burridge 12).

The strong undertow of ambivalence that is manifest in the missionaries' code of "participant observation" makes more sense the more we reflect on its origins in the system of Evangelical doctrine and sensibility. If it is true "that every version of an 'other,' wherever found, is also the construction of a 'self'" (Clifford, "Introduction" 23), the cruel, madly lascivious heathen Polynesian can be seen to play an unexpectedly potent role in his unwished-for transaction with the puritanical imagination. This fictive image can only be what De Quincey would call the missionaries' "dark interpreter," the projection of the original, innate depravity in themselves which their religion teaches them to ponder incessantly, to regard with horror and to repress with utmost vigilance. For earnest Evangelicals, every other thought is subordinate to the morbid knowledge that "the principle of evil" (Thomas Williams 103) is in every person's blood without exception, tainting even a pious Christian's worthiest actions with evil.[17] For sensibilities organized around this principle, the anomalous-seeming combination of the call for intimate acquaintance with savages and the horrified condemnation of them would have after all a compelling logic. Such a situation merely reproduces, but in a less threatening form, the structure of Evangelical introspection. The project of suppressing the superstitions and bestial practices of Polynesia must have symbolized on the psychological plane a striving on the missionaries' part to triumph by heroic exertion over their own obligatory self-doubting. To the extent to which relations between missionaries and their potential converts were in fact based in this undeclared way upon exploitation of the natives' supposed wickedness to allay the moral distress of their European visitors, it would appear that there could be little room in these relations for reciprocity or for an attempt at unprejudiced observation.

One can lend credence to these thoughts and set them in a somewhat wider context by noting how clearly the pattern just guessed at in the case of mission ethnographers finds expression in Malinowski's field diary, where his loathing for the Trobrianders and his revulsion from their "whorish" women (*Diary* 225) are inseparably mingled with his own relentless self-condemnation—notably for his guilty erotic fascination with these same women (*Diary* 255, for example). Malinowski's bad conscience expresses itself in diametrically opposed form from what we seem to see in missionary texts, of course. Rather than venting itself in condemnation of "savages," it does so in proclaiming the principle of moral relativism: in *suspending* moral condemnation and in arguing the underlying similarity of cultures. But the two moves are closely equivalent to the degree that they both seem to represent attempts to assuage moral anxieties. For Malinowski, effacing his true hostility toward his subjects and replacing it with displays of empathy in the text of *Argonauts of the Western Pacific* amounted in an obvious way (obvious once we know the *Diary*) to an effacing of his hostility toward himself and his own ungovernable desires. Without supposing that Malinowski's psychic condition is typical of anthropological fieldworkers (given the rarity of documents like his diary, it is impossible to know), we are entitled, I think, to wonder how far this conflicted emotional structure, the distinctive sign of a characteristic religious sensibility, may exert a determining influence upon ethnographic ideology in general. To put this issue in the sharpest possible terms: does the principle—central to the idea of culture—that one is never justified in passing judgment even on the most offensive practices of another society trace some of its historical origins to the doctrine of original sin, which asserts that none of our actions or ideas ever possess uncompromised validity? A sense of the incurably equivocal nature of all our own doings would at all events dictate just that strangely decentered posture vis-à-vis foreign practices and values that is the essence of "ethnographic subjectivity." To grasp this point is perhaps to gain insight into how it was that nineteenth-century missionaries found themselves (even as they tightened their grip upon various Pacific societies) undermining their own rhetoric of moral absolutism and laying the groundwork for what was to become in the era of professional fieldwork a comprehensive doctrine of cultural relativism.

In the dizzying pattern of intimate contact and appalled rejection that defines their relations to their native clients, one significant factor must have been their consciousness of the affinity of the cardinal idea of taboo in Polynesian religion to central themes in their own religious thinking. Evangelicals and heathens alike lived under the constant sway of much the same panicky belief in processes of contamination by deadly metaphysical forces (conceptualized alternatively as moral evil or as the lethal sacredness called *mana*) through contact with unclean objects. Indeed, the missionaries' tactics of defense of their psychic and cultural integrity in their wildly disorienting new surroundings focused sharply on this complex of metaphors and lent it a heightened emotional charge. As we shall see more fully in a moment, they lived in fear that they or their children might contract moral "pollution" through exposure to Polynesian indecencies, especially sexual ones, and they set up their own taboos to guard against such dangers.

One need hardly say that the homology of aboriginal superstition in Polynesia and Evangelical British Protestantism goes unstated by mission ethnographers, yet they seem aware of it, indeed they almost compulsively hint at it, Raskolnikov-like, as though daring the reader to detect this scandalous secret (which was fully expounded by a later generation of anthropological theorists including Spencer, Robertson Smith, and Frazer). Ellis, for example, at one point describes as a grotesque superstition the decontamination ceremonies performed at the funerals of deceased members of the *Areoi* society, ceremonies "designed to divest the body of all sacred and mysterious influence" imparted to the members of the society by their patron, the evil god Oro. But this contaminating influence is quite real, as we learn just a few pages later, when Ellis recounts in a different rhetorical key the story of a high-ranking *Areoi* converted to Christianity. "From all the moral pollution and guilt then contracted," says Ellis earnestly, echoing closely the theory of heathen superstition, "he was washed and removed" (*PR* 1:326, 330). Similarly, Polynesian priests offered bloody sacrifices and prayed to their perverted gods "to cleanse the land from pollution," Ellis informs us (*PR* 2:215), being careful not to note how similar these practices are to the missionaries' own prayers that the heathen would be "purified from their moral defilement, in that blood which cleanseth from all sin" (*PR* 1:329). In another essay on the Polynesians' "false religion" (*PR* 2:208), Ellis focuses his disparaging rhetoric on the natives' belief in evil spirits. "No people of the world . . . appear to have been more superstitious than the South Sea Islanders, or to have been more entirely under the influence of dread from imaginary demons, or supernatural beings," he informs us (*PR* 2:225)—and in his remarkable next paragraph asserts his own belief, "recognized in the declarations and miracles of our Lord and of his apostles," that "satanic agency affects the bodies of men," and that wicked Polynesian idolaters are in fact subject to persecution from demonic spirits! If there is in these writers—how could there not have been?—an unavowed consciousness of the continuity of thinking between their religion and its dark interpreter, the satanic one of the Polynesians, it undoubtedly lent special urgency to the insistence in missionary discourse on the absolute and unquestionable difference between them; yet it must also have played its role in the creation of a fieldwork system based on the principle of intimate self-identification with savages.[18]

Nineteenth-century missionaries were by no means fully cognizant of all the implications of their own ethnographic practice, and they expressly denied, indeed, one of the key principles of the creed which later writers distilled from such practice: the principle that living for a long while in the midst of a primitive culture produces a psychic "sea change" (Junker 70) in a visitor from Western society, and that it is this change that enables him or her truly to gain access to the inner world of the people under study. Field experience, says Lévi-Strauss, is the necessary means to "that inner revolution" which makes the anthropologist "a new man" endowed with new insight into exotic forms of social life (*Structural Anthropology* 373). "What comes out of a study of a primitive people," says Evans-Pritchard, "derives not merely from intellectual impressions . . . but from its impact on the entire personality, on the observer as a total human being" (*Social Anthropology* 82). Such language—fully elaborated long before by Harriet Martineau, as we noticed—expresses in extreme terms the myth of the anthropological vocation as moral emancipation: ethnographic research actually liberates us from our own previous selves, its practitioners declare. It is important to understand that this proposition is more than merely an instance of "the romanticism that has always been in ethnography, no matter how desperately repressed" (Tyler 128); it is a necessary adjunct of the idea of culture as a structure of implicit or occult meanings not perceptible to the naked eye. Once this idea is accepted, it follows that nothing short of mental revolution can enable an outsider to gain access to cultural truths. This is the theoretical substructure of modern versions of the rhetoric of cultural intimacy first elaborated by the missionary ethnographers (though we should not exclude the possibility, as suggested above, that the theory may have been a kind of back-formation which emerged out of an existing system of research procedures). "To get that depth of understanding [which Boas] required meant submerging his thinking in that of another," writes his student Marian Smith, for example. "It meant learning to think in another's terms and to view the world through another's eyes. The most intimate knowledge of an informant's thought processes was mandatory and could only be obtained by intensive work over a long period" (M. Smith 58).[19] This is just the ideal which John Williams claims to have attained in having so immersed himself in Polynesian language that it has become more familiar to him than English—as though it were not the natives who were destined to undergo a transforming conversion experience, but their "civilized" visitor instead.

Such a conversion, if it occurs, must be fraught with tension and incompleteness, for "actually going native . . . is taboo for anthropologists" (Pratt 38) and can only be experienced in a kind of hypothetical way.[20] Nineteenth-century missionaries in Polynesia declared themselves exempt from any such tension by frequently emphasizing that their mission required of them the strictest fidelity to all the principles which they brought with them from their churches and chapels in England. There was no ostensible room in their program for the ideal of "mutual metanoia" (Burridge 20) that a more sentimentalized, more defensive, and less coherent latter-day missionary ethos would invoke. On the other hand, their activities were bound to be influenced, if only in a half-conscious way, by the "emphasis on transformation of character" (Welch, *Protestant Thought* 1:28) which formed the distinctive feature of their creed. Personal salvation for a nineteenth-century Evangelical was to have "undergone that change of mind, which our Lord himself . . . called being 'born again', and without which he had declared no man can enter into the kingdom of heaven" (Ellis 2:314). It is consistent with this principle (though not at all with their overt rhetoric) that men of Ellis's and John Williams's religious disposition should have developed a system of ethnographic work based on the rules of total cultural immersion, linguistic fluency, and the attainment of intimacy with the most alien personalities, and which in its deep logic seems to conduce as much to the personal transformation of the fieldworker as to that of native populations. Evangelical fieldwork procedures could scarcely have taken another form, and the "scientific specialists" who later perverted these procedures to serve the cause of the godless gospel of "culture" (linking this move to a specific campaign of vilification directed at missionaries) are evidently the direct heirs of the likes of Ellis and John Williams, Evangelicals under the skin.

The cultural anthropologist's idea of the necessity of undergoing "an extremely personal traumatic kind of experience" (Leach, *Rethinking Anthropology* 1) as the prerequisite to shedding prejudice and thus attaining ethnographic truth (defined as entering into another conceptual world) reproduces closely the Evangelical salvation narrative in which an influx of awareness of sin is imagined to be the prerequisite of the shedding of egoistic selfhood and of the spiritual new birth which follows. The confluence of the two supposedly antagonistic systems is made almost too plain in Roy Wagner's narrative of the typical fieldwork experience. The anthropologist newly arrived in the field is stricken, he says, with acute "culture shock," feels "lonely and helpless," and is filled with a sense of extreme personal inadequacy that leaves him "depressed and anxious." He undergoes in this dark night of the soul what Wagner speaks of as "a loss of the self" through the loss of his normal social context. ("Strip thyself naked of thy own works and thy own righteousness," exhorts John Wesley. "Let us be emptied of ourselves" [quoted Southey 113, 117].) But this traumatic loss is the means to shedding the "elitist self-images" that bar the path to personal transformation and thus to the fieldwork equivalent of salvation. This final stage consists in nothing less, says Wagner, than the revelation of "the concept of culture" itself, which occurs in the career of the neophyte researcher "generally [as] something of a 'conversion experience'" (*Invention of Culture* 1–8). Anthropology may on one level have used the culture theory to wage its declared war upon Evangelical thought, but it has evidently carried on all along a covert operation aimed at reclaiming and revitalizing the salvation scenario which forms its central idea. A plainer example of how a society's mobile army of metaphors disperses and then regroups itself from one historical period to the next, producing both renovation and continuity of thought, would be hard to find. Some of the equivocal status and the suppressed emotional charge of the concept of culture can probably be explained, one concludes, with reference to its origins in born-again Christianity.

Of all the early Polynesianists, the one who explored most daringly the issue of the possible transformation of the "civilized" Christian visitor through contact with barbarous heathens was the Wesleyan Thomas Williams, whose missionary post was in Fiji, a fiercely warlike nation where cannibalism and other, to European eyes, equally ghastly customs were practiced more intensively than anywhere else in the Pacific.[21] In Fiji the regime of anomic primitive passions could apparently be documented in its worst imaginable forms. Yet like other writers of his day and his religious disposition, Williams forecasts the twentieth-century ethnographic creed by declaring in *Fiji and the Fijians* that the precondition of understanding such a people is the attainment of genuine intimacy with them—that a purely external view of them is valueless—and that this in turn demands, as the price of admission to the mental world of a primitive society and to a new way of seeing and understanding, that we shed European preconceptions. "There are very few who have had the opportunity of long and intimate acquaintance" with the Fijians, says Williams, "and who, at the same time, have been either able or disposed to give a fair and unprejudiced statement of what they have witnessed" (*FF* 116–17). It is almost superfluous to remark at this point that the goal of being "unprejudiced" seems impossibly discordant with the mission of a Methodist clergyman preaching the gospel to a people addicted to what he is bound to regard as abominable depravities. Should we shed our prejudices against promiscuous sexual intercourse, cannibalism, ritual murder of widows, infanticide, wars of extermination? Williams brings such issues repeatedly to the fore as he stresses again and again the need to strive to look at people like the Fijians without imposing our own distorting notions of value upon them. This state of perception can scarcely be achieved by an act of will, however; it can only be achieved, he makes clear, by taking the vertiginous existential leap of actually living among them and thus to some extent—though Williams does not put it in these words—becoming one of them, with potentially unpredictable results. "Some familiarity is needed to picture a Fijian justly; for strangers cannot look on him without prejudice. They know that the history of his race is a scandal to humanity, and their first contact with him is certainly startling." The European visitor "experiences a strange and not easily described feeling when first he sees a dark, stout, athletic, and almost naked cannibal, the weird influence of whose penetrating glance many have acknowledged." Yet "personal intercourse," Williams assures his readers, allays the disgust aroused initially by knowledge of the Fijian's "abominable practices" (*FF* 90, 91).

This is a perilous and rhetorically very unstable argument, and each time that Williams invokes it, he risks giving the impression not only that the sinister Fijians are less depraved after all than they may seem from a distance, but that his own prolonged "intimate acquaintance" with abominations has had the effect of causing him to regard them with diminished horror, or even to accept them as potentially legitimate customs. Far from evading this risk, he seems to court it in ways that sharply problematize the whole official scheme of mission discourse. It would be an error, he maintains, for instance, to conclude from the rampant murder occurring in Fiji that the natives are devoid of genuine affection. "Allowance must be made for the manner in which custom and training have directed the expression of their affections, or we shall be in danger of denying the existence of the principle, because developed in a manner different from that to which we are accustomed" (*FF* 115). Hence, the prevalence of such practices as strangling a dead man's widows or his mother, burying alive aged or infirm parents, or killing babies at birth does not mean, Williams insists, that Fijians do not care for one another (*FF* 116). Elsewhere he partly contradicts his own subversive argument, stating that Fijians only feign domestic affections while in fact they kill one another out of sheer callous laziness and selfishness (*FF* 157–58), but that is not the point here. The point is, first, that Williams's determination to achieve an impartial and unprejudiced view of these people stained with crimes leads him to postulate something approximating what anthropologists call "culture": a set of irresistible collective forces by which an individual is unconsciously molded. In one striking passage, he suggests, in language that might have been taken from a twentieth-century textbook of anthropology, that the supposed moral differences between our own society and that of Fiji are simply the effects of different cultural imperatives. "Any portraiture . . . of a people living, for many generations, under the uninterrupted power of influences different from any which we daily feel, and strangers to those motives and forces which have, more than anything else, modified the development of our own individual and social character, must convey instruction, imparting, as it does, revelations which shed new light on the difficult study, —Man" (*FF* 117). As hortatory Evangelical rhetoric falls away in such a passage, we find ourselves unexpectedly contemplating the Fijians not as a spectacle of the anomic depravity of heathens, but as a mirror of ourselves. In the basic paradox of all anthropological thinking, one defines another people as radically alien—obeying as they do different cultural influences—and by the terms of this very definition they are found to be just like us after all. This twofold principle is at the heart of "ethnographic subjectivity," and opens upon the possibility of a relativistic ethnography conceived in existential and indeed self-sacrificial terms: one in which the observer divests himself by a kind of deliberate psychic violence of his own conventional ideas and feelings in order to gain access to the ideas of another people.

From this equivocal new perspective, the data which one seeks to observe and record *seem to be transformed,* as Thomas Williams says. Thus, for example, that initial European impression of being confronted by an "almost naked cannibal" turns out to be, viewed from the Fijian angle of vision, an obtuse misinterpretation. "In their dress, scanty as it is, the Fijians display great care and pride," says the sophisticated Williams, who never loses an opportunity to hint at the sociological character of perception and knowledge. "In judging of this matter, it is very difficult for a civilized stranger to form a right opinion, influenced, as he must be, by the conventionalities of costume to which he is accustomed. Hence the natives are frequently spoken of as naked; but they only seem so when compared with other nations" (*FF* 132). If we learn to look at them with Fijian eyes, they are revealed as in fact a richly dressed, rather dandified people—their costume being centered largely, for example, in their fantastic art of hairdressing, in which they display the "originality and versatility of genius," as well as in their intense pride in their fetishized national garment, the *masi* or loincloth, in their taste for fanciful bodily ornamentation, and in their cultivation of decorative scarification and of tattooing (*FF* 134, 104, 137–38). To think of such a people as naked is, for one who has entered their perceptual universe, so preposterous as to be nonsensical.[22] Perceiving ethnographic fact is thus problematic and difficult, and demands, above all, strenuous mental discipline that can only be acquired on the spot, existentially, through immersion in the native mentality. "So-called empirical observations," according to Thomas

Williams, scarcely exist. Murder is not murder, nakedness is not naked-ness, but thinking makes it so. We will not find so morally seditious a principle stated openly in *Fiji and the Fijians,* any more than it had been stated twenty years before by Harriet Martineau, but the trend of Williams's thought moves distinctly in this direction. Very likely it was this persistent suggestion, and not just his attempt to describe Fijian sexual customs in uneuphemistic terms, that caused his superiors in the Missionary Society to submit his surprising manuscript to an Evan-gelical editor (the Rev. George Stringer Rowe) for thorough revision prior to publication. The moralistic exclamations that repeatedly in-terrupt Williams's ethnography have very much the look of contribu-tions from another hand; they fail, however, to obscure the troubling and modernistic moral doctrine that his work implies.[23]

This doctrine, which leads directly to anthropological notions of culture that turn missionaries into villains and to a principle of moral neutrality—the principle, as Lévi-Strauss puts it, that all human socie-ties are "equally valid" (*Tristes tropiques* 386)—may never come to full expression in Thomas Williams, but it notably does in the earlier text of the *Account* of Tonga which John Martin compiled from William Mariner's testimony. Custom, Martin asserts again and again, recalling *The Theory of Moral Sentiments,* is the supreme determinant of all values (*NTI* 2:186, etc.). Debating the state of moral virtue among the Tongans (whose Machiavellian treachery and cruelty, among other vices, have been amply documented in Mariner's narrative), Martin lays down a definite principle. "If we were to measure their conduct by the notions of virtue, honour, and humanity received among civilized nations," he says, "we should do them great wrong, and forfeit our own titles to the epithets of just and honourable: we shall therefore endeav-our to ascertain in what *their* notions of honour consist, and judge them upon their own principles" (*NTI* 2:150). With regard to the supposed virtue of chastity, for instance, the only proper method is first to determine what are the Tongans' "own ideas respecting this matter," and then "[to] take those ideas as the standard by which to judge them" (*NTI* 2:157). Martin does not shrink from following his relativistic principle to its logical conclusion, going so far as actually to justify the treacherous unprovoked massacre of scores of British officers and men aboard Mariner's ship as proper and reasonable by Tongan standards (*NTI* 2:151–52).

The trends that we are noticing in this body of literature lead at last to signs, staged sometimes as moments of almost hallucinatory crisis, of an anxious sense that by becoming immersed in Polynesian culture as the missionaries' ethnographic code requires, and by relaxing one's grip on absolutist moral principles, one risks actually becoming infected with savagery one's self. Ellis recounts the melancholy story of a missionary named Lewis, who had arrived in Tahiti in 1797 aboard the first missionary ship, and who at length scandalized his colleagues by deciding with great solemnity to marry a native woman. On the grounds that she was "an idolatress," Lewis was strictly ostracized by his fellow missionaries, despite his exemplary conduct in all other respects, until one day he was brutally murdered by unknown assailants (*PR* 1:94–95). Another missionary confesses to deistical sentiments and chooses, again, to live with a native woman as his wife; he, too, is summarily tabooed, lest contamination infect anyone else (*PR* 1:103). These anecdotes give us glimpses of what was inevitably—as Malinowski's *Diary,* along with Cook's and other accounts of South Sea exploration remind us—an ever-present and extremely volatile, risky factor in the intimate relations which the missionaries cultivated with their Polynesian clients: the bewitching erotic allure and ready availability of Polynesian women. Describing the South Seas in 1795 as an ideal field for mission work, the Rev. Thomas Haweis had proclaimed the region uniquely free of hazards for missionaries "except . . . such as may arise from the fascination of beauty, and the seduction of appetite"; "avoid to the utmost every temptation of the Native Women," counselled the official instructions to the missionaries who departed for Tahiti in 1800 (Davies xxix, 18). The sexual difficulties of missionaries form the forbidden subject of most missionary literature,[24] but it is clear that great vigilance and severity were felt to be necessary to counter carnal temptation, which must often have reminded even the morally purest missionaries of the truth of Wesley's doctrine of the ineradicable persistence of sin in the born again.

Showing his acute sensitivity to the contagion of heathen uncleanness, Ellis worries repeatedly about the corrupting influence which the proximity to tabooed native indecencies can exercise upon even the most rigidly virtuous Christian. The common talk of the Tahitians, he says, making clear that he has in mind their free allusions to the pleasures of sex, "was often such as the ear could not listen to without pollution, presenting images, and conveying sentiments, whose most fleeting passage through the mind left pollution"—effects rendered all the more pernicious, evidently, by the natives' beguiling personal characteristics, "the apparent mildness of their disposition, and the cheerful vivacity of their conversation" (*PR* 2:25). Dreading "the awfully polluting character of their most common communications," the missionaries strictly segregate their children from natives in the Sandwich Islands; Polynesians again are pictured as carriers of ideas "whose most rapid passage through the mind must leave pollution" (*PR* 2:543). For someone like Ellis, the ideal of ethnographic intimacy and full linguistic fluency was thus in this immediate, urgent way frighteningly contradictory: one was required both to enter unstintingly into the native mentality and strictly, anxiously, to insulate oneself from it for fear of contamination. This is nothing but the Evangelical version of the paradox that has always been central to the ethnographic idea of culture, though expressed not as a logical/epistemological contradiction (that which is inherent in being inside and outside the sphere of study at the same time) but in the characteristic Evangelical mode of moral and existential crisis.

Signs of these anxieties appear in other missionaries' works as well. Explaining his determination to live in Samoa in a thoroughly respectable European-style house, John Williams shows his sense of potential danger by reminding his readers, for example, that "the Missionary does not go to barbarize himself, but to civilize the heathen" (*NME* 477). Yet "pollution" by barbarizing influences can occur in insidious ways. Williams puts in a telling footnote the anecdote of the missionary's wife who upon returning to "civilization" after ten years' residence in the islands finds that she is nauseated by the taste and smell of beef. She "burst into tears, and lamented bitterly that she should have become so barbarous as to have lost her relish for English beef" (*NME* 409). The same process takes more disturbing form in James Calvert's remarkable acknowledgment that once he and his fellow missionaries and their wives became accustomed to life in Fiji, "cannibalism soon lost its dreadful novelty, and began to be regarded as a matter of course" (*Missionary Labours* 249). Such moments bring into focus the idea that in entering a foreign society one enters a field presided over by patterns of thought able to impress themselves even upon the most recalcitrant minds and to give to any practice whatever the character of a natural thing—this being the essential element, as we have seen, of the concept of culture.

The hint of dread detectable in such examples takes on a full charge of panic elsewhere in this literature. The case of William Mariner as transcribed by John Martin provides a striking example. A young British sailor whose life was spared when Tongan warriors seized his ship, the Port au Prince, and slaughtered the crew, Mariner lived for the next four years on a footing of intimacy among the natives, becoming fluent in the Tongan language, before escaping at last aboard a passing British vessel. Martin realized that the mode of cultural observation which Mariner fell into against his will held the potential of a new level of detailed insider's knowledge of primitive society and of a new mode of ethnographic discourse; he recognized also that such discourse entailed necessarily a new type of potentially drastic experimentation with the observer's own selfhood. The central place in *Natives of the Tonga Islands* is held by the Tongan king Finow, and the book's main strategy lies in the suspension of moral judgment concerning this man (who organized the attack on the Port au Prince) in the name of close study of his personality in its minutely transcribed social and cultural context. One corollary of this project is the nearly complete suppression of information about Mariner's view of his own radically disoriented position as he enters Tongan society, becoming a loyal lieutenant of the king (at one point taking a hand in his treacherous assassination of a potential rival [*NTI* 1:278–79]) and ultimately his adopted son. If his deepening and affectionate intimacy with this murderous "savage," who had massacred his own shipmates before his eyes, seemed to Mariner morally problematic or caused him any pangs of ambivalence, no mention of this issue is ever made in the book—a glaring omission which in fact seems designed to draw attention to itself and in this way to highlight the psychological and spiritual risks of a method of participant observation in which the ethnographer, in his quest for the principle of culture, agrees "to abandon himself without reserve" to local ways of thought. If there is a dimension of existential panic in this story, it is therefore studiously obscured—with a single striking exception.

After one brutal military victory, owed largely to the effect of the guns which Mariner operates on behalf of his patron Finow, some young Tongan chiefs, imitating the martial habits of the Fijians, kill a number of prisoners and indulge in a cannibal feast. Mariner declines to join in, "though the smell of [human flesh], when cooked," he amazingly notes, reversing the anecdote of the missionary's wife cited above and bringing out its implications, "was exceedingly delicious." Ravenously hungry after two and a half days without eating, he eagerly accepts a piece of pork liver offered to him by one of the warriors, and "was raising [it] to his mouth, when he saw, by the smile on the countenance of the man, that it was human liver; overcome by disgust, he threw it in the man's face, who only laughed" (*NTI* 1:110). Edgar Allan Poe appears to replay this scene ten years later in his own fantastic account of a voyage to the South Seas, the *Narrative of A. Gordon Pym*. The starving Pym finds himself suddenly enticed by "a portion of clotted and liver-like substance" torn from the dead body of a sailor by a sea gull. "May God forgive me, but now . . . there flashed through my mind a thought which I will not mention, and I felt myself making a step toward the ensanguined spot. I looked upward, and the eyes of Augustus met my own with a degree of intense and eager meaning which immediately brought me to my senses. I sprang forward quickly, and, with a deep shudder, threw the frightful thing into the sea" (Poe 810). If Poe did have Mariner's account in mind here, as seems likely, he had correctly diagnosed the horrified awareness of implication in Polynesian obscenities that Mariner's brush with cannibalism implies. The linkage of the two texts illustrates in especially clear form, one might add, the close nexus between emergent ethnographic literature and the emergence of dislocated modernist sensibility at large.

But it is in *Fiji and the Fijians* that the traumatic awareness of a crisis of identity is dramatized with the greatest distinctness in the books which we are surveying. If practicing scientific ethnography amounts to and depends on personal participation in the culture being described, or at least entails tacitly conferring a patent of normalcy upon it, Thomas Williams is the most culpable of all the early Polynesianists. His lavishly and one can only say lovingly detailed descriptions of every aspect of the traditional life of the dreaded Fijians, from their exquisite canoe-building techniques to the interior arrangement of their neat and elegant houses, nullifies nearly all the effect of his own occasional outbursts of rhetoric—or those of his Evangelical editor— about how "the principle of evil" reigns unchecked in the islands. He confesses, as John Williams had before him (*NME* 520), that he is himself deeply affected by such things as the nobility of Fijian warriors on the eve of battle or by the contagious delight of the *yaqona* (*cava*) ceremony (*FF* 48, 123). That he has been "barbarised" to the extent of finding much to admire in Fijian life and of being able to enter spontaneously into its world of feeling is the most pervasive implication of this book, in other words. His treatment of the culture of cannibalism is especially remarkable, for he describes all its practices and associated ideas with the same calm objectivity with which he treats Fijian furniture. If one desires, for instance, to know in anatomical detail precisely how a human body is carved for different methods of cooking, Williams the Methodist missionary tells us (*FF* 177–78), adding that "the heart, the thigh, and the arm above the elbow are considered the greatest dainties" (*FF* 180). There can be no doubt that his role as missionary author is profoundly compromised by so much ethnographic detachment—or is it the reverse of detachment, participation? No wonder John Calvert felt it necessary to submit Williams's disquieting text to revision before allowing it to go to press.

These strains of ambiguous feeling converge upon the astonishing scene in *Fiji and the Fijians* where Thomas Williams, having for nearly two hundred pages pursued his ethnographic project from the point of view of nearly complete scientific impersonality, suddenly surges into the scene in his own person as an anguished participant. Hearing of the death of the aged king Tuithakau (who in fact, however, is still alive, as he only discovers later), Williams rushes to his house to try to prevent the ritual strangling of the deceased man's wives which Fijian custom decreed, but arrives a moment too late. One woman lies dead, and another is in the very act of being strangled by the customary groups of people pulling on opposite ends of a ceremonial white cord looped around her neck. "The effect of that scene was overwhelming," says Williams, even though he "was but too familiar with murders of this kind":

> Scores of deliberate murderers, in the very act, surrounded me, yet there was no confusion, and except a word from him who presided, no noise, but only an unearthly, horrid stillness. Nature seemed to lend her aid to deepen the dread effect; there was not a breath stirring in the air, and the half-subdued light in that hall of death showed every object with unusual distinctness. All was motionless as sculpture, and a strange feeling came upon me, as though I was myself becoming a statue. To speak was impossible; I was unconscious that I breathed: and involuntarily, or, rather, against my will, I sank to the floor, assuming the cowering posture of those who were not actually engaged in murder. My arrival was during a hush, just at the crisis of death, and to that strange silence must be attributed my emotion. . . . (*FF* 165)

The story continues for several macabre pages, but its crux is Williams's gesture of sinking down as though entranced to take his place in the horrible tableau vivant, assuming the ritual posture of the onlookers. This gesture is left unexplained, but it can only signify his acknowledgment of the hollowness of professing at such a moment to be simply a detached foreign observer. As an ethnographer if not as a Christian missionary, he discovers with a shock of recognition that he has become "against [his] will" personally and radically entangled in the culture which he has made it his life's work to discover and to record in detail for posterity. His work is inescapably an apologia for that culture, which here, he discovers, exercises its power over him as though by means of an hypnotic spell. The scene records that moment of invasion called "sympathy" by Harriet Martineau, and thus acts out in condensed form the "inner revolution" or experience of personal metanoia through cultural dislocation which causes the anthropological fieldworker, in Lévi-Strauss's phrase, to be reborn as "a new man." We do not know, so far as I am aware, what further evidence of this change there may have been in Williams's later life—John Martin significantly says that William Mariner's friends "could scarcely recognise him to be the same person" after his return from Tonga (NTI 1:xxxvi)—but one conjectures that its effects on a nineteenth-century Methodist could only be profound. It is a relatively conventional exercise for a twentieth-century intellectual like Lévi-Strauss, steeped in the doctrine of the inherent validity of "culture," and addressing an audience equally steeped in it, to argue the moral acceptability of such a practice as cannibalism (Tristes tropiques 387–88), but for Thomas Williams, strenuously working out the beginnings of this sort of doctrine for himself, such an idea could only be, to quote Poe's protagonist Pym, "a thought which [he] will not mention."

The Language Model

For all its melodramatic rhetoric, mission ethnography fails signally to bear out its originating proposition that pre-Christian Polynesia was ruled by ungovernable desire and thus that primitive society gives empirical support to original-sin theology. Increasingly this literature brings forth, indeed, a fundamentally different paradigm of savage life: that of a "complex whole" composed of elements of elusive symbolic import. Foucault charts the nineteenth-century evolution of the human sciences as centered on a "vast shift" away from biological models with their hypotheses of instinctual force and leading to "the reign of the philological (when it is a matter of interpretation and discovery of hidden meanings) and linguistic model (when it is a matter of giving a structure to and clarifying the signifying system)"

(*Order* 360, 359). This is the shift enacted in compressed form in missionary literature, where the development of a quasi-linguistic notion of cultural materials seems to spring directly from the writers' arduous experience of learning previously unstudied languages nearly from scratch.

The Polynesian missionaries "were the first in modern times," says their historian, "to grapple with a savage language, reduce it to grammatical order, represent its sounds, so difficult to catch from the lips of the natives, by the proper letters, and unravel the mystery of its complicated syntax" (Lovett 1:162). Having selected the South Seas for proselytizing largely from a belief that the "primitive" Polynesian languages could readily be mastered in a few weeks' time by an intelligent European,[25] the missionaries were profoundly impressed by the discovery of the complexity of these languages, which taxed their intellects nearly to the breaking point. Even the bigoted George Turner exclaims over the intricate subtlety of Polynesian tongues. "It is worthy of remark," he says, for instance, "that these dialects [of the island of Tanna in the New Hebrides] are copious, euphonic, and have some of the niceties of language; a triplial as well as a dual in the pronouns, for instance" (*Nineteen Years* 84). Unriddling such difficulties of language at the cost of "gigantic work" (Lovett 1:162) carried several implications. It involved each missionary in a totally unforeseen, totally absorbing project of intensive ethnographic investigation: like it or not, they could not simply intervene as moral and religious reformers in native life at once as they had anticipated, but had to begin by acquainting themselves in minute detail with at least this dimension of the natives' system. Their own indoctrination had to precede that of their intended converts. Entering to this extent into the natives' mental world could not fail to throw in doubt the mythological premise that Polynesian life was based almost exclusively on "the gratification of monstrous lust" (Lovett 1:148), and to bring home to them the principle that even these licentious savages inhabited first and foremost a world of *meanings* and of articulated symbolic systems. In the realm of language at least, what manifested itself was not at all the pandemonium of "unrestrained indulgence and excess" but symmetry, refinement, and flawless order. This discovery seems to have altered their perception of Polynesian life in a fundamental way, though the alteration was in good measure unconscious and never caused them to abandon the rhetoric of "unbridled passions."

In an early passage praising the prodigious linguistic achievements of the first Tahitian missionaries, William Ellis emphasizes the near-uselessness of the fragmentary lists which they possessed of the meanings of individual Tahitian words, and evokes the ludicrous results of their first blundering attempts at verbatim translation from English. In order to use the separate words meaningfully, he declares, in order, that is, to set them "in their proper collocation," one needs to master the whole integrated system of the language in question (*PR* 1:71). After the great effort of accurately discriminating words phonetically, another missionary complained in the same vein, "there is as great a labour to arrive at the true sense and meaning of a word, or its various meanings; for one word is used to express very opposite things in different sentences" (quoted Lovett 1:162). Such insights into the nature of linguistic values give a foretaste of the revolutionary Saussurean principle that "everywhere and always there is [in language] the same complex equilibrium of terms that mutually condition each other" such that no accurate definition of a linguistic term is possible if we "isolate a term from its system" (Saussure 122, 113); they register at the same time the missionaries' receptiveness to the great principle of the systematic character of cultural phenomena in general. Meanings of the kind described in the above quotations cannot be learned abstractly or reduced to simple tables of equivalences: they can only be made accessible experientially, through actual personal immersion in the many lived contexts, permeated with affective values, that govern the senses of words. One subsequent theorist of fieldwork makes just this point in discussing "the wide and complex considerations into which we are led by an attempt to give an adequate analysis of meaning." "Instead of translating, of inserting simply an English word for a native one, we are faced by a long and not altogether simple process of describing wide fields of custom, of social psychology and of tribal organization which correspond to one term or another" (Junker 29).[26] In other words, the practical project of learning an unknown language cannot be carried out in a vacuum; it almost inescapably requires one to begin to conceive the society in all its bearings as a "culture" of inseparably interlocked symbolic elements and to think of the language and the whole economy of extralinguistic cultural materials (customs, tribal organization, and so forth) as exact equivalents of one another. If the language proves, as of course it does, to be "a regular grammatical system" (Ellis 1:449), the milieu of customs and values to which it exhaustively refers must therefore have the same character of logical organization. This process of reflection or intuition is largely abridged for a person learning a language as a preanalyzed artifact in a textbook, but the original South Sea missionaries must have been obliged to undergo it in its full extent.

Acquiring this experience has as a further consequence that of necessarily dealienizing the society which one confronts. By learning savage languages, the missionaries discovered to what was clearly their immense surprise, one comes perforce to hear them not as animal-like gabblings, but as a normal medium of communication. In their repeated exclamations over Polynesian eloquence, this is what they essentially mean: that Tahitian or Fijian or Tongan, once you learn it thoroughly and are able to speak it spontaneously (which means having learned to experience Polynesian social life much as a Polynesian does), is *just like English,* equipped with a full range of expressive nuance and affective potency, and so perfectly attuned to the consciousness of native speakers that it seems almost to bring that consciousness into being. Given all this, how could an earnest British missionary fail to be at least subliminally aware that his deep immersion in Polynesian language tended to implicate him willy nilly in the whole vile array of "savage" things that he condemned? Only when we have grasped the intensity of these men's conviction that the whole of Polynesian life was saturated with depravity will we be able to guess at the disorientation which they must have experienced in laboring to master local languages, in submitting docilely to months of instruction from native speakers—and then in hearing the language of cannibals issuing at last from their own lips, and even becoming, as John Williams declared, more familiar to them than their own native tongue. The pathos and the existential drama of missionary fieldwork, as well as its philosophical resonances, surely begin in the labor of language acquisition.

As for what particularly interests us here, the intellectual drama of reconceiving the logic of primitive culture, William Ellis provides an especially rich documentation. In the early sections of *Polynesian Researches,* he gives the heaviest possible stress to the importance of the language factor in ethnography and to the elaborateness of the linguistic culture of the Tahitians (*PR* 1:72–76), and the rest of his narrative continuously reasserts the paramount role of language in the conversion of the natives, highlighting as decisive influences in this process such things as King Pomare's fascination with writing, the establishment of a printing press on the island, and so forth. He singles out as a pivotal event in Tahitian history, for instance, the official adoption of a Tahitian alphabet on March 6, 1805. All in all, his book testifies plainly to a growing sense of language not merely as a convenient device of exchange, like money in Adam Smith and Mill, but as an agency that powerfully governs social life. It also seems to become for Ellis a powerful ethnographic metaphor, a model for the representation of the whole range of social phenomena. We can best illustrate this effect by looking at a representative passage of his text.

In the course of narrating an epochal voyage (*PR* 1:163–64) to set up the original printing press in the Society Islands—an occasion in which ideas of intercultural translation and the diffusion of language are uppermost in his mind—Ellis gives his readers a typical lesson in purely linguistic matters. "Mrs. Ellis, and myself, with an infant and her nurse, set out in a native canoe. . . . Mr. Crook and family preceded us in a fine large double canoe, called '*Tiaitoerau*,' literally 'wait for the west wind,' from *tiai* to wait, and *toerau* west wind." In the next sentence, as though passing merely to another branch of the same theme, he begins a detailed analysis of this canoe, considered now as a construction not of linguistic but of culturally fashioned physical materials (though he cannot exclude linguistics altogether from his account):

> It was between thirty and forty feet in length, very strong, and . . . well built. The keel . . . was formed with a number of pieces of tough Tamanu wood, *inophyllum callophyllum,* twelve or sixteen inches broad, and two inches thick, hollowed on the inside, and rounded without, so as to form a convex angle along the bottom of the canoe; these were fastened together by lacings of tough elastic cinet, made with the fibres of the cocoa-nut husk. On the front end of the keel, a solid piece . . . so contrived as to constitute the forepart of the canoe, was fixed with the same lashing. . . . This front piece . . . was called the *ihu vaa,* nose of the canoe. . . . The joints or seams were not grooved together, but . . . fitted with remarkable exactness by the adze of the workman" (*PR* 1:163–65).

The passage continues for another eighteen pages, minute physical description of *Tiaitoerau* leading successively into explanation of the various categories of Tahitian canoes and all their many ritual, military, and everyday functions, of the principles governing the names bestowed on them, of canoe manufacturing methods and systems of payment, of the dangers to native mariners from sharks, of their superstitious cults of shark gods, and of other related matters as well. Such a passage is not at all a mere learned miscellany of data (though it might be misread as one). First and foremost, it is designed to dramatize the peculiar sensibility of this observer whose gaze rivets itself with such intensity upon every detail of Tahitian life. (He becomes in effect so absorbed in studying a specimen of native canoe design that he forgets about the adventurous voyage which he had begun to narrate.) This is a text charged with affective values, in other words, though they may not be easily intelligible at first glance and may in the final analysis refer less to Tahiti than to Ellis's real subject here, a certain mode of ethnographic interpretation.

Its essential principle, never stated but vividly portrayed in practice, is that every cultural formation such as a canoe or a god must be viewed *as a system* intricately constructed according to an internal logic of its own which an interpreter, if he wishes to understand it, must painstakingly bring to light. Such a system needs further to be viewed as an element in a larger system of systems which, if we followed all their ramifications as far as they go from any single point (an individual canoe, for example), would at last encompass nothing less than the whole of an efficiently integrated way of life, each part of which is "fitted with remarkable exactness" to all the others. Tahitian carpentry, economics, art, religion, and social structure all turn out to be interconnected and inseparable: this is the point of presenting all these disparate-seeming materials in the guise of a single train of thought. Ellis's passage transcribes an evident will to reveal what Adam Smith called "the invisible chains which bind together . . . disjointed objects" (Astron 45) in the field of culture—though the only specifiable chains here, just as Smith would insist, are those of the interpreter's own mental associations as he strings together one item after another in his own discourse. It is no accident that this meditation leading to an idea of the complex wholeness of culture takes the form of a gigantic extrapolation from an etymology, for Ellis seems intuitively to model his discourse on canoes on the linguistic paradigm, seeing them in all their inflections of form, size, ornamentation, and function as grammatically ordered figurative expressions and constituents of Tahitian consciousness, itself graspable only when its many elements have been set "in their proper collocation."

To understand this implicit argument is to see how such a passage as the account of canoes prefigures and interlocks with a series of analyses of other branches of what emerges at last in *Polynesian Re-*

searches as a vast Tahitian symbol-system, grounded ultimately in this people's language and reduplicating its "complicated syntax" in one figurative idiom after another: that of the "complex and intricate" structure of sorcery beliefs (*PR* 2:24–25); of the amazingly elaborate Tahitian system of numbers (*PR* 2:423); of the institution of the battle-priests and their wonderful metaphorical oratory (*PR* 2:488); or, above all, of the Tahitian religion, which Ellis, despite his official loathing of it, typically recognizes to be, "as a system, singularly complete," and admirable—like the language or a canoe—for "the fabrication and adjustment of its several parts" (*PR* 1:vii). One especially resonant passage in this context, since it broaches in such clear form the problem of decoding enigmatic cultural imagery, is Ellis's discussion of the Society Islanders' cherished institution of tattooing (*PR* 2:463–77). Originally invested with specific symbolic meanings, the conventionalized motifs of tattooing as practiced in modern times appear to Ellis to be purely "decorative." Sensing the symbolic values which remain attached in spite of everything to tattoo markings, however, the missionaries make a concerted effort to outlaw this practice; they see that by literally inscribing themselves with these ancestral signifiers, the Tahitians, earlier misdescribed as "destitute of letters, hieroglyphics, and symbols" (*PR* 1:vii), are in fact symbolizing their fidelity to the entire way of life which the missionaries' arrival has placed in jeopardy. Ellis dwells on the stubborn defiance of the ban on tattooing which long persists among the islanders, who clearly realize, for their part, that to abandon this branch of their representational language is tantamount to abandoning all native values whatever.

The intellectual fascination and the historical significance of a work like *Polynesian Researches* thus concentrate themselves in the unstated insight that all the many systems of phenomena described ultimately constitute a unified semiological structure, a "culture," the elements of which, one might speculate, would be symbolically transposable from one field to any other (as all commodities are transposable into all others inhabiting the same market system in the theory of political economy). At the final level of analysis, the level which Ellis's text despite its poverty of philosophical vocabulary seems to strive to attain, the Polynesian language system and that, say, of Polynesian canoe thinking or of the order of Polynesian divinities would turn out to be not merely formal analogues of one another but identical structures of metaphor, and ethnographic description would inevitably become *interpretation* aiming to reveal the underlying system of value which enables symbolic transposition to occur.

In its articulation of just this principle nine years later, Martineau's *How to Observe* furnishes a running gloss on Ellis's ethnography, bringing to explicit formulation all its implicit assumptions. For one thing, since people are unconscious of the meaning of their own cultural practices, personal testimony in this field is inherently unreliable. "The grand secret of wise inquiry into morals and manners," she therefore declares, "is to begin with the study of THINGS, using the DISCOURSE OF PERSONS as a commentary upon them" (*HO* 63). In the impersonal realm of "things," by which she means institutions and customary objects of all kinds, we discover "manifestations of the common mind" (*HO* 63). All things, in other words, are to the ethnographic eye *symbolic* and interpretable, and by the same token all at some level represent one another, expressing the same continuous meaning. For the "philosophic" observer, "everything that he looks upon will instruct him, from an aqueduct to a punchbowl, from a penitentiary to an aviary, from the apparatus of a university to the furniture of an alehouse or a nursery" (*HO* 65). No element in this inventory of items, properly construed, is merely practical or trivial; each is an expressive part of a semiology, and open to the kind of minute analysis which Ellis performs upon the eloquent surface of *Tiaitoerau*. Martineau invokes the common mind as though it were an autonomous reality in which cultural symbolism is grounded, just as the political economists whose works she studied long attempted to preserve "absolute value" as a reality independent of the relativism of the exchange system and the symbolic marking of price. (It was around 1823 that Ricardo and his school concluded, as we saw, that the quest for absolute value was a fool's errand into "the transcendental part" of political economy.) Still, the clear tendency of Martineau's argument is to absorb that highly equivocal theoretical entity, the common mind (which has no reliable correlation at all, she insists, with conscious psychology), altogether into the figurative structures which "manifest" it.

Something close to this absorption is what seems to occur in the portrayal of the most characteristic of all Polynesian institutions, the *cava* ceremony, in Martin/Mariner's *Account of the Natives of the Tonga Islands*. Fully twenty-five pages are given over to this description (*NTI* 2:172–96), which is striking, first and foremost, for that obsessive minuteness of detail which it shares, say, with Ellis's description of *Tiaitoerau* and is in fact the stylistic signature of what we see emerging in these texts, the ethnographic concept of culture. This is the repertorial idiom which implicitly corresponds to—or itself brings into being—the idea that a plenitude of (necessarily obscure because unconscious) meaning inhabits each cultural item and "even the smallest of the co-existent parts of [social life]" (A. Smith, *TMS* 289). Phenomenologically speaking, such a technique represents a state of mind both mesmerized by the spectacle before it—in this case a thoroughly routine occasion in Tongan society—and straining with almost agonized intensity to grasp its meanings, not daring to let the tiniest particle of data escape unrecorded. "The ethnographic subjectivity," we have seen, predicates itself on a radical self-suppression; but passages like these make clear that this process can yield an almost morbid heightening of perceptual power in the light of which primitive ways seem all at once to radiate unsuspected significance.

The participants in the *cava* ceremony sit in a circle—though "it is in general not an exact circle, the greatest diameter dividing the top from the bottom, which last is rather less curved than the top" (*NTI* 2:175)—to watch the preparation of a beverage made from an infusion of chewed *cava* or pepper-plant root, cups of which are then distributed to everyone according to an elaborate system of order and precedence. It takes Martin four dense pages to "unravel the . . . complicated syntax" of the system of protocol governing who sits where in the three zones which he defines as the superior, inferior, and exterior circles. "No person, though he be a chief of high rank, can sit in the superior circle at the same time that his father is there, (or any superior relation), even though he be at a considerable distance; and if he be already seated there, when his father comes, he must necessarily retire to the inferior or exterior circle, no matter which, out of respect to his superior relation: in either of the other circles, however, father and son may sit near to each other if they please" (*NTI* 2:177). The method of this approach is exactly that of the exposition of a system of grammar, and clearly its ultimate referent is the abstruse, hypercomplicated Tongan theory of personal relations which the seating code, like the parcelling of tribal space into a schema of irregular circles, signifies. The *cava* ceremony is thus a scene of symbolic representation, an enactment of the whole system of relationships upon which Tongan society is based.

Martin's method of analysis takes a different and yet closely related form when he comes to the preparation of the drink itself, devoting two full pages to tracing, one by one, the smallest bodily movements of the preparer. "In the first place, he extends his left hand to the farther side of the bowl, with the fingers pointing downwards, and the palm towards himself; he sinks that hand carefully down the side of the bowl, carrying with it the edge of the *fow* [a thatch of fibrous material floating on the surface of the infusion]; at the same time his right hand is performing a similar operation at the side next to him, the fingers pointing downwards, and the palm presenting outwards" (*NTI* 2:183). Each stylized movement is made to seem an element in a cryptic, seamlessly integrated gesture-language, though Martin offers no reading of whatever symbolic meanings may in fact underlie the performance. The brew once prepared, there comes into play another complex set of statutes dictating who is served in what order. Martin/Mariner lays these out with the same exhaustive completeness and the same sense of intricate grammatical relations that govern the style of the rest of the passage. "1st. Where the cava is a present, and the giver is in company, the order is thus: the giver; the mataboole; the president. 2nd. The cava not being a present, or the giver not in company, but there being a visitor, thus: the visitor; the mataboole; the president. 3rd. There being two or more visitors of nearly equal rank, and the master of the ceremonies not knowing how to choose without giving offence, thus: the president; the mataboole; the chief next below the president in rank" (*NTI* 2:190–91). And so forth.[27]

What is striking in this passage, apart from its continuing stress on the principle that all the features of savage customs are "fitted with remarkable exactness together" (and thus are the very opposite of a spectacle of chaotic personal impulses), is the immense proliferation of observed detail coupled with a near absence of interpretive commentary. Especially notable by its absence is any invocation of a *conscience collective* as an independent or transcendent reality in which the profusion of Tongan symbolism is grounded. "We have been particular in the description of the ceremony of preparing and drinking this infusion, because it sets in so strong a light the manners and customs of the people": this opaque comment is Martin's sole response to a reader's bewilderment at confronting such a mass of "the imponderabilia of daily life." What is set in the strongest light in such passages, we may say, is the emergence of a sensibility (as exotic as Tongan society itself) which registers awareness of social phenomena in a strange new way. Martin's reconstruction of Mariner's story makes him the classic instance of the fieldworker's transformation according to Roy Wagner's scenario of traumatic dislocation and solitude leading to the revelation of "the idea of culture." From the point of view of the ethnographic observer this idea causes every customary practice to seem to participate in a great self-enclosed system of metaphor; it implies for Martin that Tongan consciousness is constructed not by instinctive passions but by its immersion in this galaxy of symbolic signifiers, which unfolds itself in a structured play of inflections and recombinations of affectively charged motifs; and by implying the difficulty of any interpretive intervention in such a system (since every element in it refers to everything else), it impels one to try to register its smallest detail. The danger of this mode of writing is obvious, and it is the one that has haunted modern ethnography, and the work of Boas and Malinowski in particular: that masses of unrationalized empirical data may at last stifle cultural understanding in the way that masses of devalued commodities may stifle an economy in a Malthusian "general glut." As Clifford has said in reference to Malinowski, the ethnographer's "obsessive inclusion of data . . . may be seen as a desire to unmake as well as to make a whole" ("Ethnographic Self-Fashioning" 152). Martineau foresees this dilemma as lucidly as she foresees so much else in interpretive ethnography: in amassing data, she says, "the wearied mind soon finds itself overwhelmed by the multitude of unconnected or contradictory particulars" (*HO* 16). This has been a hard problem to avoid, for once one conceives of a culture as an integral whole, there is no ready way to limit a potentially anomic proliferation of information. "When can one be sure of having all the data that would warrant definitive interpretation?" asks Robert Lowie, in reference to Boas (*History* 152).[28] "If one set out to note all the facts about a single grain of sand," cautions Marvin Harris, "all of the computers in the world could not store the information which could eventually be collected on that subject. . . . 'Complete descriptions' of anything are impossible" (Harris 288).

Martin/Mariner's account of the *cava* ceremony gives a clairvoyant prefiguring of how a certain cryptolinguistic paradigm of culture can impel ethnography toward just this futile aspiration to completeness, to the endless piling-up of ever more microscopic facts, and ultimately to a Derridean awareness that in a system of differential relations, the proliferation of interpretation is an interminable process. But the cumulative effect of this passage, which even now seizes a reader's attention as a rather flamboyant exercise in experimental prose, is quite the reverse of "taxonomic description for its own sake, without a redeeming point or argument" (Marcus 188). Martin possesses scarcely any technical vocabulary for analyzing the symbolic properties of all the imponderabilia he inventories here; but the need for producing some such vocabulary forms the subtext of the whole passage. It is because the smallest detail of the ceremony is perceived as a node of concentrated meaning, as in effect a synecdoche for a whole way of life, that not a detail can be omitted. This the reader is made to understand without the point being anywhere stated explicitly, and a close reader in 1818 could hardly have missed the feeling of being in the presence of a strong new paradigm. Its essential idea (if I may state it once more) is that the *cava* ceremony—and by extension the whole society of which it is one of the characteristic formations—is not a random array of separate features, but a configuration the organizational principles of which are somehow immanent in its every detail. This, surely, is the elusive sense in which the *cava* ceremony "sets in so strong a light the manners and customs of the people."

The principle that all the disparate-seeming customs of a people ought in theory to be "reducible to systems" is still more distinctly invoked in negative terms by early Polynesianists: that is, in the attention which they repeatedly draw to seeming anomalies or logical disjunctions in the Polynesian way of life. Perceiving eruptions of cultural illogic involves a tacit measuring of a foreign society against the conventional arrangements of our own. But focusing on such problems can be the first step not only toward recuperating outlandish- and defective-seeming foreign societies as coherent systems through the development of ever more sophisticated methods of analysis, but toward imagining that nearly all customs and all combinations of customs are possible for human societies, and that no one arrangement can claim after all to possess more logical coherence than any other.[29] It would of course be possible to conclude from the juxtaposition of the thought-systems of different peoples that all human societies are equally irrational rather than equally rational, that "representations" evolve individually and cluster together in a haphazard way, and that theories of their organic interrelations in the case of any given society are as a result the delusive fictions that Adam Smith's "History of Astronomy" essay would declare them to be.[30] But in the literature which we are at present surveying, it is precisely the stress on seemingly irrational combinations that marks the movement away from any such conclusion.

CHAPTER THREE

For observers with as deeply moralized a world-view as the one held by the first South Sea missionaries, the most profound and most encompassing anomaly of Polynesian life was bound to be that of the conjunction of habitual depravity and blind, uncontrolled "passions" with refinement, intelligence, and civic order. The anomaly stood out so glaringly in Polynesia as to constitute a shock to the very foundations of the European, especially the British, view of the world. How could a people be saturated with sadistic wickedness and every animalistic vice, with original sin in its nearly unmitigated form, as the missionaries declared them to be, and at the same time, for instance, be capable of long ocean voyages by celestial navigation, possess admirable poetic traditions, display urbane and elegant manners, and be full of witty merriment in their daily intercourse with one another? Scarcely any of these writers fails to exclaim about the intelligence of the "naked savages" of Polynesia, and they repeatedly declare that in truth they are absolutely the equal of Europeans in this regard (Ellis 2:22, for example). Mariner makes the point vividly by reporting in great detail his long conversation about money with Finow and his attendant Filimoëatoo; at first completely befuddled by the concept of money, the two Tongans quickly grasp it, and launch into a subtle philosophical discussion of the perplexities of the theory of value, and then into an analysis of how the institution of money determines the European moral character, that might have come from Adam Smith (*NTI* 1:248–52). This is just the kind of surprise emphasized by C. F. Gordon Cumming in her introduction to the 1884 edition of *Fiji and the Fijians,* a book, she says, "which, years ago, thrilled the reading public of Britain . . . with amazement, that a race should really exist who combined such inconceivable and habitual barbarity with such punctilious etiquette in ceremonial observances, such extraordinary richness of language, and so large a share of the artistic faculty . . . and who altogether presented so remarkable a problem to the student of divers races" (Cumming v). This remark bears witness that moral presuppositions, rather than blocking cultural speculation, may strongly excite it or even be its indispensable element. The contradiction sharply underlined by Cumming made conscious and problematic the previously untheorized assumption that the various constituent elements of the life of a people were, so to speak, equivalent—and led at length to the development of analytical principles ("relativism" in its various guises first and foremost) able to salvage the original assumption that the elements of social life are logically consistent with one another, *bound together in a uniform system of relations.*[31]

The ethnography of Polynesia had in fact long stressed just this "problem" of seemingly illogical combinations of traits. Ellis, for instance, focusing as always on paradoxical signifiers and on the attempt to imagine culture in linguistic terms, tries at one point to get to the bottom of the Tahitians' "strange and contradictory usage" of lacerating themselves to express joy as well as bereavement. His native informants, themselves perplexed by his perplexity (for to their eyes there is of course nothing at all illogical about this practice), can only give him the all-sufficing answer that "it was the custom of Tahiti" (*PR* 1:530). He does not draw from this conundrum the conclusion that the conceptual system which declares "joy" and "grief" to be logical antitheses and thus unable to be represented by the same sign is itself just the custom of Europeans, no more valid or self-evident than the alternative customary logic of Tahitians, which evidently categorizes states of feeling in altogether different ways: but he so lucidly sets up the interpretive problem and pursues it so tenaciously that some such conclusion is made to seem implicit in it, at least in retrospect. Analysis of this kind pointedly defines ethnography as an attempt to unriddle the symbolic interrelations of customs, and it hints persistently, as so much does in the literature which we are considering, at the problematic character of interpretation. In the same spirit, Ellis analyzes elsewhere "the most striking contradictions" in the Tahitians' "moral character," as evidenced in their rules of hospitality (*PR* 2:22). Their attitudes respecting marital fidelity likewise exhibit "a most unnatural mixture of brutal degradation [as shown in the sharing of wives with brothers and friends], with infuriated and malignant jealousy" (*PR* 2:369–70).

Other writers energetically pick up the same crucial topos. In his attempt to explicate logically "the system of tapu, or rendering sacred," William Brown notices so many apparent inconsistencies that he wonders "how much is really a fixed law or custom," and how much the observances of taboo in fact fluctuate according to circumstances (*New Zealand* 10).[32] He highlights elsewhere the baffling anomaly, as it seems to him, of the New Zealanders' displaying great "propriety of conduct" in sexual matters yet relishing "very obscene songs." "So eccentric and anomalous are their feelings, —a strange mixture of vanity, liberality, and cupidity," he says in another place. He stresses "their kindness and sympathizing nature"; however, "another anomaly in their character is their ingratitude, which is manifested to a great extent" (*New Zealand* 36, 70, 72–73). Thomas Williams's sophisticated account of the Fijians is especially rich in such discoveries. "One of the strange and almost anomalous blendings of opposite traits in the Fijian character," he declares at one point, for example, is that the love of agriculture exists "side by side with the wildest savagism" (*FF* 49). Similarly, Fijians, though they are addicted to the practice of murdering their own newborn children, often adopt orphans and shower them with parental tenderness: they "are made up of contradictions" (*FF* 155).

The persistence of this rhetoric of disjointedness and incoherence is thus a further sign of the process the elusive traces of which I have been attempting to recover: a momentous yet almost unconscious shift of focus in mission ethnography from its nominal project of reporting the foregone conclusion of primitives' wickedness and stupidity to that of using the vantage point of intimate acquaintance to try to make rational sense of them. The world of savage mentality and savage customs increasingly presents itself in these texts, in other words, in the guise not of a foregone conclusion at all, but in that of an interpretive riddle, one even harder to decipher than that of their language, requiring even more extreme efforts of empathy, yet (if only by implication) similar to it at bottom and able to be rendered intelligible at last if only one could "unravel the mystery of [the] complicated syntax" which will cause the many contradictions and anomalous combinations to resolve into "their proper collocation," that of an expressive unity.

These writers propose, in fact, a distinct thesis asserting the unity of Polynesian culture, even if they fail to apply it systematically in a detailed way to the problematic cultural materials which they so copiously document. They come to this thesis from the angle we would least expect, as a direct consequence of their aim of effecting the entire transformation of Polynesian society, and of their need of a writ for so sweeping an enterprise. They themselves, for all the horror they felt before a broad range of practices in this society, sometimes worried about the propriety of interfering with native ways beyond the realm of religious belief itself (J. Williams 140). There could be just one solution: the discovery that native life was after all an indivisible whole, and more particularly that false, "idolatrous" religion—their entitlement to abolish which few Europeans would have contested—

so imbued all areas of Polynesian life that it could not possibly be defeated without making a clean sweep of the entire culture. To allow even the most trivial-seeming custom to survive (tattooing, for instance) would be by this theory to allow the virus of "idolatry" to remain alive and potentially to break out anew in the future. The missionaries' will to power leads directly in this way to the distinct formulation of the principle of the indivisible integrity of culture.

The above is in part a hypothetical reconstruction of the missionaries' thinking, but no guesswork is necessary about the emphasis steadily placed in this literature on the all-pervading character of Polynesian religion and thus on the organic unity of Polynesian life, for these form the presiding themes of all these writers. No conscientious Christian could allow the Tahitians' traditional family system to go on unaltered, says Ellis, for example, for "idolatry had exerted all its withering and deadly influence, not only over every moment of their earthly existence, but every department of life, destroying, by its debasing and unsocial dictates, every tender feeling, and all the enjoyments of domestic intercourse" (PR 1:221). The same principle applies to the islanders' cherished sports and pastimes. "With the ancient idolatry of the people, their music, their dances, and the whole circle of their amusements, had been so intimately blended, that the one could not survive the other. When the former was abolished, the latter were also discontinued" (PR 1:281). To abolish the syntactic principle which informs "every department of [Tahitian] life" causes the individual expressive elements of the system to break into meaningless fragments, into signifiers unable to mean any longer because their essential linkages with all the others have been undone, and thus to disappear. Boxing and wrestling exhibitions, beloved by the natives, "have ceased with that system of barbarism and cruelty with which they were associated, and by which they were supported" (PR 1:293). "It is astonishing to notice," says Ellis again, summing up the point he makes often, "how intimately their system of religion was interwoven with every pursuit of their lives. Their wars, their labours, and their amusements, were all under the control of their gods" (PR 1:301). In particular, "their government, in all its multiplied ramifications, was closely interwoven with their false system of religion, in its abstract theory, and in its practical details" (PR 2:341). "Religious rites were connected with almost every act of their lives" (PR 2:216). We need only set aside Ellis's comments on the falsity of Polynesian religion to make out the modernity of this line of anthropological thought, which crystallizes into a definite thesis the implications running throughout *Polynesian Researches*. Tahitian culture in Ellis's eyes is first and foremost a totalizing semiological system; every element of Tahitian life symbolizes one fundamental scheme of meaning in which the most diverse and insignificant-seeming ethnographic data prove to be "intimately interwoven." "We are dealing then with something more than a set of themes, more than institutional elements, more than institutions, more even than systems of institutions divisible into legal, economic, religious and other parts. We are concerned with 'wholes,' with systems in their entirety": Mauss's conclusion to his watershed study of primitive exchange-systems (*The Gift* [1925] 77) is exactly in line with Ellis's grasp of a society wholly articulated by the religious principle. Anthropological theorists may well be chagrined to see the conceptual foundations of their discipline so firmly and precociously set in place by a writer using this discourse not to prove the inviolability of primitive society but to rationalize the destruction of ancient cultures in the name of Evangelical piety.[33]

Ellis's idée fixe and its distinctive metaphor of interwoven fabric become commonplaces in subsequent missionary literature, the best of which is clearly inspired by this unlikely-seeming architect of modern thought. After their conversion to Christianity, the Rarotongans needed to adopt a new code of laws, says John Williams, "for as their civil polity was intimately interwoven with their sanguinary idolatry, when the one was subverted, the other perished in its ruins." "Their civil and judicial polity, and all their ancient usages, were interwoven with their superstitions; and . . . all these partook of the sanguinary character of the system in which they were embodied, and by which they were sanctioned" (*NME* 127, 140). Edward Shortland's important discussion of the system of taboo in New Zealand, where the transmission of dangerous "spiritual essence" through physical contact is called the "fundamental law" of a whole array of superstitions extending throughout Maori society, applies Ellis's principle with new analytic subtlety. Being aware of "the singular influence which the law of *tapu* has exerted on the domestic habits of this people" gives one, says Shortland, "a clue to the interpretation of many of [their] peculiar habits," linking intimately together, as he shows, such disparate-seeming spheres as family and political structures, eating practices, haircutting, and the theory of disease (*Traditions and Superstitions* 82, 81, 92). Ethnographic study is thus a process of *interpretation* of submerged (and typically arcane) meanings, Shortland declares, and is based on the presumption (or leads to the discovery) that all the practices of a society are finally coordinated, obedient to an all-pervading syntax. His awareness of what Lévi-Strauss calls "the system of interconnections among all aspects of social life" (*Structural Anthropology* 358), or, in other words, of the principle of culture, could not be more lucid. One can guess, indeed, that the great interest in taboo among early Polynesianists and then among theoretical anthropologists at large has to do with the way the magical transmission of *mana* formed a paradigm-metaphor for the transmission of unifying themes throughout the different departments of a culture.[34]

The thesis that the principles of evil superstition were expressed in every nook and cranny of Polynesian life worked in one fundamental sense against the Evangelical discourse which it was meant to confirm. It carried the distinct implication that collective life is determined not, after all, by "the mark of the beast" inherent in human nature and evinced in uncontrollable desire, but, rather, by structures of cultural productions such as religion and all its affiliated phenomena. The special aura of dread which surrounds the concept of "idolatry" in the texts of Ellis and his colleagues may partly originate in an awareness that to accept the notion that men collectively create themselves by sacralizing their own representations—the very notion which these writers themselves promulgate in their exegesis of Polynesian religion—is inevitably to destabilize the whole Evangelical scheme of thought. One sign of this subversive process having already begun is that the thesis of the hegemony of superstition in Polynesia soon began to lead even in missionary texts to broadening and less tendentious conceptions of cultural unity. This can be seen to happen in Ellis himself, partly on an implicit level hinted at by the sheer immense accumulation of his ethnographic data and the systematic and respectful character of his treatment of it, and at times explicitly. Consider, as an illustration of Lévi-Strauss's dictum that "the customs of a community . . . always have a particular style," Ellis's analysis of the extremely "ceremonious" quality that surprises the observer of the "uncivilized people" of Tahiti. "This peculiarity appears to have accompanied them to their temples, to have distinguished the homage and the service they rendered to their gods, to have marked their affairs of state, and the carriage of the people towards their rulers, to have pervaded the whole of their social intercourse, to have been mingled with their most ordinary avocations, and even their rude and diversified amusements" (*PR* 2:10). So powerful a concept of a dominant trait, genius, or stylistic principle presiding over every dimension of the life of a people and giving every custom a primary character of *expressivity* is hard to reconcile with the thesis of deranged primitive appetites. Its equivocal moral implications come forth most clearly, as one might expect, in Thomas Williams.

This author has the strongest possible awareness of the integral character of Fijian culture, and of the need always to interpret any customary practice not as an isolated datum but holistically, or, as we might say, linguistically, with reference to others. Hence, for example, his account of the intricate code governing the crucial institution of the *vasu*, "nephew" or "niece." "Vasus cannot be considered apart from the civil polity of the group, forming as they do one of its integral parts, and supplying the high-pressure power of Fijian despotism" (*FF* 27). So too with taboo, the influence of which, Williams says, corroborating Shortland, "is wondrously diffused," affecting the whole range of "things both great and small" (*FF* 197). We get a hint of the morally destabilizing potential of this line of thought in Williams's analysis of cannibalism, which he cautions against taking as evidence of disordered personal appetites or in any sense as an aberrant, perverse, or pathological practice for Fijians. Rather, it is a cultural phenomenon, and as such it is normal and sociologically positive, being integrally linked as it is to the whole configuration of Fijian life, which has silently been installed as the appropriate ground of value for interpretation of this kind. "Cannibalism among this people is one of their institutions; it is interwoven in the elements of society; it forms one of their pursuits, and is regarded by the mass as a refinement" (*FF* 175). "It is a startling but incontestable fact, that in Fiji there exists a general system of parricide, which ranks too, in all respects, as a social institution," says Williams (*FF* 158), informing his readers at the same time that aged parents in Fiji often request their children to strangle them (*FF* 158, 156–57). In such revelations as these, one seems to see Ellis's original apologia for missionary interventions turned dizzily inside-out, or at least potentially so. The claim that evil idolatry is all-pervasive and that Polynesian society must as a result be dismantled root and branch, seen from the slightly altered angle of vision induced by the experience of discovering the complex wholeness and rich expressiveness of "barbaric" languages, becomes the claim (scarcely recognized as such by Williams himself) that shocking social practices which are "interwoven in the elements of society" can scarcely be adjudged evil, but must be construed as normal and sustaining social institutions. For one thing, they are inseparably bound up with networks of other Fijian practices and cultural trends which excite not horror but admiration. The monstrous in Williams's eyes is merely a customary pattern of thought and expression, and "custom," as Shortland declares, "sanctions the greatest enormities" (*Traditions and Superstitions* 15; see also 213–14, 253).[35]

It would be overstating the case to claim that Thomas Williams comes as close as John Martin does to the kind of systematic moral and cognitive relativism that lies at the heart of the anthropological concept of culture; but clearly *Fiji and the Fijians* moves (from a radically opposed point of departure) in this direction, and if its author draws back from explicitly professing the theory that acts deemed fiendish crimes in our society may be normal, which is to say, morally positive, in another, he stops just at the threshold. Any contemporary reader would have been bound to feel and to be disturbed by the current of moral ambiguity flowing strongly through this book, and to be aware that the mythic figure of the savage awash in "unchecked passions" had by this point been decisively displaced in Wesleyan missionaries' program of discourse. What had displaced it was the concept of a profoundly unified way of life regulated even in its smallest details by ancient codes of meaning and value and immune for this reason to the charge of being "unnatural," just as Polynesian languages had proved immune to that of being uncouth or unintelligible. This is the conceptual shift through which Evangelical ethnography, which we have considered both as a system of fieldwork technique and as an emergent structure of theoretical propositions, makes its surprising contribution to modern modes of thought.

CHAPTER FOUR

MAYHEW'S COCKNEY
POLYNESIA

T his book portrays the idea of culture not as the outcome of a train of disinterested scientific reasoning but as a product and instrument of modern imagination—which is to say, as a tactic first and foremost in a broad revulsion from Wesleyan-style Victorian thinking, and particularly from the moral ideology which grounded itself in the fantasy-theme of unrestrained desire. As what was in fact a literary mechanism, a construction of emotively laden metaphors, purporting to give a scientific account of reality, the new idea had necessarily an equivocal status from the first; as we have seen, its logical difficulties became apparent even before it had properly articulated itself, making the possibility of attaining a coherent philosophical anthropology based upon it seem in the later nineteenth and early twentieth centuries to grow more remote the more plainly it appeared. Theorists of anthropology now respond to these ineradicable difficulties by portraying the defining concept of their field as a two-fold "fiction." In the phrase of Roy Wagner, on the one hand, ethnographers are understood to proceed inescapably through a self-reflexive "invention of culture": through projecting our own values and discursive categories upon exotic others in order to render their experience intelligible to us (see also Geertz, *Interpretation* 15–16).[1] On the other hand, a culture is definable as a (realistic) "fiction" because it consists of a body of symbolism that in effect invents a persuasive, coherent imaginative world and that expresses systems of meaning in elliptical or strategically encoded forms—and thus is properly, like a literary text, an object of interpretation. Such principles are foreign to most nineteenth-century social thinking, but they are profoundly explored in what may be the most significant ethnographic text of its age, Henry Mayhew's pioneering work of urban sociology, *London Labour and the London Poor* [*LL*] (1851–61).[2]

One consults this work not so much for a lucid formulation of the culture thesis—for Mayhew, who seems to work it out intuitively for

himself as he goes along, never states it in anything like clear propositional form—as for a prophetic demonstration of the problems it entails. It would scarcely be an exaggeration to say that Mayhew's overriding theme is his own heroic search for a methodology adequate to
the task of cultural depiction and analysis, or that his chief discovery
is the one to which so many later theorists have come as well: that the
discourse of systematic ethnography, however rhetorically potent it
may be, is subject to a malign logic which causes it to become more
problematical and incoherent the more fully it elaborates itself. To
read Mayhew attentively and sympathetically from a modern angle of
vision is to be made aware of all the issues embedded in the notion of
culture which sophisticated culturalists like Benedict, Evans-Pritchard, Lévi-Strauss, and Geertz frequently obscure and suppress as the
price of producing compact, efficient, aesthetically satisfying ethnographic literature. Compared to urbane writers like these, Mayhew at
first glance seems almost grotesquely uncouth and defective, and so
inarticulate on the plane of theoretical reflection as hardly to merit
close study.

The salient stylistic features of *London Labour* are its mind-bog-
gling profusion and density of ethnographic detail and its resultant
sense of uncontrollable expansiveness, features which both give this
text its gigantic power and at the same time, paradoxically, render it
next to unreadable. (To survey the secondary literature on Mayhew is
to discover that even specialist scholars seem rarely to have been able
to read him in extenso.) According to the theory of culture which can
be inferred from Mayhew's research, achieving a full, scientifically
valid representation of a given social world requires presenting the
most detailed direct personal testimony from many informants—from
what amounts to an almost limitless number of them. Only in this way
can one hope to register the full spectrum of available experience
within the culture as well as the nuances of feeling, of values, and of
characteristic patterns of utterance which for Mayhew form the essential traits of social identity. Only in this way, too, can one hope to
preserve authentic ethnographic data from the distortions of summary, generalization, abstraction, and impressionism which, as Dan
Sperber and other critics have argued, vitiate most ethnographic literature to greater or lesser degree. But a text obedient to such a demanding principle of authenticity is bound to become almost incom-
prehensibly vast in scale, as Mayhew's notoriously is, yet always to seem
to convict itself of falling short of completeness after all, and to take

CHAPTER FOUR

on at the same time an aspect of mere haphazard data-gathering that seems to contradict the scientific spirit in another way. "An accumulation of data . . . does not make a science," says Sperber (11).

These problems of method and of rhetoric are at the origin of the confusions and contradictions, the false starts and masses of incoherent-seeming information, the section headings out of synch with the text and other such surface blemishes, which are typical of *London Labour,* as critics have said. Overarching all local defects in Mayhew's text is the miscarriage of his original scheme (preserved for posterity only in the book's anomalous title) of carrying out a general survey of the trades of skilled and unskilled London labor. What was planned as a brief introductory section on the lowest, most culturally destitute, and most marginal of all groups of the poor, the homeless "street folk," expanded uncontrollably in his hands, taking on mammoth dimensions and at last submerging all other subjects. From this and from the other plain symptoms of malorganization which *London Labour* impenitently seems to thrust upon the reader's notice rather than to try to disguise, one might well conclude with Anne Humpherys that Mayhew, lacking any but the most ineffectual interest in sociological theory, had no more philosophical motive for his work than an ungovernable personal "mania" for collecting and classifying data, and thus finally was disabled as a social scientist by his "limitless curiosity" about the alien world of the poor (Humpherys, *Travels* 74, 68).[3] In a notable aside near the end of his last volume, Mayhew shows his own keen awareness of the compulsive-seeming and extravagant, anarchic character of his text, yet seeks to shield himself from the charge of being a victim of anomic boundlessness in research. The unmanageable problem for a would-be analyst of the modern urban underclass, he claims here, is the sheer amount of crucial but unknown information needing to be brought to light about the world of poverty:

> I would rather have pursued some more systematic plan in my inquiries; but in the present state of ignorance as to the general occupation of the poor, system is impossible. I am unable to generalise, not being acquainted with the particulars; for each day's investigation brings me incidentally into contact with a means of living utterly unknown among the well-fed portion of society. (*LL* 3:301)

The pathological character of his text, he asserts here, necessarily reproduces that of the social world he studies and belongs to. We shall return to this argument of Mayhew's below, merely noting for now how clearly it ties the arduous attempt to frame a "systematic plan" for ethnographic research—a theory of culture, in short—to motives of dissidence from the respectable Victorian mentality, which expresses its respectability among other ways by its utter oblivious-ness to the life of society's unfortunates.

Not only does his conception of ethnography generate extreme problems of textual coherence and readability, it also causes his dec-larations of scientific disinterestedness and objectivity to seem increas-ingly dubious, for *London Labour* proves to be a richly literary and imaginative production at every level, full of rhetorical heightening both on the author's part and on that of the street folk whose some-times lengthy statements he tirelessly reproduces. No text affords more vivid evidence than this one of the difficulty of excluding fictive processes from would-be scientific ethnography. So novelistic does Mayhew's "survey" often seem that he has inevitably been suspected (on almost no evidence) of doctoring his informants' statements, pre-sumably to give them an enhanced Dickensian flavor, of falsifying his image of street life by dwelling at disproportionate length on weird and picturesque individuals and occupations, and of gullibly report-ing made-up stories as fact.[4] Even his statistical tables—like the famous computation of the amount of horse dung dropped per day in the London streets (*LL* 2:194–95)—seem at times to spring from a strain of grotesque imagination and to reinforce one's sense that Mayhew's ethnography, rigorously veridical as it claims to be, deploys in fact a discourse of a peculiarly ambiguous and unstable kind.

These problematic aspects of *London Labour* will be probed in what follows. Ultimately they must be seen as the symptoms of Mayhew's powerful movement toward a fully ethnographic—which is to say, a fully interpretive—concept of culture; they exhibit in all their disrup-tive glory the contradictions which that equivocal concept necessarily entails. More immediately, they signal the strenuousness of the pro-cess which Mayhew enacts definitively, the displacement by the emerg-ing idea of culture of the idea or mythological image which we are tracking in its zigzag course through the annals of modern social thought: that of a state of unbounded passional desire.

The Anomie of the Urban "Savage"[5]

London Labour pointedly identifies itself with the still embryonic dis-cipline of anthropology. "Each civilized or settled tribe has generally some wandering horde intermingled with, and in a measure preying upon, it," Mayhew declares on his first page, citing J. C. Prichard and other ethnographic authorities and claiming that his study of the "nomadic tribe" of London's street folk will illustrate laws of primitive life and personality the world over.[6] It is understandable that scholars have given no more than passing notice to his claims to be a theoretical anthropologist,[7] since the proposition about the binary interrelations of the civilized and the primitive seems never significantly developed, despite a few references to it later on. Yet it bears upon the argument of *London Labour* in a fundamental way from the moment that Mayhew, confirming Wagner's thesis in almost scandalously clear form, engages his great inquiry by means of a sweeping, peremptory "invention of culture": that is, by stamping upon his subjects, the derelict street folk of Victorian London, the lineaments of a fabricated conception of his own. He does not invent the London poor out of whole cloth, however, but out of existing ethnographies of primitive peoples (themselves highly prejudicial, ideologically and textually saturated inventions to begin with). At least partly aware of his own originating maneuver, he is frank in suggesting that his image of the urban proletariat is calqued upon that of "many savage tribes" (*LL* 1:43), but the tantalizing suggestion is hard to assess or verify, since he is unspecific almost to the point of mystification about his ethnographic references. Having just surveyed the early ethnographic literature of Polynesia, we can undoubtedly retrieve some of the most significant of these, and in the process get a vivid example of how empirical reality constitutes itself for early sociology in the form of that "mobile army of metaphors" which Nietzsche says passes for truth in any age.

Polynesianist literature, as we saw, founds itself upon the axiom that the unconverted South Sea islanders lived in a state of limitless desire, knowing no rule but that of "the unbridled influence of their passions" and of "unrestrained indulgence and excess"; thus they naturally were filled with "enmity to the moral restraints" of Christian religion and could be counted upon to rebel against any "restraint . . . imposed upon their evil propensities" (Ellis 1:37; 2:359, 315, 462). These stereotyped formulas, through which the Evangelical mind channeled its phobic aversion to the "primitive" (and its pride in its own moral power), were reiterated almost incessantly in the missionary narratives which chiefly revealed Pacific societies to nineteenth-century Europeans, and they pass with surprising directness into

Mayhew's sociology. His point of departure and the theme to which everything in his work directly or indirectly refers is the idea that the homeless "nomads" of London are monsters of anomie.

Thus he claims to have discovered and very often notes in the early sections of his study "how perfectly unrestrained are the passions and appetites of [costermonger] youths" (*LL* 1:39). This whole category of the London poor, "unused to the least moral and prudential restraint" (*LL* 1:55), is ruled, he declares with monotonous insistency, by "habits of life in which passion is the sole rule of action, and where every appetite of our animal nature is indulged in without the least restraint" (*LL* 1:43). The costers (street vendors of fruit, fish, and vegetables) have "nothing but their appetites, instincts, and passions to move them" (*LL* 1:213); a man of this class is driven, Mayhew reports more specifically, "by his passion for stupefying herbs and roots, and, when possible, for intoxicating fermented liquors— . . . by an immoderate love of gaming," and much worse besides (*LL* 1:2). All this language, suffused as it is with Wesleyan-style injunction, obviously amounts as much to a prefabricated program of rhetoric as it does to a record of empirical observation. Giving a racialist cast to this set of "findings," Mayhew theorizes at various points that the costers' "indomitable . . . hatred of the least restraint or controul" (*LL* 1:214), and thus their "impatience of steady labour" (*LL* 3:369), express the innately "restless and volatile disposition" (*LL* 3:373), the erratic, wandering propensities, natural to nomadic peoples. In this he picks up the theory aired twenty-five years earlier by William Ellis, who complained that even after much indoctrination in the work ethic, his Tahitian clients retained "their impatience of control" and their debilitating devotion to their "fugitive and unsettled mode of life" (Ellis 1:474). Nomadism directly expresses a state of anomic desire, in other words.

Evangelical observers dwelt with particular emphasis upon the "notorious licentiousness" of the Polynesians (Ellis 2:446), referring endlessly to their love of "very obscene songs" (Brown 36), their "unsightly gesticulations and lascivious songs" (J. Williams 60). Unequipped as these writers were to view sympathetically a form of religion based on fertility worship, or even to identify it for what it was, they took Polynesians to be lewd and profligate, subject to "all the evils of the most licentious sensuality" (Thomas Williams 115). Edward Shortland, for example, speaks in horror and bewilderment of the "disgustingly lascivious" dances performed at the New Zealanders' funeral rites (*Traditions and Superstitions* 123–27). "The words of the women's song may not be translated," says Thomas Williams, describing a victory celebration in Fiji. "Nor are the obscene gestures of their dance . . . fit to be described" (*FF* 42–43). The worst of all these infamous practices were the Tahitian festivals presided over by the itinerant aristocratic *Areoi* society, a "dissipated and wandering fraternity . . . addicted to every kind of licentiousness" (Ellis 1:320, 321), reports of which, as Malthus said as early as 1803, "have justly occasioned so much surprise among civilized nations" (*EP* 50). Ellis describes the "often obscene exhibitions" of this society, which included, let us note for future reference, a range of theatrical and quasi-theatrical performances such as ballad-singing, oratorical prologues, dancing, wrestling shows, and satirical drama; invoking the common turn of phrase, however, he declares that exact details of the *Areois'* spectacles could not be reported "without violence to every feeling of propriety" (Ellis 1:319, 311).

Again, this whole tendentious discourse recurs in Mayhew, almost unaltered in its apparently direct transposition from the South Seas to the East End. An especially clear instance of transposition would be his long report on the pornographic theaters called the "penny gaffs," which he portrays as a central institution of the London poor and where, as he declares in the formulaic phrase, one witnesses "the unrestrained indulgence of the most corrupt appetites of our nature" (*LL* 1:40). Replicating ancient Polynesia as seen through missionaries' eyes, the penny gaffs offer programs of shockingly smutty songs and dances—"the smuttier the better," says one coster lad (*LL* 1:39)—as the basis of the entertainment, and in fact a "love of libidinous dances" is said by Mayhew to be one of the chief passions of the London poor (*LL* 1:2). He then describes at length a performance climaxed, just as a Polynesian funeral was, by a copulatory dance in which "the most disgusting attitudes were struck, the most immoral acts represented" (*LL* 1:42), producing a frenzied response in the audience: "lads jumping on girls' shoulders, and girls laughing hysterically from being tickled by the youths behind them, every one shouting and jumping, presented a mad scene of frightful enjoyment," reports the appalled ethnologist (*LL* 1:41). He is even more preoccupied by the wickedness of the "low" lodging houses, virtual brothels where sexual vice, he declares, goes uncontrolled, though the details of the "orgies" and the "gross profligacy" that occur in these places are "too gross to be more than alluded to" (*LL* 1:254).

In giving such a heavy stress to the supposedly ungoverned sexual and other appetites of the street folk, Mayhew picks up the broad trends of anthropological thinking that issued in Victorian theories of "primeval promiscuity," the state of "group marriage" imagined to prevail in rudimentary societies. Among such lovers of "riot and confusion" as the costers, the vagrants, or the chimney sweepers, he tells us, for example, "there is a promiscuous intercourse continually going on" (*LL* 2:370), while in the lodging houses, "boys and girls are all huddled promiscuously together" (*LL* 1:412), like an amazing modern-day "survival" of the primitive pre-social horde theorized by writers such as Bachofen, Morgan, Tylor, Lubbock, and McLennan.[8] But specifically Polynesian echoes continue to be evident in Mayhew's exposition, as, notably, in his treatment of the "caste" (*LL* 1:249) that chiefly frequents the lodging houses, "the pattering fraternity"—the "vagrant fraternity" of street orators and mountebanks of every sort, including "jugglers, showmen, clowns, and fortune-tellers," all of them, Mayhew says, "much given to intemperance" and every other sort of vice (*LL* 1:245, 250, 309). The men of this "fraternity," who consider themselves "the haristocracy of the streets" (*LL* 1:213), are certified by Mayhew to be the most depraved of all the street folk, "demoralised to the last degree," adepts in "horrid, extravagant, and far-fetched" immorality (*LL* 1:217). His redaction of the London patterers picks up almost to the smallest detail, it will be seen, the Polynesianists' accounts of the "dissipated and wandering fraternity" of the Tahitian *Areois*.

Likenesses only slightly less striking multiply between Mayhew's street folk and the passionate "savages" of early Polynesian ethnographies. The London poor are not alleged by Mayhew to practice the infanticide and cannibalism that formed in the eyes of Europeans the most horrific Polynesian customs of all, but he uses an audacious literary device to insinuate even these themes into *London Labour.* This device is an increasingly distinct metaphorical link between the street folk and an emblematic animal often invoked in this text in a way that dramatizes almost too plainly for comfort the psychic urgency of early sociological investigation: the London brown rat. The rat hordes which "prey upon the garbage in the common sewers" (*LL* 1:450), devouring, as Mayhew says, "a great quantity of sewer filth and rubbish" (*LL* 3:19), give an easily interpreted allegorical form to the proletarian crowds who feast avidly on the "filth" of the smutty humor at the penny gaffs, for example (*LL* 1:40). "This destructive animal is continually under the *furor* of animal love," he says, declaring that the exponential population increase caused by the rat's insane sexual drive is checked only by another "insatiable appetite, that impels them to destroy and devour each other." The male rat in particular is said to be driven by "an insatiable thirst for the blood of its own offspring" (*LL* 3:3–4). Thus the cannibalism and infanticide practiced with fiendish avidity in Polynesia, as early ethnographers reported, have their London equivalents also, even though the human street folk are guilty of these crimes only by metaphorical association. Rats inscribe vividly in Mayhew's text the fundamental Wesleyan figure of fallen man as insatiably lustful beast and as slave of "our animal nature": the rat in effect is original sin incarnate.

Since the subject here is the deployment of metaphorical programs—habits of discourse—in the guise of scientific observation, we can perhaps follow the rat motif in *London Labour* a step further. Its importance for Mayhew's argument is registered with phantasmagoric clarity in a passage at the opening of volume 3, where he evokes the menace of this lust-ridden animal in apocalyptic Malthusian terms. "If . . . rats were suffered to multiply without the restraint of the most powerful and positive natural checks," he asserts here, "the whole surface of the earth in a very few years would be rendered a barren and hideous waste, covered with myriads of famished grey rats, against which man himself would contend in vain" (*LL* 3:4). Contemporary readers, preyed on by deep-running fears of "the dangerous classes," could hardly have missed the sociological import of this imagery;[9] even so, it is expounded at the conclusion of the volume, where Mayhew, yielding to caste phobias which, though they obviously catalyze his imagination, he usually keeps in check, declares that there exists in England a savage, lice-infested criminal army of professional vagrants. These vagabonds carry typhoid from one workhouse to another and, through this and other forms of contagion, truly endanger civilized society. "There are, then, no less than 100,000 individuals of the lowest, the filthiest, and most demoralised classes, continually wandering through the country; in other words, there is a stream of vice and disease—a tide of iniquity and fever, continually flowing from town to town, from one end of the land to the other" (*LL* 3:397). The themes of the proletarian nomad and the filthy horde of rats fuse here with another of Mayhew's leading themes, the polluted river, into a single hyperbolic image which itself crystallizes, it seems likely, around yet a further reminiscence of the classic accounts of the *Areoi* society of Tahiti. According to William Ellis, members of this depraved infanticidal cult "spent their days in travelling from island to island, and from one district to another, exhibiting their pantomimes, and spreading a moral contagion throughout society." To support themselves, they plundered the districts through which they passed, leaving them afterwards, like the earth's surface infested by rats, "a scene of desolation and ruin" (Ellis 1:316, 319). Whether or not Mayhew's horde of ratlike criminal vagrants contains a specific reference to Ellis's Tahitians, it is evident that the two ethnographers systematically construct their subjects in terms of just the same repertoire of stereotypical literary imagery, and that the books of both writers are driven to a large extent by the same fantasy of extravagant forces of desire somehow breaking free of all structure, all restraint.

In invoking and giving so sensationalistic a character to this array of themes, Mayhew thus grounds his sociology deeply in the distinctive tropes of Victorian Evangelical discourse (tropes used here as elsewhere as vehicles of class anxieties). Yet his instinct for close systemic analysis coupled with his own hostility towards respectable Victorian society leads him to carry out at last a radical revision of the Wesleyan discourse which sets his project in motion. The result is a text marked by deep contradictions between much of its overt rhetoric and the thinking which in fact propels its great program of social investigation.

As the first stage of this process of revision, Mayhew offers an increasingly complex account of the mental state of the street folk, who are infested, he comes to believe, not only with the energy of pathologically expansive libido, but with a subtler, almost more debilitating disorder, a compulsive malaise and a state of persistent disorientation. To highlight this point is to locate very specifically in this text the transition from the Evangelical story of boundlessly active "animal" desires to its successor, the Durkheimian story of anomie.

The urban "nomad," Mayhew reports, "has naturally an aversion to any regular occupation, and becomes erratic, wandering from this thing to that, without any settled or determined object" (*LL* 3:368). We have seen that this state of anomic irresoluteness, earlier diagnosed by J. C. Prichard in just the same language under the heading of "moral insanity" and later named by Hardy "the modern vice of unrest" (*Jude the Obscure* 87), has its own long (and ambivalent) history in modern discourse. The word *restlessness* holds in fact a crucial place in Mayhew's lexicon, as when he speaks of "that restlessness of spirit which is so marked a characteristic" of the patterers (*LL* 1:264), or of a certain laborer as "afflicted with the restlessness of the tribe" of street people (*LL* 1:464). Such phrases indicate the powerful thematic confluence of *London Labour* with modernist fiction and modernist literature at large: Mayhew studies so intensively the psychic condition of his obscure and marginal street folk, just as Dostoyevsky studies his "underground man" (who in many respects closely resembles them), as a figuring of the characteristic features of morbidly agitated modern sensibility itself. To highlight the technical, diagnostic significance of his special term for this state, he at times italicizes it, as he does in reporting a statement from a "scurf" scavenger: "I don't know just what made me come back, *but I was restless*" (*LL* 2:237; see also 2:448, 501; 3:153, 372, 373, 428.). In laying so much stress on this word as the sign of a chronic condition of modern people, Mayhew prefigures Bagehot's theory that moderns are preyed upon by "a mere love of activity" pathologically in excess of real needs. But where does "restlessness" originate, and what are its links to the state of unappeasable, morbidly inflamed desire, the addiction to sex, drink, violence, and other vices that he professes to see among the homeless poor?

Making this link intelligible involves Mayhew in several different lines of analysis. It involves him, for one thing, in drawing a crucial distinction—more problematic than he says—between different *stages* of desire, or, more exactly, between what he terms "appetite," a blind bodily drive, and what he technically terms "desire," a construct of social and cultural life (*LL* 3:301). *London Labour* marks out its special ethnographic territory by fixing rigorously upon existence lived below the apparent threshold of "desire": upon the lives, that is, of a class of people plunged into such degrading destitution and afflicted by such intensity of bodily distress—by what Mayhew calls "the wear and tear of poverty and privation" (*LL* 1:395)—that meaningful social experience seems virtually denied to them. His original presumption is that in entering the dismal world of the poorest of the poor, one enters the world of sheer primitive appetite. However, by considering the frontier of "appetite" and "desire" not as a theoretical abstraction but as a field of lived experience, he uncovers among the London poor a wealth of provocative material that the original distinction seems inadequate to explain. This material increasingly controls the course of his research, bringing increasing pressure to bear upon its fundamental assumptions and upon the rhetorical strategy they produce, the subsuming of the London street folk into stock imagery of the Polynesian "savage."

Degenerationism

The life of appetite among his urban South Sea "nomads" splits, Mayhew finds on closer inspection, into two apparently contradictory syndromes: what Ruth Benedict would term "Dionysian" licentiousness and its opposite, a nearly complete *collapse* of libido. Elaborately documenting the latter state, he stresses the almost cretinous blankness and stupidity characteristic of many of the nomadic poor, especially among the most deeply degraded: the bone-grubbers, the mudlarks, the "pure"-finders (scavengers of dog manure), the nightmen, the "lumpers." Among these contemporary urban equivalents of Victor of Aveyron or of Malthus's torpid primeval savage, desire seems to all intents and purposes nonexistent, and appetite itself reduced to a craving for the food and warmth necessary for mere organic survival. Such a state risks being an impossible literary subject precisely because it is so undifferentiated, so primitive, and so urgently monotonous. But Mayhew, who made it his calling to redeem from oblivion materials unsuitable in various ways for literary representation (being too offensive or too trivial-seeming), is not deterred by this risk from concentrating on that fathoms-deep level of London society inhabited by people whose harsh experience appears to have put most of their faculties out of commission.

His observation that "the sense of smell is actually dead" in many outdoor laborers (*LL* 1:132) is only a mild example of the theme. A fuller image (to cite only one), where the range of impaired faculties is much broader, is that of one coster lad "with a face utterly vacant. His two heavy lead-coloured eyes stared unmeaningly at me, and . . . he did not exhibit the slightest trace of feeling. He sank into his seat heavily and of a heap, and when once settled down he remained motionless, with his mouth open and his hands on his knees—almost as if paralyzed" (*LL* 1:39; see also 2:136). We could not well be further from the exhilaration which latter-day polemical writers have sometimes associated with the experience of emancipation from social structure and with "the dissolving of fixed identities." The contrast between this state of vacancy and inertia, in any case, and that of anarchic libido is evident, but it is crucial to Mayhew's argument that they be recognized as complementary, not contradictory images; indeed, their strongly polarized and absolute quality is enough to tell us at once that they cling together as the two aspects of a single fictive or mythic idea. This idea is the one that presides over the several branches of nineteenth-century "degenerationism," the adverse counterpart of the idea of evolutionary progress which formed part of the schizophrenic official ideology of the age. According to degenerationist theory, as touched on in chapter 1 above, human society has in many regions followed its natural tendency by progressively deteriorating from an original higher stage of civilization, its cultural repertoire becoming more meager and its moral consciousness more coarse and brutish.[10] "All savages are the degenerated remnants of more civilised races," declares in 1855 the leading advocate of this doctrine, Richard Whatley, Archbishop of Dublin (Whatley 22), and he quotes almost verbatim (Whatley 11) a famous formula originally stated, it would appear, by his disciple W. Cooke Taylor in *Natural History of Society*. "No savage nation," Taylor asserted, "ever emerged from barbarism by its own unaided exertions; . . . the natural tendency of tribes in such a condition is to grow worse instead of better" (Taylor 1:309; see also 1:197).[11] This long-influential trend of thought, resonant with original-sin theology and Protestant moral judgment as it is, expresses itself plainly in the distinctive literary feature of *London Labour*, Mayhew's immense constellation of imagery of human beings sinking down into lower social realms and into degenerate states of character, often seeming in the process to undergo a kind of evolutionary regression.

Giving the theme of degeneration maximum emphasis, Mayhew employs as one of his most prominent motifs (one that plays a correspondingly large role in the Victorian novel as well) the narrative of the Fall from comfort and respectability to the destitution and "sheer necessity" (*LL* 1:103), the "fatigue and despair" (*LL* 2:136), of street life. Literally scores of refined gentlewomen, classical scholars, and clergymen sunk to the lowest social depths figure among his informants.[12] One of these is a squalid old woman "resembling a bundle of rags and filth" who had been the daughter of a rich dairy farmer and had fallen step by step to the lowest echelon of all, that of the scavenger of dog manure ("pure"). "She was characterized," says Mayhew, "by all that dull and hardened stupidity of manner which I have noticed in the class" (*LL* 2:144). At times he states the lessons which he derives from such cases in propositional terms which echo the formulas of Taylor and Whatley, citing the depraved "patterers" in particular as giving clear evidence of "a propensity to lapse from a civilized into a nomad life" and observing that "ethnology teaches us, that whereas many abandon the habits of civilized life to adopt those of a nomadic state of existence, but few of the wandering tribes give up vagabondising and betake themselves to settled occupations" (*LL* 1:213–14). He spares no labor in correlating the degenerate state of the London poor with its various outward symptoms (immorality, "restlessness," mental vacancy) and its practical causes.[13] At the same time, *London Labour* is impelled by an urge to gain a deeper understanding of this state, at once more experiential and more philosophical, than the citing of half-baked theories or the notation of symptoms and causes can afford. It is at this point in his argument that Mayhew takes his decisive step toward an eventual recantation of degenerationist anthropology and toward forming—in a negative reflex, as it were—the idea of culture "in its wide ethnographic sense."

One locus of this development is his inquiry into the many different commodities which London "nomads" peddle in the streets. He studies the trade in each one in the most detailed way in order nominally to demonstrate how the item in question comes to acquire its particular quotient of economic value. But what this line of analysis serves chiefly to reveal, rather than a process of the creation of value, is one by which values of all kinds in the world of the homeless poor are negated. It is not just that money values are next to nil, barely adequate to sustain life, in this hand-to-mouth world, but that the symbolic and affective values which normally accrue around material things and give them their power to express a collective mentality turn out to be radically depleted as well. Mayhew's nomadic street folk experience as a result a condition equivalent in important respects to an earlier vision of a state of cultural nullity, the Malthusian nightmare of a "general glut" of commodities whose value has somehow, from a broad entropic failure of desire, dissipated below the level necessary for the maintenance of coherent structures.

With rare exceptions, the items traded by Mayhew's informants are (from their own point of view) culturally sterile, void of any significance or capacity to activate desire beyond the pittance of money they will fetch. The woodcut of one of his most famous subjects, "the crippled street-seller of nutmeg-graters," shows this catastrophically afflicted man hung about with his stock of graters and funnels, but his account of himself displays no awareness that the item upon which his life depends is one thing rather than another (*LL* 1:329–33); if he knows what nutmeg is or how the graters work, his statement gives no sign of it, and he portrays his previous career as an undifferentiated sequence of commodities. "I sold tin-ware, and brass-work, and candlesticks, and fire-irons, and all old furniture, and gown-prints as well," he reports. "[Later on,] I sold baking-dishes, Dutch ovens, roasting-jacks, skewers and gridirons, teapots, and saucepans, and combs. I used to exchange sometimes for old clothes" (*LL* 1:331–32). This passage resembles various others in *London Labour* where Mayhew unfolds catalogues of commodities listed pell-mell, as though in great heaps, and where the near-illegibility of the prose makes the point about the unraveling at this level of Victorian society of the kind of semiological codes that normally bind cultural fabric together. Hence, for example, the surreal account in volume 1 of the "miscellaneous" and "heterogenous" merchandise displayed in "swag-shops": "dirks . . . a mess of steel pens . . . and of black-lead pencils, pipe-heads, cigar-cases, snuff-boxes, razors, shaving-brushes, letter-stamps, metal tea-pots, metal teaspoons, glass globes with artificial flowers in the feathery part, fans, side-combs, glass pen-holders, and pot figures (caricatures) of Louis Philippe, carrying a very red umbrella, Marshal Haynau, with some instrument of torture in his hand," and so on (*LL* 1:334). In this allegorical tableau, we seem to see all of culture—literature, art, domestic comfort, ornament—decomposing antically before our eyes into a jumble of alien and alienating objects, which themselves appear to be rapidly decaying into mere rubbish. The same theme is sardonically accented and keyed distinctly to the idea of a degeneration of *meaning* in the statement of the street-buyer of waste paper, who evokes for Mayhew the spectacle of the decomposition of world literature into so much "waste": "I've had Bibles—the backs are taken off in the waste trade, or it wouldn't be fair weight. . . . I've dealt in tragedies and comedies, old and new, cut and uncut—they're best uncut, for you can make them into sheets then—and farces, and books of the opera. I've had scientific and medical works of every possible kind, and histories, and travels, and lives, and memoirs. . . . Poetry, ay, many a hundred weight" (*LL* 2:113). *London Labour* contains numerous other examples of this distinctive trope in which welters of commodities are equated with mere meaningless rubbish. The world intimated in this concerted absurdist imagery is more than anything else one of semiological entropy, in which cultural artifacts lose their power to represent social values, become inarticulate, and sink in macabre fashion to the level of significance of "rags, broken metal, bottles, glass, and bones" (*LL* 2:104).[14]

Mayhew thus brings insistently before us the idea of the degeneration of social order into a crazily unstructured state which value and meaning have deserted, a state of anticulture lower and more appalling than "savagery" itself. One face of this idea is the demented euphoria of the "penny gaff"; the complementary one is the narcoleptic imagery of a passage like the one describing tribal life in Church-lane, Bloomsbury, where the intrepid ethnographer has gone in search of information concerning the street sale of salt:

> The street literally swarmed with human beings—young and old, men and women, boys and girls, wandering about amidst all kinds of discordant sounds. The footpaths on both sides of the narrow street were occupied here and there by groups of men and boys, some sitting on the flags and others leaning against the wall, while their feet, in most instances bare, dabbled in the black channel alongside the kerb, which being disturbed sent up a sickening stench. Some of these groups were playing cards for money, which lay on the ground near them. Men and women at intervals lay stretched out in sleep on the pathway; over these the passengers were obliged to jump; in some instances they stood on their backs as they stepped over them, and then the sleeper languidly raised his head, growled out a drowsy oath, and slept again. Three or four women, with bloated countenances, blood-shot eyes, and the veins of their necks swollen and distended till they resembled strong cords, staggered about violently quarrelling at the top of their drunken voices. (*LL* 2:90)

Archbishop Whatley himself, if he read Mayhew, must have been startled by the intensity of his special form of "degenerationism," a form that does not reassuringly isolate this process in primitive tribal societies of other hemispheres, but detects it raging out of control like a cholera epidemic in the midst of Victorian London. He would quickly have recognized, in any case, that the powerful myth of degeneration, at once biblical, anthropological, and Malthusian, drives all the elaborate empiricism deployed in *London Labour,* and anchors this work profoundly in the mentality of its age.

The evil process of de-signification is charged in *London Labour* with strong emotional overtones, but they are largely projected onto a closely adjacent array of imagery, that of organic decomposition and of every possible form of intensely polluting filth. It would lead us deep into the pathologies of the Victorian middle-class mind if we could thoroughly analyze Mayhew's almost obsessive fixity upon imagery of slime, dirt, decay, garbage, noxious effluvia, and especially, the summation of all these themes, human and animal bodily wastes. We would need in particular to try to account for the mingling of horror with a kind of fascinated delectation; the latter is evident, for example, in Mayhew's detailed inspections of maggots, which swarm in "the dead and putrid flesh" of horses (*LL* 2:8) and excite "disgust and nausea" when one observes them "wallowing . . . in the midst of a mass of excrement" (*LL* 3:24). Undoubtedly these materials reflect in the first instance the ambiguous obsession with contaminating moral "filth" which is a key feature of Evangelical sensibility (and was vividly displayed, as we saw, in the writings of mission ethnographers). But Mayhew imparts to them some sharply revised rhetorical values which mark in fact a growing revulsion from the cultural scapegoating that forms the principal motive of Wesleyan and Whatleyan anthropology.

His fixation on "sewer filth" (*LL* 3:19), "'offal,' or 'refuse,' or 'waste'" (*LL* 2:7) is thus a function, for one thing, of a determination to testify polemically to the horrors of the everyday experience of the poor. Some aspects of this experience may be "too gross to be more than alluded to," but he makes it his vocation as a writer and as a social scientist to allude to them none the less in startling detail, consciously running the risk as he does so of making his text too ugly, distressing, and scandalous to be read. (We can gauge something of this risk by means of a comparison with Dickens's portrayals of the same materials, which alongside *London Labour* usually seem euphemistic and almost sentimentalized.) We see Mayhew's wretched outcasts on many occasions eating garbage in the streets (*LL* 1:339, 340, 356; 2:146, 334, 464; 3:419), imagery which fuses shockingly with that of the maggots, rats, and other garbage-eating vermin that figure so prominently in the book.[15] And the environment the street folk inhabit is consistently shown as pervaded by filth and pestilential odors from which middle-class eyes and nostrils recoil uncontrollably. This is the environment epitomized in the lodging houses, places of "dilapidation, filth, and noisomeness" where the only toilet is a bucket in the middle of the room (*LL* 1:252), or in the "casual wards" of the workhouses, where one sees young girls so infested with lice that their heads look "as if they were full of caraway seeds—vermin, sir—shocking!" (*LL* 3:395): "No one can imagine, but those who have gone through it, the horror of a casual ward of a union; what with the filth, the vermin, the stench, the heat, and the noise of the place, it is intolerable" (*LL* 3:402). The culmination of these themes comes in a tableau of the public cesspool basins of Paris, where naked men are seen swimming in vast rat-infested lakes of urine, scavenging for rotten fish dumped by market inspectors (*LL* 2:441). Degeneration and cultural annihilation can hardly take more extreme form than this.

The rotten refuse that obsesses Mayhew stands then as objective correlative for the sickening moral rottenness of the professedly Christian and philanthropic society which allows such conditions to exist in its midst, and it serves the rhetorical function in his text of affronting as harshly as possible the codes of genteel refinement that he saw to play a key role in maintaining Victorian structures of neglect and exploitation. In this respect, as in many another modernist text, *London Labour* draws on imagery of dirty obscenity as a source of liberating or cleansing power. Mayhew moves beyond his starting-point in the mythology of conventional Victorian anthropology and social theory no less scandalously by expounding in a new way the connection between the decay of value-bearing symbolism (which, along with many other forms of decay, holds such broad sway in the world of the poor as he represents it) and the pathological trends of behavior typical of London's derelict population. His analysis of this relation implies a new intellectual structure for the study of human culture and generates, practically speaking, a precociously modernistic mode of ethnography alongside which most of the work of the early Polynesianists (with which it otherwise has so much in common) looks old-fashioned. His insight is that the wild excesses of appetite and desire that mark the life of the urban poor need to be reinterpreted not as signs of "depraved propensities" but as symptoms of a desperate collective attempt somehow to recapture value in a set of circumstances where value seems preyed upon by a "natural tendency" to deteriorate, and where as a result the hunger for it seems unable to express itself except in a radically paradoxical language of nihilism and "moral insanity." This conception of the active forms of street life as a fierce, hazardous, self-contradictory striving *to invent cultural value almost out of nothing* becomes Mayhew's paramount theme, though it is always to some degree a cryptic one. The idea of culture which gradually takes shape in this text thus is predicated at every point upon a very elaborately articulated idea of socioexistential crisis: culture for Mayhew—

at least at the "primitive" level represented by the London poor—is an organized struggle of consciousness against its antithetical principle, the degeneration of meaning.

We need in what follows to illustrate Mayhew's thesis regarding "the invention of culture" in specific terms. However, there is no way to isolate this strand of argument in *London Labour* from the complementary one centering upon the crisis of the practice of ethnography itself and upon the paradoxes inherent in the production of a new vein of ethnographic subjectivity. To this dimension of the argument we need now to return.

Basketry and the Rhetoric of Microscopic Facts

The picture Mayhew constructs of the degraded London poor, showing them partly driven by an animalistic "furor" of desire and partly sunk in helpless vacancy and numbness, is a severely unstable one for several reasons, but chiefly because both classes of phenomena so strongly imply a cultural void—and thus the incapacity of sociological study to tell us anything about them. To suppose on the one hand that the poor have "nothing but their appetites, instincts, and passions to move them" both renders them morally unsuitable (possibly even dangerously contaminating) subjects for intimate study and at the same time denies the possibility that their social life might possess the kind of meaningful structure that an ethnographer could investigate in a systematic way. At the start of his expedition into the interior of "the undiscovered country of the poor" (*LL* 1:xv), Mayhew imagines the homeless, irreligious street folk to compose not a society at all but an anarchic "horde," a vortex of disconnected and therefore unregulated individuals. "The only thoughts that trouble [lustful young costermongers]," he says, "are for their girls, their eating and their gambling—beyond the love of self they have no tie that binds them to existence" (*LL* 1:39). This state of amorphousness and personal disconnectedness seems to offer no possible foothold for sociological analysis. And what kind of society could exist among the likes of the somnambulistic bone-grubbers or the denizens of Church-lane? Like the missionary ethnographers, though for somewhat different reasons, Mayhew seems to have embarked on a self-contradictory project.

We can gauge his sense of a methodological crisis in his own text by the energy with which he seizes upon the one principle of structure that seems potentially able to give intelligible shape to the social world of the "nomadic" poor: that of the economic system. This is the basis of his great taxonomy of the poor, whom he classifies primarily by occupation—which is to say, by the commodities in which each group trades: foods, manufactured goods, "found" articles, entertainment. Surveying the array of street occupations in exhaustively detailed fashion, Mayhew reveals that each item of street commerce has its own highly specialized mode of sale—its own corresponding social institution, so to speak. It may be a makeshift expedient, but it is none the less a brilliantly original and a richly productive one to bring so marginal a realm of commerce as that of the despised street "nomads" under the aegis of political economy and to treat transactions involving economic values on what is often an infinitesimally small scale (the resale of the few lumps of coal which a "mudlark" may be able to scrounge up from the river muck at low tide, for example) as elements of a definite system of institutional relations. One effect of this move is that of seeing the usual index of value and significance in political economy—that is, the quantitative index, measured by the amount of wealth involved in a given market—sharply displaced. The result of this legitimation of supposedly valueless people and activities is to render the "horde" of street folk representable as a complicated structure of occupational categories and, in place of phantasmagoric imagery of unbounded passions, to cause to emerge in the portrayal of the activities of the London underclass a new aspect of regularity and normalcy. Mayhew's mammoth tables of street commodities are in fact tables of a well-established social organization.

Given the pervasive incoherence of *London Labour,* it is not self-evident that this strategy of analysis ever enables him to gather the multitudinous phenomena of street life into anything like a "complex whole." We saw that he himself ascribed the perpetual breakdown of "system" in his text to the proliferation of raw new data which his researches among the poor produced. One might say that he registers most broadly the dubious character of all schemes of verbal representation aspiring to impose the semblance of simplicity and logical order upon the avalanche of sociocultural phenomena which comprises any society—or, rather, to impose upon the reader the comforting sense of having intellectually mastered reality. Impositions of this kind carry heavy political significance, Mayhew saw lucidly, in the case of a society organized, as Victorian Britain was, around a system of class divisions, zones of strategic social unawareness, and large-scale institutions of social engineering such as the workhouse system. (The same principles apply just as fully, of course, to ethnographic literature associated with cases of colonial usurpation of "primitive" societies in faraway lands.) These are topics that deserve much elaboration, but if our goal is chiefly to situate Mayhew's work in reference to the history of the ethnographic concept of culture, the immediate point is to observe how clearly the organizational disarray of *London Labour* exemplifies that intellectually chaotic period which according to Fleck and Kuhn always precedes the emergence of a new scientific "fact." In such a period, data (generated by ideas which have yet to be cogently stated) seem to overflow the conceptual frameworks available for classifying them. This is what seems to occur in the work of such founders of modern anthropological method as Boas and Malinowski, who have long been criticized, as we noted, for a supposed addiction to that "obsessive inclusion of data . . . [which] may be seen as a desire to unmake as well as to make a whole" (Clifford, "Ethnographic Self-Fashioning" 152), to "thick description" carried to the point at which it becomes "taxonomic description for its own sake, without a redeeming point or argument" (Marcus 188). So when Ruth Glass, for example, declares of Mayhew's work that "there is no theme" in it, and that it mostly contains mere "description without selection and analysis" (Glass 43), she associates him with a chronic difficulty of writers in his field. We might say that "culture" is the name invented to stand for the missing sense of thematic order in early ethnographic texts.

Formulas like Glass's may, however, obscure the crucial point—crucial to a reinterpretation of Mayhew, at all events—that would-be exhaustive sociological description does *not* occur in a spontaneous way merely as the consequence of the absence of a guiding theory. Quite the contrary, it represents a highly specialized style of examining the world and one which is scarcely intelligible except by reference to a particular philosophical and scientific conception of social life—the conception which after 1871 or so defines itself as the theory of "culture." This is why Mayhew's is such a significant text for the history of ethnographic imagination. The style of expository discourse in his work is fully enough formed to remind us consistently of sophisticated twentieth-century anthropology, which often declares its allegiance to the "exhaustive survey of detailed examples" (Malinowski, *Argonauts* 17) and to a "microscopic" method devoted to "exceedingly extended acquaintances with extremely small matters" (Geertz, *Interpretation* 21); yet the theory which the microscopic style implies can only be read in Mayhew between the lines. *London Labour* seems to mark in this way the emergence of a new structure of social thought; it gives us at the same time the insight that the fundamental stylistic trend of modern ethnographic writing, the trend of "thick description," can perhaps best be understood to signal a persistent anxiety that the enterprise of cultural interpretation is structurally unsound after all and cannot possibly attain substantial conclusions. This is the anxiety which Adam Smith clearly foretells in "The History of Astronomy," though without predicting that it might manifest itself in the compensatory form of a "mania" for an ever-expanding collection of data.

It is awkward to illustrate by quoting passages the sheer ethnographic density of *London Labour,* that trait that seems to run counter to the attainment of meaningful interpretation, but since this effect is the crucial one in Mayhew's work, and since its awkwardness and extravagance are precisely the point, I offer here a representative sample of his prose:

> Another mode of conveying the goods through the streets [by costermongers] is by baskets of various kinds; as the sieve or head basket; the square and oval "shallow," fastened in front of the fruit-woman with a strap round the waist; the hand-basket; and the "prickle." The sieve, or head-basket, is a round willow basket, containing about one-third of a bushel. The square and oval shallows are willow baskets, about four inches deep, and thirty inches long, by eighteen broad. The hand-basket is the common oval basket, with a handle across to hang upon the arm; the latter are generally used by the Irish for onions and apples. The prickle is a brown willow basket, in which walnuts are imported into this country from the Continent; they are about thirty inches deep, and in bulk rather larger than a gallon measure; they are used only by the vendors of walnuts. (*LL* 1:27)

Rhetorically speaking, the salient feature of such a passage and of a thousand others like it in *London Labour* is the challenge it very deliberately poses to a reader's ordinary notions of literary significance and to his or her patience. If the "fictive" or literary dimension of ethnographic writing corresponds to the need to render empirical data in intelligible and interesting (that is, emotionally stimulating) form, the account of costermonger basketry seems designed primarily as an empirical scientist's stringent corrective to fictionalizing: these, nominally, are facts in their raw state, as devoid of emotional inflection as they are of interpretive significance. Yet although the passage masquerades as an assemblage of inert factual information, it contains after all a multifaceted argument, if we are willing to make the effort to spell it out. Doing so schools us in the new method of reading which the new ethnographic discourse requires.

The passage argues, first of all (and this with a calculated intent to disrupt settled habits of thought in its readers), the intense involvement of the life of the poor with material reality. It is a convention of popular literature, and in the first instance nothing less than a foundational principle of bourgeois sensibility, that physical practicalities per se occupy the bottommost rung in the hierarchy of human things. They are granted significance only insofar as they can be seen to carry spiritual, aesthetic, or intellectual values or to express qualities of individual personality: these being the dominant ideal themes of middle-class culture, which as almost its defining activity strives on every discursive front to mark itself off from the sphere of the uncouth masses who do physical work.[16] Victorian (and much post-Victorian) anthropology cooperates with this program, installing as its fundamental proposition the principle that the advance of "civilization" means a transcendence of the physical and an ascent into the realm of mental and spiritual refinement.[17] But no such self-gratifying disdain for the world of material objects is possible when one seeks authentically to grasp the experience of the severely disadvantaged, Mayhew insists—hinting plainly as he does so that such a principle of disdain works strategically to shield "the well-fed portion of society" from having to reflect on or take responsibility for its own implication in numerous unpleasant aspects of contemporary life. To designate baskets a subject lying below the threshold of significance and interest may be an aspect of confining below the same threshold the human beings whose livelihoods depend on such appliances. Mayhew implies that it can only be a form of bad faith for a bourgeois reader to find so much detail on the subject of costermonger baskets objectionable. In refusing to submit to this code, he must be seen as transgressing his readership's taste in much the same way that he does more sensationalistically in his constant gravitation to imagery of obscene, filthy, and repulsive things. He implies further in his close inspection of baskets that the hankering for totalizing theories (as opposed to the registration of particularized data) in ethnography may be the sign of nothing more elevated than impatience or revulsion before the experiential reality of an inferior and thus distasteful people.

These are not obscure implications in Mayhew, even though he never states them as explicitly as I just have, for they follow from the oppositional trend basic to all his work. The urban poor, he declares, constitute the *"proscribed class"* (*LL* 2:3) of Victorian society. This proscription takes many cruel forms (one of which is the myth of boundless lower-class desire that Mayhew himself at first professes, then devotes a career of research to refuting), but the ultimate one is a systematic attempt on the part of the well-fed to preserve their peace of mind by *suppressing awareness of the very existence of the poor.*[18] This system of radical denial expresses itself unmistakably, for instance, in the fact that the presence of the costermongers, a population estimated by Mayhew to number at least 30,000 in London alone and at least 40,000 in total, goes unrecorded in the national census (*LL* 1:xv, 6). He sees the whole "civilized" order of the nation as implicated in a conspiracy to transform these "hordes of vagabonds and outcasts from their own community" (*LL* 1:1) into ghostly nonentities, and he consciously practices his sociological calling as a response to this wicked system: each pungent, vividly observed detail that he records of the life of his subjects amounts to a polemic against it. A discourse which calls for entering into such minute detail in the analysis of costermongers' baskets is first and foremost a declaration that these tabooed people truly exist, that their most banal appurtenances have that density and richly particularized texture by which we recognize our own reality. The abundant registration of surplus detail has long served as a principal device for creating verisimilitude in "realistic" fiction, and it functions in just this way in Mayhew, giving anti-fictional materials a fictionalizing role after all.

His extreme and very early—essentially unprecedented—use of the method of "microscopic" fieldwork gives us, therefore, a striking confirmation of the principle that "so-called empirical observation" does not occur spontaneously in an intentional vacuum or as the consequence of mere "curiosity," but is inherently a *motivated* and leveraged activity, a positive rhetoric loaded from the first with ideological and emotional, as well as practical, implications. To see the concept of (primitive) culture taking shape in his "survey" as a byproduct of his complexly antagonistic relations with his public is to recognize anew— as we can no less clearly in the work of writers like Boas, Malinowski, or Benedict—the extent to which this concept has from its inception served specifically as an instrument of activist attack upon "Victorian" prejudice. Michel Foucault and his disciples are apt to take for granted that close sociological study is a form of "surveillance" and a way of exercising hegemonic social power; Mayhew turns this argument around, and portrays exhaustively close observation of the exploited poor as the one way of redeeming them from their wretched limbo of unreality.[19]

Baskets: Mayhew's analysis of them opens in another way on the modern doctrine of "culture." The essential argument of the passage quoted above is that costermonger baskets make up not an undifferentiated or an amorphous mass, as a more casual mode of observation might allow one to suppose, not an anarchic proliferation of basket types, but a few stylized forms. Mayhew's microethnography springs from his grasp of this fact as deeply significant, for it testifies to the existence of definite code or structure in the seeming atomistic confusion and fantastic variety of street life. Such a passage implies what we are in search of throughout this study: an emergent theory of culture according to which the most minute particle of social life—a distinction between types of street baskets, for instance—is presumed to be a significant part of some large organized whole and thus cannot be allowed to escape unrecorded without jeopardizing the logic of the whole system. "To the ethnologist," Boas declares, stating not merely a rule of methodological caution but almost the defining principle of his science, "the most trifling features of social life are important" (*Race, Language and Culture* 632). In fact, the more "trifling" the materials invested with interpretive importance, the more the analytic power of the science is demonstrated. On the scale on which this method is put into practice by Henry Mayhew, it carries the disconcerting hint that the organizing principles of a way of life lie at so profound a level and take such fantastically condensed forms that they may finally be bound to escape definite formulation: they may finally be incommensurate with any data, however detailed and voluminous, which a social scientist could possibly assemble.

This kind of methodological vertigo aside, Mayhew's painstaking taxonomy of baskets and his correlation of the different types with the different professional and ethnic categories of costermongers embody a sociological imagination of a kind that forecasts later veins of thought. Baskets for Mayhew are not physical things after all, even though their dimensions can be measured so precisely; rather, they are social institutions, and as such they are inscribed deeply with a semiological character. Apart from fulfilling purely practical functions (if any such category can be said to exist), they are "collective representations" which signify a highly organized way of life obedient to traditional forms and possessing, as the study of costermongering in *London Labour* goes on to reveal at great length, its own elaborate structure of values, customs, and folkways. Mayhew does not attempt to decipher, as Lévi-Strauss would, the symbology that might reside in the geometrical imagery of baskets, even though his careful specification of round, square, and oval forms hints intriguingly at the need to attempt just this kind of interpretive analysis. What he does make amply clear is that in assuming one of these baskets, a costermonger performs the resonant symbolic act of signifying identity with an established social group, and it is in virtue of their symbolic property that Mayhew inspects them as closely as he does, rhetorically impregnating them, so to say, with cultural value. Seen in the context of his great sociological poem as a whole, they manifest their possession of "value" by their sheer power to maintain their distinctive forms and thus to set at naught the degenerative tendencies which transform material and human things across a broad field into shapeless, useless, valueless refuse.

In other words, basketry exemplifies in little the principle upon which all of *London Labour* rests: that the world of the London poor is not that of a chaotic, randomly promiscuous "horde" at all, but an organized structure of distinct occupations, each of which (Mayhew amazingly reveals) has not only its own sociology and political economy, but its own personality profile as well.[20] He reveals in other passages his keenly historical understanding of the various callings of the poor, every now and then proposing deep researches into the evolutionary morphology of these institutions. "It would be . . . a curious inquiry," he remarks in one place, "to trace the origin of the manifold occupations in which men are found to be engaged in the present day, and to note how promptly every circumstance and occurrence was laid hold of, as it happened to arise, which appeared to have any tendency to open up a new occupation, and to mark the general progress, till it became a regularly-established employment, followed by a separate class of people, fenced round by rules and customs of their own, and who at length grew to be both in their habits and peculiarities plainly distinct from the other classes among whom they chanced to be located" (*LL* 2:147). Evidence of this process of cultural articulation— which runs sharply against the grain of the "degenerationist" thesis of a world of random libido—is to be found in a kind of fossilized imagery in current institutions, Mayhew sees, though only in the form of an obscure code needing to be unravelled by an ethnological science of interpretive close reading of cultural detail. Pondering in one striking passage the subtle differences between the Saturday-night market and the Monday market, for example, he has a flash of intuition. "It appears to me," he says, "that in all these little distinctions—of which street-folk tell you, quite unconscious that they tell anything new—there is something of the history of the character of a people" (*LL* 2:13). He does not often attempt actually to decode this cryptic history (despite frequent historical digressions on the occurrence of this or that calling in earlier times), but the principle stated here underlies all his painstaking notations of the "rules and customs" peculiar to categories of street people so obscure that they were never known to exist before he discovered them; it is present in sharply compressed form, in particular, in his disquisition on costermonger basketry. Equipped with the necessarily clairvoyant insight (so Mayhew hints to a receptive reader), an interpreter might discover even in such opaque-seeming materials as these baskets "something of the history of the character of a people," and in the process throw open an altogether new vein of social science.

Having stressed all along the inseparable connection linking the theoretical concept of culture to the practical vocation of fieldwork, we need to emphasize one further element of the basket passage—the expression, that is, of what it may seem at first glance to efface entirely: the experiential and psychic origins of ethnographic discourse. Such a massing of inaccessible cultural detail dramatizes willy nilly the ethnographer's passion for collecting a kind of specialized data which to the uninitiated would appear almost ludicrously insignificant, and it bears a vivid trace of the arduous activity of exploring unknown social territory which producing such data was bound to have required. It testifies in fact to the project theorized at an early date by missionary ethnographers, if only carried into execution in carefully hedged ways by them: that of seeking virtually total knowledge of the life of an alien people through "participant observation" and full immersion in their milieu and even, as far as this is possible, in their mentality—that is, through expressly putting one's own selfhood in jeopardy, a drastic, inherently perplexed enterprise which easily can seem to amount to "mania" on the part of the observer. Mayhew articulates this enterprise more fully than ever before and draws out its implications for what he knows himself to be involved in, the larger enterprise of constructing a distinctively modern subjectivity.

His investigative work impressed upon him every day the truth that "so-called empirical observations" do not spring into being of their own accord, but imply, rather, the laborious manufacture of a whole enabling system of thought and research, and in fact he steadily emphasizes the riskily experimental and existential character of his project. Like his missionary predecessors in ethnography, he announces in his preface that in setting out to explore the world of the London poor he is engaged in founding an altogether new mode of study, the essential feature of which is the personal presence in the field of an adventurous observer who strives, paradoxically, to guarantee the purity of his data by expunging from his written report all traces of his own point of view. His is the first book ever, Mayhew declares, "to publish the history of a people, from the lips of the people themselves . . . in their own 'unvarnished' language; and to pourtray the condition of their homes and their families by personal observation of the places, and direct communion with the individuals" (*LL* 1:xv). Such a declaration glosses over the epistemological problems attaching to data gathered in this way (problems which it was one of the chief functions of the culture concept to try to resolve); more to the point here, it glosses over the precarious, ambivalent position which so impassioned a participant observer seems fated to occupy in the midst of the "primitive" people whom he seeks to study. However, in the rest of *London Labour* this ambivalence is registered so vividly that the predicament of the observer threatens at times to become the principal theme of the book.

We have seen that Mayhew regards the lewd, riotous street folk with a dislike and moral disapproval that he is unable to suppress; yet he increasingly declares his sympathy with them and devotes his professional career to proclaiming and defending their interests and to learning the most intimate details of their lives. He attains in the process a more unstinting "direct communion" with his subjects than perhaps he ever anticipated. In emphasizing their bitter hatred of the upper classes and their love of lawlessness and indecency, he projects ever more plainly his own acute disaffection from the respectable middle-class world of his origins; and his absorbed interest in the many categories of London scavengers, pariahs who make their livings by recovering every possible form of repulsive refuse, seems increasingly to reflect an awareness that in his own professional work he too was expressly a scavenger, collecting, expertly sifting, and then selling the most repellent materials—and inescapably becoming tainted to some degree by the unclean milieu in which his vocation obliged him to live. At the end of his life, he reflected on his long immersion in the most disreputable spheres of society, ruefully confessing to a fear that his pose of scientific objectivity had not sufficiently insulated him from the contaminating effects of this experience. "I had been every-where—seen everything which maybe a gentleman should not," he said (quoted Humpherys, *Travels* 197). The presiding fictional struc-ture of *London Labour and the London Poor* turns out to be that of a distinctively modernist fable, the exploration of selfhood through conscious self-alienation and through dangerous experimentation with forbidden and perverse areas of experience. If at the end of his life Mayhew read Stevenson's *Doctor Jekyll and Mr. Hyde,* for example, he surely sensed the affinity of his own career to that of Jekyll, the respectable man of science who seeks to discover himself by releasing a deep part of his own psyche to go out at night to haunt the world of criminality—and who finds at last that his identity has been perma-nently compromised by this experiment. Mayhew helps us to discover that the invention of ethnographic subjectivity and of the sort of knowledge and literary modes it yields largely takes place under the auspices of this archetypal modernist plot, which informs in a surpris-ing way, at its final level of meaning, his bland-seeming discourse on the several styles of street-vendors' baskets.

The Culture of Vagabondism

The best way to demonstrate the "complex wholeness" of Mayhew's ethnography, and thus to reveal him as one of the first practical expounders of the doctrine of culture (the doctrine of an all-inclu-sive, integrated system of collective phenomena) is to trace in specific terms the logic of some main themes developed in his work. This means engaging in an active process of interpretation, at times divin-ing ideas which the writer never formulates explicitly and filling in unstated connections among seemingly disparate and incongruous clusters of data. The risk of this approach from a scholarly point of view is that of unjustifiably imposing later canons of interpretation upon an early text; but we must run this risk if we hope to gain knowledge of that supremely interesting phase of intellectual history when amorphous "proto-ideas or pre-ideas," in Ludwik Fleck's phrase, come to the verge of crystallizing into definite principles of analysis.

At first conceiving the study of poverty as a problem of political economy, Mayhew sets out to trace in detail the commerce of goods and services carried on by the street folk and thus to confirm his presupposition that the economic world of the very poor, which from one point of view seems one of hand-to-mouth individual expedients for survival, in fact constitutes a well-established *system*, each component institution of which is linked in a complex network with all the others.[21] As he did in his original reports for the *Morning Chronicle*, Mayhew pores over this system to extract its economic "laws,"[22] but finds himself carried quickly into a more speculative order of analysis focused on the customs, attitudes, and expressive style of his subjects. Transposing the hypothesis of an elaborately ramified economic system into that of a similarly organized system of symbolic devices through which is carried on a (thriving) commerce not of things but of *meanings*, he increasingly organizes his study around the problem of semiological rather than material scarcity. How do the ignorant street folk, destitute as they seem to be of nearly all the resources of culture, manage to *express themselves?*

William Ellis and his fellow missionaries gave a rudimentary form to holistic cultural analysis in arguing that the all-pervading principle of "idolatry" bound even the most disparate-seeming elements of Polynesian life into an indivisible system; but this thesis remains in most of their work merely a generalized formula (one aimed chiefly at justifying their own activity of wholesale cultural demolition), not a method of analysis. In Mayhew, the intuition that even an impoverished primitive culture can be seen as a complex symbolic system emerges with unprecedented clarity. As we shall see, one of its key points of focus in *London Labour* is imagery of *performance*. Against the backdrop of a waste land where symbolic order seems to have deteriorated beyond recall, Mayhew portrays the street folk as building it up anew by deploying a collective genius for theatrical and quasi-theatrical spectacle and by stamping a distinctive expressive style, full of densely coded meanings, upon every aspect of their lives.

In order to pursue investigations along these lines, he needs as one of his first tasks to dispel the myth of rampant instinctual desire, a myth that disables sociological reasoning from the outset. He never abandons categorically the theory that some classes of people are genetically preprogrammed for street life, having inborn "libidinous propensities" and a naturally "restless and volatile disposition" (*LL* 1:321), and he persists in invoking that imaginary creature of early anthropology, the uncontrolled savage, speaking, for example, of "the impulsive costermonger, . . . approximating . . . closely to the primitive man, moved solely by his feelings" (*LL* 1:213). But this set of presumptions, pressed into service mainly to explain the cases of respectable "settled" citizens who descend into hedonistic "nomadism," is made ever more peripheral to his research on "the tribe *indigenous* to the paving-stones," who acquire their character, as he clearly sees, through cultural imprinting, imbibing "the manners and morals of the gutters almost with their mothers' milk" (*LL* 1:320). In fact, certain key passages of *London Labour* flatly contradict earlier ones by defining human beings as "instinctless animals" with an urgent bodily need to eat but otherwise little or no determinate nature; "the greater part, if not the whole" of what we are has been taught to us by others, he declares (*LL* 1:101). We are in effect cultural artifacts. What flows from this revision is the prospect of thoroughgoing sociological analysis through which the world of the streets, rather than being a field of atomized human particles scattering anarchically from the force of uncontrolled instinctive desires, can be perceived to be a dense, integrated social world with a strong organizational logic—a world that can be studied methodically and made the object of literary representation. So when Mayhew speaks of what one sees in the lodging houses as "a system of depravity" (*LL* 1:412), the word *system* gets an implicit stress that to some extent nullifies the overt stress on *depravity;* it implies, at least, a method of structural analysis rather than mere moral commentary, and Mayhew in fact pursues this method to a degree that seems a transcendent achievement in the context of Victorian ethnological ideas.

We thus witness in *London Labour and the London Poor* the significant episode in modern thought that occurs when the model of human desire basic to Victorian Evangelical doctrine, according to which desire is a phenomenon alien to and invasive of social life and naturally without limits, is displaced by an idea of desire as a social formation, a collective rather than an individual dynamic and one transmitted entirely along circuits of highly specific symbolic forms. Thus the costers' wild promiscuity is found not to be spontaneous and innate after all, all Mayhew's rhetoric to this effect notwithstanding, but to be *learned* in various institutions set up in effect to perpetuate the distinctive costermonger way of life. Mayhew dramatizes the new paradigm by giving sharp, repeated emphasis to the process of enculturation by which street children unavoidably "[get] a relish for that sort of life" (*LL*

1:410). The pornographic entertainments of the penny gaff, for example, "[force] into the brains of the childish audience before them thoughts that must embitter a lifetime, and descend from father to child like some bodily infirmity" (*LL* 1:42). Anomic primitive desire is after all a thoroughly social, thoroughly institutionalized phenomenon in a milieu where licentiousness is not deviant but standard.

Other no less coercive forms of conditioning produce the distinctive personality types of street folk, according to Mayhew. He particularly stresses the linkage between habits of depraved carnality among proletarian "nomads" and the sharp, unpredictable swings from famine and destitution to semi-prosperity which they continually undergo. Thus "a journeyman baker's life drives him to drink, almost whether he will or not" (*LL* 1:179), according to the same logic which causes periods of famine or pestilence to give rise predictably to a "spirit of reckless extravagance" and indulgence in "the wildest excesses" (*LL* 2:325; see also 1:101, 158–59; 2:326–27). Conditioning engraves itself so deeply upon individuals that it actually alters their bodily constitution: this is the lesson of Mayhew's account of the case of an Irish coster girl who grudgingly took an indoor position as a domestic servant in order to maintain her mother, but could never reconcile herself to "the loss of her liberty" and of the right to go barefoot in the streets.

> After a girl has once grown accustomed to a street-life, it is almost impossible to wean her from it. The muscular irritability begotten by continued wandering makes her unable to rest for any time in one place, and she soon, if put to any *settled** occupation, gets to crave for the severe exercise she formerly enjoyed. The least restraint will make her sigh after the perfect liberty of the coster's "roving life." (*LL* 1:44)

Mayhew's insistence in such passages on the overwhelming stress of cultural circumstance in generating tendencies to wildness, vagrancy, and immorality in the London street folk runs so strongly against the thesis of a natural propensity to vice that it threatens indeed to turn them into automatons whose social and psychic existence reduces to little more than a mass of conditioned reflexes. To this extent, one sort of determinism seems to replace another. But this implication is more than overshadowed by Mayhew's gradual revelation of the system of cultural values and of collective imagination that

---

*All italics in quoted passages appear in original texts.

underlies all the seeming anarchy and moral nihilism of street life. His decisive discovery is that the London "nomads," supposedly marked by "an innate aversion to every species of . . . moral [law]" (*LL* 1:214) and supposedly goaded by bodily needs alone, in fact possess a genuine tribal constitution which the least articulate among them is fully conscious of, intensely loyal to, and quick to express. Its fundamental principle (the one functionally equivalent to "idolatry" in missionary analyses of Polynesian life or to "moderation" in Benedict's analysis of the Zuñi) is their fierce antagonism toward the respectable "settled" society amid which they live as persecuted aliens. From this principle derives a richly elaborated system of distinctive institutions.

The street folk's dissident impulse takes its most overt form in the sadistic tribal conflict which, as Mayhew observes at the beginning, the costermongers carry on with the police and in which "they resemble many savage nations, from the cunning and treachery they use" (*LL* 1:16). Mayhew's further insight is that the wild hedonism of the street folk needs to be interpreted in analogous terms, not as the result of a biological disposition to carnality and vice, but as a cultural program full of ideological content symbolically expressed. Whatever else it may be, the depravity of the poor is a form of defiance, a rejection of bourgeois moral coercion and a proclamation of their "fixed hatred to all constituted authority" (*FF* 2:370); as such, it can almost be seen not as animalistic or as pathological after all but as a legitimate response to their status as the victims of police persecution and economic exploitation. Mayhew cannot make so scandalous an argument openly, but it is implicit, for example, in the evident connivance with which he quotes his informants' scornful dismissal of attempts to indoctrinate them with respectable Christian morality. As one of them tells him, "tracts is no good, except to a person that has a home; at the lodging-houses they're laughed at" (*LL* 1:412). "Sermons or tracts," a costermonger states, "gives them the 'orrors" (*LL* 1:26).[23]

The leading article of the counter-code professed by the street folk, according to Mayhew, is their idealization of the state of unfettered vagabondism. Rather than being simply excluded from "settled" society, they despise it and consciously rebel against it—or tell themselves such a fiction, at least—by choosing a "nomadic" existence instead. They have "*taken* to it from a natural love of what they call 'roving'" (*LL* 1:213) or "'shaking a loose leg,' as the vagrants themselves call it" (*LL* 1:407). In laying such stress upon the costers' "innate 'love of a roving life'" (*LL* 1:213), Mayhew shows, first, that this predilection is not innate at all, but a collective response to a set of social conditions: it is in fact an institution. But chiefly he emphasizes the insistency with which the street folk symbolize their vagrant condition and their shared mentality in the form of a certain repertoire of poetic figures. Fixing upon these stock locutions because they throw so much light upon the agency of "culture," he repeats almost endlessly the street people's talismanic phrase in its several variants. Coster boys, he says, "must be perpetually on the move—or to use their own words 'they like a roving life'" (*LL* 1:36); some individuals are especially strongly marked by "this passion for 'a roving life' (to use the common expression by which many of the street-people themselves designate it)" (*LL* 1:321); "I longed for a roving life and to shake a loose leg," says an informant (*LL* 1:407); "My mind was bent upon costermongering and a roving life," says another (1.414). A returned convict begins his reminiscences with the stereotypical formula: "When I was young I was fond of a roving life" (*LL* 3:386). "I then ran away," says a vagrant boy, "for I had always a roving mind" (*LL* 3:390). In volume 2, Mayhew begins highlighting the stylized character of this and related phrases by putting them significantly in italics. "I was rather frolicsome in those days, I confess," says a street-sweeper, "and perhaps *had rather a turn for a roving life*" (*LL* 2:262).

Mayhew never offers a specific analysis of the cult of "roving" among the street folk, partly because he would not have known how, but partly, too, because he has rendered the meanings of this codified symbolism so transparent. On one level, the street folk's almost obsessive penchant for homelessness is another manifestation of their loathing of upper-class culture, for it has to be seen as a concerted revulsion from the sanctifying of Home and of domesticity upon which the British bourgeoisie lavished such excesses of sentiment in the eighteen-fifties and sixties. It evidently carries as well a more specific reference to the liabilities of their own lives. Subject as they perpetually are to the cruellest, most inescapable social, economic, and natural forces, the street folk for this very reason glorify the idea of "freedom from every restraint" (*LL* 1:410). Held fast in the grip of "sheer necessity," they transcend their condition on the level of fantasy, at least, by the audaciously counterfactual cultural device of declaring themselves figures of "perfect liberty." This amazing invention bestows upon the costers and other street folk a sense of tribal identity, of being not helpless, isolated vagrants but of possessing the vastly magnified power which comes from belonging to a collectivity of people who think, live, and speak like themselves. At the same time, it transfigures the world they inhabit from a phantasmagoric void of "fatigue and despair" into a theater for enacting their own symbolically meaningful and thus unexpectedly glamorous and moving satirical drama. It is a performative speech-act in an especially specific sense of the term, in other words: it is what allows them to *perform*.

Mayhew's original discovery, then, is that the street folk are very richly endowed with what Fleck calls "the style-permeated thinking of a collective" (Fleck 181n), and that this kind of thinking is so closely bound up with styles of expressive metaphorical speech that it scarcely seems possible to separate them. This implication forms the rationale of Mayhew's decision to build his study around innumerable verbatim transcriptions of the "oral autobiographies" of individual informants—the result being that his book continually dramatizes and in effect takes as its primary theme the spectacle of men and women seemingly doomed to catatonic muteness *expressing themselves*. The euphoria typically released in these speakers as they perform, deploying their racy eloquence, artfully piquing the interest of their audience, is obvious and well remarked by Mayhew himself. The mesmerizing effect of their stories, on the other hand, is the surest signal we could have that the ostensibly factual recitals produced by Mayhew's "ingenious and wordy" (*LL* 1:214) Cockney narrators (and painstakingly verified by him, as he insists several times) need to be classed as fables, fictions, performances, stylized cultural texts.

The essentially fictive, representational status of these accounts is what their heavily stressed literary turns of phrase ("I was fond of a roving life") continually imply, and what is implied on another structural level in their recurrent narrative patterning. Dramatizing the most prominent pattern of all, one speaker after another takes over the charismatic role of roguish picaresque hero, portraying his or her life as a long sequence of adventures and singing all the time the conventional liturgy of praise—qualified more often than not by rueful moral commentary—of the life of "freedom and license" (*LL* 1:322). A couple of narratives in which this scheme and the fictionalizing motive it expresses stand out with particular distinctness would be, for instance, the mini-novel of the career of "Chelsea George" the dog thief (*LL* 2:51–52) or the tale of the returned convict (*LL* 3:386–88). Into one statement of a runaway vagrant boy, Mayhew, hinting fairly plainly at his undeclared point, interpolates a long made-up story about a runaway trickster told by the speaker, the runaway boy—the point being that it takes a keen eye to trace the line of separation between the professedly factual autobiography and the picaresque fiction (*LL* 3:389–90). One is bound to be assailed by doubt as to the strict factual veracity of these and many similar narratives, which read like the cultural myths they are. Yet for all his claims of strict scientific factuality, Mayhew gives his gifted storytellers their head and is careful to quote their phraseology verbatim, for he understands the workings of their imaginations and discursive styles—their stylized techniques of self-representation—to form an essential dimension in any portrayal of their world of experience.

Space does not permit here a survey of the fictive machinery employed by Mayhew's informants, but we can cite briefly by way of illustration the statement of the boy street-reciter known as "Shakespeare" (*LL* 3:151–54). "He had a bright, cheerful face," says Mayhew, willingly collaborating in the production of this tale, "and a skin so transparent and healthy, and altogether appeared so different from the generality of street lads, that I felt convinced that he had not long led a wandering life, and that there was some mystery connected with his present pursuits." From this prompt, we are made to feel that we have stepped abruptly from scientific sociology into a real-life version of *Oliver Twist*. The strangely fascinating boy then recounts his career of itinerant playacting to great effect. Duplicating in a remarkable way the narrative pattern of the early books of Rousseau's *Confessions,* he reports to Mayhew that he had been established in one prosperous situation after another, but abandoned each one in turn when seized by his wanderlust and his compulsive love of theatrical performance. "It's as if a spell was on me," he says (*LL* 3:152). He recounts his career very self-consciously, we may say, as a parable of nomadic "restlessness." This is the condition that he seems to epitomize not only in his footloose wanderings from place to place but even more pointedly in his daily oscillations from one fictional scenario to another: "'The Gipsy's Revenge,' 'The Gold Digger's Revenge,' 'The Miser,' 'The Robber,' 'The Felon,' . . . 'The Highwayman,'" and many other pieces besides (*LL* 3:154). Mayhew's interjections, typically, stress the boy's highly cultivated narrative and declamatory style, "a style evidently founded upon the melo-dramatic models at minor theatres" (*LL* 3:151). "He had picked up several of the set phrases of theatrical parlance, such as, 'But my dream has vanished in air;' or, 'I felt that a blight was on my happiness;' and delivered his words in a romantic tone, as though he fancied he was acting on a stage" (LL 3:151). This autobiography, an explicit fable of "roving" as a mode of theatrical self-production, amounts at the same time to a case history of anomic desire, seemingly boundless but in fact quite literally scripted by a repertoire of culturally significant texts. Its central theme is the construction of individuality from fictive materials and from concerted strategies of self-invention.

Extending this line of thought, Mayhew stresses in many places one of his key discoveries, the addiction of the London street folk to certain types of popular literature, notwithstanding the high levels of illiteracy which prevail in this stratum of the population (LL 1:220). The writing favored by his informants is devoted overwhelmingly, he reports, to glorifying lawlessness and to pandering to the "morbid feeling about criminals" which he alleges to form a leading strain of popular sensibility (LL 1:230). A street-seller of back numbers of cheap periodicals testifies accordingly that the bulk of his booming trade is "works about thieves, and highwaymen, and pirates" (LL 1:290). Foremost among these subversive works are the famous Newgate romances of Harrison Ainsworth, Rookwood and Jack Sheppard, the influence of which on the "thought style" of the urban poor Mayhew shows to be profound. Fiction of this kind permeates their lives. Dick Turpin (the outlaw hero of Rookwood) and Jack Sheppard are mentioned in passing by Mayhew's informants again and again (LL 3:383, 389, 391), he notices illustrations of them hanging on the walls of their rooms (LL 2:85), and when he raises this topic at a meeting of thieves organized by himself, he gets striking replies. Sixty-three of the 150 present could read and write; of these, fifty had read Ainsworth's novels; the others had heard them read aloud at lodging-houses. "Numbers avowed that they had been induced to resort to an abandoned course of life from reading the lives of notorious thieves, and novels about highway robbers" (LL 1:419). Mayhew bitterly attacks Ainsworth for using literature to promote "the lowest licentiousness" and for "pandering to the most depraved propensities" (LL 3:370), but his moral indignation here is obviously subordinate to his fascination with tracing the logic of certain cultural themes in street society.

He pursues this logic into one department of street life after another, ever more lucidly prefiguring the doctrine that "the customs of a community . . . always have a particular style and are reducible to systems" (Lévi-Strauss, Tristes tropiques 178). One cognate of the literary style-system of the street folk appears, for instance, in their clothing fashions, another topic upon which Mayhew lavishes a concentrated attention only explainable with reference to an emergent theory of culture. He emphasizes that despite their professed devotion to anarchic freedom, to that "common aversion to anything smacking of regulation" deplored by Durkheim (*Moral Education* 54), certain classes of street folk are ardently attached to a conventionalized, obscurely symbolic costume which is described in minute detail, down to the several styles of buttons (plain brass, sporting buttons with raised fox's or stag's head design, black bone-buttons, or mother-of-pearl) currently in fashion, along with the sartorial rules governing which type goes with each type of fabric. "The costermonger," he reports, "prides himself most of all upon his neckerchief and boots. Men, women, boys and girls, all have a passion for these articles" (*LL* 1:51):

> A yellow flower on a green ground, or a red and blue pattern, is at present greatly in vogue. The women wear their kerchiefs tucked-in under their gowns, and the men have theirs wrapped loosely around the neck, with the ends hanging over their waistcoats. Even if a costermonger has two or three silk handkerchiefs by him already, he seldom hesitates to buy another, when tempted with a bright showy pattern hanging from a Field-lane door-post. (*LL* 1:51)

Mayhew does not venture a specific exegesis of all this coded imagery—of floral designs, particular combinations of colors, wrapping techniques—but he does show clearly how important a role such imagery plays in the creation of a tribal mentality and how crucial the sense of collective identity which it symbolizes is even to these outcast vagabonds. "To be a man," one of Lévi-Strauss's informants told him, "it was necessary to be painted; to remain in the natural state was to be no different from the beasts" (*Tristes tropiques* 188). To be human— to be not an animal such as a rat, or not an utterly vacuous derelict—is to be imprinted with or enveloped in culture: this is the philosophical intuition expressed in Mayhew's treatment of the costermongers' cult of boots and silk handkerchiefs. This principle carries of course a special urgency for these dispossessed people who live so perilously on the margin of a subhuman condition; for a costermonger to be without a silk handkerchief or to be obliged to wear secondhand boots "is felt as a bitter degradation by them all" (*LL* 1:51). The flashiness of the costers' style of dress is proportionate, we easily see, to the strength of the obliterative forces to which they are perpetually subjected, and it expresses a collective "passion" to maintain a posture of cocky unsubdued dignity in the face of such forces. Mayhew's painstaking investigation into the economics of street commerce gives a context for this kind of insight into the economics of cultural symbolism, a system in which values turn out to be fully as subject to the logic of "proportionality" (in the Malthusian phrase) as they are in the trading of material goods. Receptiveness to this logic is what causes Mayhew to describe with so much ethnographic precision, for example, one coster lad "dressed in all the slang beauty of his class, with a bright red handkerchief and unexceptionable boots" (*LL* 1:39), or another street character "decently enough attired in a black paletot with a flash white-and-red handkerchief, or 'fogle,' as the costermongers call it, jauntily arranged so as to bulge over the closely-buttoned collar of his coat" (*LL* 3:151). The "nomads'" self-dramatizing production of themselves in gaudy, "showy" costume has again in Mayhew's eyes the stylized, self-conscious, emancipatory character of a theatrical performance.

The symbolic logic of street culture imprints itself in subtler metaphorical imagery upon the secret national language which Mayhew reveals the costermongers to possess, and which makes fully explicit for once the principle that cultural devices, arbitrary as they may seem to be, are properly to be treated as coded communication. The basic cryptographic rule of the costers' language is the backward pronunciation of English words ("fivepence," for example, being pronounced "ewif-yenep"); "complicating the mystery of this unwritten tongue," however, is its incorporation of a multitude of slang terms of no apparent origin, added to the principle that "any syllable [may be] added to a proper slang word, at the discretion of the speaker" (*LL* 1:23). As in his account of the costers' system of dress, it is the highly codified, intricate, stylized character of their patois that Mayhew stresses, implying as he does so that its strange formal principles may not be merely arbitrary or accidental at all, but may themselves have expressive and affective value and may bear some formal or economic—that is, "proportional"—relation to other customary practices of these people. He is explicit, in any case, in reporting the costers' sense of their esoteric language as a precious identifying attribute invested with the same emotional significance possessed by silk handkerchiefs or by the cherished phrase "a roving life." In accordance with what seems to be the key principle of their culture, they employ it as the vehicle of yet another mode of theatrical performance, "[boasting] of their clever-ness and proficiency in it" (*LL* 1:23): like their other distinctive insti-tutions, it carries the telltale inflection of a "passion" for extravagant self-display.

The symbolic schema embedded in the costermongers' fabricated lingo seems relatively easy to read, even though Mayhew, whose grasp of the complex wholeness of street culture is intuitive and incipient rather than explicitly stated, again does not spell it out. Its leading principle of structure is satirical antistructure, the playfully subversive *reversal* of respectable speech: at every utterance, the flashy coster patois expresses in this way the dominant impulse of its speakers, that of the renegade inversion of bourgeois values. What Mayhew docu-ments is a pure instance of the linguistic phenomenon called "heteroglossia" by Mikhail Bakhtin, and an instance in particular of the kind of parodic language that may, as the latter says, be "aimed sharply and polemically against the official languages of its given time" (Bakhtin 273)—this one being not, however, reserved for use at cer-tain festive occasions, like the ones Bakhtin specifies, but perma-nently, exuberantly active as an element of an established dissident (sub)culture. Mayhew shows that the way of life developed for them-selves by the London "nomads" is the bourgeois way turned with pro-grammatic violence inside out, with license exalted in place of disci-pline, rascality in place of rectitude, gaudiness in place of sobriety, mobility in place of fixity, carnality in place of spirituality. All this is symbolized with theatrical vividness in their speech, which thus testi-fies, like other analogous phenomena of street culture, to the princi-ple defined classically in Evans-Pritchard's study of the Nuer: the ten-dency of social groups to coalesce largely or entirely around antagonism to other groups.

The more distinctly one defines this binary principle, the more its ambiguities come into view. It implies, we have noted, that there is "always contradiction in the definition of a . . . group, for it is a group only in relation to other groups" (Evans-Pritchard, *Nuer* 147). This contradiction, inherent in the principle of the proportionality of cul-tural value, gnaws at the base of communal identity, and it is flagrant in the case of the costers, who, though all their cultural representa-tions project an ideal of anarchic freedom, in fact are bound in their very anarchism, just as their secret jargon is bound to the patterns of regular English, to the "settled" society amid which they live and from which, parasitically, they derive their sense of identity by despising it and subjecting it to profanation. Their lawlessness is very largely an illusion in any case: this, we have said, is Mayhew's central insight, as it is increasingly the central theme of portrayals of "primitive" peoples in ethnography of the later decades of the century. Ostensibly a chaos of lewdness and disorder, street life takes on ever more clearly in *London Labour* the aspect of a *replication* of the norms of respectability, though in the form of a travesty, in parodic reversal. The adorning of slang words with random syllables according to the whim and inventiveness of the speaker signifies the street nomads' deep collective urge to valorize rampant individualism, seemingly even to the point of anarchy. But this style of willed individualism is belied by the realities of dependency and finally suggests a basic illogic in a symbolic system founded as this one is on the ironic principles of guerrilla theater.

The same equivocation shadows a broad range of more explicitly theatrical street institutions investigated by Mayhew: for example, the many varieties of street oratory and mountebankery known as "pattering"; street juggling and street musicianship; the exhibiting of the drama of Punch (*LL* 3:43ff); or, one of the most remarkable of all, the gymnastic tumbling shows traditionally performed after hours by juvenile crossing-sweepers (*LL* 2:494–503). Mayhew's sustained emphasis on this cluster of related occupations reflects his consciousness of the spiritually creative character of such institutions for the gifted rogues who practice them and for their street audiences as well. Yet he makes plain how limited and precarious their symbolizing gestures of emancipation are bound to be, and suggests that the impassioned, extravagant character of these gestures may ultimately testify to their inherent shortcomings. At this level of his argument, he registers "the invention of culture" in its most intimate and pathos-laden symptoms. He is full of admiration for "the king" of the tumbling crossing-sweepers, who proudly puts on for his ethnographic visitor a show of "his wondrous tumbling powers," which image in symbolic physical gestures the code of reckless euphoric freedom that pervades street life; yet "his royal highness was of a restless disposition," Mayhew significantly notes (*LL* 2:501). Even this brilliant performer, whose theatrical skill has endowed him with so firm an individuality, is subject to that state of morbid malaise which *London Labour* identifies as the special affliction of the poor and which it lets us see as bearing witness at last to the structural flaw at the heart of their communal fiction.

Spicy Pleasures

The argument which we are tracing in Mayhew takes especially clear form in his prolonged inquiry into the eating habits and the culture of food among the poor, which he focuses upon as the site of the most intimate nexus of all between biological "appetite" and collective representations—a nexus charged with the strongest possible emotions for people constantly menaced, as the street folk of Victorian London were, by hunger and even by starvation. As their penchant for anomic excess in other areas would predict, the street people are characterized, says Mayhew, by proneness to "an inordinate or extravagant indulgence of the palate" (*LL* 1:462); but this trait, which he portrays as one of the central factors in their lives, proves to have nothing to do with mere ratlike gluttony. It constitutes, in fact, one more highly inflected sign-system for a structure of cultural values. Mayhew studies gastronomic desire partly as a surrogate for other forms of carnality which decency forbids analyzing in the necessary "microscopic" detail. His unpacking of the semiological dimension of food offers a paradigm, in other words, of the mode of interpretive ethnography by which one may reach the very heart of human desire.

He notices that the tastes in food of the street folk follow a consistent pattern and present, in particular, certain striking anomalies. One of these proves to be the key to a constellation of vital elements in the life of these people: the anomaly that, familiar as they are with the pangs of starvation, they habitually long not for solid, nourishing food, as one would expect, but for various kinds of highly seasoned "dainties." One informant reveals that during a period of thirty-eight hours without food, his hunger was "gnawing" rather than "ravenous," and that "some tasty semi-liquid was the incessant object of his desires" (*LL* 1:158–59). Mayhew glimpses a structure of unconscious thought in this odd wrinkle of desire, which he sees to be yet another cultural conundrum needing to be analytically unravelled. Initially he theorizes that the street folk, who in periods of famine are obliged to consume the most repulsive food, inevitably suffer one more form of organic degeneration, a severe impairment of their sense of taste. "Therefore, [they] prefer something that 'bites in the mouth,'—to use the words of one of my informants—like gin, onions, sprats, or pickled whelks" (*LL* 1:120). This principle of street gastronomy evidently strikes Mayhew as a significant discovery, for he later repeats the point that the costermongers' sense of taste is fixated upon things "of a *strong* flavour," since their palates, used to "that which is somewhat rank," are incapable of appreciating delicate tastes (*LL* 1:195). Readers schooled by *London Labour* (or by subsequent anthropological literature) to be alert to economic relations among different elements of a culture will spot the hint of an analogy between the taste of Mayhew's subjects for sharply flavored food and their tastes for high levels of pungent stimulation in other areas such as costume and literature—a hint that Mayhew follows out in linking food questions to broadly symbolic themes of warmth and cold.

No other insight in *London Labour* is more profoundly registered than Mayhew's awareness of the cruelty of cold weather for the derelict poor and of the influence exercised over their minds in all seasons by the dread of exposure to cold. He returns obsessively to this supreme affliction of poverty, driven in the first instance by empathy and compassion for his subjects, but increasingly, too, by the ethnographic motive of discovering how this theme expresses itself in various interlinked cultural representations. "I have often had occasion to remark that the poor, especially those who are much subjected to cold in the open air, will sacrifice much for heat," he comments, for example, explaining why costermongers' rooms are typically kept "oppressively close and hot" and reeking with "a fetid smell" (*LL* 1:71)—another instance of his prevailing method of focusing his analysis on the deciphering of what seem to be aberrant, irrational, or opaque cultural phenomena. His discovery of the exorbitant craving for heat among his informants leads him then to ponder in several key passages what he claims to be the virtual interchangeability of the problem of cold and that of food for those he calls "the famishing poor." In one of these passages, he undertakes a long nutritional analysis of their diet, based on laborious computations of goods sold at the street markets. He stresses that the dietary insufficiency to which the poor are subjected is above all a caloric insufficiency and has one primary effect: "they become more susceptible of cold, and, therefore, more eager for all that tends to promote warmth" (*LL* 1:118–19). This deadly problem of street life is compounded by the fact that "nearly all trades slacken as the cold weather comes on"—economic systems (in the narrow sense of the term) linking themselves in Mayhew's analysis to chemical and biological as well as social ones—making it doubly hard for the poor to get a proper diet just at the season when they need it most. It is only the providential cheapness of fish that enables London's street folk to escape what he calls, quoting a telling phrase from the Arctic explorer Sir John Ross, the "starvation from cold" which "follows but too soon a starvation in food" (*LL* 1:119).

One would need to cite impossibly long masses of quotation to evoke at all adequately the intensity and also the analytical acuity of Mayhew's continuing discussion of the influence exercised by cold weather upon all dimensions of street life. His informants allude to it again and again, as in the comments of an old woman living just at the starvation line by selling watercress in the streets: "I was [at the market] this morning at five, and bitter cold it was, I give you my word. We poor old people feel it dreadful. Years ago I didn't mind cold, but I feel it now cruel bad, to be sure" (*LL* 1:149). "I am *so* sick of this life, sir," says a young man whose occupation is selling ham sandwiches at theater doors. "I *do* dread the winter so" (*LL* 1:178). Such testimony continually underlines Mayhew's claim to have discovered that "the ill-paid and ill-fed workpeople prize warmth almost more than food" (*LL* 2:82). This theme reaches its climax in the passages on the Asylum for the Houseless Poor at the end of volume 3, where he describes the appalling spectacle of the applicants for admission waiting outside in the cold, wind, and snow, "with their bare feet, blue and ulcerous with the cold, resting for hours on the ice and snow in the streets, and the bleak stinging wind blowing through their rags" (*LL* 3:417). Then he pictures the group of "houseless wanderers" gathered around the stove in the sleeping ward, avidly warming themselves. "One and all are stretching forth their hands, as if to let the delicious heat soak into their half-numbed limbs. They seem positively greedy of the warmth, drawing up their sleeves and trousers so that their naked legs and arms may present a larger surface to the fire." One poor wretch with the ague crouches "with his legs near as a roasting-joint to the burning coals, as if he were trying to thaw his very marrow" (*LL* 3:428–29).

In the language of synesthesia that runs through this passage, the heat that drives away the numbing cold is "delicious," reminding us again of the symbolic and physiological interchangeability of the two primitive needs for warmth and food. The poor of the Asylum, victims of "starvation from cold," gluttonously devour the stove's heat to drive away deadly numbness, and nothing less than a scorching intensity of heat will do. All this stress on the unexpected correlation of two physiological drives and on the ambiguous crossovers that affect sensory experience in these areas brings us back to Mayhew's analysis of the street people's craving for heavily spiced foods. More than a mere physical reaction caused by damaged taste buds, this craving, he strongly implies, is in its deep logic a symbolic formation based on little more than the figure of speech which designates such food as "hot." The longing for certain foods expresses in a radically figurative mode the longing for warmth and sensation and the terror of the numbing effect of cold, and to this extent is as much an object of interpretive decoding as is costermonger patois. Indeed, it is essentially a linguistic phenomenon, a pun charged with so much affective force that it takes sensuous form. We can recall here Malinowski's striking definition of symbolism as "the modification of the original organism which allows the transformation of a physiological drive into a cultural value" (*Scientific Theory* 132). This synesthetic transformation, this infusion of value and meaning into physical sensations and outward objects simultaneously, is exactly what Mayhew shows to occur under the auspices of the metaphor of "hot" food.

I have cited Harriet Martineau's *How to Observe* (1838) as evidence of the early appearance of the idea of treating cultural products as elements of unconscious symbolic systems; even so, there is next to nothing in the language of sociocultural analysis current in the eighteen-fifties that could serve as warrant for the thesis on street gastronomy sketched in above, or that probably could have allowed Mayhew himself to state it in propositional terms; as a result, he sets it forth only by implication. Yet the implication is plain enough in his elaborate study of the compulsive taste of the street folk for the kind of spicy treats provided, for example, by Jewish street-sellers of hot elder wine, some of whom spike their brew heavily with raspberry vinegar to lend "a sharp pleasant twang," while others increase "the heat and pungency" of the wine by adding whole black pepper (*LL* 1:190). The urgency of the need for stimulating warmth and the mediation of this need by figurative language stand out with particular clarity in the rhetoric associated with other spiced delicacies traditionally purveyed to the poor by street vendors. "Hot spiced gingerbread! hot spiced gingerbread! . . . sm-o-o-king hot!" is the cry of one (*LL* 1:160); "One a penny, two a penny, hot Chelsea buns! Burning hot! smoking hot! r-r-r-reeking hot! hot Chelsea buns!" cries another (*LL* 1:102), in a traditional formula appealing evidently to a dread that street people carry in their "very marrow," yet transforming it into the exhilarating discourse of still another flamboyant public performance. (Even food is a theatrical, which is to say a symbolic, medium for the London poor.) Hot eels are served in the streets, like other such items, with pepper and vinegar, and "the street-boys are extravagant in their use of vinegar" (*LL* 1:161). "The pies in Tottenham-court-road are very highly seasoned," Mayhew remarks, quoting a rival pieman who lost his customers to the purveyors of these treats so fiercely peppery that one "nearly took the skin off my mouth" (*LL* 1:196). "It ain't such bad wine," comments a choosy street lad at an elder-wine stand, "but not the real spicy" (*LL* 1:190).

This gustatory code based on the craving for spiciness, like the sartorial one based on the gaudiness of "flash" silk handkerchiefs, has the character of an organized public institution: this is Mayhew's point in examining at great length its outward manifestation, the amazing system of establishments which has come to exist in London for the vending of succulent "street luxuries" (*LL* 1:160, 197), mainly of the hot and spicy kind: roasted apples and chestnuts, hot eels and hot peas-soup, cough drops, oranges, ginger-beer, plum pudding, sweet-meats, baked potatoes, hot coffee, pickled whelks, meat and fruit pies of every description, brandy balls and peppermint sticks, buttered muffins and crumpets, sherbet, lemonade, and a great deal more. In his densely detailed ethnographic survey of these materials, Mayhew, by revealing the profound emotional value with which hot, tangy, spicy foods are invested in the eyes (on the palates, rather) of the poor, lets us see the great array of the London nomads' spicy treats ever more clearly in the aspect of "a galaxy of signifiers," of what Durkheim calls collective representations. Far from being mere physical and commercial entities, they are mental ones above all, constellated imagery of some of the deepest currents of imaginative life of this people. At the same time, Mayhew further prefigures Malinowski by giving an overriding stress to the significance and value of customary pleasures, "of the *joie de vivre*, . . . of all the bonds of intense interest . . . which bind members of a human community to existence." One wonders if Malinowski in writing that phrase (*Argonauts* 466) could conceivably have had a reminiscence of the phrase of Mayhew's, quoted already, from the opening of *London Labour:* "the only thoughts that trouble [the coster youths] are for their girls, their eating and their gambling—beyond the love of self they have no tie that binds them to existence" (*LL* 1:39). What Mayhew comes to discover is that it is precisely such ordinary pleasures, morally disreputable though many of them may be in the case of street people, which "bind them to existence" in society, the binding filaments being, we have seen, networks of stylistic effects charged with cryptically expressed meaning. In giving the most pro-

found and most deeply sociological expression of this pleasure principle to be found in Victorian literature, Mayhew dissents sharply from
the received idea of his age that restraint, discipline, and work were
the forces of social cohesion, and that pleasure and desire, which arise
from "animal instinct" and never free themselves from the taint of
their base origins, were those of disintegration. Victorian assumptions, we have seen, survive tenaciously in latter-day theories, deriving
more or less immediately from Freud, that social order is achieved
only at the cost of "an impoverishment of desire" (Bersani 6);
Mayhew's book offers among other things an immensely sophisticated, though always ambivalent, correction to such a view.

The point still to be made about the theme of "spiciness" in *London Labour* is that this principle, far from being confined to the gastronomic realm, pervades the whole culture of many sectors of the homeless London poor. Mayhew makes the point explicitly a few times, then
leaves the reader to follow out its wider ramifications. One informant
tells him, for instance, that costermongers in their reading habits "like
something spicier" (*LL* 1:25) than the kinds of educational literature
that philanthropists try to get them to read. Street book-auctioneers,
testifying in eloquent fashion to "the style-permeated thinking of
[the] collective" to which they belong, accordingly hawk their wares
by employing just the rhetoric of the Chelsea-bun-sellers. "They are all
recommended as explanatory of every topic of the day, and are often
set forth as 'spicy'" (*LL* 1:297). Here the fetishized term means, of
course, smutty, as it does in the street cries for the titillating item
known in the trade as "indecent snuff-boxes": "spicy snuff-box, very
cheap" (*LL* 1:441). These phrases bring our reconstruction of
Mayhew's argument full circle by making evident the symbolic correspondence between the street folks' passion for peppery, vinegary
food and their deep collective attraction to lawlessness, obscenity, and
vice, their idolization of criminality, their bitter defiance of the police,
their craving for entertainments that "outrage all decency" (*LL* 1:298)
and in general for all things "political, libellous, irreligious, or indecent" (*LL* 1:239). Habitual immorality among the street folk is evidently to be interpreted as one more means of metaphorical expression of their craving for the invigorating warmth that drives away the
"cold"—that is, the whole array of numbing, deadening influences,
including middle-class norms of virtue and propriety, to which destitute outcasts are subjected.

The more closely we read Mayhew's text, the more "animal passions" and biological needs among the poor tend to resolve into chains or clusters of unconscious signifiers of this kind, and to call for a mode of interpretation that draws the most disparate-seeming elements of street life—sex, cuisine, language, politics, costume—into a stylistically coherent "complex whole," each particle of which finally implies a system of figurative equivalences with all the others. Mayhew brands the illicit trends in the culture of the poor as signs of a degradation needing to be counteracted by agencies of moral improvement—though he always insists that attempting to impose upper-class respectability on the poor through coercive means is cruel and futile. But *London Labour,* from the ethnographic angle of vision which it takes on social problems, continually hints at a more scandalous register of thought by giving to the moral depravities of the homeless poor the character of a desperate communal resistance to annihilation and by showing the chaotic-seeming world of these people to be organized in a remarkably cohesive ensemble of institutions, a unified way of life which implicitly is immune, if only for this reason, to moral evaluation from an external set of standards. The increasing flow of Mayhew's sympathy toward his often disreputable and even criminal informants, and his increasingly harsh indictment of the cruelties and hypocrisies of his own native sphere of the population, are after all the plainest things of all in this book.

If he extends so much of the tolerance of "moral relativism" to the culture of the London poor, it is finally on the grounds that this culture is what enables many of his poverty-stricken informants not to succumb to "degeneration," but to produce themselves against all odds as variegated, cultivated, self-aware personalities endowed with what Jean Itard terms "the characteristic faculties of their species": wit, intelligence, imagination, sensuality, emotion. In making or at least pervasively implying such an argument, *London Labour* offers a remarkable gloss upon Mary Douglas's analysis of the cultural symbolism regularly attached to tabooed pariah castes, "persons," in her words, "in a marginal state ... who are somehow left out in the patterning of society, who are placeless" (*Purity and Danger* 95). Despised as carriers of pollution by those within the official social hierarchy, such groups represent, according to Douglas, "both danger and power," and are especially prone to be invested with "spiritual power" and black magic, even with "sacredness" (*Purity and Danger* 94, 112).[24] The officially nonexistent street folk portrayed in *London Labour* seethe with just this kind of ambiguous power, which seems at first to be that of a "furor" of sheer libido in a monstrously pure, unmodified, ungoverned state. But in exploring his fundamental insight that desire can scarcely assert itself in the world, which is to say, in human society, without suffering translation into a mode of symbolic expression, a "fiction" laden with a cargo of meaning, Mayhew lets us guess that the aura of frightening spiritual power which seems to surround marginal, drastically impoverished, culturally dispossessed populations may spring from the idea that their predicament imposes upon them the need actually to manufacture their own collective humanity for themselves. The enterprise of manufacturing humanity has inevitably a sacrosanct or desecrating character—see Mary Shelley's *Frankenstein*—and it means calling into play sociopsychic forces radioactive with contaminating energy (the energy clearly registered in *London Labour* in Mayhew's troubled fascination with proletarian vices and with the polluting filth that pervades proletarian life) and prone at every moment to fly destructively out of control in one or another form of "moral insanity." From this point of view, the nearly demented desires of London's "nomadic tribes" seem to signify not an anarchic denial of social order after all, but almost the opposite: a strenuous labor to project ordered meaning and value into a singularly terrible world where meaning and value can scarcely survive.

THE NOVEL OF CULTURAL SYMBOLISM: DOCTOR THORNE

The Metaphorics of "Depth" and the Role of the Novel

The theory of culture in the "wide ethnographic sense" has been portrayed in this book not as an issue of objective knowledge or as a disinterested, rhetorically neutral logical construct, but as a highly motivated discursive formation whose advent is registered, even before it has assumed distinct form, by the turbulence it generates within various nineteenth-century fields of thought. It acts in particular as a focus of revulsion from the Evangelical mentality that exerted so broad an influence throughout this period—and that seemingly lent its paradigm of an all-pervading, meticulously organized system of law and discipline, and its myth of the traumatic spiritual new birth of the believer as well, to the culture theory itself. But while we have tried to guess at the convoluted relations which thus link the emerging theoretical entity, "culture," to a widely disseminated "thought style," the analysis has tended to run against its own logic by localizing the culture idea in fairly specialized fields of scholarly and speculative discourse. It is true that, in the nineteenth century, technical fields like political economy, ethnology, sociology, and linguistics were at once far more accessible to nonspecialist audiences and more visibly marked with moral and other themes of popular thought than they have been since. Even so, the goal of this concluding chapter is to witness something of the immediate impact of the culture thesis upon popular imagination, and also to examine the logic of the decisive reaction of the latter upon the former, by considering as a final realm of discourse that particularly sensitive indicator (and instigator) of nineteenth-century popular consciousness, the novel.

This will entail by way of introduction a brief discussion of the metaphor of "depth" and its necessary correlate, "superficiality" or "shallowness."

Without broaching the question of when and how the figurative sense of "deep" can be said to have originated and to have acquired its commanding function in Western discourse,[1] it seems likely that its intensive exploitation in the nineteenth century and after owes much to Wesley and to the Christian tradition of original-sin theology that his evangelism helped inject into modern awareness. Wesley's chief postulate (which was given even more extreme stress in Whitefield's Calvinistic Methodism) was in effect that outward conduct and conscious motives are merely signs of or masks for a more significant level of phenomena, "the folly and wickedness which are deep rooted in [our] souls" (Wesley, *Works* 9:280)—the "subterranean" forces of primitivism which, as Frazer put it long afterward, lie permanently "beneath the surface" of civilized life (*Golden Bough* 1:236).[2] At least among the unregenerate portion of humanity, no amount of apparent respectability and good works, no amount of selfless Christian virtue, could ever be more than a delusive surface appearance laid over the "unfathomable depth of wickedness" (Wesley, *Works* 9:463) in the human spiritual constitution. All experience was interpreted in Evangelical homiletics by reference to this radical polarity of superficiality versus depth, seductively empirical-sounding terms which came to be synonymous with falsity and truth respectively, and which for purposes of practical morality were closely correlated with the polarity of the worldly versus the spiritual, and further, by an imperceptible extension, with that of the collective versus the individual. From this clustered concatenation of terms, two closely related principles derive (and pass historically from puritanical theology into middle-class moral doctrine, guaranteeing that modern experience will be infested with self-contradiction): first, that a more or less radical emancipation from the regime of conventional social values (pride of wealth and station in particular) is necessary to spiritual renewal, and that those unregenerate citizens who persist in devotion to social conventionality and worldly pursuits lack spiritual "depth."

Given the strong hold that conventionality has upon us, emancipation from it can only come about through an agonizing experience of solitude, introspection, and self-annihilation figured most easily as a descent into the depths of the self: so "deeply" ingrained is this mythic configuration in nineteenth-century thinking that even avowedly antireligious texts like Mill's *Autobiography* or Butler's *The Way of All Flesh* distinctly play it out. So too, in a form peculiarly germane to our topic, does Beatrice Webb's *My Apprenticeship*. In the crucial episode of this book, the author describes herself as discovering her sociological vocation by temporarily suppressing her conventional identity—"let us be emptied of ourselves," said Wesley (Southey 1:117)—in order to carry out an initial experiment in "participant observation" among working-class folk. This is no mere data-gathering technique for Webb, but a spiritual exercise of radical self-renewal, and it is carried out under the immediate auspices of the metaphorical themes that we are tracing here. Her life in upper-class worldly society was invalid, she says, for the specific reason that it afforded merely "surface impressions without depth" and stimulated only "the superficial part of my . . . intellect"; there remained "lurking in the depths of [my] nature a profound discontent" with worldly life. From such ideas come her increasingly extreme self-alienation from "Society," her symbolic shedding of her identity, and her self-consecration to the scientific project of "research into the constitution and working of social organization" (*My Apprenticeship* 64, 145, 146). With the help of such a text, we can glimpse clearly in the nineteenth-century metaphorics of "depth" the conceptual link bonding together such diverse fields of discourse and practice as Methodist theology, ethnographic fieldwork, psychoanalysis, and popular fiction: all institute mechanisms through which one sheds or pierces social conventionality in order to reach knowledge of deeper-lying truths and thus some version of what Wesley called "justification."

In all these contexts, "deep" is a radically metaphorical value word, a rhetorical intensifier, rather than the descriptive one which it claims to be. Insofar as it has any empirical reference at all, it designates that which is ulterior or occult, that which, to quote again Spencer's characterization of the subject matter of sociology, "cannot be manifest to perception" (Spencer, *Principles* 1:436). As at many other points, the language of sociocultural analysis coincides here with that of the evangelical religion it opposed. Sounding for all the world like Durkheim on the metaphysics of "sociological method," Wesley stresses that the function of Methodist discipline is to cultivate "faculties suited to things invisible," things "not perceivable by these gross senses": for instance, the presence of unconscious "sin" in every act of unredeemed men and women (Southey 2:66, 301). To grant a royal privilege to this category of invisibility as we automatically do, to define as most authentic that which is least accessible to direct observation, signals (apart from the residual influence of religious mythology) a huge investment of prestige in various mechanisms of investigation—essential truth must be deeply hidden, otherwise what function can be performed by strenuous technologies of discovery like psychoanalysis?—even as it signals yet more clearly, perhaps, the

determining power of figurative diction once the process of reification has acted upon it. This power authorizes Michel Foucault, for
instance, to dismiss out of hand all possible evidence of nondisjunctive
evolution of thought as "doubtless only a surface appearance"—such
evidence seems disqualified by the very fact that it *appears*—and to
validate his own interpretive paradigm as one which has reference to
"the deepest strata of Western culture," those lying at "a level that I
have called, somewhat arbitrarily perhaps, archaeological" (*Order* xxii,
xxiv, xi). A trope endowed with so much coercive rhetorical power that
it can reverse the categories of the visible and the invisible before our
eyes must derive that power ultimately from unconscious lines of association laden with great emotional value.

Still, for all its later efficacy, the mystifying figure of "depth" bore
ambiguous significance for social sciences in their early phases. Not
only did these sciences strive to preserve a rigorously empirical character based on study of the factual surface of society, but they also
tended to focus upon precisely those factors in human life traditionally classed as superficial, valueless, and despiritualized (political
economy being guiltiest of all in this regard, of course). Since these
were the very things that moral hygiene required one to disavow, the
social sciences thus readily took on an ignoble character. Mayhew
seems defiantly to advertise this problem by loading his sociology with
the basest and most repellent imagery possible. Beatrice Webb herself
was dismayed by the destruction of idealizing religious values by "the
cult of science." On the other hand, it was precisely by laying claim to
the all-authenticating rhetoric of depth, as Foucault so imperiously
does, that the scientific culture thesis came into its own and, despite
its hostility to key aspects of Wesleyan belief, associated itself inseparably after all with Wesleyan and what we can call post-Wesleyan sensibility. To study culture as such was to delve below surfaces and to reveal
deep patterns, deep trends, deep structures. Various features of social
life, even the most meaningless- and dysfunctional-seeming institutions, took on authenticity as objects of study along several axes of the
metaphor of depth. First, they were proclaimed to possess a dimension
of *historical* depth, representing as they do the outcome of long historical formations which can be reconstructed through exercises of the
kind that McLennan, Tylor, Spencer, Frazer, Durkheim, and Mauss
produced in abundance. Tylor made a point of comparing this sort of
reconstructive work to excavations below the earth's surface to retrieve vestiges of paleolithic life and skeletal remains of extinct ani-

mals (*Primitive Culture* 1:59). Cultural time is specifically marked by its property of "depth," in other words: Foucault's equation of cultural study with archaeology was (of course) not "arbitrarily" chosen at all. Second, institutions possess *psychological* as well as temporal depth, according to the emerging theory—prefigured in Wesleyan doctrine, as we noticed—that members of a society are necessarily unconscious of the "deep" logic of their devotion to customary ideas and practices; and they possess *hermeneutic* depth, once we recognize the primacy in human life of symbolic meaning obscurely embedded in ordinary cultural items, meanings only recuperable at the cost of much interpretive digging. The more of this that is required, the "deeper" the meaning is said to lie, thus the truer and more significant it is taken to be. We recall that Lévi-Strauss identifies Mauss's supposed transcending of mere empirical data in the name of an effort to reach "deeper realities" (*Introduction* 38) as the point of origin of modern ethnographic analysis. However accurate his historical account or his reading of Mauss may be, he accurately defines in this statement the rhetorical formula whose unique prestige has long been relied upon to secure the plausibility of cultural interpretation.

The role played by the novel in nineteenth-century Britain was likewise strongly mediated by the trope of depth, which appears in this context, we shall see, with its primitive Wesleyan valences scarcely obscured at all. The norms to which the novel was subject in this period implied, however, a nearly unbridgeable gap between novelistic style and the kinds of representation which flow from the ethnographic theory of culture. Wolf Lepenies has fully documented the tension that was felt to exist between imaginative literature and the new social sciences in the nineteenth century: sociologists, he shows, waged a long campaign to rid their discipline of the taint of the literary and thus to conquer as best they could their chronic, disorienting sense of being ambiguously suspended "between literature and science." Novelists had a more secure charter and could afford to take more for granted the antagonism of their own guild to the mentality of social science; even so, the antagonism comes out now and again in cruelly satirical fictional portraiture of exemplars of this mentality: Gradgrind, the fetishist of Malthusian "fact" in *Hard Times,* Casaubon the hapless theorist of the origins of mythology in *Middlemarch,* or the dreary sociological Baileys (caricatures of Sidney and Beatrice Webb) in Wells's *The New Machiavelli* are instances of this revealing motif. All these grotesques are indicted for their shallowness of human feeling and—what appears to be the same thing—for being tyrannized by pseudoscientific patterns of thought. They appear as effigies of the novelists' sense of a fundamental incompatibility between social science and their own province.

The main factor in this incompatibility is the novel's overriding commitment, through its always central function of generating empathetic identification with imaginary (usually idealized) characters,[3] to the principle of individual personality and of the primacy of personal will. Freud is surely right to declare that at the center of all fiction there stands its true organizing element, "His Majesty the Ego" ("Creative Writers and Day-Dreaming," *Standard Edition* 9:150).[4] Thus, in its dominant bias toward achieving "truth to individual experience" (Watt 13), the novel is incorrigibly *psychological,* reproducing and reinforcing John Wesley's fixation, which left so deep a mark on Victorian subjectivity, upon the spiritual drama of individual conscience, reflection, and introspection. We have come back to where we began, for the novelistic effect known as "depth" has always been closely correlated with the narrative of solitary individual character, particularly at moments of crisis or even of breakdown—Fagin in the condemned cell, Dorothea on her disillusioning honeymoon in Rome, Jane Eyre dreaming of escape from drudgery and servitude—that bring secret facets of the mind into view and create with this device the wonderful novelistic illusion of individuality generating itself before our eyes. (The principle that the breakdown of self and self-discovery are the same event is of course the Wesleyan principle par excellence.) A nineteenth-century reviewer succinctly formulates the role of the trope of "depth" in the theory and practice of Victorian fiction. "Almost every nature has depths about it somewhere, with all sorts of moral curiosities at the bottom, if one has plummet deep enough to sound them," declares this writer, who goes on to identify the greatest novelists, like Charlotte Brontë and George Eliot, with exactly this function of fathoming psychological depths; and it is this operation, the reviewer asserts, that reflexively gives such writers' works "so deep a hold over the interests and affections of the reader" (Smalley 171).

In sharpest possible contrast to the novelistic cult of deep, singularized individuality, the culture theory decrees, as Malinowski says, a portrayal of human life confined to "stereotyped manners of thinking and feeling." The cultural anthropologist, he warns his readers, is "not interested in what A or B may feel *qua* individuals" (*Argonauts* 23). The student of social experience as such, Durkheim announces in the same vein, stressing his sharp divergence from ingrained prejudice, "must abandon psychology as the center of his operations," for "there is a deep line of demarcation between the social and the psychic" (*Rules* 75, 106). The realistic novel is characterized by detailed portrayals of the social environment, as has very often been observed, but it needs to be observed as well that society appears in fictional literature endowed with overwhelmingly negative significance only: as static background to the narration of individual characters' experience and (just as in *My Apprenticeship*) as an oppressive, stultifying, inauthentic system of life, typically a system of prejudice and respectable hypocrisy, from which the hero and heroine must in some fashion free themselves in the name of personal values. Individuality is effectively defined within the rhetorical system of nineteenth-century novels as one's capacity for resisting social pressures of conformity.[5] To incorporate into fiction in any concerted, explicit way the ethnographic thesis that individual personality is parasitic upon standardized or stereotyped cultural patterns, that emotions are not the antithesis of social institutions but *are* social institutions themselves, and that events spring not from personal will but from the "subtle and complex [causation] which runs," as Spencer said, "through the actions of incorporated men" (*Study of Sociology* 4), would undo at its root the vital principle of novelistic imagination.

At every point which follows from this fundamental opposition of modes, the novel and the discourse of cultural analysis appear as irreconcilable-seeming antitheses. The novel, with its fixation on individuality and its absorption in empathetic identification, deploys a rhetoric of pathos and sentiment, while it is something like the very condition of the discourse proper to social science to banish such effects: the sociologist, as Spencer said, must strive to contemplate his field of study through the lens of an "almost passionless consciousness" (*Principles* 2:232). Such a phrase suggests that modern social science, no less than other modes of modernist art and thought, was impelled by a nauseated reaction against the long Victorian regime of extravagant sentiment—a regime associated especially closely with the fictional literature of the age. Novels by the same token create dramatic structures, trains of events bound together at every junction by the principles of suspense and climax, while cultural analysis is ideally vacant of events and so closely wed to the hypothesis of a system in a state of static equilibrium that critics like Gellner and Archer have charged it with manifest impotence to account for social change.[6]

Novelistic emotion and the activity of sympathetic identification are inseparable, too, from the invocation of binding moral rules; the science of culture, by contrast, has always taken as its own principle of integrity a relativistic suspension or even disavowal of moral rules. In all these ways and in others as well, the novel and the study of culture appear irreconcilably at cross purposes.

Could the culture idea come into ascendancy in a novel, it could only do so, one imagines, in an anomalous fictional type that would be marked not only by dramatic inertia and by shallowness, but by an affective privation altogether at odds with the richness of pathos and of titillation that marked Victorian novels in both their respectable and sensational varieties. This hypothetical genre would (like orthodox realistic fiction) be profuse in sociological detail, but in order truly to express the idea of culture, it would above all need to find ways of insisting distinctly upon the *symbolic* character of sociological features, and, what is in fact the same thing, upon their systematic integration. To some extent the idea of the unconscious symbol is inherent in that of a society as, in Mill's phrase, a closed code "containing within itself all that is necessary for its own interpretation" (*Bentham* 80), and we have seen in previous chapters something of the emergence of a symbolically oriented social analysis in political economy and in Mayhew. But given the all-importance of the principle of symbolism for the culture concept, we need here to pause briefly to describe how this principle crystallized in early anthropological literature. Then we can turn to a nineteenth-century popular novel for illustration of the issues just surveyed.

The Anthropology of the Symbol

In light of the domination of nineteenth-century anthropology by the evolutionary hypothesis, it would seem at first glance that cultural awareness could hardly have emerged in this field. Marc Augé pointedly says that "evolution and culture are two terms that ought, properly speaking, to be mutually exclusive" (Augé 51). Evolutionary theory emphasizes in effect the inadequacies of each society's system of life so as to explain the laws of progressive development of higher, more complex "civilized" forms from low primitive origins; the postulate of culture, on the other hand, sees each society as a fully integrated unity and as a significant object of study in its own right, and rejects any hierarchical classification of societies as more or less "advanced." Furthermore, "by the sixties, anthropology and racial determinism"—the very antithesis of culturalism—"had become almost synonyms" (Harris 101). And yet one can make out fairly clearly in nineteenth-century evolutionist literature the emergence of the concept of institutions as systems of unconscious symbolism—the concept which in the generation of Mauss, Boas, and Benedict would become the core of the explicit culture idea and would send Victorian social-evolutionary thinking into obsolescence. The main vehicle of this development (and, it seems likely, of the dismantling of racialist theories) was the evolutionist doctrine of *survivals.*

According to this doctrine, each advanced society is honeycombed with ideas and practices which are explainable not, so to speak, empirically, in terms of present function or of any significance which might consciously be ascribed to them by members of the society, but only as the unconscious residues of past stages of historical development. "The meaning even of familiar thoughts and practices" is likely to escape analysis altogether, says in 1865 the leading survival theorist, E. B. Tylor, unless we are able to rediscover their origins in primitive culture (*Researches* 1). In other words, the most banal items of social life are conceived from the point of view of survival theory as symbolic formations expressing their true "meaning"—their occult reference to forgotten primitive institutions—in obscurely coded form requiring an intensive work of quasi-linguistic interpretation to decipher. The idea of function as a principle of social analysis is thus sharply displaced by that of meaning. As survival theory comes into focus in this way as essentially a semiology, a theory of the signifying character of social practices, we are able to see its continuity with Tylor's early attempts to unriddle "the relation between idea and sign" (*Researches* 11) in various modes of human language—a category to which he gives a greatly expanded definition—and to understand why, dissenting from another authority, he should have asserted "*Man* is essentially . . . not 'the speaker,' but he who thinks, he who *means*" (*Researches* 58). Tylor says this, although the main thrust of all his work is to show that the distinctive characteristic of *Homo significans* is *not to know,* in effect to have forgotten, what he "means," since much of the "original expressiveness" which Tylor postulates for human sign-systems "has no doubt disappeared beyond all hope of recovery" (*Primitive Culture* 1:229). Thus the operations of evolutionary theorists upon "things which seem to have outlived the recollection of their original meaning" (Tylor, *Researches* 126), however incompatible their theory may at last have been with the doctrine of culture, in fact laid the groundwork for latter-day cultural interpretation. As is true for exegetes of culture, the key principle for evolutionists was that social life is a dense matrix of symbolic signifiers, and that in utilizing them, people are unconscious of their own figuratively represented meanings, "meaning" being a function vested not in personal psychology (a field that drops out of this discourse) but in representational codes.

Spencer's *Principles of Sociology* offers many brilliant proto-Fraserian analyses based on this concept. The widely prevalent rite of self-bleeding in funeral ceremonies thus is traceable, he speculates, to forgotten origins in cannibalism, and is symbolically equivalent to multifarious practices of symbolic mutilation, scarification, tattooing, and other forms of marking the human body (*Principles* 2:70ff.). Cultural meaning runs along proliferating linkages of signs, and escapes ordinary knowledge: this is Spencer's chief anthropological principle.

John McLennan's important writings base themselves in the same way on the idea that evolving societies carry along elements of primitive life "disguised," as he puts it, "under a variety of symbolical forms." To study a society from an anthropological point of view is therefore to unravel its institutionalized symbols. "In the whole range of legal symbolism there is no symbol more remarkable than that of capture in marriage ceremonies," he declares, focusing his research on the occurrence of this feature in marriage practices in diverse and far-flung societies. He brings modern cultural anthropology into being almost at one stroke by denying out of hand that "the mere lawlessness of savages" or "the mere instinctive desire of savages to possess objects cherished by a foreign tribe" could ever have been "consecrated into a legal symbol": "it must have been *the system* of certain tribes to capture women," and the system itself must have originated "in their circumstances, their ideas of kinship, their tribal arrangements." Social symbolism refers ultimately not to "instinctive desire" or even to isolated practices but to deeply integrated systems of ideas, values, and conventional practices, McLennan thus argues (*Primitive Marriage* 7, 11, 20).

Given their fixation upon diachronic rather than synchronic relations, and upon anomalous "survivals" rather than effectively functioning institutions, the evolutionists' investigations of symbolism in social life may seem to remain largely foreign to an ethnographic idea of culture. This is scarcely true, however, of the treatment of the symbol offered by Harriet Martineau in her prescient book on fieldwork method. If an ethnographer lack the vital faculty of imaginative sympathy with his subjects, Martineau warns, "the most important things will be hidden from him, and symbols (in which every society abounds) will be only absurd or trivial forms"; for one alert to the symbolic character of social productions, on the other hand, "everything that he looks upon will instruct him" (Martineau 50, 65). Martineau's interpretive model, in which every social item "from an aqueduct to a punchbowl" acquired symbolic status, suffered from an excess of intellectual audacity, and, having largely disappeared from view in the interim, only came to full articulation in Durkheim. Still working squarely, as one is inclined to forget, within an evolutionist framework, Durkheim fuses and extends the ideas of writers like Spencer and McLennan (and, notably, Robertson Smith) and lays down at last the basis of a full-blown semiological theory of culture.

The key text of Durkheim's in this connection is *The Elementary Forms of the Religious Life* (1912) [*EF*]. His search for such forms, he makes clear, amounts to nothing less than a quest for the original principle of culture itself (*EF* 87, 234, 255).[7] Totemism, which figures in this book as the most primitive phase of religion, is according to Durkheim radically a function of symbolic representation. The most striking manifestation of the mentality of totemic peoples, he declares, is their habit of inscribing the image of the taboo totem animal ubiquitously on and inside houses, on canoes, on every sort of utensil, on ceremonial objects, and on their own bodies (*EF* 135); symbolic tattooing in particular he declares to occur "almost automatically" among people at the totemic stage of development (*EF* 264). Culture in its quintessential form is thus a proliferation of one dominant symbolic representation throughout the life of a society. Without quite making the point explicit, Durkheim's analysis implies that the insistent marking process of culture causes all customs and objects within a given social field (human bodies included) to be at some level symbolic equivalents of one another: a single meaning pervades all and gives to the most diverse-seeming things a single conceptual structure. His signal finding as he develops this analysis is that in totem societies the most sacred thing is the stylized totemic image itself—often so cryptic that it bears no overt relation whatever to the thing supposedly represented (*EF* 148–49)—and that the real totemic animal designated in tribal imagery occupies a distinctly inferior position. "*The images of totemic beings are more sacred than the beings themselves*" (*EF* 156). From this discovery of the unique prestige with which "figured representations" (*EF* 216) are endowed among primitives, Durkheim boldly extrapolates the view not only that social life in general consists in "a vast symbolism" but indeed that mentally speaking, "a man is nothing more than . . . a system of representations" (*EF* 264, 259). What these representations ultimately all refer to, he argues here as in other works like *Primitive Classification,* is nothing other than *the structure of society itself.* Totemism therefore is not a system of animal worship at all, but "a system of ideas with which the individuals represent to themselves the society of which they are members, and the obscure but intimate relations which they have with it" (*EF* 257). The collective life is summed up and made possible by a proliferation of conventional symbols the true interpretation of which is again supposed to escape the knowledge of those who live under their sway.

The line of thought which we have traced in its early avatars extends historically at least as far as Clifford Geertz's *Interpretation of Cultures,* where he repeatedly professes his adherence to "the extrinsic theory of thought," which treats human thought as essentially "public" rather than private and as manifested legibly in visible, tangible, overt social phenomena (*IC* 214, 45). Thought, says Geertz, in language evocative of a lot of Victorian speculation of such themes, is "a traffic in significant symbols—objects in experience (rituals and tools; graven idols and water holes; gestures, markings, images, and sounds) upon which men have impressed meaning" (*IC* 362). This argument is best understandable as a (futile) attempt to evade the issues raised once social science, in its theory of structures and internal relations and its preoccupation with the ambiguous category of "meaning," commits itself hazardously to "a principle alien to the domain of the visible" (Foucault, *Order* 227), and it is the same one that Harriet Martineau long before placed at the theoretical center of her essay on fieldwork.

I come back to the primary materials of this chapter by repeating the point that this constellation of anthropological themes seems inaccessible to sustained treatment by a popular novelist. What would become of the requisite mythic drama of the struggle against egoism and natural desire, and what of the function of idealized portrayal and moral instruction, once human beings have been redefined via the culture thesis as bundles of institutionalized symbolism automatically tattooed, if not upon their bodies, upon their personalities? What standing could be accorded a hero or heroine who by virtue of participation in culture is oblivious to his or her own "meanings," which are intelligible only to expert interpreters? How could such fiction, in which ethnographic notation would take precedence over narrative and "things" over persons, in which the most banal customs would be pored over as symbols of "the common mind," in which the roles and personalities of individual actors would be submerged in social conventionality, hope to generate the kinds of dramatic and psychological interest that novelists, courtiers of "His Majesty the Ego" as they are, need to create? It is safe to say that this hypothetical category of novel-writing is bound to be for all practical purposes nonexistent. Yet in the eyes of many readers in the age of Martineau, McLennan, Tylor, and Spencer, one novelist seemed conspicuously prone to just the kinds of deviant fictional practice that we have posited. This was Anthony Trollope.

Trollope and His Reviewers

As Donald Smalley's compilation of Trollope reviews in the *Critical Heritage* series attests, reviewers complained endlessly about what seemed to them to be Trollope's conscious, deliberate "sacrifice of the usual means of exciting interest" in fiction (Smalley 108). For one thing, he was judged to be addicted to depicting "almost perversely prosaic" characters (Smalley 523), thereby failing to gratify, and in fact insulting, the longing of readers for idealized portraiture. This was the "vulgarity" in his writing which decades of reviews vehemently condemned (Smalley 76, 178, 185, 233–37, 249). He seemed further to be trying to produce fiction in which plot structure and dramatic tension, the sine qua non of the Victorian popular novel, were reduced as close as possible to nothing. "Perhaps Mr. Trollope carries his aversion from everything melodramatic to an extreme," says E. S. Dallas, who imagines this allegedly dissident novelist declaring to his public, "I will do what novelists never yet have done; I . . . will sacrifice all the interest of [heavily plotted fiction]" (Smalley 104, 105; see also 51, 63, 125, 242, 329). No less important in Trollope's apparent disregard for the canons of fictional art is his oft-alleged deficiency in the presentation of character, a deficiency invariably couched in the prestigious metaphorics of "depth." Rather than deep psychological explorations, he gives, we are told, only external and thus superficial views of character: "he paints exclusively from without" (Smalley 171); "he photographs the . . . exterior accurately; he does not go below the surface" (Smalley 165). This great failing, Trollope's fixation upon "social surface" and his relative obliviousness to "depth of private character" and "strictly individual life" (Smalley 310, 311), say many commentators, is what produces—is virtually synonymous with—his telltale characteristic, the affective flatness that marks and disables nearly all his work. Incapable as he is of delving down to "the roots" of a character's "passions and affections" (Smalley 311), he offers a "sort of writing [which] can never produce a profound emotion" (Smalley 171). Unlike, say, Scott, Trollope is never "lost in the passion" of the scenes he portrays; "passion . . . is but scantily served" in his novels; "deep . . . passion is not in them" (Smalley 147, 234, 286). Knowingly or not, Trollope in his want of "depth" seemed to have betrayed his calling by coming as close as a novelist could to achieving that "almost passionless consciousness" that Spencer holds up as the ideal of sociological investigation.

One hostile reviewer, in fact, specifically identifies Trollope's affective flatness with a sociological turn of thought, blaming him for devoting his fiction to the tedious notation of a "huge mass of conventionalism" rather than to that which novelists are particularly commissioned to study and to glorify, human individuality; his characters, says this reviewer, "are never viewed as men and women; but only in their relations to Society" (Smalley 131). The phrase makes Trollope's work sound indeed like fiction conceived exactly according to the prescriptions of Spencer, Durkheim, and Malinowski. And on at least a couple of occasions, reviewers glimpsed with great clarity the possibility that the apparent shortcomings in this writer's fiction might amount not just to failings of art and imagination but to signs of a concerted attempt to reconstruct fictional discourse along the lines of cultural analysis. Such reviews are worth citing not only as evidence of sophisticated contemporary appreciation of Trollope as something more than a (failed) popular entertainer, but as signs of the articulation of the concept of cultural analysis itself at a relatively early date. Thus one reviewer, rehearsing yet again the commonplace that Trollope "dealt . . . chiefly with the surface of society," and again lamenting this depthlessness, none the less declares that he has carried out this project with such unprecedented fulness and precision as to constitute an epochal achievement. His novels will for future generations, says the reviewer, "picture the society of our day with a fidelity with which society has never been pictured before in the history of the world" (Smalley 507, 508). This image of an uncompromisingly "empirical" novelist (Smalley 258) almost compulsively driven, as Mayhew, Boas,

and other ethnographers have been said to be, or as Charles Booth
was said to be by Beatrice Webb (*My Apprenticeship* 234), by "an infinite
love of detail" (Smalley 528) in the recording of social phenomena
and by the desire to achieve new standards of fidelity in ethnographic
portrayal: this is the sign of the emergence of a new sensibility in a
field of discourse to which it had been essentially alien. For the reviewer just cited, Trollope does "what novelists have never yet done":
he conceives the social order not as the backdrop for the adventures
of his characters, and not as a system of confining strictures against
which individual personality asserts itself, but as the primary subject
of his "fiction."

The reviewer who grasped the new sensibility most clearly published a clairvoyant essay on Trollope in the *Spectator* in 1865 (the
watershed year which also saw the publication of McLennan's *Primitive
Marriage* and Tylor's *Researches into the Early History of Mankind*). With
other novelists, says this writer, "the creative effort is spent upon the
characters themselves," whereas with Trollope, a new tactic is employed: the interest is decisively shifted to the social environment,
which the characters seem designed in effect simply to illustrate.
"[Trollope's] creative effort is chiefly spent on the little mental and
moral reflectors in which we catch a new glimpse of his characters'
nature and essence"; he "is engaged much more upon elaborating the
infinitely varying social occasions for reflecting character than on creating character itself." Rather than on individual personality considered as a phenomenon unto itself, he dwells on the dynamics of "conventional knowledge and artificial custom" and "seems the more
skilful the more minute and complex are the conventional *nuances*
through which his characters express themselves." "Mr. Trollope is
always strongest," the reviewer declares in a memorable formulation,
"when painting individuals through the customary manners of a class,
and even of classes he paints those manners best which are almost an
artificial language in themselves, which it almost takes an art to interpret" (Smalley 222–23). With great precociousness of vocabulary, the
Spectator reviewer in effect attributes to Trollope the Durkheimian
doctrine that "a man is nothing more than . . . a system of representations" constituted in some fashion by the "vast symbolism" of the so-
ciolinguistic field which he inhabits—a doctrine that brings with it
necessarily a radical revision of novelistic method.

The task of this chapter is to try to vindicate the above reading of
Trollope with reference to one representative novel of his, *Doctor*

Thorne [*DT*] (1858). We shall try in effect to read the book as though it were not a novel at all, but an ethnography of modern England based on a Durkheimian theory of culture. Even if treating the text in this way makes it seem upon reflection to be an anomalous fictional type destined to remain in certain regards without many literary descendants, its appearance, if indeed it bears out the *Spectator* reviewer's thesis, can be taken as signal evidence of the moment of the almost unconscious emergence of the culture idea and of its ambient sensibility in the mid-nineteenth century—and of the sharp pressure which this development exerted upon the Victorian field of discourse at large. There will inevitably remain a gap between the often elusive empirical evidence which can be culled from the text and the general characterization which my argument leads one to draw from it. No modern reader will easily be convinced of the shocking, almost depraved aspect of this writer who most commonly has been faulted (as he sometimes was in his own day as well: Smalley 123, 254–58, 352) for an excess of bland conventionality. Yet we have no choice but to believe the evidence abundantly provided by his reviewers that his work did in fact have the power to scandalize his contemporaries. That this power lay in things in his work that have become at many points almost invisible to us only testifies the more fully to the original disruptiveness of cultural thinking and to how thoroughly that thinking has now become our own.

Symbols of Taboo

We meet in this text our final example of the set of tropes which regularly manifests the reaction of Wesleyan-derived thought against the tendencies of modern cultural analysis. One of the striking features of *Doctor Thorne* is thus the almost melodramatic contrast, as pronounced as in various missionary reports on Polynesian "savages," which it imagines between the theme of anomic appetite on the one hand and that of normal, orderly social existence on the other. The plot originates with a tale of alcoholism, illicit sexual lust, rape (or something close to it), and vengeful murder; and much of the rest of the story hinges on the theme of the suicidal alcoholism, first, of the uncouth self-made millionaire Sir Roger Scatcherd, and then of his doomed son Louis Philippe. Anomie takes somewhat more respectable but no less distinct form in the career of Squire Gresham, who ruins his estate by his uncontrollable expenditure of money on futile election campaigns and on his mania for foxhunting. On the other hand, other characters of the novel, including those clearly intended by the author to stand as models of virtue, display an almost extravagant regard for propriety, self-control, and decorum, and spend what may seem an abnormal amount of time consulting with each other on the interpretation of principles of conduct. This novel thus forms an almost paradigmatic instance of the fable of ungoverned desire confronting its antithesis, the principle of "restraining discipline," or, in nineteenth-century ethnological terms, of the primitive confronting the civilized.

Trollope sets up this schema only to revise it sharply. Increasingly it becomes clear that the pathological drives which operate so destructively in the story are to be interpreted not as "mere instinctive desire" running out of control or as evidence of individual moral depravity, but as an essentially sociological phenomenon. Specifically, they are the symptoms of the cultural dislocation and the flux of social categories, and thus the crisis of personal identity itself, that Trollope presents as endemic to nineteenth-century society and tirelessly illustrates throughout the book—so tirelessly, as we shall see, as almost to turn his novel into a treatise on contemporary social trends. Outbreaks of exaggerated desire are the signs of pervasive, often psychologically unendurable, institutional disorder, which at heart is a perturbation of the symbolic field of British society. At least in retrospect, the "anthropological" character of Trollope's treatise on such themes is striking, for its analysis surveys a broad spectrum of the questions that students of primitive societies would elaborate in ever more technical language in the decades immediately following: caste and kinship structures (centering indeed on the great issue of the avunculate, the institution of paternal and maternal uncles, that soon becomes a crux of anthropological research and debate); social ritual of all kinds; anachronistic "survivals"; and, especially, taboos and ideas of defilement. The deepest affiliation of *Doctor Thorne* with latter-day theories of culture lies, however, in its strand of meditation on how a certain social and psychological environment is bound together, in ways of which the inhabitants of that environment are largely unconscious, by clusters of emotionally saturated symbolic imagery. This tendency in *Doctor Thorne* displaces the issue of anomie and puts novelistic values in jeopardy as it does so.

By far the dominant trait of Victorian society, according to this novel, is the caste system. Everything in the plot (such as it is) hinges on the conflict of love and caste, and the theme of caste is touched on in explicit or indirect form, it is scarcely too much to say, in virtually every line of dialogue. Every human relationship in this society, Trollope reports, is imprinted with people's obsessive awareness of their positions on a minutely differentiated hierarchical scale and with the complex of emotions which this awareness produces: snobbery, social resentment, the longing to migrate upward on the scale. But much of the special imaginative texture of this book, and the aura of potentially subversive thinking which hovers about it, come from Trollope's disinclination simply to treat this theme in terms of the usual polarized moral allegory in which love stands as the locus of the natural, the personal, the profound, and the sacred, and class consciousness as that of the artificial, the merely social, the shallow, and the morally base. Trollope in fact alters the usual schema in radical fashion, as we shall see, by partly siding with the principle of class as against that of young love. But more to the point here is simply his insistence on treating Victorian snobbery, the most banal reality of everyday life, not as a given and a pretext for sentiment but as an enigmatic social formation calling for an intensive process of analysis and explication.

Trollope's analysis focuses on the paradox that people worship the doctrine of caste distinctions and key their whole lives to it to the degree that even their most private and passional experience falls under its sway, *when in fact no one really believes it at all.* Only the most egregious snobs are willing to state such doctrine in so many words, and these very people are the ones most eager to violate it when, say, practical expediency impels them to do so. Lady Amelia De Courcy sends to Augusta Gresham a long philosophical letter explaining to her that since "it has been God's pleasure that we should be born with high blood in our veins," ladies like themselves would suffer "pollution" by marrying attorneys (*DT* 402–5)—and promptly marries the attorney Mortimer Gazebee herself when Augusta, intimidated by her letter, turns down his proposal. We have no reason to think that Lady Amelia's incongruous behavior will cause her snobbery to be any less virulent in the future. Conversely, the many characters in the novel who long to enter the aristocratic orbit from below are full of contempt for the theory of upper-class supremacy. Dr. Thorne himself forms almost the most telling instance of this irrational state of affairs. Not only a man of great moral refinement but also an intellectually advanced man of science, he is fully aware of the ugly absurdity of

but why participation observation

upper-class claims of inherent superiority, an awareness exacerbated by the cruel plight of his beloved illegitimate niece, Mary. "It is hardly too much to say that he naturally hated a lord at first sight." Yet he has aristocratic blood in his own veins, and his own snobbery is after all the elemental force in his personality. His pride in his "good blood," observes the narrator, "made him believe himself to be better and higher than those around him, and this from some unknown cause which he could hardly explain to himself" (*DT* 29, 22). This striking phrase ties Trollope's thinking about social life closely to all the language of invisible agencies and "metaphysical phantoms" which comes to pervade theoretical writing on culture in subsequent decades, and to the ever more dominant stress, which Foucault calls the crucial factor in the human sciences of the late nineteenth century (*Order* 364, 378), on the *unconscious* character of cultural systems. What is the nature of the "unknown cause" which acts irresistibly on every member of Trollope's fictional society, charging with superstitious force a set of ideas which no one regards as intellectually or pragmatically valid? This is the question addressed in a surprisingly concerted way throughout *Doctor Thorne.*

Trollope comes via the medium of literary imagination to essentially the answer reached by another route by evolutionary anthropologists of his time: that the binding principle of social life is symbolism. It is by condensing its organizing ideas, and particularly its key idea of caste hierarchy, in a system of symbolic forms that Trollope's imaginary society endows them with their mysterious coercive power, channelling them, it seems, straight to the unconscious[8] and evading in this way all the problems which they entail on the level of conscious ideology. It follows from this principle that the surest way to discover the "common mind" or *conscience collective* of such a society is by a close interpretive scrutiny of symbolic objects, which is just the activity to which a disproportionate-seeming portion of Trollope's text is devoted. No later than the evocation of the aristocratic estate of Greshamsbury Park in the novel's opening chapter, he distinctly identifies the symbolic motif that turns out to preside over the whole range of social relations depicted in *Doctor Thorne:* the motif of the forbidden threshold.

The focus of the Greshamsbury passage falls on the entrance gates leading both to the house itself and into the park. What dominates the scene is a crudely intimidating display of imagery of prohibition and of the aristocratic family system. "There was an entrance with large gates at each end of the village, and each gate was guarded by the effigies of two huge pagans with clubs, such being the crest borne by the family" (*DT* 8). Opposite each guarded house gate stands an "entrance" to the park where the same ensemble of symbolism proclaims an unambiguous Keep Out. "At the entrance there were four savages and four clubs, two to each portal, and what with the massive iron gates, surmounted by a stone wall, on which stood the family arms supported by two other club-bearers, the stone-built lodges, . . . the four grim savages, and the extent of the space itself, . . . the spot was sufficiently significant of old family greatness" (*DT* 9). We need to read further into the novel to pursue Trollope's idea that systems of semiologically loaded representations like this one are not merely elements of an external decor, but are the junction of the collective and the personal, conduits along which currents of energy pass from codes of public, official values to the unconscious minds of individuals, molding their subjectivity in ways bound to seem unfathomably mysterious. The problematic character of "meaning" in such a process—the theme elaborated by Tylor several years later—is, however, immediately stressed by Trollope. This is his point in having his narrator scrutinize at some length the enigmatic family motto inscribed again and again, like the image of a sacred animal in totem society, about the Greshamsbury gates: "Gardez Gresham."

The motto makes overt the implication that characteristic cultural artifacts like architectural structures need to be given a linguistic character and seen as symbolic texts to be deciphered. To study social "things" ethnographically, the passage intimates, is to try to *read* them. However, this text, though plainly written out in words, proves to be equivocal. Originally the sense of "Gardez Gresham" must have been readily intelligible, the narrator speculates, but now "men were not of one mind as to the exact idea signified" (*DT* 9). The phrase has been attacked by the "disease of language" or semantic decay that Max Müller and his school claimed to be the germinating principle of mythology, and it stands in need of exegesis to restore to it a semblance of meaning. Some interpret "Gardez Gresham" as an exhortation to the symbolic savages to protect the house of Gresham, but the narrator prefers the alternate "signification": that it advises all who might impiously challenge aristocratic supremacy to "beware the Gresham" (*DT* 9). The motto allows a third conjectural reading, unmentioned by the narrator but powerfully indicated by the story of the Greshams' decline as a family and by all that transpires in the novel afterward: "Beware, Gresham." To be a Gresham is to occupy a perilous state, one vulnerable to the vicissitudes of social and political history and perhaps only preservable by self-contradicting acts that strike at the whole upper-class mystique (such as refurbishing family finances, as young Frank Gresham does, by seeking to marry socially taboo heiresses).

Given the undecipherability of this text, which in any of its variant readings epitomizes the ambiguous status of the aristocratic caste in modern-day England, it is all the more striking that the narrator reasserts the importance and value of anachronistic symbolism like that in which the Greshamsbury gates are encrusted. The fact of aristocratic superiority is now highly dubious, he agrees, "but the old symbols remained." They make possible interpretive cultural history: "to him who can read aright, they explain more fully, more truly than any written history can do, how Englishmen have become what they are" (*DT* 9). A dozen years before John McLennan expounded the theory of "survivals" by explaining that "symbols are facts in decadence" ("Worship of Animals" 210),[9] Trollope thus proposes that decoding vestigial symbolic formations is the one authentic way for an interpreter "who can read aright" to rediscover origins and in this way to grasp, at what Foucault would call "the archaeological level," the essential mentality of a society. The hint is clear that some such project underlies the entire novel which we are about to read. Moreover, these supposedly dysfunctional and only obscurely legible symbols continue to exercise a profound influence upon modern sensibility: they in fact are nothing other than the occult "unknown cause" which forms people's beliefs independently of all rational thought. Contrary to what is often said, the narrator thus proclaims, "England is not yet a commercial country"; at heart "she might surely as well be called feudal England, or chivalrous England." The sign of this persistence of the primitive national soul in the modern day is that "merchants as such are not the first men among us; though it perhaps be open, barely open, to a merchant to become one of them" (*DT* 10). We notice that this principle of social organization again crystallizes around the idea of the occluded threshold, the seeming entrance that in reality is "barely open," a principle of exclusion.

In a corresponding passage in chapter 19, Trollope examines the Duke of Omnium's country seat, Gatherum Castle. Focusing particularly on the magnificent façade and entrance, he shows again in this specimen of analysis his grasp of Harriet Martineau's principle that

one uncovers a culture most effectively through close readings of constellations of symbolic things. Newly built of white stone in pseudo-
Italianate style and on the grandest possible scale, Gatherum is "a very
noble pile" (*DT* 206). In fact it amounts to a kind of architectural
definition of the meaning of the term "noble," particularly in its crucial conjunction with the term "house." Since aristocratic rank in this
society is in effect conferred according to how long one's family has
lived in the same ancestral house (the house itself being conceived as
the repository of the sacredness with which a family invests itself
through the metonymy of calling itself a "house"), domestic architecture is bound to be charged with symbolic values, as Gatherum almost
too blatantly is. The grandiose entry hall "was . . . hung round with
various trophies of the house of Omnium; banners were there, and
armour; the sculptured busts of many noble progenitors; full-length
figures in marble of those who had been especially prominent; and
every monument of glory that wealth, long years, and great achievements could bring together" (*DT* 206). This ensemble of figurative
imagery makes an argument which because of its superstitious character cannot be explicitly phrased in words, but only symbolically represented: that the sacred essence called "noble" status derives from the
ancient glory of one's "house" and expresses itself in a mystical energy—a "glory" in the sense of an almost visible radiation, the phenomenon for which Durkheim uses the ethnographic term *mana*—
lodging itself in holy relics like trophies and ancestral images. As these
ideas, survivals of primitive pagan religion (as the pagan savages on
the Greshamsbury portals remind us), ramify in modern society, they
become laced with the manifold ironies which it is the leading task of
Trollope's story to unravel. For one thing, though it is the ancient
status of one's "house" in the sense of family or clan that confers
nobility, this house, Gatherum, is in fact newly built, and in a foreign
style to boot: is authentic culture here on display, or, as Bagehot would
claim in his discussion of these same practices, a mere manipulative
simulacrum of it? Also, in one sense particularly stressed by Trollope's
narrator, this house is an anti-house, for its deliberate magnificence
has made it so uncomfortable as to be utterly useless as a dwelling, and
its noble owner as a result occupies it as little as he possibly can. He
feels none of that direct affective bond with one's house that ought to
certify one's own possession of nobility. There is also the irony particularly elaborated by Durkheim: that symbolic representations of society, such as totemic emblems, are more intensely sacred than the real

beings and objects they nominally represent. Awed though they are by the "glory" transmitted to the Duke of Omnium by his environment of architectural and other symbolism, his visitors regard the man himself with only very moderate deference and respect. It is precisely in this gap between sacralized signifiers and the secular things which they only nominally represent, one may say, that all the disequilibrium (and much of the entertainment value) of Trollope's fictional society originates.

But it is the irony surrounding the entrance-imagery of the house that Trollope once again most emphatically stresses, for the portico and the front door at Gatherum amount in fact to a quite legible symbolism of *refused* entry. "This portico was supported by Ionic columns, and was in itself doubtless a beautiful structure. It was approached by a flight of steps, very broad and very grand; but . . . an approach by a flight of steps hardly suits an Englishman's house," and the front door as a result is closed to ordinary use; the door actually used by the duke and his company is a more modest one located in one of the wings (*DT* 205). "A carriage, however, could on very stupendously grand occasions . . . be brought up under the portico," despite the "rather stiff ascent" necessitated by the castle's entrance road (*DT* 205–6). Gatherum, we may sum up by saying, is erected in Trollope's story as a massive symbol of the principle of inherited social hierarchy, a principle condensed with particular force in the figure of a tabooed threshold designed to discourage and inhibit rather than to allow access. This configuration, reinforced as it is in *Doctor Thorne* by recurrent talk of the danger of "contamination" and "pollution" through improper contact across caste lines (*DT* 28, 403), accords closely with the logic of primitive taboo as explicated by Victorian ethnographers, the central rule of which is that things and places infested with the dangerous radioactivity of *mana* must never be physically touched by common mortals. As we noticed in an earlier connection, indeed, the etymology of the Polynesian word *taboo*, "marked thoroughly," was said to refer specifically to the posting of symbolic insignia to warn unauthorized persons away from radioactive ground (Shortland 81). All the grandiose imagery of entrance at Gatherum—portico, flight of steps, (unused) front door, entrance hall—serves to signify the prohibition of entrance, and subliminally to instil in every beholder's mind the awareness that the key principle of nobility in this society is the one forbidding all outsiders to transgress the sacred precincts.

How this latent idée fixe may actualize itself in public life is spelled out, say, in Trollope's account of the parliamentary election fought between two parvenus, Mr. Moffat and Sir Roger Scatcherd. The episode is an evident sociological allegory dramatizing the aspiration of the nouveau-riche class to inclusion in the national elite; but Trollope, showing again his special slant of understanding, keys the allegory interestingly to the dynamics of political publicity, and particularly to the symbolism of election procedures themselves. Each candidate campaigns under a motto, which in Sir Roger's case is "displayed on four or five huge scarlet banners, and carried waving over the heads of the people" (*DT* 179–80)—another modern survival of ancient ideas of the magical powers of mottos and insignia. Like "Gardez Gresham," the political mottos ("Peace abroad and a big loaf at home" for Scatcherd, "England's honour" for Moffat) are notable mainly for their egregious failure as texts. Rather than being semantically ambiguous, however, they are immediately recognized by all onlookers as semantically vacant: no voter is "so fatuous as to suppose" that either phrase possesses real significance. The signifier has in effect fallen into the lethal gap between itself and its own referent; here again, in other words, official public ideology is a poor index of cultural forces. So, "seeing that language fell short in telling all that was found necessary to be told," both camps change their semiological register by resorting to the fabrication of defamatory cartoons, in which "every possible symbol" of the victim's political shortcomings "was displayed in graphic portraiture on the walls and hoardings of the city" (*DT* 180). The narrator describes these images in detail, for all the world like an ethnographer recording for posterity the curious rituals through which the public life of a remote people is conducted. The process of effecting political "representation," he shows, is at every level a manufacturing of the society's characteristic repertoire of symbolic representations.[10] The scurrilous cartoons take as their main theme therefore the impropriety of lower-class men attempting to claim membership in the nation's traditional ruling elite. That a former stonecutter and the son of a tailor are contesting a seat in parliament is a public joke and a public scandal. Thus the unfortunate Moffat "was drawn with his goose, with his scissors, with his needle, with his tapes; he might be seen measuring, cutting, stitching, pressing, carrying home his little bundle, and presenting his little bill; and under each of these representations was repeated his own motto, 'England's honour'" (*DT* 180). What is projected by this multiplex array of symbolic "representations" which "mark [so] thoroughly" the walls of the town, as by the architectural ones of Gatherum or by the Greshamsbury stone savages, is at bottom once more the pervading idea of forbidden thresholds, the idea according to which Trollope's fictional England intensively organizes its social territory, investing it with its characteristic logic and its characteristic affective valences.[11]

Because Trollope is a novelist and not a theorist of politics, he tracks the ramifications of the principle of caste, "disguised under a variety of symbolical forms" (McLennan), throughout his fictional world in order to highlight at last the irresistible inscription of these forms upon personal experience. Experience at this level in *Doctor Thorne* is markedly patterned, for the emotional syndromes typical of the characters in the story have a definite logic, and it is again and again the logic of the semiology of forbidden entrances which we have sketched. Hence, for example, the episode in which Scatcherd's hard-won seat in parliament is taken away from him for election fraud. "He had made so much of the power of walking into that august chamber"—of crossing the prohibited boundary separating the profane from the sacred, as Durkheim would say—that when he is expelled at last from it by the election judges, the stone savages in real-life form, he is "a broken-hearted man" (*DT* 239). A corresponding scene in which the emotional values are exactly inverted is the one of the illegitimate Mary's arrival at age twelve in her aristocratic uncle's house, an event treated as a euphoria of free threshold-crossings. "He took her first into the shop, and then to the kitchen, thence to the dining-rooms, after that to his and her bedrooms, and so on till he came to the full glory [n.b.] of the new drawing-room, enhancing the pleasure by little jokes, and telling her"—to defuse the anxiety that crystallizes around the twin ideas of tabooed uncleanness and forbidden access—"that he should never dare to come into the last paradise without her permission, and not then till he had taken off his boots" (*DT* 35). The considerable poignancy of the scene depends on its implicit reference to all the most emotively laden symbolism of this society.

We meet the same concentrated set of themes, to cite just one more illustrative scene almost at random, in the episode of the arrival for dinner at Doctor Thorne's of Sir Roger's vulgar alcoholic son Sir Louis. Mary Thorne views him with "aversion" and the doctor with "unutterable disgust"—he is an unclean taboo object in their house, charged (thanks to the reversal of the taboo-theme that seems to occur in modern society) with a kind of metaphysical power of contamination—and they agonize together that he is sure to "come up [to that sacrosanct drawing room] after dinner" and that Doctor Thorne, bound as he is by obligations to the young man's father, "could not turn [Sir Louis] from his door" as he would otherwise do (*DT* 363). Read in the context of what by 1858 was already a rich ethnographic literature on the mechanisms of taboo (a literature which would expand much further still in the works of Frazer and Robertson Smith), this episode seems like many another in *Doctor Thorne* to be forcing readers to try to unpack the strange mental complex, evidently a crux of British culture, in which the idea of illicit entry, symbols of prohibition, and the response of something like physical nausea are intimately intertwined. With "the entrance of the baronet," we are faced with interpreting another array of stylized cultural representations, for Sir Louis is "dressed in what he considered the most fashionable style of the day," and the narrator, typically, pauses to describe this imagery in detail, finding here a perfect instance of "the conventional *nuances* through which . . . characters express themselves." Sir Louis "had on a new dress-coat lined with satin, new dress-trousers, a silk waistcoat covered with chains, a white cravat, polished pumps, and silk stockings, and he carried a scented handkerchief in his hand; he had rings on his fingers, and carbuncle studs in his shirt, and he smelt as sweet as patchouli could make him. But he could hardly do more than shuffle into the room" (*DT* 363). The unfortunate young man is "marked thoroughly" with a vengeance. There is much talk in the novel about the supposedly natural, inherent superiority and refinement of the upper classes; but Trollope's novelistic method everywhere insists, as it does here, that entitlement to cross restricted thresholds like that of the doctor's drawing-room is more than anything else a matter of mastering an almost infinitely complex code of symbolic imagery designed to testify to one's freedom from lower-class contamination. Sir Louis, with his ill-chosen showy costume, his obnoxious perfume, his perpetual violations of etiquette (mentioning unmentionable topics as he compulsively does in polite company), betrays in glaring fashion his unfamiliarity with the secret code and arouses in all his beholders the intense sensation of "disgust" which in modern upper-class England, as in ancient Tahiti, are the instinctual-seeming responses to unauthorized minglings of the sacred and the profane. We may seem far, in the aristocratic drawing-rooms of *Doctor Thorne,* from the heaps of fecal matter and imagery of rats and maggots that occupy so central a place in *London Labour and the London Poor,* but the truth is that as investigators of contemporary taboo-themes and of the logic of civilized disgust, Trollope and Mayhew are closely akin.

Anomaly and Legalism

The national consciousness and unconsciousness may be enmeshed according to *Doctor Thorne* in highly coherent, compulsively self-replicating patterns of symbolic imagery, but incoherence is after all just as strong a factor in Trollope's ethnographic tale. His theme is that the social structure of modern England has undergone a profound shift, causing it to become severely discordant with the structure of cultural values embodied in "the old symbols."[12] With the concentration of wealth in the new entrepreneurial class personified by Scatcherd, and with the economic decline of the landowning gentry represented by the Greshams, the old caste lines, which hitherto distinctly marked the boundary between the clean and the unclean, have become ambiguous, according to Trollope. They remain in force none the less. The result is not the terrible evacuation of cultural value (with its unconscious linkage to Malthusian economics) which menaces the London poor in Mayhew, but, in a sense, the reverse of this: a *surplus* of cultural value in the form of vestigial survivals unable to be psychically or pragmatically assimilated into people's lives. Parvenus buy estates and ape the gentry, but are tormented all the while by the guilty awareness of being impostors. Aristocrats pontificate about the sanctity of "high blood," then writhe with embarrassment as they hunt for rich spouses, no matter how socially ineligible, for their sons and daughters, and brood on the thought that possibly their status in society derives not from a mystical essence of superiority after all, but simply from inherited wealth. Doctors and lawyers dangle agonizingly in an undefined social realm having the most equivocal and ambivalent relations to the upper class. Inhabiting a social order obsessed with caste gradations and profuse in its symbolism of them, yet which in fact is full of internal discrepancies, Trollope's characters typically must endure the fate of being "without a legitimate position in which to stand" (*DT* 83), without "a fixed standing-ground in the world" (*DT* 85), having "no recognised station" (*DT* 257). To feel secure of one's "place in the world" (*DT* 143) is both their most urgent longing and their most elusive goal.

This state is illustrated, for example, by Doctor Thorne, who believes in the sacredness of upper-class blood and is himself related to the ultra-aristocratic Thornes of Ullathorne; but he is "only a second cousin; and, therefore, though he was entitled to talk of the blood as belonging to some extent to himself, he had no right to lay claim to any position in the county other than such as he might win for himself" (*DT* 16); and moreover, he exercises the relatively lowly profession of a country doctor. His honorifically styled "niece" Mary forms an even more extreme instance of anomalous social identity: the illegitimate child of a working-class mother, she thinks of herself as fully entitled to mix socially with the upper classes, paradoxically upholding all the while the doctrine of the mystical purity of aristocratic society. Trollope dramatizes this regime of equivocal or divided social roles with single-minded insistency.[13]

It is clearly one result of this condition of ideological and emotional instability that so much anxious energy is channelled by Trollope's characters into their obsessive activity of policing entryways and denying admittance to whatever or whomever is deemed unclean. It is the reason also for the very noticeable displacement of plot interest in *Doctor Thorne* toward the decoding and exegesis of ambiguous symbolism. Trollope's characters, in fact, seem scarcely to have time in their lives for any other activity than those of theorizing in a quasi-anthropological way about the "old prescriptive principles" (*DT* 404) that regulate social relations and of trying to determine the applicability of these principles to litigious particular cases. There may well be a suggestion here that the development of anthropological imagination in the nineteenth century had its origin in the peculiar social disequilibrium of the age. Trollope turns his characters in any case into compulsive analysts and interpreters of their own culture, and what emerges is again a view of culture in which private experience and public conventions turn out to be indissolubly fused together at every moment.

In one typical episode spanning chapters 6 and 7, for example, the initiating impulse of erotic desire is immediately usurped by, or transformed into, the activity which gives the special genius of Trollope's characters in this novel its fullest play, that of cultural hermeneutics. Having received a reckless proposal of marriage from Frank Gresham, Mary begins reflecting anxiously about the problem of her clouded parentage. The narrator digresses to discuss Beatrice Gresham's responsibility for fostering the intimacy of Frank and Mary even though she has all "the De Courcy veneration for blood" (*DT* 74)—blood, of course, not here in the sense of the bodily fluid that among other things carries charges of sexual impulse, but in the very opposite sense, that of a metaphor of the subservience of "the body and its desires" (Arnold) to the theory of social categories. There follows a long passage analyzing Mary's own thinking on this point. "Mary was also proud of blood" despite uncertainty about her own origins. She is certain that "if she were born a gentlewoman" she is entitled by the unwritten laws of caste to marry any "gentleman," whatever her rank, wealth, or level of fashion may be. But abruptly she realizes that the meaning of these crucial terms has never been fully spelled out to her:

> If she were born a gentlewoman! And then came to her mind those curious questions; what makes a gentleman? what makes a gentlewoman? What is the inner reality, the spiritualised quintessence of that privilege in the world which men call rank, which forces the thousands and hundreds of thousands to bow down before the few elect? What gives, or can give it, or should give it? (*DT* 75)

She finds herself impelled to try to decipher a complex of conventional signifiers, to interpret just as a modern cultural anthropologist would the submerged, unconscious theory on which outward social forms such as the existence of an "elect" caste entitled to worship are grounded:

> And she answered the question. Absolute, intrinsic, acknowledged, individual merit must give it to its possessor, let him be whom, and what, and whence he might. So far the spirit of democracy was strong within her. Beyond this it could be had but by inheritance, received as it were secondhand, or twenty-second hand. And so far the spirit of aristocracy was strong within her. (*DT* 75)

The logical/syntactic vagueness of the key phrase "beyond this" obscures somewhat the fact that Mary's answer to the problem of rank in society is sharply self-contradictory, and that it signals a basic cultural dilemma. The symbolic code of her society, which she here discovers to form the unconscious foundation of her own emotional life, is not unified but divided against itself. Under these vexing circumstances, she refuses Frank's offer, but proceeds none the less to interview her uncle with the aim of learning whether her own family background could ever entitle her to enter into such a marriage. Their conversation takes the form of a detailed survey, much too long to quote, of the quasi-legal technicalities governing rank and marriage taboos in upper-class society. Is the law of caste being violated in Augusta Gresham's upcoming marriage to Mr. Moffat? Does the man confer his own rank automatically upon his wife? Are the Thornes "as grand a family as the Greshams?" Only at the end of all this labored exegesis, "almost perversely" emphasized by Trollope at the cost of sentimental effect, does Mary at last pose a blunt question about her own family background, and receive a veiled but sufficiently clear reply.

According to Foucault, there occurred in the human sciences of the late nineteenth century a decisive "transition from an analysis in terms of functions, conflicts, and significations to an analysis in terms of norms, rules, and systems" (*Order* 361).[14] The passage just cited from *Doctor Thorne* is an early harbinger of this new mode of thought, and it typifies the incessant process in Trollope's novel of analysis and interpretation of the cultural rule-system, from trivial-seeming nuances of etiquette to major conventions of social life and codified legal principles, all of which Trollope plainly sees as forming a single continuous fabric of thinking. To try to grasp the rationale of even the smallest rule of manners is implicitly to try to find out the fundamental system of value which binds all the culture together and by the same token to try in effect to discover what one's own unconscious feelings about the rule in question are. Durkheim makes this kind of interpretive activity, and the necessary role of commissioned experts in performing it, the very sign of the nature of social life. "How often does it happen that we are ignorant of the details of the obligations that we must assume, and that, to know them, we must consult the legal code and its authorised interpreters!" This activity, he declares, forms a constitutive activity of society, clarifying and reaffirming "the symbols in which it thinks of itself" (*Rules* 50, 40). No motif is more insistently stressed in *Doctor Thorne*, in fact, than that of consultation with experts in social rules of all kinds: experts like "Lady De Courcy, who thoroughly understood that portion of the world in which she herself lived" (*DT* 191), or Mr. Athill, "a man who thoroughly understood dinner-parties" (*DT* 207) and who takes Frank under his guidance at Gatherum Castle, or, especially, the lawyers to whom characters in this novel habitually turn for advice. Trollope goes so far as to insert an amazing passage—another stylistic perversity meant to throw into relief the novel's fixation on the decoding of "norms, rules, and systems"—proposing that modern novelists pool funds to retain a lawyer, "if a counsellor adequately skilful can be found to accept the office," to advise them on the legal technicalities that arise in their fiction (*DT* 476). Such an advisor would have had a lot to do in connection with the present story, so much of which concerns the "continual litigation" (*DT* 356) and the masses of "purely legal discussion" (*DT* 478) that arise from Scatcherd's financial dealings with the Greshams, from the interpretation of his will, from the petition regarding election malpractice, and so forth. The regime of legalistic rules extends with undiminished force into more personal or domestic levels of experience as well: for example, into all the anxious adjudication of the issue of whether Mary, "tabooed" (*DT* 330) and "forbidden to enter [the Greshams'] domain" (*DT* 284) as she is, will be entitled to be a bridesmaid at Beatrice's wedding, or into the long sequence in which Mortimer Gazebee, the manager and legal advisor of the Gresham estate, elucidates for Lady Arabella the intricate issues of protocol, etiquette, and caste relations involved in inviting Doctor Thorne to dinner despite his official exclusion from the house, and in which Doctor Thorne and *his* advisor, Mary, then consult together just as meticulously about all the problems of precedent and protocol that the invitation entails (*DT* 366–70).

To dwell on such issues as intensively as Trollope does carries the obvious aesthetic risk of shunting too much imaginative energy away from the story, from the play of personality and of dramatic tension, and into material which readers are likely to find trivial and tedious. The same stylistic problem infects this text, in other words, as infects William Mariner's detailed account of the Tongan *cava* ceremony or William Ellis's of Tahitian canoe construction, except that Trollope's subject matter lacks the redeeming appeal of exoticism. This potential deficiency of entertainment values forms a clear symptom, one which Trollope seems determined to make as conspicuous as possible, of strain between ethnographic imagination, focused as it is upon the banal and the stereotypical, and Victorian popular sensibility. One can guess that this strain is traceable in turn to sources of philosophical disquietude in this text, the disquietude which the culture idea still provokes to this day. Indulging in so much anxious analysis of the social code can only mean that the code itself, the principle of caste and the network of special applications that radiates out from it, is endowed with irresistible authority. Personal moral character has a role to play in this novel, but its overriding function is to try to conform to the (often ambiguous) code as most wisely interpreted; private feelings and individual conscience are not allowed to be a law unto themselves. This is true even when the code appears shockingly irrational and devoid of legitimacy, as is suggested, for example, in the sessions of legalistic interpretation in which Frank Gresham and his father the squire engage to determine precisely the nature of the young man's familial duty to "marry money":

> "You must take [the world] as you find it, Frank. . . . If Porlock [the eldest son of the Earl De Courcy] were to marry the daughter of a shoe-black, without a farthing, he would make a *mésalliance;* but if the daughter of the shoe-black had half a million of money, nobody would dream of saying so. I am stating no opinion of my own: I am only giving you the world's opinion." (*DT* 415)

Trollope's failure to reject such a view, in which personal judgment and official ideals are alike overruled by cultural norms, is what has caused him sometimes to be dismissed out of hand as a mere snob and (in the same way that Durkheim has sometimes been dismissed) as a publicist of politically driven "dominant ideology." Any such judgment needs to notice that Trollope is at pains to advertise, rather than sweep under a rhetorical carpet, that sympathy with upper-class values means embracing a set of ideas that often seem wildly self-contradicting and morally dubious. It should notice, too, that this awkward position is nothing other than the one implied (and often expressly stated) by the relativistic doctrine of culture, which takes for granted that the only possible ground of value is the one defined by the conventional usages of one's society. Seemingly intractable logical incongruities such as the one involved in simultaneously worshipping "blood" and money are from this point of view, to quote Foucault again, "doubtless only a surface appearance" which it is the specific task of ethnographic reasoning to restore to order within the "complex whole" of culture.

What we are seeing is that Trollope's perception of the Victorian social scene as a fabric of symbolic imagery leads him by its own logic, as a similar perception led missionary ethnographers in Polynesia, toward a potentially scandalous social philosophy and at the same time toward a discursive style more or less antagonistic to the taste of his public. We can gauge how far this movement carries him by looking briefly at his treatment of the three closely clustered terms which every reader in 1865 would have taken to define the realm of positive moral value: love; the natural; the individual. Each element in the holy triad is subjected, we shall see, to much the same process of

deconstruction in *Doctor Thorne*—necessarily so, given that the three
categories overlap so much as to be at some level almost interchangeable. This process emerges ever more clearly as comprising the essential agenda of Trollope's novel.

Love, Nature, and the Individual

Can personal feeling transcend the dictates of culture, and ought it
to do so? Trollope does not give just the orthodox sentimental reply
to this question, and his failure to do so is the sign of the affront
which the culturalist imagination always offers to sentimentalism,
precisely because of the burden of ambiguity which it inflicts on the
concept of the individual. Often *Doctor Thorne* expounds, as we would
expect it to, the pious theory that true love and personal sincerity are
supreme values, and that undue concern with social conventionalities, including the value given by worldly people to wealth and position, is morally base. Miss Dunstable, the daughter of the Oil of Leb-
anon millionaire, acts as the specially appointed spokeswoman of this
theory. As though to appease readers who might even so be in doubt
as to his views, Trollope goes so far as to insert a personal denunciation of mercenary marriage as "sneakingly mean" (*DT* 484–85). Such
appeasement was called for, since he in fact takes a surprisingly ambivalent position on this great subject, supposedly the litmus test of
sound moral feeling. He tends at first to treat Frank's infatuation with
Mary as an amusing extravagance of youth rather than as transcendent passion, and he increasingly makes clear that the young man's
determination to marry a penniless girl in the face of the anguished
disapproval of all his family (including sympathetic figures like the
squire and Beatrice), and despite the certainty that such a marriage
would result in the final ruin of the Gresham estate, would be a
deeply dubious act at best. In fact Dr. Thorne, the moral touchstone
of the novel, expresses this judgment quite unambiguously. "Even
he—he the doctor himself, much as he despised the idea for money's
sake—even he could not but confess that Frank, as the heir to an old,
but grievously embarrassed property, had no right to marry, at his
early age, a girl without a shilling" (*DT* 391). To seem to countenance
such a judgment amounts for a mid-Victorian popular novelist almost
to a sacrilegious breach of taste, a defiance of the whole ethic of
spiritualized, purified feeling that the novel in this age was commissioned to uphold. To some very considerable degree collective and

conventional values take precedence over love, Trollope here tells his readers, in the kind of taboo-violating move that caused his fiction to be condemned by many offended reviewers as "vulgar," "odious," and "absolutely repulsive" (Smalley 76, 231, 237).[15] The miraculous inheritance enables the marriage to go on without difficulty at last, but before this occurs, the cult of what is derisively referred to at one point as "the sentimentation of romance" (*DT* 277) and, in general, of the sanctity of personal feeling, has been severely infringed in *Doctor Thorne*.

It is infringed more subtly by the growing intuition, implied by all the ethnographic logic of the novel, that the phenomenon of idealized young love among the English upper classes (as mythologized in popular fiction, at least) is after all merely another stereotyped cultural syndrome possessing approximately the same degree of moral sanctity as prevailing codes of table manners, fashions of dress, or caste hierarchies—and indeed as one inseparably intertwined with all of these. We can glimpse the emergence of some such thesis (which Trollope could hardly express openly without blighting his novel beyond recall) in the contrasting effects of two noteworthy passages. In the first of these, the narrator wonders how it is that Mary has fallen in love with Frank, the mediocrity of whose character and intelligence relative to her own has made the love theme of the novel keenly problematic from the start. "Her innate desire for the companionship of some much-loved object [was] as strong as his," he remarks; but this assertion of an innate (radically individual and noncollective) basis of love is promptly made the subject of irony:

> Had she been able to walk heart-whole by his side while he chatted his commonplaces about love? Yes, they are commonplaces when we read of them in novels; common enough, too, to some of us when we write them; but they are by no means commonplace when first heard by a young girl in the rich, balmy fragrance of a July evening stroll. (*DT* 243)

Even the most intimate and profound-seeming feelings in the domain of love are not innate at all, this passage suggests, but enactments of "commonplaces," of stereotyped cultural formulae which are transmitted through institutional media like popular novels and which retain their full bewitching potency only so long as we are naive with reference to their real nature. So great is their coercive effect that they can persuade a shrewd young woman that she loves a rather dimwitted young man whose shortcomings as an object of passion are plain to see. Like belief in the caste system, erotic sentiment appears to be governed by an "unknown cause" which no one under its sway can possibly comprehend. Before the novel ends, Trollope carries the demonstration further by providing a memorable specimen of just the kinds of commonplaces which it is the function of Victorian novelists to utter:

> Frank had once held [Mary] close to his warm breast; and her very soul had thrilled with joy to feel that he so loved her. . . . She had acknowledged him to be master of her spirit; her bosom's lord; the man whom she had been born to worship; the human being to whom it was for her to link her destiny. Frank's acres had been of no account; nor had his want of acres. God had brought them two together. (*DT* 448)

But it is impossible to take the hyperbolic sentimentality of this passage and its language of mystical destinies at face value. Especially in contrast to the spicy, richly personalized speech with which Trollope's characters are endowed, its highly formalized rhetorical figures are easy to identify as an illustration of the kind of idealized cultural code that *Doctor Thorne* has analyzed from the start. The passage contains in fact a satire on the mystifying rhetoric deployed in this society to suppress consciousness of all the material interests and other social determinants with which erotic sentiment is inescapably pervaded. To assert that "Frank's acres had been of no account" in Mary's love for him is to strive (with telltale defensiveness) to mask the truth that all the personal qualities she presumably admires in him—his dashing, unconstrained manner, his refined politeness, his ethic of gallantry and loyalty—form part of an aristocratic male ideal proper to a privileged class founded very squarely on the possession of hereditary "acres" (an ideal quite different, say, from the concurrent middle-class ethic of seriousness, respectability, and hard work). To deny the all-importance of the factor of caste in any human relation in this society would simply be to deny the lesson preached on every page of *Doctor Thorne*. By the same token, if Sir Louis Scatcherd seems to Mary and her uncle "so totally of a different class" that he is like "a Hottentot, or an Esquimaux" (*DT* 305), and thus a disgustingly inappropriate suitor for Mary's hand, it is because of his own unexpunged taint of lower-class origins. Mary loves Frank not because "God had brought them two together" but because she has been reared to venerate the ideal of the "gentleman" and its whole mystique of innate superiority, an ideal which it is pure self-delusion to imagine as unrelated to the possession of family wealth. We shall see in a moment how plainly Trollope spells out this implication in his account of Mary's upbringing.

The notion of "culture" being almost synonymous with seditious-seeming reconfigurations of the "natural," probably the clearest sign of the philosophical bearing of all the cultural notation in *Doctor Thorne* is the constant invocation of the term "nature" throughout the text (where it occurs, often capitalized, on at least twenty-five significant occasions). Inquiring in an elliptical yet quite systematic way into the status of this concept, Trollope hints at a sophisticated explanation in sociological terms of why it plays the dominant role it does in nineteenth-century discourse. What he emphasizes first and foremost, however, is its equivocal, inconsistent character. Like "Gardez Gresham," the word "nature" proves to be rife with ambiguity, a crucial signifier breaking up before our eyes under the pressure of historical change, yet seeming to acquire from this very process a heightened emotional urgency.

In its sentimentally positive sense, the word is closely bound up with the idealized mythology of love, and it is frequently cited in *Doctor Thorne* in this sense, as the warrant of instinctive sentiment believed to occur spontaneously, independently of sociological causation. "Deep as was her cause for anger against the man who had so inhumanly used her, still it was natural that she should turn to him with love rather than with aversion," the narrator says of Mary Scatcherd (*DT* 20); she is grateful for Dr. Thorne's offer to adopt her illegitimate baby, "but Nature, she said, would not let her leave her child" (*DT* 22); and so forth. However, this idealized Rousseauistic usage of the term is unstable in *Doctor Thorne;* it shades off into a potentially much less reassuring one in which "Nature" is conceived as a set of essentially biological, "animal," forces which inhabit minds and bodies. "In this matter of [seeking a mate], Nature gives her own lessons thoroughly," and sets social prudence altogether at defiance, says the narrator (*DT* 192). Sir Roger seems at one crisis of illness to be at death's door, "but it soon became evident that Nature was using all her efforts to make one final rally" (*DT* 252). What grows out of these ambiguous personifications of "Nature" is one of the most surprising features of Trollope's text:

the eruption, in the midst of what is nominally a social comedy, of powerful, shockingly discordant themes of bodily physicality.

Usually bodily and organic motifs are menacing in *Doctor Thorne;* they remind us of the natural perils that culture strives to defend us against, and more basically of the ties to physical nature and to animality that "civilized men of today," as Freud said ("Preface to Bourke's *Scatalogic Rites of All Nations," Standard Edition* 12:335), try desperately to repress and designate as the very locus of tabooed indecency. This is the context within which Trollope focuses, for instance, upon the bodily frailty that causes the death of the four Gresham babies, upon Lady Arabella's cancer, upon the devastating and grotesque effects of the alcoholism that destroys Sir Roger and his sickly son in turn, or upon the sexual lust that triggers the story by driving Henry Thorne to rape and impregnate Mary Scatcherd, in revenge for which her brother Roger crushes his skull with a club. The unseemly details of Dr. Thorne's medical practice are rarely described directly (except in his attendance upon Sir Roger), but we are always aware of them just outside our field of vision. He keeps some scarcely decent objects on display in his study: a pair of human thighbones which he handles absentmindedly when deep in conversation, and a "little child's skull" which grins down at startled visitors from the mantelpiece (*DT* 279). This is a tale that makes us constantly aware of the flesh, of semen, of genetic as well as legal inheritance, of bodily organs, of the excretions of disease. Even the incessant invocation of aristocratic "blood"—"the blood had come naturally to [Frank]," says the narrator wittily (*DT* 58)—takes some of its effect from its ironic linkage to themes of physical bodies, themes which throughout the novel play in counterpoint against its far more pervasive and insistent notation of the governing of the characters' lives by symbolic mental forms (architectural and other imagery, imperious and yet ambiguous codes of etiquette, rules of rank and precedence, mystified conventions of love).

Are human beings in the last analysis creatures of the flesh and of instinctive appetites, of what Trollope speaks of as "the cravings of Nature" (*DT* 31), as the Wesleyan model asserts, overlaid with a thin veneer of social conventionality, or is a man in his very being "nothing more than a system of representations"? To focus upon this issue, *Doctor Thorne* suggests, is to respond in particular to the crisis in the idea of "the natural," a term that has evidently become so problematic as to be more or less obsolete, however insistently it may be cited. On two noteworthy occasions, it is specifically declared null and void as

Trollope invokes the principle often cited by theorists of "culture" as the basis of the theory: that habit is second nature. At one point, Dr. Thorne tells Sir Roger Scatcherd that he must abstain from brandy:

> "Is that all you know of human nature, doctor? Abstain. Can you abstain from breathing, and live like a fish does under water?"
> "But Nature has not ordered you to drink, Scatcherd."
> "Habit is second nature, man; and a stronger nature than the first."
> (*DT* 111–12; see also 270–71)

Giving a slight extension to the term "habit," which here seizes ascendancy over "nature," we can see that Scatcherd's lesson applies not only to pathological compulsions like his own but to the whole system of conventions which Trollope has shown to govern life in the world of the novel. We recall his prefatory essay on the Greshamsbury gates, the moral of which lay in the almost unconscious heritage of ancient symbolism persisting in modern life. This line of thought implies the need to substitute for the quest for hypothetical laws of "human nature" a particularized study of how social habits have originated and perpetuated themselves—a study that can hardly fail to yield an ethnographic theory of culture and of the power of symbolic representations. It implies, too, a realization of how crucial a role is played by mythological rhetoric of the natural in sustaining the structures of taboo and caste privilege that form the central subjects of *Doctor Thorne*. The idea that nature decrees human feelings turns out to be in effect yet another powerful symbolic representation analogous in function to those of the Gatherum portico and the stone savages of Greshamsbury: like them, it serves to intimidate those who might be tempted to violate established principles of classification.

Some such underlying awareness seems evident in the description of the Greshamsbury dinner for Frank's coming of age:

> oth of the drawing-room and dining-room, looked out on to the lawn; and it was only natural that the girls should walk from the former to the latter. It was only natural that they, being there, should tempt their swains to come to them by the sight of their broad-brimmed hats and evening dresses; and natural, also, that the temptation should not be resisted. The squire, therefore, and the elder male guests soon found themselves alone round their wine. (*DT* 66)

The sophisticated joke of this passage is of course that the scene described, evoking as it minutely does the interwoven configurations of architecture, landscaping, erotically suggestive clothing, and highly studied etiquette governing after-dinner arrangements and the relations between the sexes, all coming together to yield a choreography of courtship as mannered and stylized as a minuet, is as far from the "natural" as could possibly be conceived. Every particle of the scene is imprinted with social conventionality, "naturalness" in such a context being simply the sensation of perfect harmony with one's social surroundings. No doubt the novel suggests a significant linkage between the biological drive that impels Henry Thorne to rape his friend's sister and this decorous congregation of young ladies and gentlemen, but all the stress in this scene and throughout *Doctor Thorne* falls on how this drive is mediated and transformed almost beyond recognition, transformed into a kind of ceremony, by the elaborate formalities of culture. Trollope points only a little less obviously at the significance of such an episode and of the rhetorical medium through which it is refracted for the perpetuation of the system of class hierarchies so much at issue in the novel. This idealized imagery of courtship functions both to facilitate the arranging of necessary future marriages and to shed an aura of justification upon the system itself—for if the domestic life led in aristocratic households is "only natural" in all its spontaneous emotional rhythms, how could the quasi-sacred standing and the power of the social elect be illegitimate? The overinsistent stress on the term, which the novel has shown to be invested with such a large quota of value, hints therefore at both the difficulty and the urgency of representing upper-class conventions as patterns dictated by Nature.

Since my argument is that Trollope's critique of a series of privileged terms flows from an initial insight into the symbolic character of culture, it is worth noting that the mood of bliss evoked in this scene originates in imagery of thresholds not erected for once to interfere with passage, not to impose a taboo prohibition, but to facilitate easy movement. It is a moment when the characteristic anxieties of life in this world are briefly set aside, leaving in their wake a euphoric but doubly illusory sense of "naturalness"—illusory not only because conventionality and habit are represented as Nature, but because the enjoyments of such a scene are dependent after all on the very system it appears to dispel, the system of phobic exclusion of uncleanness which is symbolized and enforced, even as the young ladies and gentlemen drift out onto the lawn, by the nearby gates of Greshamsbury. We can derive from this scene, if we follow its unspoken logic by setting it in its full context in *Doctor Thorne,* the insight that it is almost the defining function of human culture to block awareness of the mechanisms which give a sense of spontaneous rightness to what in fact are ingrained social habits—and the defining function of cultural analysis to make such awareness possible.

As Roland Barthes says in his own unravelling of just such themes in collective representations of a later era, semiology is bound to be "semioclasm" from the moment that it reveals sacralized pseudonatural ideas to be in fact accidents of human history (*Mythologies* 9). The semioclastic strain of Trollope's fiction directs itself perhaps most pointedly to the term which couples together "love" and "Nature" and forms, as we began by saying, the novelist's fundamental principle: the term of individual personality. Is personal behavior the expression of unique inward character, or is it a series of stereotypical gestures which refer to and signify at last nothing but the organizational scheme of one's society? Mary Thorne raises this philosophical issue too distinctly for any reader to overlook it, hinting as she does so that the whole novel of which she is the heroine should be read as an extended meditation on precisely this problem. "She said to herself, proudly, that God's handiwork was the inner man, the inner woman, the naked creature animated by a living soul; that all other adjuncts were but man's clothing for the creature" (*DT* 86). She registers in this atypically elevated diction the tremendous emotional investment of modern people in the "cult of the self" (Durkheim, *Moral Education* 72), and thus highlights the way in which modern social theory, in which personal inwardness tends to become a socially induced formation, has seemed to strike dangerously at the roots of orthodox ideas of spirituality. According to Mary's phraseology, belief in God and belief in the primacy of the deep inner self (and therefore in the relative shallowness and insignificance of cultural "adjuncts") are practically the same thing. She picks up here the word used half a century before by Malthus in his own treatment of this issue, though she robs cultural "adjuncts" of the all-determining force which Malthus, the very type of the scandalous modern theoretician, gave to them in his argument that human sexual desire has nothing to do with biology or nature and everything to do with symbolic associations. But by raising this issue so distinctly in this way, Trollope, rather than dispelling it as he seems to do with the invocation of an essentialist idea of "the inner man, the inner woman," only compels the reader to ponder its upsetting ramifications, which is to say, to recognize the difficulty of ever disentangling that wholly hypothetical being, "the naked creature," from the matrices of cultural "adjuncts" in which all humans are deeply embedded, and which his characters, as we have seen, spend their time meticulously studying and interpreting.

Trollope gives lip service on rare occasions to the idea that personality is an emanation of "God's handiwork," but the plainest thing of all in his fiction, and the plainest sign of his disaffiliation from much of the fiction of his day, is that personality is presented there as a sociological phenomenon through and through.[16] "His Majesty the Ego" in Trollope is never a regally free-standing entity but, like the day-laborer's wool coat in Adam Smith's famous analysis (*WN* 1:15–16), a nexus of institutional forces; it is marked above all by the trait of *complexity* because it is produced by social institutions and enacted in a social environment, and because Victorian society is itself, as Trollope insistently demonstrates and declares, an almost infinitely complex network of categories and interrelations. Hence, for example, his disquisition on the subtly differentiated subclasses of the genus "Whig" (*DT* 165), his never-ending exegeses of the elusive category "gentleman" (*DT* 114), his account of the subtle gradations of caste status that regulate the legal profession (*DT* 357–58), or his survey of the almost ineffable caste distinctions which bestow the status of gentility on some clergymen and deny it to others (*DT* 403). One's personal identity is bound up to a great extent, according to Trollope, in the social category which one occupies in this labyrinth of categories, hence in the complexly nuanced relations which that category has with all the other categories and which express themselves in one's every word and gesture through the inflections of an elaborate code of manners. (It is the inescapability of this principle in Trollope's fiction that led so many reviewers to accuse him of having a perverted conception of character.) Moreover, one individual may, almost must, occupy plural categories, which may themselves be discordant with one another, or may be ambiguously suspended between categories, giving to his or her experience an added multiplier of complexity or even leading to extreme outbreaks of irrationality and inconsistency. For Trollope, the unconscious is a powerful factor in character, but it lies open to detailed analysis because, rather than originating in the metaphysics of the psyche, it is produced in effect by a calculus of institutions: it corresponds to all those component factors of one's social self which are screened from view, though not deprived of force, by other component factors.

Being the hero of the novel and its leading figure of moral excellence does not at all exempt Doctor Thorne, for example, from the principle of the complicated social construction of character. The key to the logic of his personality is his simultaneous occupancy of the two largely incompatible categories of doctor and aristocrat, each of which proves to be fraught with complexity in its own right. Trollope thus spends much time not only studying the gradations of caste and status which make up the complicated sociology of the medical profession, but stressing as well the diversity of roles which any doctor plays relative to society at large, to colleagues in the profession, to patients, to the human body and its illnesses. Being an aristocrat with a keen sense of "blood" greatly complicates some of these relations for Trollope's hero, whose status is doubly problematic in view of the technical dubiousness of his pedigree (being as he is merely second cousin to the Thornes of Ullathorne). This compounded and recompounded ambiguity of social identity fairly plainly exerts its exacerbating force upon all sides of Doctor Thorne's personality, stimulating his campaign against the sacrosanct etiquette of the provincial medical profession (a campaign which all unconsciously gives vent to a compulsion to show his superiority to the rules of a professional guild which he considers socially beneath him), his morbidly proud severing of contact with his grand relatives, his insistence on showing to Lady Arabella on every possible occasion his sense of social equality with her, his acute sensitivity to slights, his horror at the idea of Mary's ever being claimed as a blood relation by the socially taboo Scatcherds. This is a man who beneath his urbane surface is driven by unconscious demons, but they are simply the symptoms of rifts and contradictions in the complex social code which his entire personality expresses.

For the most part, Trollope takes for granted the process of acculturation by which characters acquire their individuality and learn to read the symbolic text of their society, but he makes a very significant novelistic exception in the case of his heroine, whose education is recounted in some detail. The "unknown cause" of the ideas of social rank prevalent in this milieu turns out to be nothing more (or less) mysterious than the process by which one absorbs the semiology of one's native social habitat:

> And so Mary Thorne learnt music at Greshamsbury, and with her music she learnt other things also: how to behave herself among girls of her own age; how to speak and talk as other young ladies do; how to dress herself, and how to move and walk. All which, she,

being quick to learn, learnt without trouble at the great house.
Something also she learnt of French, seeing that the Greshamsbury
French governess was always in the room.
And then, some few years later, there came a rector, and a rector's
sister; and with the latter Mary studied German, and French also.
From the doctor himself she learnt much; the choice, namely, of
English books for her own reading, and habits of thought somewhat
akin to his own. . . . (*DT* 36)

To understand the calculated effect of this passage upon contemporary readers, one needs to be sensitive above all to its "semioclastic"
tenor. Strongly erosive of quasi-religious notions of individuality,
which the novel in its subtlest effect of all reveals as a cultural "survival" lying at the heart of our moral awareness, it depicts personal
identity in strictly ethnographic terms, as a tight mesh of conventional symbolism in which every human function, down to "how to
move and walk," must be *learned* (for the most part through unconscious osmosis, apparently) according to a highly codified set of "prescriptive principles." In every facet of her personality, Mary, her
standing as a paragon of moral refinement notwithstanding, is subject to rigorous cultural determination; she has no other way of becoming herself than that of becoming in effect a representation of
those about her. There scarcely seems any room left for the "natural"
in Mary, or for any purified sensitivity to ideas of virtue untainted by
worldly origins, so imbued is she, according to this passage, with the
social habits proper to aristocratic culture: every particle of her behavior and sensibility is inscribed with the conventions of caste
(among other things, she is at least as devout a believer in the superstitious mystique of "blood" as are snobs like Augusta Gresham or her
uncle the doctor). Thus the passage is doubly scandalous for the way
it collapses the vital distinction, in which so much cultural capital is
invested, between those aspects of selfhood, of "the inner woman,"
which we rank as spiritually superior and those other external, conventional, worldly aspects ranked as inherently base. (All the themat-
ics of taboo violation in *Doctor Thorne* converge here in a sense upon
Trollope's own transgression of the boundary between sacred and
profane.) The lesson of the passage is that anomalous-seeming con-
junctions between moral values and worldly "adjuncts" such as mastery of the style of walking prescribed for upper-class females *cannot
possibly be undone,* and indeed, that the moral principles exemplified
by this heroine cannot properly be assessed except as conventions of

a certain social caste. By submerging his fiction so deeply in sociology and by prefiguring so clearly Lévi-Strauss's dictum that "the customs of a community, taken as a whole, always have a particular style and are reducible to systems," Trollope gives the moral argument of his novel a decentered, ambiguous, anti-transcendental character almost unheard of in Victorian popular fiction.

At the risk of appearing to be merely an apologist for class interests, he asks us to view the process of acculturation exhibited in the case of his heroine without philosophical dismay. To think, in the interests of a residually religious mythology of "depth" or of an ideology proclaiming "the free development of individuality" (Mill, *On Liberty* 56), of an "inner man" or "inner woman" as a sanctuary where there originate feelings undictated by social habitat is to indulge in a delusion in any case. Trollope offers a negative allegory of this principle in the cases of the Scatcherds, whose extremely severe cultural dislocation leads to acute personal distress and to nothing less than a disintegration of personality. A person who truly could divest himself of his native cultural forms, says Durkheim, would "no longer [be] considered a human mind in the full sense of the word," would "cease being really human" (*Elementary Forms* 30). Trollope can hardly deploy within the idiom of a sentimental comedy of manners the radical metaphors of this mythic state available to writers like Jean Itard or Henry Mayhew, or to those in the tradition of Hobbes and Wesley, in which the myth of the subhuman human, the person as beast, took one of its original forms. But Trollope surprises us by calling after all upon quite extreme examples of such rhetoric in his fable of the Scatcherds. When Sir Roger's incurable estrangement from upper-class society is confirmed by his expulsion from parliament, leaving him, as he feels, bereft of social identity, he undergoes just the dehumanization theorized by Durkheim. "[Lady Scatcherd] had never known him so savage in his humour as he was now, so bearish in his habits, so little inclined to humanity, so determined to rush headlong down, with his head between his legs, into the bottomless abyss" (*DT* 240). Abandoning himself to despair and alcoholism, he dies "like a beast" (*DT* 275). Sir Louis, even more severely deprived of cultural identity than his father, disintegrates even more rapidly, and Mary speaks of him in this condition of cultural indeterminacy "as though he were some wild beast" (*DT* 363).

Once again we see in this text, therefore, the configuration which we have studied in one variation after another: the linkage of an emerging modern idea of culture, an idea never fully articulated in its positive form in *Doctor Thorne* but everywhere suggested, with the traditional themes of anomic desire which it is perhaps the key historical function of the culture idea to absorb in some fashion or other. The keynote of Trollope's modernism here is the way he almost entirely sets aside the idea of "civilization" as a set of disciplining restraints imposed upon natural propensities to desire, replacing it with the idea of culture as a symbolic system which in effect is prior to any human nature at all. It is no later than chapter 3 that he devises a way to stress this line of implication by introducing a discussion of the reigning theory of education, which holds, says the narrator, that the prevalence of "natural depravity" even in children requires all people to be "controlled" by social coercion—a theory which Trollope's alter ego Dr. Thorne rouses scandal by (qualifiedly) denying (*DT* 33–34). Anomie is no manifestation of boundless innate drives, according to this novel, it has nothing in common with "the obscure . . . violence of desire battering at the limits of representation" (Foucault), but is, rather, a purely sociological phenomenon arising from structural incoherences within a society. It is the precipitate of a disordering of codes of representation (for example, the code that defined as identical the categories of great wealth and of aristocratic "blood") by the stress of social realignment.

The Recovery of Depth

Pursuing the above line of thought as systematically as he does in *Doctor Thorne* involves Trollope, as we have said, in cultural dissonance of his own, for it means putting the novel to uses that are incompatible with the "natural" characteristics of the medium—since Trollope, rather than inventing largely new modes of discourse to accommodate the nascent idea of culture, as the political economists, the early ethnographers, or a social investigator like Mayhew were keenly conscious of doing, attempts to incorporate it into an established form with its own defining protocols. What unfolds in *Doctor Thorne* is a vision of a society in which largely unconscious ideas pervade all of experience and take shape, as if they were "almost an artificial language in themselves," in a system of analogical imagery binding together in a "limitless process of equivalences" (Barthes, *S/Z* 40) architecture, politics, table manners, erotic love, moral values, and every other function of social life. I have argued that the

development of such a thesis—essentially the thesis of culture—
amounts in this book to a defection from nineteenth-century moral
ideology, with all its stress on the drama of the individual personality,
on the primacy of the natural and the spontaneous, and on the need
to master instinctual desires. What it specifically lacks, as so many
reviewers protested, hinting at a streak of something insidiously subversive or even nihilistic in a writer often cited as an example of
blandness and conventionality, is the crucial inflection of "depth."
Doctor Thorne shocks the sensibility of its original audience by presenting itself to an abnormal degree for a nineteenth-century novel as an
observation of impersonal social surfaces, of the public signifiers
which Trollope perceives to be the true constituents of the self.

One might guess at the affiliation of his fiction with the self-conscious emphasis on "surface" which was increasingly to form the signature of modernist style, culminating perhaps in Joyce and again in
Andy Warhol.[17] In the context of the present study, what *Doctor Thorne*
primarily bears witness to is the potentially lethal estrangement of the
ethnographic culture-idea from the imagination and sensibility of its
day. Not to be afflicted with "the futility of work that is isolated from
the spirit of the age" (Fleck 45), in order, that is, to develop from the
impressionistic and largely indefinite state in which it is rendered in a
text like Trollope's to the codified theory of the "complex whole," and
in order to carry out its historical mission of insurgency against
Wesleyan thinking, the culture doctrine needed to reconcile itself with
the overriding stylistic norm of "depth." Reading the file of Trollope
reviews, one gets an idea, then, of the urgency of all the rhetoric of
depth which the official framers of the culture doctrine used to give it
the stylistic form and the emotional resonance it required to achieve
fixity, even at the risk of veering with this move into the metaphysics
and logical dilemmas which have plagued it ever after. In his searching
discussion of the problematics of cultural theory in *The Study of Sociology* (1872–73, fifteen years after *Doctor Thorne*), Spencer directs attention to just this issue. "We are liable [in sociological analysis] to be led
away by superficial, trivial facts," he says, as though echoing Trollope's
reviewers, "from the deep-seated and really-important facts they indicate. Always the details of social life . . . will, if we allow them, hide
from us the vital connexions . . . underneath" (*Study* 96). The positing
of a hierarchical distinction between surface and depth, and the identification of the latter as the domain of reality, is thus to form the
necessary basis of the stylistics of modern social science, hard though

it may be, as we saw in the introductory chapter of this book, to square this principle logically with that of empirical observation.

The speedy success of the move prescribed by Spencer is suggested in Wittgenstein's comments on Frazer's *Golden Bough*, where he very precisely identifies the effect of "depth" as the essential factor in this text and emphasizes the way the doctrine of primitive "survivals" functions here to guarantee what Trollope's "superficiality" was said to prevent, the emotional involvement of a reader.[18] The positing of "depth" thus establishes a charter and a rhetorical method for the imaginative ethnographic study of "the details of social life." Once instituted, this principle can readily sponsor many variant suppositions about the character of the "vital connexions" assumed to lie deep "underneath" visible appearances: causal-functional, genetic, symbolic. It can even, as in Clifford Geertz's widely cited interpretive reading of the "deep play" of the Balinese cockfight, sponsor the resurgence, as though from the "deep" origins of the culture theory itself, of curiously Evangelical-sounding language about "the animalistic demons that threaten constantly to invade [society]" (*IC* 420). Geertz's rhetorically resonant explication of the category of what he calls "interesting" or "deep" fights claims to discover in passions "normally well-obscured from view" (*IC* 444) what he calls "the substance of [the cockfights'] depth" (*IC* 432). Whether or not Geertz's essay succeeds in this, it lets us observe, simultaneously with the attempted deciphering of an exotic social practice, the process to which cultural theorists since Trollope's day have almost single-mindedly devoted themselves, as though the survival of their discipline depended upon it: the retransfusion into social study of all the Wesleyan and Victorian rhetoric of depth that has been experimentally drained off in *Doctor Thorne*.[19] The mobile army of metaphors, we may say, musters itself anew in a text like Geertz's and redeploys itself in one of its traditional strategic formations.

CHAPTER SIX

CONCLUSION

T he inquiry carried out in this book has been an involved one and resists a summary statement, but I shall recapitulate briefly some of its main findings, then conclude with one or two remarks on problems of method which it raises.

We began with a riddle: how did so philosophically problematic (and erratically defined) a notion as that of "culture," unstable amalgam of empiricism and metaphysics as it is, come to occupy a central place in modern thinking? There is no reason to assume that any one explanation could account for the wide range of manifestations which this idea takes on in the course of its emergence in nineteenth-century writing; indeed, it is hard to show that many of these manifestations, ambiguous as they necessarily are at this early stage of development, in fact are cognates of one another. Yet evidence from various fields of discourse indicates that culturalist thinking takes form at surprisingly early dates as the agency of a movement of disaffection from an ideological system rooted in the original-sin theology which John Wesley was chiefly instrumental in impressing upon modern consciousness: disaffection, in particular, from the doctrine that social order depends on imposing controls upon potentially boundless and anarchic human desires. Constructing an alternative to the doctrine of desire and control became, this evidence lets us see, the crucial project of progressive social theory. However, Wesleyan-style thinking on this score was invested with so much affective and imaginative power and, in particular, so much moral urgency, that it could hardly be purged altogether; even the most determined insurgents against it (writers like Mill, Freud, Durkheim, or Malinowski) could hardly avoid borrowing the conceptual machinery of their ideological adversaries and being preyed upon as a result by chronic ambivalence and self-contradiction. Thus ethnographic theories of culture which outwardly deny what we have elliptically called "Wesleyan" principles often prove no less easily readable as insidious refigurings of these very principles and as reinscriptions of the moral rhetoric which they specifically claim to banish; so at least I have argued.

The literature of political economy is treated accordingly in this book as a sustained response to the theory of illimitable desires, and one that lays the groundwork for ethnographic interpretation of cultures by elaborately working out a model of society as a self-enclosed system of symbolic equivalences in which the grand principle of order is exchange rather than control. The economists formulate at the same time, and wrestle with long and inconclusively, the philosophical dilemma inherent in culturalist reasoning, naming it the dilemma of "value." In roughly contemporary mission ethnography of the South Seas, the problem of value, anchored now in an emergent romance of risky personal observation closely tied to themes of born-again Christian theology, takes overwhelmingly existential form, implicating the ethnographic observer himself in various forms of ambivalence so acute as to render this whole body of writing severely self-contradictory. Even as they give lurid expression to the myth of limitless primitive lusts, these writers develop their own conception of society as an integral semiological system, evidently coming to this line of thinking by way of an analogy with the structure of language.

In its transposition of Polynesian imagery directly onto the inhabitants of London's East End, Mayhew's *London Labour and the London Poor* forms an exhibit of the almost uncontrollable contagiousness, for the nineteenth-century mentality, of "Wesleyan" metaphors of desire; it forms a remarkably vivid exhibit at the same time of how these metaphors acted to stimulate the development of a mode of ethnographic interpretation the most potent impulse of which was a revulsion from the moral absolutism of Evangelical thinking. In Mayhew we see the emergence of cultural theory in its patently dissident, anti-Victorian aspect, which allows the theme of anomic desire to be radically refigured as the sign of a concerted resistance waged by a destitute caste against the menace of a disintegration of symbolic order itself. Mayhew's project of observation and analysis involves him in an analogous struggle of his own: that which stems from the tendency of ethnographic science to issue in a deeply unstable form of discourse which may become more incoherent the more intensively it examines its special data. Trollope, finally, works through similar rhetorical difficulties in a different literary register, treating the problem of anomic desire in modernistic terms as symptomatic of purely sociological and cultural disjunctions, and in the process making evident the potentially scandalous effect for a nineteenth-century public of even the most innocuous-seeming ethnographic study in which interpretation is allowed to take precedence over the framing of moral judgment.

From this range of evidence, several broad conclusions can seem to emerge.

First, one concludes that the culture idea was the product of a broadly diffused movement of thought, a general reorganization of sensibility which very gradually, and always in self-divided forms, articulates itself in the course of the nineteenth century. This model suggests the delusiveness of assigning the discovery of "culture" to any single theorist, Herder, Tylor, Mauss, Boas, or whomever, and implies that great-man theories in this connection are perhaps not ideologically innocent: they lend a persuasive semblance of unity and an authenticating aura of inspired genius, not to mention the charm of a dramatic fable of scientific discovery, to a concept always weakened, for those who look closely into it, by seemingly incurable vagueness and incoherence. The alternative model developed in the present book implies that the incipient culture idea can be detected in the sentences of many writers scarcely conscious of it, and that particular avenues of transmission are likely not to be specifiable or for that matter overly significant. It implies too what written evidence seems often to bear out: that appearances of the culture idea in early texts are likely to be sites of intellectual disorganization rather than coherent and distinctly legible statements, disorienting though this state of affairs may be for the historian of ideas.

Most generally perhaps, the argument proposed here carries implications for the philosophical status which one may accord to the notion of culture. It presents this notion as, so to say, the residue of an adversarial project native to the nineteenth century, and sees its later codification in explicit philosophical theories of the "complex whole," and its enactment in a voluminous literature of ethnographic interpretation, as the consolidating of an historical revulsion from "Wesleyan" thinking. This, I have meant to suggest, was an equivocal genesis from which the culture idea has never been able to extricate itself so as to find a footing in the sheer empirical objectivity to which it so often, with obvious defensiveness, has laid claim. Its logic appears to be as much a function of the intellectual and emotional needs and of the habitual metaphorical constructions of a period as it is a function of real structures in human societies. How much of its appearance of scientific validity will survive, one is entitled to wonder, once the philosophical and moral anxieties which agitated the nineteenth century, and particularly those arising from the fantasy of human nature as a mass of unruly animal desire, have been definitively displaced by others?

I have called my study of these things "intellectual history," but it may seem hardly to deserve this honorific name. It presents no very coherent narrative, indeed, scarcely any consecutive narrative at all; and it leaves largely in abeyance the question of the causes of intellectual change in order to focus on uncovering sometimes intricate structures of thought and implication in particular texts. If this is a deficiency in my account, I do not see how it could effectively be overcome (given the nature of my materials and the slant which I take upon them) except by resolutely closing one's eyes to the epistemological difficulties inherent in historiographical conventions of proof. It seems best to figure the apparent congruencies among different sorts of texts which I have stressed as varying manifestations of a general trend of thought of indeterminate origins developing by a logic which it would be rash to formulate in schematic terms, given its embroilment in masses of unconscious and incalculable mental material. I have portrayed the culture idea as a negative response to metaphors of illimited desire and social control; but in constructing this schema as a context for individual *explications de texte*, I do not profess to know "why" this ensemble of metaphors came to lose its original stability (to the extent that it ever was very stable), nor to know "why" the metaphor of the complex whole, rather than some other, became the dominant one in its stead. Guesses at nontautological answers to such questions lie so far from any possible conclusive proof or disproof by empirical evidence that they seem almost to be better left open as a matter of principle. At least in the context of the philosophical situation within which current scholarly research is compelled to operate, it is well to acknowledge the wide domain of the unknowable in the past world that we have the audacity to manufacture out of historical documents.

It may seem finally a flagrant error of method, even a species of moral impropriety, to proceed as I have in this book: to insist on the illogic inherent in the ethnographic culture concept and then to portray it as deriving historically from configurations of emotionally saturated symbolic imagery which ramify throughout disparate fields of nineteenth-century thought, from economics to popular fiction—in effect, to base my argument throughout on the dubious theory of culture itself. In explaining the great persuasiveness of the modern culture idea as a cultural effect or a cultural delusion, do I not utter a manifest paradox? But it can hardly be called an error, except in the most scholastic sense, to do what scholarly or scientific investigations can never escape doing: to derive demonstrations from conceptual "paradigms" whose truth is demonstrable only by reference to data which in effect are functions of the paradigms to begin with. "Proof" under such circumstances is a device of exposition, a figure of speech. To follow this skeptical line of reflection on the functioning of our own organizing concepts is to become aware that logical circularity is their fundamental law, and thus to recognize the always provisional, conditional nature of our results, the futility of seeking ever to grasp a permanent truth that lies outside mutable signifying systems. Truth of this transcendent order is a rhetorical construct in which contemporary trends of analysis scarcely allow us to believe any longer. But if we are not to be disabled intellectually and stricken mute by this awareness (and there is no reason we should be), we have no choice but to explore the world as best we can with the most productive and compelling paradigms we can discover, knowing all along that we can hope to attain only a relative mode of truth devoid of positive terms. Operating in this way, we make logic our servant, not our tyrant master. This is what Adam Smith does in showing all philosophical and scientific systems without exception to be "imaginary machines" vouched for by nothing beyond the esthetics of elegant logical demonstration, then proceeding in *The Theory of Moral Sentiments* and *The Wealth of Nations* to build theoretical systems of especially bold and imaginative elaborateness; it is what Ruth Benedict does in pronouncing the idea of flawlessly coherent social systems to be an unprovable "superstition," then writing *Patterns of Culture;* it is what Jacques Derrida does in observing that philosophical deconstruction "always in a certain way falls prey to its own work" (*Grammatology* 24; see also 4); and it is what we inevitably do, at pain of lapsing into the idiotized condition of Victor of Aveyron, in recognizing the moral values we live by to be nothing but the curious customs of the society in which we happen to have been reared, yet clinging to them despite this knowledge as though they rested on a bedrock of necessary truth. In seeking to demystify the concept of culture by means of techniques of cultural interpretation, I perform this same characteristic maneuver. If it involves me in a logical dilemma, I can only plead in my own defense that it is the one to which ethnographic imagination and modern consciousness itself tend inescapably, and from which no escape can for the time being be discerned.

NOTES

INTRODUCTION

1. "The concept of culture," says Roy Wagner, "has come to be so completely associated with anthropological thinking that . . . we could define an anthropologist as someone who uses the word 'culture' habitually" (Wagner 1).

2. One such area is on the way to achieving quasi-disciplinary status in American universities under the name of "cultural studies." The streams of interdisciplinary research called "new historicism" and "the new cultural history" are two more modes in which the culture idea has been heavily exploited by present-day scholarship. For an introduction to the latter, see Lynn Hunt, ed., *The New Cultural History*.

3. Malinowski, having devoted a lifetime to championing the functionalistic interpretation of culture that originates in Spencer and Durkheim, comes in the posthumous *Scientific Theory of Culture* to a remarkable concession: the concept of "function" in culture is logically circular, as critics have charged, and is valid "primarily as a heuristic device" (170).

4. In the opening paragraph of *Marxism and Literature*, Raymond Williams calls for exactly such an inquiry into the idea of "culture." He carries out this project in *Culture and Society 1780–1950*, which is discussed below.

5. In *Culture and Agency: The Place of Culture in Social Theory*, Margaret S. Archer demonstrates the persistence throughout the most varied schools of thought of what she calls "the myth of cultural integration," which "perpetuates an image of culture as a coherent pattern, a uniform ethos or a symbolically consistent universe" (Archer xv).

6. She fails to highlight the discrepancy of the fact that Zuñi take enemy scalps and collect them in scalp-houses with her assertion that they are "never violent," for instance; and her argument that Zuñi society is virtually without agencies of authority and discipline is strangely at odds with her statement that any strong personality in this society is likely to be branded a sorcerer and put to the torture. For her assertion that alcoholism was unthinkable among the Zuñi, when in fact alcoholism was a severe problem on Zuñi reservations, see Harris 406.

7. See, for example: Sperber 41, 49; Archer 126; Augé 11, 77, 83.

8. Ernest Becker charges that anthropology in Lowie's generation em-

braced a morally empty "positivism" and that "the purpose of anthropology became that of furthering itself as a discipline" (*The Lost Science of Man* 101). One need not share his moral commitment to see the applicability of this analysis to the way in which academic anthropology seized upon the unverified hypothesis of "culture" as the basis of its disciplinary program.

9. Clifford Geertz paints a very different portrait of Evans-Pritchard as the practitioner of a resolutely commonsensical mode of ethnography devoted to eliminating conceptual ambiguity and to representing African society as "orderly, straightforward and levelheaded, firmly modeled and open to view" (*Works and Lives* 70). How one could so describe *The Nuer,* which dwells in a nearly obsessive way on themes of relativity and indeterminacy in cultural analysis, is a puzzle.

10. See Lepenies, *Between Literature and Science* 129, for a discussion of the "deep-rooted distaste for theory" which prevailed among the Webbs and other socialist sociologists.

11. A half century later, Freud exactly recapitulates this argument in *Moses and Monotheism*—though if he has a reminiscence of Spencer here, it goes undeclared. Still operating in 1937 within the supposedly defunct Victorian paradigm of an evolutionary "advance in civilization," Freud identifies the decisive overcoming of primitivism with the moment at which "human beings found themselves obliged in general to recognise 'intellectual' forces—forces, that is, which cannot be grasped by the senses (particularly by the sight) but which none the less produce undoubted and indeed extremely powerful effects" (*Moses* 114). Modern thought is directly akin, he says, to animism and superstition, even though science labors to expunge these very tendencies.

12. For critiques of Lévi-Strauss along these lines, see Mary Douglas, *Natural Symbols* 66–67, Marvin Harris 496. Unflinchingly drawing the consequences of his position at the outset of *The Raw and the Cooked* (1964), Lévi-Strauss declares that it is immaterial in the interpretation of a cultural expression such as myth whether the structures analyzed actually are present in the myths or are being concocted by the analyst himself. "What matters is that the human mind, regardless of the identity of those who happen to be giving it expression, should display an increasingly intelligible structure" (13).

13. "Fundamentally 'feeling' and 'meaning' are one," he remarks in a tantalizing aside (*IC* 135), but the point is not expounded further.

14. Geertz seems at various points to tackle directly the issue that runs through modern cultural theory: is culture something that exists in external reality and actually impinges upon men and women, or is it a hypothetical construct existing solely in the domain of anthropological theory? Alert as this sophisticated writer is to the fallacy of reifying abstractions, he strongly disclaims the idea of culture as having any capacity of effective action. "Cul-

ture is not a power, something to which social events, behaviors, institutions, or processes can be causally attributed," he says categorically, but simply "a context within which they . . . can be intelligibly . . . described" (*IC* 14). Yet he routinely contradicts this position by using the explicit language of agency to interpret elements of culture. Culture, he says elsewhere, is "a set of control mechanisms . . . for the governing of behavior" (*IC* 44). Culture patterns are "the mechanisms by whose agency" human indeterminateness is narrowed to "actual accomplishments" (*IC* 45); they exercise "governance" over man (*IC* 48). This is something altogether different from an interpretive "context" and something more substantial than a "web" of "pseudoentities" that disintegrate the more we know about them; it is a set of coercive, quasi-tangible realities.

15. Mill cogently illustrates this principle by showing the impossibility of computing the labor which goes into the production of such a commodity as a loaf of bread: "for if, as a part of the labor employed in making bread, we count the labor of the blacksmith who made the plough, why not also (it may be asked) the labor of making the tools used by the blacksmith, and the tools used in making those tools, and so back to the origin of things? But after mounting one or two steps in this ascending scale, we come into a region of fractions too minute for calculation" (*Principles* 1:38).

16. In the course of an extended critique of the literary methods deployed by ethnographic writers to create the illusion of cultural homogeneity, Dan Sperber reasserts Lowie's point: "Anthropological evidence does not warrant the assumption that particular beliefs are integrated into coherent, all-embracing culturally transmitted world-views." The typical "world-view format" of anthropological accounts, he argues, amounts merely to "an expository device, a way to order and organize generally heterogeneous and scattered data" (*On Anthropological Knowledge* 46). Taking a somewhat different slant on the same issue, Margaret S. Archer has followed Ernest Gellner and others in assailing the culture doctrine on the grounds that it fails to account for social change, and on the empirical grounds that the assumption of coherence is refuted by the manifest inconsistencies of belief and social practice that prevail within any "culture." (It is worth noting, however, that the insistence of such theorists on the role of "cultural contradictions" in producing social change testifies strongly in spite of everything to the tenacity of what Archer calls "the myth of cultural integration": to detect a "contradiction" in a system is to assert the determining reality of the system after all, and to assert the state of coherence, integration, and logical consistency as the theoretical norm.)

17. John Burrow notes occasional evidence in Victorian writing, notably in Spencer, of an awareness of the possibility of "the analysis of working social systems" according to the principles of structural-functionalism, but argues that the implicit "seeds of modern sociological theory" which can be detected in Victorian anthropology "were stifled by the overriding needs of . . . evolu-

tionism," to which Victorians clung for reassurance in the face "the weakening of traditional religious belief" and the seeming threat of "total relativism" (*Evolution and Society* 83, xiii, 97, 98). George W. Stocking, Jr. argues convincingly that Tylor himself never in fact employed the culture concept in the (apparent) sense of his own definition, and that it became operative as a means of technical ethnographic analysis only in the early twentieth century, largely under the influence of Franz Boas (*Race, Culture, and Evolution* 81–84, 202–3). Claude Lévi-Strauss corroborates the late dating even as he nominates another founding father, very precisely identifying the birth of the new concept with the publication in 1923–24 of Marcel Mauss's *The Gift* (*Introduction to the Work of Marcel Mauss* 38). I do not dispute this version of the record as it applies to the practice of formal anthropology, but in this book I argue that Tylor's and Mauss's doctrine (whenever exactly it was codified) only crystallized a complex of ideas illustrated fairly fully in documents predating *Primitive Culture*, in some cases by many decades.

18. Does this assertion mean that the psychology of every nineteenth-century believer in social evolutionism really was determined in just this way? Or does it mean that a certain large percentage of converts to the theory followed this course of reasoning? Or that some such logic contributed in some degree to many individual adherences to evolutionism? Any of these distinct formulations could form the basis of an empirical test, but the way in which the assertion is phrased (causing human actors to drop entirely out of what seems to be an interplay of ideas only) makes it impossible to know just what factual statement, if any, is being asserted. But how could such a claim as to motivation ever be proven by factual evidence, even in a single case, even if the subject had explicitly stated (as none probably ever did) that the reason alleged by Burrow was indeed "the specific attraction" of evolutionism for him or her? What evidence could suffice to prove a sequence of thinking which presumably would not be fully conscious to begin with, or to eliminate from contention other possible explanations for the choice of adherence to a doctrine—the personal appeal of a teacher, for instance, or the perception of the institutional prestige of one theory as opposed to another, or sheer intellectual infatuation? Do we know clearly why we believe what we do? Burrow never does offer an evidentiary case history designed specifically to demonstrate the chain of logical and emotional operations which he hypothesizes to explain the appeal of evolutionism; but if he did, how could one say that such a case history represented a proof of the thesis, and not merely an illustration of it? The difficulty is not just that Burrow, in stating his thesis, is simply guessing in the absence of empirical evidence; it is that ideas in this kind of account are not empirical, which is to say psychological, entities at all, but hypothetical or mythical generalizations playing out dramatic scenarios according less to documentable evidence (which in this case, as I have said, is close to nil) than to the norms of plausibility of historical narrative.

19. This approach distinguishes the present book from Foucault's magis-

terial survey of some of the same ground in *The Order of Things*, where radically coherent *epistemes* spring into being without cause and without antecedents, and where all sense of the internal dynamics of the thought of a period is eclipsed. If these are flaws in Foucault's work, they spring directly, we should note, from his extreme fetishizing of culture, which in a sense he only carries to its logical conclusion. "In any given culture and at any given moment," he claims to have discovered, "there is always only one *episteme* that defines the conditions of possibility of all knowledge, whether expressed in a theory or silently invested in a practice" (*Order* 168). One may feel various kinds of uneasiness at the promulgation of this sort of theoretical totalitarianism, which at the outset declares as a point of dogma that any possible contradictory empirical evidence is merely a "surface" effect (*Order* xxii) and that undeviating obedience to a single system of thought is as obligatory for scientific researchers as obedience to the cultural system is for ordinary members of a society.

20. See, in addition to Burrow's *Evolution and Society*, for example, Harris, *The Rise of Anthropological Theory* (subtitled *A History of Theories of Culture*); Evans-Pritchard, *A History of Anthropological Thought*; Manicas, *A History and Philosophy of the Social Sciences*; Stocking, *Race, Culture, and Evolution* and *Victorian Anthropology*; Kuper, *The Invention of Primitive Society*.

CHAPTER 1: FROM ORIGINAL SIN TO ANOMIE

1. Elisabeth Jay has emphasized that for all nineteenth-century Evangelicals, not just Methodists, "the concept of Original Sin . . . was the linchpin of the Evangelical creed" (Jay 54).

2. This need is made explicit in Dr. Andrew Ure's *Philosophy of Manufactures* (1835). For an analysis of Ure's "satanic" text, see E. P. Thompson, *The Making of the English Working Class* (359–62).

3. This is just the spectacle evoked, for instance, in a Methodist proclamation of 1819, a year of widespread social unrest. At various "tumultuous assemblies," declares this text, many have come under the influence of "infidel principles, . . . wild and delusive political theories, and . . . violent and inflammatory declamations," the ultimate tendency of which is "to bring all government into contempt, and to introduce universal discontent, insubordination, and anarchy" (quoted Thompson 353).

4. The notion that society sets boundaries for individual impulses is, according to J. D. Y. Peel, "the linchpin of modern sociology" (Peel xxxiv).

5. The idea of "an unceasing war between biological impulse and social restraint" has been criticized, for example, by Robert K. Merton, who observes that "the image of man as an untamed bundle of impulses begins to look more like a caricature than a portrait" (*Social Theory and Social Structure* 131).

6. We should note, though, Mill's quick transition to a very different idiom in this same passage. Strikingly prefiguring Durkheim's *Elementary Forms of the Religious Life*, he goes on to say that social order is guaranteed also by shared loyalty to whatever "fundamental principles" the society has designated as "sacred," and thus by a sense of collective identity (*Bentham* 122–26).

7. For discussions of this system, see Southey 1:284, 306; 2:274.

8. Foucault comments intriguingly on the late-eighteenth-century displacement of vegetable by animal figures as the predominant imagery of living beings in the field of natural history and also on "the ambiguous values assumed by animality" in this period (*Order* 276–78), but he does not discuss the ways in which this imagery impinged on ideas of human nature during the same period.

9. Stark devotes a six-volume study to the illusory project of proving empirically that social order "rests on the reduction and the control of animal propensities, not on their free unfolding" (Stark 1:vii), and cites by way of supposed demonstration many cases of insane-seeming civil disorder breaking out the moment that agencies of control relax their vigilance. This demonstration ignores all the sociocultural and thus purely human factors—race and class animosities, resentment of the agencies of control themselves, and so on—that invariably underlie outbreaks of disorder like the riots and lynchings studied by Stark. To speak of such events as evidence of "animal propensities" makes little sense; no animal has ever participated in a riot or a lynching.

10. See, for example, J. C. Prichard, *Researches* 1:183.

11. See Gallagher, *Industrial Reformation* 13.

12. Spencer closely echoes Robert Owen's claim "*that the character of man is, without a single exception, always formed for him; that it may be, and is, chiefly, created by his predecessors*; that they give him . . . his ideas and habits, which are the powers that govern and direct his conduct" (quoted Gallagher, *Industrial Reformation* 13).

13. No text illustrates the pattern here suggested more conclusively than *Civilization and its Discontents*, which resuscitates puritanical moral discourse in almost too plain a form. Discovering "the original nature of man," says Freud, for example, "reveals man as a savage beast to whom consideration towards his own kind is something alien." Aggressiveness, he declares (without any evidence), invoking the trope of boundlessness central to puritan moral discourse, "reigned almost without limit in primitive times" (*Civilization and its Discontents* 59, 60). In all such speculations on "the original nature of man," Freud follows Wesley's language very closely.

14. For a fine survey of these dissident strains in current anthropological theory and practice, see James Clifford, "On Ethnographic Authority." See also Clifford and Marcus, eds., *Writing Culture: The Poetics and Politics of Ethnography*.

15. Lewis Henry Morgan closely identified the emergence of centralized state power with the development of writing (Augé 19); Lévi-Strauss has in turn greatly elaborated this thesis (*Tristes tropiques* 296–300).

16. This analysis exactly confirms Foucault's axioms that power and knowledge, rather than being essentially incompatible, "directly imply one another" (*Discipline and Punish* 27), and that the constitution of modern human sciences is the historical correlative of the development of new modalities of social domination. My speculation that the theory of culture is readable in part as an allegory of ideal discipline is highlighted by the close congruence of many of Foucault's formulations with the habitual language of ethnographic theorists. The real aim of judicial and penal reform in the eighteenth and nineteenth centuries, he states, for instance, was not to render the system of punishment more humane, but to institute a more efficient and continuous system of controls capable of "operating everywhere, . . . down to the finest grain of the human body," of effecting "the penetration of regulation into even the smallest details of everyday life," into "the most elementary particle, the most passing phenomenon of the social body" (*Discipline and Punish* 80, 198, 214).

17. Well-known cases include: the story of Omai or Mai, the native of the Polynesian island of Huahine brought by Captain Cook in 1773 back to England, where he was entertained by aristocracy and caused a sensation, and returned by Cook to his homeland in 1777, where his subsequent history of lapsing back into "barbarism" was recorded by the missionary William Ellis (*Polynesian Researches* 2:90–102); the case of Kaspar Hauser, who in 1828 emerged at Nuremberg after many years' solitary confinement, gabbling unintelligibly and seeming to onlookers "an idiot or a madman, or . . . a kind of savage" (Zingg 286); and the accounts of wolf children in India published by Sleeman in 1855. The voluminousness of this literature and its great significance for nineteenth-century speculations are well indicated in E. B. Tylor's lead article for the inaugural issue of *The Anthropological Review* (1863), "Wild Men and Beast-Children." All such reports, he argues, need to be regarded with great suspicion.

18. Clifford Geertz's speculations on the same themes more than 150 years later point up the special significance of this line of Itard's work for the modern theory of culture. "Undirected by culture patterns," says Geertz, "man's behavior would be virtually ungovernable, a mere chaos of pointless acts and exploding emotions, his experience virtually shapeless"; men without culture, he remarks elsewhere, would be "unworkable monstrosities" (*Interpretation of Cultures* 46, 39). One can guess that some conscious or unconscious recollection of Itard's descriptions of Victor underlies this argument.

19. See Stocking, "From Chronology to Ethnology" xvii–xxi, for an argument that Prichard, originally a Quaker, came increasingly under the influence of the Evangelical movement.

20. Gallagher traces this ambiguity in its specific application to attacks by radical reformers upon the liberal political tradition. Thus the key failure of liberal apologists for industrialism and the system of "free labour," declares Cobbett, is that they fail to "tell us what [they] mean by the word *freedom*" (quoted Gallagher, *Industrial Reformation* 10).

21. Lévi-Strauss (*Structural Anthropology* 353–54) and Geertz (*Interpretation of Cultures* 46–48) extend the principle to the process of biological evolution itself, claiming that the very structure of the human cerebral cortex was determined by the cultural environment of early man.

22. A Barthian concept of reading as an uncovering or an engendering of a scarcely limitable "process of equivalence" inflects (infects?) the present inquiry in ways which by now should be evident and which render it at last, in a circularity bound to elude full explication, an inquiry into its own conditions of possibility.

23. See especially Whatley's noted 1854 essay "On the Origin of Civilization."

24. The anthropologist Thomas Gregor has lately revived the subject, studying a Brazilian tribe that seems to practice unrestrained promiscuity in sexual matters; he concludes that sex among the Mehinaku is in fact not free but inhibited by a network of prohibitions and deep anxieties.

25. As Lewis Coser has pointed out (xx).

26. Calling it the distinctive illness of modern people, Freud identified this state with an unappeasable "craving for stimulation," and declared that it led infallibly to "an endless series of substitutive objects none of which, however, brings full satisfaction" ("On the Universal Tendency to Debasement in the Sphere of Love," *Standard Edition* 11:189).

CHAPTER 2: DESIRE, WEALTH, AND VALUE: ANOMIC THEMES IN POLITICAL ECONOMY

1. See Burrow, *Evolution and Society* 16–18.

2. Adam Smith, for example, is unmentioned in Lowie's *History of Ethnological Theory*, and, except for a few passing mentions of his name in other contexts, in Harris's *Rise of Anthropological Theory* as well; in Voget's *History of Ethnology*, Smith is touched on in a couple of brief paragraphs (75, 78–79). Philip Abrams convincingly argues that "the rise of sociology in Britain must be treated first in terms of the vicissitudes of political economy" (Abrams 8), but the theory of culture lies outside the scope of his book. In contrast to Burrow and to Raymond Williams, who both portray the growth of nineteenth-century anthropological thinking as a reaction against the tradition to which political economy belonged, Stocking (*Victorian Anthropology* 30ff.) discusses the relevance of political economy to the history of nineteenth-cen-

tury evolutionist anthropology, stressing the idealization of the Malthusian doctrine of prudential restraint and of the Victorian gospel of work in theories of the progress of civilization; but again, he is not concerned in this book with the development of the ethnographic theory of culture, which appears to me to emerge precisely in opposition to the Victorian moral ideology which evolutionism embodies.

3. Bagehot ventures the guess that the increasing prosperity of the nation caused the study of economics to seem less urgently necessary (*ES* 155). Philip Abrams (77–79) situates the decline of political economy somewhat later than does Bagehot, and offers an opposite thesis: that the economic downturn of Britain in the 1870s caused a loss of faith in the economists' doctrines (see also Manicas 198).

4. This implied lesson is clearly stated at last in a late passage of Mill's text where he disavows Adam Smith's doctrine that a healthy capitalist economy needs to maintain a state of continuing expansion. Stating his own preference for "the stationary state of capital and wealth," Mill vividly evokes the ugliness and futility of a furious competitive struggle for riches (*Principles* 2:313–14).

5. "No one could have looked closely into the sources of fallacious thinking," says Mill, "without being deeply conscious that the coherence, and neat concatenation of our philosophical systems, is more apt than we are commonly aware to pass with us as evidence of their truth" (*Some Unsettled Questions* 154).

6. W. P. D. Wightman stresses that for many thinkers of Newton's day and before, notably Leibniz, gravity was "regarded as either an inexplicable miracle or as an 'occult' property of matter itself," and posed a "fundamental dilemma" in philosophy (Wightman 22).

7. The transposition of Humean epistemology into a cultural theory based on habitual association is frequently implied, if never fully analyzed, in D. A. Reisman's admirable *Adam Smith's Sociological Economics* (26, 35).

8. This reflexive process is just the one implied throughout *The Golden Bough* by Frazer's thesis that religious myths are invented to account after the fact for the accrued sacred status of practices whose original rationales, if any, have been forgotten; and it is the one argued more explicitly by Boas in a crucial text of twentieth-century anthropology, *The Mind of Primitive Man* (226–52).

9. This principle stands out clearly in Freud's definition of the function of "Eros." "Civilization is a process in the service of Eros, whose purpose is to combine single human individuals, and after that families, then races, peoples and nations, into one great unity, the unity of mankind. Why this has to happen, we do not know; the work of Eros is precisely this" (*Civilization and Its Discontents* 69).

10. Novelists throughout the nineteenth century pick up this thesis in fictional essays on bad conscience which tell us, with Adam Smith, that the peculiar anguish of this state is rooted in the hallucinatory sensation of splitting into two different people. This is just the theme of the brilliantly phantasmagoric episode in Dickens's *Martin Chuzzlewit* describing the guilty agonies of a murderer who, brooding on the thought of the room where he pretended to be while out committing his crime, becomes "in a gloomy, murderous, mad way not only fearful *for* himself but *of* himself for being, as it were, a part of the room, a something supposed to be there, yet missing from it." Ultimately, says Dickens's narrator (making overt the occult theme in Adam Smith's fable of the man who "becomes in some measure the object of his own hatred and abhorrence"), "he became in a manner his own ghost and phantom, and was at once the haunting spirit and the haunted man" (chap. 47).

11. It is this aspect of Smith's theory of value that Foucault, drawing all his references from the opening pages of the first volume of *The Wealth of Nations*, stresses to the exclusion of all others, portraying it as a sharp departure from classical ideas of "representation" (*Order* 221 ff.): Smith's conception of labor value is "irreducible to the analysis of representation" (*Order* 225). Smith's theory as developed at length is more ambiguous than Foucault says, and more entangled in ideas of socially produced symbolism.

12. So too with the closely related institution of totemism. The Ojibwa word originally means "mark": one's totem animal is the marked animal, and in turn one's own mark. See on this theme Durkheim's striking discussion of the sacred imagery of totemism in *The Elementary Forms of the Religious Life*. "In themselves, the churinga [ritual instruments] are objects of wood and stone like all others; they are distinguished from profane things of the same sort by only one particularity: this is that the totemic mark is drawn or engraved upon them. So it is this mark and this alone which gives them their sacred character" (*Elementary Forms* 144).

13. Setting the labor theory of value in an explicitly anthropological context, Smith declares that "if among a nation of hunters, . . . it usually costs twice the labour to kill a beaver which it does to kill a deer, one beaver should naturally exchange for or be worth two deer" (*WN* 1:53). The example shows by its seemingly deliberate implausibility that the notion of "labour" as a kind of natural absolute quantity in a cultural vacuum leads to nonsensical conclusions. Obviously, unless there existed compelling sociocultural reasons for valuing beaver to begin with, no hunter would ever invest in killing a beaver the same amount of labor which would yield far greater rewards if otherwise employed; so Smith's hypothetical example seems moot, and the pure labor theory seems undercut rather than elucidated by it.

14. In order to minimize distractions, let us make a point of bypassing "the Adam Smith problem," that of measuring the degree of self-contradiction

there may be between his earlier stress on "sympathy" and his later stress on self-aggrandizement. For a survey of the literature on this issue, see Raphael and Macfie 20–25, and Macfie, *The Individual in Society* 59–81.

15. It is a near-quotation too of Hume's discussion of "the avidity . . . of acquiring goods and possessions," which he describes as "insatiable, perpetual, universal, and directly destructive of society" (*Treatise* 491–92).

16. Smith does note that this ideal state is not currently realized, given the frequent distortions of the market which result from restraints on freedom of trade. But the individual's constant exertions to invest capital most advantageously are supposed by Smith's theory to continue unabated even once such restraints have been eliminated and equilibrium achieved.

17. References to the first (1798) edition of Malthus's *Essay* will be abbreviated *EP*, references to the sixth (1826) edition, the last published in the author's lifetime, will be abbreviated *EP6*, followed by volume number in the Wrigley-Souden edition (2 or 3) and page number.

18. In thus intimating the theory of "survivals" in culture, Malthus echoes Adam Smith's still earlier suggestion of it in *The Wealth of Nations* (1:408). Neither writer is mentioned in Margaret Hodgen's historical survey of this theme, *The Doctrine of Survivals*.

19. Long after, Durkheim closely reproduces Malthus's argument. "After all, what is marriage?" he asks in *Suicide*. "A regulation of sexual relations, involving not merely the physical instincts which this intercourse involves but the feelings of every sort gradually engrafted by civilization on the foundation of physical desire. For among us love is a far more mental than organic fact" (270).

20. Coleridge was scandalized by this line of argument in Malthus. See Himmelfarb, "Introduction" xxvii.

21. Except where noted, references are to the 1836 edition (volumes 5 and 6 of the Wrigley-Souden edition of Malthus's works).

22. "If the scientific study of culture has lagged," says Clifford Geertz, "it has been in large part because its very subject matter is elusive. The initial problem of any science—defining its object of study in such a manner as to render it susceptible of analysis—has here turned out to be unusually hard to solve" (*Interpretation of Cultures* 362).

23. See V. E. Smith, "Malthus's Theory of Demand and its Influence on Value Theory," for the history of Malthus's development of the concept of "intensity of demand" as reflected in his correspondence with Ricardo.

24. This correspondence is published as volumes 6–9 of *The Works and Correspondence of David Ricardo*, ed. Piero Sraffa and M. H. Dobb.

25. Winch (55) interprets Malthus's "doctrine of proportions" as referring merely to the need to discover a "golden mean" in balancing economic factors so as to achieve optimal results.

26. For a survey of Ricardo's treatment of this issue in his *Principles of Political Economy and Taxation* and in his unfinished *Absolute Value and Exchangeable Value*, see Caravale and Tosato, *Ricardo and the Theory of Value Distribution and Growth* 54–58.

27. "I believe [the wants and tastes of mankind] to be unlimited," wrote Ricardo to Malthus. "Give men but the means of purchasing and their wants are insatiable" (*R* 6:148).

28. Mill devotes a long section of text (*Principles* 90ff.) to refuting this "absurdity" (2:96).

29. "Abundance without increase of value," Malthus wrote to Ricardo, "would . . . lead to a stagnation of demand" (*R* 7:194).

30. Mill had made the same point. Political economy is often hampered, he declares, by "the error . . . of not distinguishing between necessities arising from laws of nature, and those created by social arrangements" (*Principles* 1:520).

31. Bagehot did not originate this theory. It was fully set out, for example, in Mill's *On Liberty*. "The greater part of the world has, properly speaking, no history," says Mill, "because the despotism of Custom is complete" (71).

32. "The political economist inquires," says Mill, "what are the actions which would be produced by this desire, if . . . it were unimpeded by any other" (*Some Unsettled Questions* 139–40).

33. We get shrewd preliminary glimpses of such a science in the course of Bagehot's discussion, as, for example, where he emphasizes that some societies do not, like our own, inculcate an awareness of "luxury" or a desire for it, and where he notes how this idea of the desirability of luxury couples itself in our society with certain feelings of parents for their children to generate economic behavior (*ES* 172).

34. This is the theme of Manicas, *A History and Philosophy of the Social Sciences*.

35. Sir Henry Maine had stated Bagehot's principle some years previously. "It is not the business of the scientific historical enquirer to assert good or evil of any particular institution. He deals with existence and development, not with its expediency" (quoted Lowie, *History* 51). Mill takes the same position, asserting that political economy "has nothing to do with" moral judgments of different uses of goods; but he compromises the supposedly value-neutral character of his science by declaring capitalist free enterprise to be the best known system for filling human needs (*Principles* 1:521, 255).

36. Forty-four years later, Franz Boas elaborately theorized this same principle in *The Mind of Primitive Man*. People of all cultures, he says, picking up the argument made by Adam Smith in *The Theory of Moral Sentiments*, regard what is customary and traditional as sacrosanct, invest every rule of etiquette, however trivial, with moral significance, and regard, for instance, other table

manners than their own with "feelings of displeasure which may rise to such an intensity as to cause qualmishness" (*Mind* 229). Whatever deviates from the customary instantly triggers powerful emotion.

37. See Huxley, *Evolution and Ethics* (49) for a similar statement as to how the imitative nature of human beings causes us automatically to adopt "the hue of passion of those who are about us."

38. See, for example, Lévi-Strauss (*Structural Anthropology* 353) and Geertz (*Interpretation* 46–48) on the theory that the evolution of the cerebral cortex was to some degree conditioned by the original phases of human culture.

39. Freud surprisingly lends credence to this Victorian legend that advancing civilization means a progressive erosion of libido: see "Why War?" *Standard Edition* 22:214.

CHAPTER 3: SAVAGERY, CULTURE, AND THE SUBJECTIVITY OF FIELDWORK

1. Anthropological definitions of institutions as functionally interrelated social units, says Malinowski, "in reality . . . are condensed formulae which contain extensive recipes for the organization of perspective in field-work. And this really is the hallmark of scientific definition. It must principally be a call to a scientifically schematized and oriented observation of empirical fact" (*A Scientific Theory* 115). Rosalie H. Wax has noticed "the possibility that Malinowski developed [the] new functionalist school partly as an academic justification for his monumental and, professionally speaking, highly unusual piece of fieldwork" (*Doing Fieldwork* 37).

2. Everett C. Hughes similarly declares his "conviction that field work is not merely one among several methods of social study but is paramount" (Hughes vii).

3. For a Victorian anthropologist to have had the idea of studying primitive people through extended personal contact with them "would have required," says John Burrow, "an almost superhuman leap of imaginative curiosity" (Burrow 85).

4. Malinowski does once qualify his indictment of this class by a passing reference to "the few intelligent and unbiassed missionaries to whom Ethnography owes so much" (*Argonauts* 18).

5. The fieldworker, declares B. H. Junker, "will experience something given to few others in a well-ordered society, namely, an opportunity to escape from the particular variety of ethnocentrism to which each . . . is very likely to be bound" (*Field Work* 5). Roy Wagner speaks in the same way of the "evangelistic message" of anthropology, which, he says, "draws people who want to emancipate themselves from their culture" (*Invention of Culture* 10).

6. According to the OED, the word "ethnography" entered the English language only in 1834.

7. Published reactions to Malinowski's diary include the following: F. L. K. Hsu, "The Cultural Problem of the Cultural Anthropologist"; E. Leach, "On reading *A Diary in the Strict Sense of the Term*"; George W. Stocking, Jr., "The Ethnographer's Magic"; Clifford Geertz, "Under the Mosquito Net"; James Clifford, "Ethnographic Self-Fashioning."

8. For an excellent collection of essays dealing with these themes, see Clifford and Marcus, eds., *Writing Culture: The Poetics and Politics of Ethnography*. Marc Augé touches pungently on the alliance between anthropology and both ethnocide and genocide (*Anthropological Circle* 78, 90). See also Jarvie 179: "It is a sentimental dream to talk of understanding what (other) people do and think in terms of their own cultural values and categories."

9. For a venomous denunciation of early missionary work in Polynesia, see Norman Lewis, *The Missionaries* 1–8. The relation of this recklessly libellous polemic to scholarly research is parodic at best. Drawing his information almost wholly from the testimony of the renegade missionary J. M. Orsmond, Lewis asserts, for example, that the missionaries in their dealings with the Tahitian chief Pomare pursued a deliberate scheme of "stupefying him with spirits" (Lewis 7). In the mission history of John Davies, published in the same volume with Orsmond's account, there is much evidence that in fact the missionaries strove in vain to prevent the introduction of alcohol into Tahiti (Davies 227–31). Lewis never makes the slightest reference to this evidence or to any other—needless to say, there is a mountain of it, even though it needs to be approached with skepticism—that fails to match his diabolical portrait of the missionaries. Nor does he ever question the credibility of Orsmond, whose bitterness toward the London Missionary Society stemmed in part from his having been dismissed from it in 1845 for insubordination.

10. One order of 1813, for instance, enjoined under threat of severe punishment that Europeans "shall properly demean themselves towards the natives; and not commit acts of trespass on their gardens, lands, habitations, burial grounds, tombs, or properties, . . . or at all interfere in their quarrels, or excite any animosities among them, but leave them to the free enjoyment of their rites and ceremonies" (quoted Ellis 1:100). The missionaries' project set them sharply at odds with the spirit and letter of such an order, and in fact they violated every provision of it, especially the last, in the most extreme fashion.

11. Bernard Smith has spoken of the important role played by missionaries and by the Evangelical mentality at large in overturning the eighteenth-century cult of the noble savage, a cult that had mythologized Tahiti in particular as a paradise of natural virtue (*European Vision* 137).

12. Bernard Smith obscures this motive by categorically distinguishing

documentation of the "ignoble savage" idea from supposedly truer scientific investigations.

13. James Calvert describes himself and his (undoubtedly severely respectable) wife pulling down the blinds of their hut in Fiji to screen their view of cannibal feasts occurring just outside—much to the indignation of the villagers (*Missionary Labours* 254).

14. Mary Louise Pratt has discussed premonitions of contemporary ethnographic discourse in early travel narratives: "Fieldwork in Common Places" 34. K. O. L. Burridge intriguingly suggests that Malinowski's animus toward missionaries reveals "an unresolved oedipal problem" toward those who had "fathered" ethnographic study, but he does not pursue the point (5).

15. "We must insist," wrote Franz Boas in 1911, "that a command of the language is an indispensable means of obtaining accurate and thorough knowledge, because much information can be gained by listening to conversations of the natives and by taking part in their daily life, which, to the observer who has no command of the language, will remain entirely inaccessible" (quoted in Lowie, *History* 132).

16. It does largely paralyze George Turner, who expresses it quite plainly in introducing his very perfunctory survey of Samoan mythology. "The mythology of Samoa, like that of all heathen nations, whether savage or civilized," he declares, "abounds in obscenities and absurdities. An hour, however, is not altogether lost in turning over the heap of rubbish." The best reason he can give for such an activity is that primitive myths can occasionally provide "corroboration" of biblical history (*Nineteen Years* 244).

17. Wesley devotes one of his most impassioned sermons, "On Sin in Believers," to arguing this essential point of doctrine (*Sermons* 2:360–78).

18. Following a hint of Franz Steiner's, I have explored more fully elsewhere the correlation between Polynesian theories of magical contamination and Victorian dirt phobias. See Herbert, "Rat Worship and Taboo."

19. "It is evident that [the fieldworker visiting a foreign people] can only establish [the necessary] intimacy," says Evans-Pritchard in the same vein, "if he makes himself in some degree a member of their society and lives, thinks, and feels in their culture. . . . To understand a people's thought one has to think in their symbols" (*Social Anthropology* 79).

20. For references to the anthropological literature on the issue of "going native," see Jarvie 154.

21. See Stocking, *Victorian Anthropology* 87–92 for a thoughtful appraisal of Williams's ethnography.

22. Landing for the first time on a Polynesian island, George Turner was struck by the "ludicrous," elaborate face-painting of the natives, which gives him the very mistaken impression of being amid "a nation of Merry-Andrews." The natives give him a lesson in ethnographic perception, though it

is wasted on him. "As to clothing, of the men I may say they had none. 'Why do you put that paint on your faces?' we would ask, and presently one would smartly reply, 'Why do you put these clothes on? This is our way of clothing, that is yours'" (*Nineteen Years* 5).

23. We shall never know exactly what Rowe did to Williams's manuscript. Calvert in his preface (xxiv) implies that Rowe's revisions of both his own work and Williams's were extensive, but gives no indication of their nature in the case of the latter. John McLennan, lamenting the loss of potentially vital ethnographic data, declared in 1896 that "we may assume that Mr. Rowe's discretion was exercised throughout to make the book a good readable and saleable record of missionary work" by suppressing improper sexual materials (*Studies in Ancient History* 207). A later Fijianist, Basil Thomson, portraying Williams as a fearless empirical scientist whose work was "ludicrously out of keeping with the spirit of the missionary publications of those days," gives a more elaborate account of what happened. "In his simple love of truth, Mr. Williams had forgotten to point the usual moral," says Thomson, and this caused the Missionary Society to appoint "a Bowdler" in the person of Rowe, a "maiden-modest editor" whose main task was removing Williams's frank discussion of Fijian marriage laws. The manuscript of *Fiji and the Fijians* thus suffered a "sinister fate" (Thomson 56–57). Thomson's indictment of Rowe is apparently based on sheer conjecture. It embroiders without any warrant upon McLennan's comments, which themselves were conjectural to begin with. It is possible that the self-contradictory discourse of Williams's work, which combines strong intimations of moral relativism with equally strong outbursts of Evangelical moralism, and combines minutely detailed ethnography with occasional fits of reticence, is the sign of the author's own deeply conflicted attitudes toward his materials, rather than the sign of sinister editorial intervention. Were this the case, it would in no way diminish the glory of Williams's achievement.

24. The forbidden subject is exposed with a vengeance by the dissident missionary Orsmond (Davies 351, 358, 359).

25. A belief continued to prevail until much later in the rudimentary, uncouth character of "primitive" languages. See, for example, Tylor, *Researches* 62ff.

26. Or, as Evans-Pritchard puts it, "when one has fully understood the meaning of all the words of [the natives'] language in all their situations of reference one has finished one's study of the society" (*Social Anthropology* 79–80).

27. The modernity of Martin's text can best be highlighted by collating it with such examples of twentieth-century cultural exegesis as, say, Lévi-Strauss's obsessively detailed studies of the geometrical patterning of Caduveo body painting (*Tristes tropiques* 191–95) or Bororo village layouts (*Structural Anthropology* 141–47), Victor Turner's analysis, replete with dia-

grams, of the spatial symbolism of the *Isoma* ritual of the Ndembu (*Ritual Process* 30), or Geertz's "microscopic" analysis of the betting system of Balinese cockfights (*Interpretation of Cultures* 425–32). "From this proposition—that the higher the center bet the more exactly a fifty-fifty proposition the cockfight is—two things . . . follow: (1) the higher the center bet is, the greater the pull on the side betting toward the short-odds end of the wagering spectrum, and vice versa; (2) the higher the center bet is, the greater the volume of side betting, and vice versa" (Geertz, *Interpretation* 430). This is just Martin's (and, indeed, Adam Smith's) analytic method, applied to another ceremony.

28. For a sharp critique of Boas's tendency to the unlimited collection of data, his principled hostility to theory, and the chaotic results which this approach supposedly yields, see Harris 282–89. Malinowski is indicted in just the same terms by Evans-Pritchard (*History* 198).

29. Given its maximally skeptical twist, this principle implies that the very concept of "logic" in cultural analysis is delusive, and that as a result no valid interpretation of another culture is possible. "A relativist in earnest," says Dan Sperber, "should be either quite pessimistic about the possibility of doing ethnography at all, or extraordinarily optimistic about the abilities of ethnographers" (*On Anthropological Knowledge* 41). See also Augé 11, 77, 83.

30. Such in fact is much the implication of "culture complex" or *Kulturkreislehre* theorists, vigorously denounced for this reason by Malinowski (*Scientific Theory* 33–35).

31. The doctrine of "survivals," known already to Adam Smith (*Wealth of Nations* 1:408) but developed as a broad anthropological theory by Tylor, was one device for accounting for perplexing irregularities of "levels" within particular cultures.

32. The seemingly irrational logic of taboo became a crux of the development of the nineteenth-century science of culture, as writers like Shortland, Frazer, and Robertson Smith elaborated ever more profoundly the great enigma that in taboo thinking, sacred purity and pollution are identical.

33. Ellis exactly bears out Marc Augé's statement that mission anthropology "invents the myth of a society enjoying total unanimity and solidarity in order to set up recipes for modified forms of development" (*The Anthropological Circle* 84).

34. The guess is corroborated by the work of Dan Sperber and other recent theorists on the "epidemiology of ideas" within cultures, focusing on the issue of what causes some ideas to be "more contagious than others" (Sperber 30, 31). Cultural processes are thus figured explicitly as contamination. This turn of thought is particularly evident in Robertson Smith's *Religion of the Semites* (1889), where the nascent theory of the complex whole is closely tied to an analysis, reminiscent of Ellis's, of how "divine life [was] transfused through

every member . . . of the sacred circle" (Robertson Smith 312–13) in early Middle Eastern cults.

35. Such declarations foreshadow Durkheim's relativistic argument many decades later that any widely occurring phenomenon in a society—crime in our own, for example—must be defined sociologically as normal and desirable, rather than pathological (*Rules* 85–104).

CHAPTER 4: MAYHEW'S COCKNEY POLYNESIA

1. The same view is expressed more skeptically by Franz Boas as a reason to doubt the validity of grand theoretical schemes in anthropology. "Absolute systems of phenomena as complex as those of culture are impossible," he declares. "They will always be reflections of our own culture" (*Race, Language and Culture* 311; see also 317).

2. Of the four-volume version of *London Labour* published in 1861–62, only the first three volumes are by Mayhew, and only these will come under discussion in the present chapter. For a survey of the complicated genesis and publication history of Mayhew's work, see Humpherys, *Henry Mayhew* 81–139.

3. Humpherys closely echoes Ruth Glass's earlier assertions that "there is no theme" in *London Labour,* only "description without selection or analysis," and that Mayhew's sociological work is vitiated by his "endless curiosity" (Glass 43).

4. For example, F. B. Smith is at great pains in "Mayhew's Convict" to prove that at least one of Mayhew's informants probably invented at least part of his tale.

5. In this section and to a lesser extent throughout this chapter, I have borrowed materials published previously in my essay "Rat Worship and Taboo in Mayhew's London."

6. Not all of Mayhew's references to writings of anthropologists are acknowledged or, perhaps, conscious. When, for instance, he declares that the nomadic "savage" is characterized by "an immoderate love of gaming, frequently risking his own personal liberty upon a single cast" (*LL* 1:2), he is silently quoting W. Cooke Taylor's *Natural History of Society:* savages, says Taylor, have "an immoderate love of gaming," and he cites the willingness of North American Indians "to risk even their personal liberty upon a single cast" (Taylor 1:185). *London Labour* is full of such echoings, though sometimes it is hard to tell whether Mayhew is quoting a particular source or merely citing a commonplace of anthropological thinking of the time.

7. For a fine brief discussion of Mayhew's anthropology, see Yeo 86–88. See also Deborah E. Nord, "The Social Explorer as Anthropologist."

8. For various theories of "primeval promiscuity," see Harris 186, 188, 198, and 348.

9. Compare George Eliot's portrayal of the nomadic gypsies, "a race /
More outcast and despised than Moor or Jew," as

A race that lives on prey as foxes do

With stealthy, petty rapine: so despised,

It is not persecuted, only spurned,

Crushed underfoot, warred on by chance like rats,

Or swarming flies, or reptiles. . . .

(*The Spanish Gypsy* 142–43)

10. Margaret T. Hodgen documents in *The Doctrine of Survivals* the widespread influence of degeneration theory in the first half of the nineteenth
century.

11. Missionary ethnographers claimed to have confirmed this principle
through their own observations of heathen tribes. "The movement apparent
in the moral history of Fiji has been steadily and uniformly from bad to
worse," declares Thomas Williams, for example. "Old men speak of the atroc-
ities of recent times as altogether new, and far surpassing the deeds of cruelty
which they witnessed fifty years ago" (*Fiji and the Fijians* 103).

12. See, for example, *LL* 1:103, 246, 254, 264, 269, 359, 362, 395, 405, 408,
435; 2:74, 140, 144, 157, 209; 3:60, 84, 305, 306, 399.

13. On the first two pages of *London Labour* and once or twice in passing
thereafter, Mayhew floats the notion, well vouched for in the ethnology of his
day, that the degraded poor represent a low-grade racial stock biologically
predestined for a "wandering" existence. Gertrude Himmelfarb ("Mayhew's
Poor: A Problem of Identity") takes him harshly to task for this suggestion,
but the fact is that Mayhew's own text massively refutes it by stressing throughout "the degrading influence of circumstances upon the poor" (*LL* 2:157).
He dwells with particular insistency on the many wicked schemes of exploitation by which the poor are victimized and prevented from improving their lot
in life. Among the cruelest of these, for instance, would be the system of
virtually compulsory alcoholism set up by the employers of the ballast-heav-
ers, "a most vile and wicked plan for the degradation and demoralization of
our fellow-creatures" (*LL* 3:272), or the system devised by contractors for
hiring "lumpers," enabling the contractor to keep "reducing and reducing
the wages of his bretheren until all sink in poverty, wretchedness, and vice"—
a system that must infallibly, Mayhew declares, "result in the degradation of
the workmen" (*LL* 3:294). It is almost libellously misleading to claim that
Mayhew explains the sorry position of the poor through a theory of racial
inferiority.

14. Mayhew's point, obviously enough, is the one asserted some time afterward by Franz Boas: "greater lack of cultural values than that found in the
inner life of some strata of our modern population," says Boas, "is hardly
found anywhere," even among the rudest primitive tribes (*Mind* 198).

15. Catherine Gallagher has remarked in an excellent study of *London Labour and the London Poor* that "for Mayhew scarcity is not an issue" since "London seems to be overflowing with cheap food in his works" (Gallagher, "The Body versus the Social Body" 102). If one is absolutely destitute, however, food cannot possibly be cheap enough, and he never stops insisting on the constant pressure of malnutrition, famine, and even starvation for the poor.

16. Pierre Bourdieu has highlighted this characteristic function of bourgeois culture (*Distinction* 41–65).

17. In *Moses and Monotheism*, Freud presents this dogma in its baldest possible form, stipulating that "advance in civilization" consists of the "victory of intellectuality over sensuality" and the "dematerialization" of religious thought (*Moses* 114, 115)—precisely the language, say, of the Evangelical ethnographers of a century before proclaiming the manifest superiority of Europeans over various tribal peoples, especially those who worshipped idols.

18. Mayhew's analysis coincides with Engels's analysis of just the same phenomenon in *The Condition of the Working Class in England* (1845). The Victorian upper classes were remarkably successful, according to Engels, in designing patterns of life which would keep the poor from ever crossing their field of vision. "It is quite possible for someone to live for years in Manchester and to travel daily to and from his work without ever seeing a working-class quarter or coming into contact with an artisan," he says (Engels 54; see also 55, 93, 153, 190, 195, 208).

19. This caution applies, for example, to Mark Seltzer's polemical references to Mayhew in *Henry James and the Art of Power*. Invoking Foucault's ideas in doctrinaire fashion, Seltzer identifies Mayhew's research among the poor with the spirit of "policing and surveillance" that supposedly governs the development of oppressive nineteenth-century state institutions. "Watching cannot be freed from an act of violation," Seltzer declares, without bothering to offer proof of so remarkable an assertion (30); sociology such as Mayhew's "registers an expansion and dissemination of policing techniques and of the apparatus of incrimination," and it embodies "a dream of absolute surveillance" (34). In this literature, "seeing becomes the mode of power par excellence" (34). Such monstrously totalitarian writing as Mayhew's is "coextensive with . . . the expansion of the metropolitan police and the penal apparatus" (38). However just these prefabricated formulas may be in connection with later observers of the London underworld such as George R. Sims, James Greenwood, or William Booth, they yield a hopelessly distorted and tendentious reading of Mayhew, who in fact carries on in *London Labour and the London Poor* an increasingly fierce polemic against police persecution of the "proscribed class" of street folk (*LL* 1:266, 337–38, 394, 434; 2:489) and the whole system of exploitation that the police subserve, as well as against the "love of power" (*LL* 2:264) that he sees at the base of various philanthropical

schemes which seek to impose disciplined organization upon the poor. Mayhew's argument is that the Victorian authorities oppress the poor most cruelly by refusing to acknowledge their existence, that is, by a systematic *insufficiency* of "surveillance." It is not seeing but refusing to see that becomes the Victorian "mode of power par excellence." Thus Mayhew often complains that his attempts to discover the truth of the condition of the poor are obstructed by the authorities (*LL* 2:268, 3:302), and he complains that the national census, which fails to record the presence of this entire vast section of the population, serves as an instrument for concealing the "state of hopeless degradation" (*LL* 3:309) prevailing in poor neighborhoods and is "a national disgrace" (*LL* 3:234; see also 1:4). To object to Mayhew's brand of "surveillance" is to serve all the interests of the exploiters, he would maintain against a critique like Seltzer's.

20. Chimney sweeps, for example, despite their pariah status, display high intelligence (*LL* 2:364); cabmen are mysteriously prone to violent crime (*LL* 3:356–57); costermongers, for all their seeming brutality, have intense affection for their donkeys (*LL* 1:29); and so forth.

21. To see the central role of this principle in Mayhew's thinking is to grasp the significance of such a passage as the long, odd-seeming excursus in volume 3 (*LL* 3:318–27) on "the entire transit system of Great Britain," where the interconnecting networks of different modes of transport symbolize his view of the nation as a labyrinthine network of agencies of communication in which all sectors are correlated with all others into a "complex whole."

22. Some of his most striking discoveries take this form. "*It is impossible to make labourers of the paupers of an over-populated country without making paupers of the labourers,*" he declares, for example (*LL* 2:242). Later he promulgates "a plain unerring law—*over-work makes under-pay and under-pay makes over-work*" (*LL* 2:300).

23. Missionaries had to suffer the same indignities. William Ellis thus describes the derision of Tahitian onlookers during the attempt of an early missionary to preach a sermon: they "insult him by their insinuations, ridicule him by their vulgar wit," and "excite the mirth of their companions by ludicrous gestures" (*Polynesian Researches* 1:118).

24. Victor Turner has echoed this argument in his own discussions of "the structurally inferior as the morally and ritually superior," and of "secular weakness as sacred power" (*Ritual Process* 125).

CHAPTER 5: THE NOVEL OF CULTURAL SYMBOLISM: *DOCTOR THORNE*

1. In the OED, the first recorded usage of "deep" in the figurative sense of "lying below the surface; not superficial; profound"—as in the phrase "deep structure," let us say—is from the surprisingly late date of 1856. For an ex-

tended analysis of the metaphorics of depth in modern literature, see Jules David Law, *The Reflections of Empiricism: The Rhetoric of Reflection, Surface, and Depth, from Locke to Ruskin,* forthcoming. My thinking in this chapter has been greatly stimulated by Law's fascinating work.

2. This complex of thinking, which links Frazer closely to Freud, exemplifies in all respects the modern *episteme* which Foucault sees emerging around 1800, however remote Evangelical superstition may seem to be from the fields of science and philosophy surveyed in *The Order of Things.*

3. Theorists of realism consistently stressed the centrality of this function. The point is taken up more fully in Herbert, *Trollope and Comic Pleasure* (151–57).

4. Foucault historicizes the same point by describing the novel, in its determined stress on "the secret singularity" of private selves, as the chief literary agency of modern "procedures of individualization" (*Discipline and Punish* 193).

5. This formula applies even to much of Jane Austen, who among classic novelists comes closest to ascribing positive value to sheer social conformity, and to shifting the principal site of fictional dynamics from the private ego to the field of impersonal social patterns. Even in her work, as is broadly true in the great tradition of the British novel, society is typically the realm of conventional, conformist, unselfreflective robots brought forward to be satirized in the name of personal awareness and personal integrity, and the proprieties are usually masks for greed, sadism, stupidity, coldness of heart.

6. As an early instance of this problem, see Beatrice Webb's attempt to justify "the static method" of social analysis against the charge that it is blind to developmental processes (*My Apprenticeship* 252–53, 256).

7. Spencer had made the same claim about the origin of all the departments of culture in primitive religion (*Principles* 2:519); indeed, it is hard to find in Durkheim a single leading idea not previously developed in Spencer.

8. See Lévi-Strauss for the argument that only "the language of symbols" is able to "penetrate the screen of consciousness to carry [its] message directly to the unconscious" (*Structural Anthropology* 200).

9. Cf. Carlyle on much the same theme: "as Time adds much to the sacredness of Symbols, so likewise in his progress he at length defaces, or even desecrates them" (*Sartor Resartus* 210). McLennan's theory of the temporality of symbolism exactly reverses Carlyle's.

10. See Gallagher (*Industrial Reformation* 187–267) for a brilliant study of the linkage between nineteenth-century theories of political and of literary representation.

11. The electioneering scenes in *Doctor Thorne* embody just the state of affairs invoked by Foucault as "a functioning of [cultural] power, distributed throughout the social space; present everywhere as scene, spectacle, sign,

discourse; legible like an open book; operating by a permanent recodification of the mind of the citizens" (*Discipline and Punish* 129–30).

12. This pattern in *Doctor Thorne* is precisely the one analyzed by Geertz in his essay on "Ritual and Social Change" in Java (*Interpretation of Cultures* 142–69).

13. In *My Apprenticeship,* Beatrice Webb analyzes "as a good sociologist should" the upper-class milieu of her late-Victorian girlhood years and lays particular stress on the "continuous uncertainty as to social status" which plagued that society as the result of its lack of "fixed caste barriers." Among the pernicious effects of this state of ambiguous categories, she reports, were "a distressing mental nausea" and cynicism from which few were exempt (Webb 67–75).

14. Harriet Martineau gives just this emphasis to rules as a central focus of anthropological study. "A life without purpose is uncomfortable enough," she says; "but a life without rules would be a wretchedness which, happily, man is not constituted to bear" (*How to Observe* 47).

15. Parodying such reactions to his work in *The Eustace Diamonds,* Trollope highlights the sensation of nausea which is the specific symptom of taboo violations. "Why should one tell the story of creatures so base [as to be unfaithful in love]? One does not willingly grovel in gutters, or breathe fetid atmospheres, or live upon garbage" (*Eustace Diamonds* 315).

16. The case of Oliver Twist, whose endowment of moral propriety and upper-class diction demonstrates the blessed independence of his character from social impurity, forms an especially clear instance of the antisociological trends that Victorian fiction could sponsor and that were repugnant to Trollope. Dickens became subtler in his use of such effects, but they remained crucial to his work. *Great Expectations* deploys them in a systematic way, for instance. Pip's transformation in late adolescence from apprentice to an illiterate blacksmith into a fashionable, educated, urbane young gentleman occurs instantaneously and effortlessly, and although it involves him in moral difficulties, it presents no practical ones at all. There is never a hint that the character features (not to mention grammar, diction, and accent) of a village blacksmith might possess an inertia of their own and offer resistance to such a transformation. We learn from this imaginatively depleted allegory, in which all other fictional effects are subservient to the lesson of the harmfulness of pride and the saving power of love and sympathy, that the sociocultural coordinates of character are trivial surface features at most. (Trollope's version of the same fable in the story of Sir Louis Scatcherd focuses by contrast on the nearly indelible, deep-running character of social characteristics and thus gives the tale of social amphibianism a psychological and existential resonance altogether lacking in Dickens's version.) That this principle rested for Dickens upon a conscious moral ideology is shown in the same novel by the much-elaborated case of Wemmick, the man of two distinct personalities.

The personality which pertains to the public and social sphere of life (specifically, his employment at Mr. Jaggers's chambers) is robot-like, inhumane, and, we discover, ultimately a mere illusion. In his strictly personal self, the kind and morally authentic self which resides in a fantasy of isolation in Walworth (complete with moat and drawbridge to protect him from the corrupting influence of society), Wemmick has absolutely no connection with his other role, which he can set aside at will.

17. On the "disappearance of dimensions of depth in twentieth-century art" and on cognate developments in philosophy, poetry, and literary criticism, see J. Hillis Miller, *Poets of Reality* 9–11.

18. Commenting on Frazer's interpretation of the Beltane fire-festival as the diminished remains of a rite of human sacrifice, Wittgenstein argues that the effect of depth belongs not to practices like this festival in themselves, but to the interpreter's attribution to them of a certain emotional content through the vehicle of a certain historical hypothesis. Should we learn that the true origin of the festival were a perfectly innocuous one after all, "the practice . . . would in fact lose all 'depth'"; "the depth lies solely in the thought of [the festival's] ancestry," not in the ancestry itself, which in fact is usually impossible to determine conclusively. "For when I say: what is deep in this practice lies in its origin, if it *did* come about like that, then either the depth lies in the idea (the thought) of . . . such an origin, or else the depth is itself hypothetical and we can only say: *if* that is how it went, then it was a deep and sinister business. What I want to say is: What is sinister, deep, [lies] . . . in what it is that gives me reason to assume it. . . . *We* impute it from an experience in ourselves" (*Remarks on Frazer's "Golden Bough"* 14e–16e).

19. One text which enacts this key rhetorical operation of cultural anthropology with particular clarity would be Renato Rosaldo's essay "Grief and a Headhunter's Rage" in *Culture and Truth: The Remaking of Social Analysis*. Rosaldo invokes "depth" as his primary analytical category from the start, but at first he encloses it within quotation marks as though to signal its problematic, wholly metaphorical character: "In my efforts to find a 'deeper' explanation for headhunting, I explored exchange theory," he says, for example (Rosaldo 3). But by essay's end he has modulated into an emphatic, unqualified usage of the term, as though its authenticity had somehow been demonstrated. "Cultural depth does not always equal cultural elaboration," he now declares. "Think simply of the speaker who is filibustering. The language used can sound elaborate as it heaps word on word, but surely it is not deep. Depth should be separated from the presence or absence of elaboration. . . . The concept of force calls attention to an enduring intensity in human conduct that can occur with or without the dense elaboration conventionally associated with cultural depth" (Rosaldo 20).

WORKS CITED

Abrams, Philip. *The Origins of British Sociology: 1834–1914.* Chicago and London: University of Chicago Press, 1968.

Archer, Margaret S. *Culture and Agency: The Place of Culture in Social Theory.* Cambridge: Cambridge University Press, 1988.

Arnold, Matthew. *Culture and Anarchy.* Ed. J. Dover Wilson. Cambridge: Cambridge University Press, 1966.

Augé, Marc. *The Anthropological Circle: Symbol, Function, History.* Trans. Martin Thom. Cambridge: Cambridge University Press; Paris: Editions de la Maison des Sciences de l'Homme, 1982.

Austen, Jane. *Sense and Sensibility.* New York: Collier, 1962.

Bagehot, Walter. *Economic Studies.* Ed. Richard Holt Hutton. London: Longmans, 1880.

———. *The English Constitution.* Ed. Forrest Morgan. Hartford: Travelers Insurance, 1889.

———. *Physics and Politics.* Ed. Forrest Morgan. Hartford: Travelers Insurance, 1889.

Bakhtin, M. H. *The Dialogic Imagination: Four Essays.* Ed. Michael Holquist. Trans. Caryl Emerson and Michael Holquist. Austin and London: University of Texas Press, 1981.

Barthes, Roland. *Mythologies.* Trans. Annette Lavers. New York: Hill and Wang, 1983.

———. *S/Z.* Trans. Richard Miller. New York: Hill and Wang, 1974.

Bataille, Georges. "The Notion of Expenditure." In *Visions of Excess: Selected Writings, 1927–1939,* by Georges Bataille, ed. Allan Stoekl, 116–29. Trans. Allan Stoekl, Carl R. Lovitt, and Donald M. Leslie, Jr. Minneapolis: University of Minnesota Press, 1985.

Becker, Ernest. *The Lost Science of Man.* New York: Braziller, 1971.

Benedict, Ruth. *Patterns of Culture.* New York: Mentor, 1946.

Bersani, Leo. *A Future for Astyanax: Character and Desire in Literature.* Boston and Toronto: Little, Brown, 1976.

Blaug, Mark. *Economic Theory in Retrospect.* 3d ed. Cambridge: Cambridge University Press, 1978.

Bloom, Allan. *The Closing of the American Mind.* New York: Simon and Schuster, 1987.

332

WORKS CITED

Boas, Franz. *The Mind of Primitive Man*. Rev. ed. New York: Macmillan, 1938.

——. *Race, Language and Culture*. New York: Free Press; London: Collier, 1940.

Bourdieu, Pierre. *Distinction: A Social Critique of the Judgment of Taste*. Trans. Richard Nice. Cambridge, Mass.: Harvard University Press, 1984.

——. "The Market of Symbolic Goods." *Poetics*, 14 (1985): 13–44.

Brown, William. *New Zealand and its Aborigines*. London: Smith, Elder, 1845.

Bruyn, Severyn T. *The Human Perspective in Sociology: The Methodology of Participant Observation*. Englewood Cliffs: Prentice-Hall, 1966.

Burridge, Kenelm O. L. "Missionary Occasions." In *Mission, Church, and Sect in Oceania*, ed. James A. Boutilier, Daniel T. Hughes, and Sharon W. Tiffany, 1–29. Ann Arbor: University of Michigan Press, 1978.

Burrow, J. W. *Evolution and Society: A Study in Victorian Social Theory*. Cambridge: Cambridge University Press, 1966.

Calvert, James. *Missionary Labours Among the Cannibals*. 4th ed. Ed. George Stringer Rowe. London: Kelly, [1884].

——. "Preface to the Fourth Edition." In *Fiji and the Fijians*, by Thomas Williams, viii–xxii. London: Kelly, [1884].

Caravale, Giovanni and Domenico A. Tosato. *Ricardo and the Theory of Value Distribution and Growth*. London, Boston and Henley: Routledge, 1980.

Carlyle, Thomas. *Sartor Resartus and Selected Prose*. New York: Holt, Rinehart and Winston, 1970.

Clastres, Pierre. *Society against the State: Essays in Political Anthropology*. New York: Zone, 1987.

Clifford, James. "Introduction: Partial Truths." In *Writing Culture: The Poetics and Politics of Ethnography*, ed. James Clifford and George E. Marcus, 1–26. Berkeley, Los Angeles, and London: University of California Press, 1986.

——. "On Ethnographic Authority." *Representations* 1 (1983): 118–46.

——. "On Ethnographic Self-Fashioning: Conrad and Malinowski." In *Reconstructing Individualism: Autonomy, Individuality, and the Self in Western Thought*, ed. Thomas C. Heller, Morton Sosna, and David E. Wellbery. Stanford: Stanford University Press, 1986.

Clifford, James, and George E. Marcus, eds. *Writing Culture: The Poetics and Politics of Ethnography*. Berkeley, Los Angeles, and London: University of California Press, 1986.

Common, Thomas. "Introduction." In *Beyond Good and Evil: Prelude to a Philosophy of the Future*, by Friedrich Nietzsche, vii–xv. New York: Russell and Russell, 1964.

Coser, Lewis A. "Introduction." In *The Division of Labor in Society*, by Emile Durkheim, ix–xxiv. Trans. W. D. Halls. New York: Free Press, 1984.

Culler, Jonathan. *On Deconstruction: Theory and Criticism after Structuralism.* Ithaca: Cornell University Press, 1982.

Cumming, C. F. Gordon. "Introductory Notice." In *Fiji and the Fijians,* by Thomas Williams, v–vii. 4th ed. London: Kelly, [1884].

Darwin, Charles. *On the Origin of Species by Means of Natural Selection, or the Preservation of Favoured Races in the Struggle for Life.* Ed. John Burrow. Harmondsworth: Penguin, 1968.

Davies, John. *The History of the Tahitian Mission, 1799–1830.* Ed. C. W. Newbury. Cambridge: Hakluyt Society, Cambridge University Press, 1961.

de Man, Paul. *Allegories of Reading: Figural Language in Rousseau, Nietzsche, Rilke, and Proust.* New Haven: Yale University Press, 1979.

Derrida, Jacques. *Of Grammatology.* Trans. Gayatri Chakravorty Spivak. Baltimore and London: Johns Hopkins University Press, 1976.

Dickens, Charles. *Martin Chuzzlewit.* New York: Signet, 1965.

Douglas, Mary. *How Institutions Think.* Syracuse: Syracuse University Press, 1986.

———. *Natural Symbols: Explorations in Cosmology.* New York: Pantheon, 1982.

———. *Purity and Danger: An Analysis of Concepts of Pollution and Taboo.* London, Boston and Henley: Routledge, 1966.

Durkheim, Emile. *The Division of Labor in Society.* Trans. W. D. Halls. New York: Free Press, 1984.

———. *The Elementary Forms of the Religious Life.* Trans. Joseph Ward Swain. New York: Free Press; London: Collier, 1965.

———. *Moral Education: A Study in the Theory and Application of the Sociology of Education.* Trans. Everett K. Wilson and Herman Schnurer. New York: Free Press, 1961.

———. *The Rules of Sociological Method.* Ed. Steven Lukes. Trans. W. D. Halls. New York: Free Press, 1982.

———. *Selected Writings.* Ed. and trans. Anthony Giddens. Cambridge: Cambridge University Press, 1972.

———. *Suicide: A Study in Sociology.* Ed. George Simpson. Trans. John A. Spaulding and George Simpson. New York: Free Press, 1951.

Durkheim, Emile, and Marcel Mauss. *Primitive Classification.* Ed. and trans. Rodney Needham. Chicago: University of Chicago Press, 1963.

Eliot, George. *The Mill on the Floss.* Ed. Gordon S. Haight. Boston: Houghton Mifflin, 1961.

———. *The Spanish Gypsy, The Legend of Jubal, and Other Poems, Old and New.* New York: Nelson, 1906.

Ellis, William. *Polynesian Researches, During a Residence of Nearly Six Years in the South Sea Islands.* 2 vols. London: Fisher, 1829.

Engels, Friedrich. *The Condition of the Working Class in England.* Trans. and ed.

W. O. Henderson and W. H. Chaloner. Stanford: Stanford University Press, 1968.

Evans-Pritchard, E. E. *A History of Anthropological Thought.* Ed. André Singer. New York: Basic Books, 1981.

————. *The Nuer: A Description of the Modes of Livelihood and Political Institutions of a Nilotic People.* New York and Oxford: Oxford University Press, 1982.

————. *Social Anthropology and Other Essays.* New York: Free Press, 1962.

Fleck, Ludwik. *Genesis and Development of a Scientific Fact.* Ed. Thaddeus J. Trenn and Robert K. Merton. Trans. Fred Bradley and Thaddeus J. Trenn. Chicago and London: University of Chicago Press, 1979.

Foucault, Michel. *Discipline and Punish: The Birth of the Prison.* Trans. Alan Sheridan. New York: Vintage, 1979.

————. *The History of Sexuality,* Volume I: *An Introduction.* Trans. Robert Hurley. New York: Vintage, 1980.

————. *The Order of Things: An Archaeology of the Human Sciences.* New York: Vintage, 1973.

Frazer, James George. *The Golden Bough: A Study in Magic and Religion.* 3d ed. 12 vols. London: Macmillan, 1917.

Freud, Sigmund. *The Standard Edition of the Complete Psychological Works of Sigmund Freud.* Trans. James Strachey, Anna Freud, Alix Strachey, and Alan Tyson. 24 vols. London: Hogarth, 1953–74.

Gallagher, Catherine. "The Body Versus the Social Body in the Works of Thomas Malthus and Henry Mayhew." *Representations* 14 (1986): 83–106.

————. *The Industrial Reformation of English Fiction: Social Discourse and Narrative Form, 1832–1867.* Chicago and London: University of Chicago Press, 1985.

Gay, Peter. *Education of the Senses.* New York and Oxford: Oxford University Press, 1984.

Geertz, Clifford. "Distinguished Lecture: Anti Anti-Relativism." *American Anthropologist* 86 (1984): 263–78.

————. *The Interpretation of Cultures.* New York: Basic Books, 1973.

————. "Under the Mosquito Net." *New York Review of Books,* 14 September 1967, 12–13.

————. *Works and Lives: The Anthropologist as Author.* Stanford: Stanford University Press, 1988.

Gellner, Ernest. *Thought and Change.* London: Weidenfeld, 1964.

Glass, Ruth. "Urban Sociology in Great Britain: A Trend Report." *Current Sociology* 4 (1955): 5–19, 27–76.

Gregor, Thomas. *Anxious Pleasures: The Sexual Lives of an Amazonian People.* Chicago and London: University of Chicago Press, 1985.

Hardy, Thomas. *Jude the Obscure*. New York: Signet, 1961.

Harris, Marvin. *The Rise of Anthropological Theory: A History of Theories of Culture*. New York: Crowell, 1968.

Herbert, Christopher. "Rat Worship and Taboo in Mayhew's London." *Representations* 23 (1988): 1–24.

———. *Trollope and Comic Pleasure*. Chicago and London: University of Chicago Press, 1987.

Himmelfarb, Gertrude. "Introduction." In *On Population,* by Thomas Robert Malthus, xiii–xxxvi. New York: Modern Library, 1960.

———. "Mayhew's Poor: A Problem of Identity." *Victorian Studies* 14 (1971): 307–20.

Hobbes, Thomas. *Leviathan: Or the Matter, Forme and Power of a Commonwealth Ecclesiasticall and Civil*. Ed. Michael Oakeshott. New York and London: Collier, 1962.

Hodgen, Margaret T. *The Doctrine of Survivals: A Chapter in the History of Scientific Method in the Study of Man*. London: Allenson, 1936.

Hsu, Francis L. K. "The Cultural Problem of the Cultural Anthropologist." *American Anthropologist* 81 (1979): 517–32.

Hughes, Everett C. "Introduction: The Place of Field Work in Social Science." In *Field Work: An Introduction to the Social Sciences,* by Buford H. Junker, v–xv. Chicago and London: University of Chicago Press, 1960.

Hughes, Robert. *The Fatal Shore*. New York: Vintage, 1988.

Hume, David. *A Treatise of Human Nature*. Ed. L. A. Selby-Bigge and P. H. Nidditch. 2d ed. Oxford: Clarendon, 1978.

Humpherys, Anne. *Henry Mayhew*. Boston: Twayne, 1984.

———. *Travels into the Poor Man's Country: The Work of Henry Mayhew*. Athens, Ga.: University of Georgia Press, 1977.

Hunt, Lynne, ed. *The New Cultural History*. Berkeley, Los Angeles, London: University of California Press, 1989.

Huxley, T. H., and Julian Huxley. *Evolution and Ethics: 1893–1943*. London: Pilot, 1947.

Itard, Jean. *The Wild Boy of Aveyron*. Trans. Joan White. London: NLB, 1972.

James, Patricia. *Population Malthus: His Life and Times*. London: Routledge, 1979.

Jarvie, I. C. *Thinking about Society: Theory and Practice*. Dordrecht: Reidel, 1986.

Jay, Elisabeth. *Religion of the Heart: Anglican Evangelicalism and the Nineteenth-Century Novel*. Oxford: Clarendon; New York: Oxford University Press, 1979.

Junker, Buford H. *Field Work: An Introduction to the Social Sciences*. Chicago and London: University of Chicago Press, 1960.

336

Kroeber, A. L., and Kluckhohn, Clyde. *Culture: A Critical Review of Concepts and Definitions*. New York: Vintage, n.d.

Kuhn, Thomas S. *The Structure of Scientific Revolutions*. 2d ed. Chicago and London: University of Chicago Press, 1970.

Kuper, Adam. *The Invention of Primitive Society: Transformations of an Illusion*. London and New York: Routledge, 1988.

Leach, E. R. "On Reading *A Diary in the Strict Sense of the Term*: Or the Self-Mutilation of Professor Hsu." *Rain* 36 (1980): 2–3.

———. *Rethinking Anthropology*. London: University of London, Athlone, 1961.

Lemert, Edwin M. "Social Structure, Social Control, and Deviation." In *Anomie and Deviant Behavior: A Discussion and Critique*, ed. Marshall B. Clinard, 57–97. New York: Free Press; London: Macmillan, 1964.

Lepenies, Wolf. *Between Literature and Science: The Rise of Sociology*. Trans. R. J. Hollingdale. Cambridge: Cambridge University Press; Paris: Editions de la Maison Des Sciences de l'Homme, 1988.

Lévi-Strauss, Claude. *Introduction to the Work of Marcel Mauss*. Trans. Felicity Baker. London: Routledge, 1987.

———. *The Raw and the Cooked: Introduction to a Science of Mythology*, Volume 1. Trans. John and Doreen Weightman. Chicago: University of Chicago Press, 1969.

———. *The Scope of Anthropology*. Trans. Sherry Ortner Paul and Robert A. Paul. London: Cape, 1967.

———. *Structural Anthropology*. Trans. Claire Jacobson and Brooke Grundfest Schoepf. New York: Basic Books, 1963.

———. *Tristes Tropiques*. Trans. John and Doreen Weightman. New York: Atheneum, 1981.

Lewis, Norman. *The Missionaries*. New York: McGraw-Hill, 1988.

Lovett, Richard. *The History of the London Missionary Society, 1795–1895*. 2 vols. London: Frowde, 1899.

Lowie, Robert H. *The History of Ethnological Theory*. New York: Holt, 1937.

———. *Primitive Society*. New York: Boni and Liveright, 1920.

Lubbock, John. *The Origin of Civilisation and the Primitive Condition of Man*. Ed. Peter Rivière. Chicago and London: University of Chicago Press, 1978.

Macfie, A. L. *The Individual in Society: Papers on Adam Smith*. London: Allen and Unwin, 1967.

Malinowski, Bronislaw. *Argonauts of the Western Pacific: An Account of Native Enterprise and Adventure in the Archipelagoes of Melanesian New Guinea*. London: Routledge; New York: Dutton, 1932.

———. *A Diary in the Strict Sense of the Term*. New York: Harcourt, 1967.

————. *A Scientific Theory of Culture and Other Essays*. Chapel Hill: University of North Carolina Press, 1944.

————. *Sex and Repression in Savage Society*. Chicago: University of Chicago Press, 1985.

Malson, Lucien. *Wolf Children*. Trans. Edmund Fawcett, Peter Ayrton, and Joan White. London: NLB, 1972.

Malthus, Thomas Robert. *The Works of Thomas Robert Malthus*. Ed. E. A. Wrigley and David Souden. 8 vols. London: Pickering, 1986.

Manicas, Peter T. *A History and Philosophy of the Social Sciences*. Oxford and New York: Blackwell, 1987.

Marcus, George E. "Contemporary Problems of Ethnography in the Modern World System." In *Writing Culture: The Poetics and Politics of Ethnography*, ed. James Clifford and George E. Marcus, 165–93. Berkeley, Los Angeles, and London: University of California Press, 1986.

Mariner, William. See John Martin, *An Account of the Natives of the Tonga Islands*.

Martin, John. *An Account of the Natives of the Tonga islands*. 3d ed. 2 vols. Edinburgh: Constable; Londen: Hurst, 1827. Rpt. New York: AMS, 1979.

Martineau, Harriet. *How to Observe: Morals and Manners*. New York: Harper, 1838.

Mauss, Marcel. *The Gift: Forms and Functions of Exchange in Archaic Societies*. Trans. Ian Cunnison. New York and London: Norton, 1967.

Mayhew, Henry. *London Labour and the London Poor: A Cyclopaedia of the Condition and Earnings of Those That Will Work, Those That Cannot Work, and Those That Will Not Work*. 4 vols. London: Griffin, 1861–62. Rpt. New York: Dover, 1968.

McLennan, John F. *Primitive Marriage: An Inquiry into the Origin of the Form of Capture in Marriage Ceremonies*. Ed. Peter Rivière. Chicago and London: University of Chicago Press, 1970.

————. *Studies in Ancient History: The Second Series: Comprising an Inquiry into the Origin of Exogamy*. London and New York: Macmillan, 1896.

————. "The Worship of Animals and Plants." *Fortnightly Review* 7 (1870): 194–216.

Merton, Robert K. *Social Theory and Social Structure*. Rev. ed. New York: Free Press, 1957.

Mill, John Stuart. *On Bentham and Coleridge*. New York: Harper, 1962.

————. *Essays on Some Unsettled Questions of Political Economy*. 3d ed. London: Longmans, 1877.

————. *On Liberty*. Ed. Alburey Castell. New York: Appleton-Century-Crofts, 1947.

————. *Principles of Political Economy, With Some of Their Applications to Social Philosophy.* 2 vols. Boston: Little, Brown, 1848.

Miller, J. Hillis. *Poets of Reality: Six Twentieth-Century Writers.* New York: Atheneum, 1967.

Murdock, George Peter. *Social Structure.* New York: Free Press; London: Collier, 1949.

Myers, Milton L. *The Soul of Modern Economic Man: Ideas of Self-Interest: Thomas Hobbes to Adam Smith.* Chicago and London: University of Chicago Press, 1983.

Nietzsche, Friedrich. *Beyond Good and Evil: Prelude to a Philosophy of the Future.* Trans. Helen Zimmern. New York: Russell and Russell, 1964.

————. "On Truth and Falsity in Their Ultramoral Sense." *Early Greek Philosophy and Other Essays,* by Friedrich Nietzsche. Trans. Maximilian A. Mügge. New York: Russell and Russell, 1964.

Nord, Deborah Epstein. "The Social Explorer as Anthropologist: Victorian Travellers Among the Urban Poor." In *Visions of the Modern City,* ed. William Sharpe and Leonard Wallock, 118–30. New York: Columbia University, 1983.

Paulson, Ronald. *Representations of Revolution, 1789–1820.* New Haven: Yale University Press, 1983.

Peel, J. D. Y. "Introduction." In *On Social Evolution,* by Herbert Spencer. Chicago and London: University of Chicago Press, 1972.

Poe, Edgar Allan. *Narrative of A. Gordon Pym.* In *The Complete Tales and Poems of Edgar Allan Poe,* 748–883. New York: Modern Library, 1938.

Powdermaker, Hortense. *Stranger and Friend: The Way of an Anthropologist.* New York: Norton, 1966.

Pratt, Mary Louise. "Fieldwork in Common Places." In *Writing Culture: The Poetics and Politics of Ethnography,* ed. James Clifford and George E. Marcus, 27–50. Berkeley, Los Angeles, and London: University of California Press, 1986.

Prichard, James Cowles. *Researches into the Physical History of Mankind.* 3d ed. 5 vols. London: Sherwood, 1836–47.

————. *A Treatise on Insanity and Other Disorders Affecting the Mind.* London: Sherwood, 1835.

Raban, Jonathan. *For Love and Money: A Writing Life, 1969–1989.* New York: Harper and Row, 1989.

Radcliffe-Brown, A. R. "On Social Structure." *Journal of the Royal Anthropological Institute* 70 (1940): 1–12.

Raphael, D. D. and A. L. Macfie. "Introduction." In *The Theory of Moral Sentiments,* by Adam Smith, 1–52. Oxford: Clarendon, 1976.

Reisman, D. A. *Adam Smith's Sociological Economics*. London: Croom Helm; New York: Barnes and Noble, 1976.

Ricardo, David. *The Works and Correspondence of David Ricardo*. Ed. Piero Sraffa and M. H. Dobb. 9 vols. Cambridge: Cambridge University Press, 1952.

Robinson, Joan. *Economic Philosophy*. Chicago: Aldine, 1962.

Rorty, Richard. "Solidarity or Objectivity?" In *Post-Analytic Philosophy*, ed. John Rajchman and Cornel West, 3–19. New York: Columbia University Press, 1985.

Rosaldo, Renato. *Culture and Truth: The Remaking of Social Analysis*. Boston: Beacon, 1989.

Rousseau, Jean-Jacques. *The Confessions*. Trans. J. M. Cohen. Harmondsworth: Penguin, 1971.

Saussure, Ferdinand de. *Course in General Linguistics*. Ed. Charles Bally, Albert Sechehaye, and Albert Riedlinger. Trans. Wade Baskin. New York, Toronto, London: McGraw-Hill, 1966.

Seltzer, Mark. *Henry James and the Art of Power*. Ithaca and London: Cornell University Press, 1984.

Shortland, Edward. *The Southern Districts of New Zealand: A Journal, with Passing Notices of the Customs of the Aborigines*. London: Longman, 1851.

———. *Traditions and Superstitions of the New Zealanders: With Illustrations of their Manners and Customs*. London: Longman, 1854.

Simmel, Georg. "Exchange." In *On Individuality and Social Forms*, by Georg Simmel, ed. Donald N. Levine, 43–69. Chicago and London: University of Chicago Press, 1971.

Singh, J. A. L. and Robert M. Zingg. *Wolf-Children and Feral Man*. New York and London: Harper, n.d.

Smalley, Donald. *Trollope: The Critical Heritage*. London: Routledge; New York: Barnes and Noble, 1969.

Smith, Adam. "The History of Astronomy." In *Essays on Philosophical Subjects*, by Adam Smith, ed. W. P. D. Wightman and J. C. Bryce, 31–105. Oxford: Clarendon, 1980.

———. *An Inquiry into the Nature and Causes of the Wealth of Nations*. Ed. Edwin Cannan. Chicago: University of Chicago Press, 1976.

———. *The Theory of Moral Sentiments*. Ed. D. D. Raphael and A. L. Macfie. Oxford: Clarendon, 1976.

Smith, Barbara Herrnstein. *Contingencies of Value: Alternative Perspectives for Critical Theory*. Cambridge, Mass.: Harvard University Press, 1988.

Smith, Bernard. *European Vision and the South Pacific, 1768–1850*. 2d ed. New Haven and London: Yale University Press, 1985.

Smith, F. B. "Mayhew's Convict." *Victorian Studies* 22 (1979): 431–38.

Smith, Marian W. "Boas' 'Natural History' Approach to Field Method." In *The Anthropology of Franz Boas: Essays on the Centennial of His Birth,* ed. Walter Goldschmidt. *The American Anthropologist* 61 (1959): 46–60.

Smith, V. E. "Malthus's Theory of Demand and its Influence on Value Theory." *Scottish Journal of Political Economy* 3 (1956): 205–20.

Smith, W. Robertson. *The Religion of the Semites: The Fundamental Institutions.* New York: Schocken, 1972.

Southey, Robert. *The Life of Wesley and the Rise and Progress of Methodism.* Ed. Maurice H. Fitzgerald. 2 vols. London: Oxford University Press, Humphrey Milford, 1925.

Spencer, Herbert. *The Principles of Sociology.* 3d ed. 3 vols. London: Williams and Norgate, 1897–1906. Rpt. Westport, Conn.: Greenwood, 1975.

———. *The Study of Sociology.* 22d ed. London: Kegan Paul, n.d.

Sperber, Dan. *On Anthropological Knowledge: Three Essays.* Cambridge: Cambridge University Press; Paris: Editions de la Maison des Sciences de l'Homme, 1982.

Stark, Werner. *The Social Bond: An Investigation into the Bases of Law-Abidingness.* 6 vols. New York: Fordham University Press, 1976.

Stocking, George W., Jr. "The Ethnographer's Magic: Fieldwork in British Anthropology from Tylor to Malinowski." In *Observers Observed: Essays on Ethnographic Fieldwork,* ed. Geroge W. Stocking, Jr., 70–120. Madison and London: University of Wisconsin Press, 1983.

———. "From Chronology to Ethnology: James Cowles Prichard and British Anthropology 1800–1850." In *Researches into the Physical History of Man,* by James Cowles Prichard, ix–cx. Chicago and London: University of Chicago Press, 1973.

———. *Race, Culture, and Evolution: Essays in the History of Anthropology.* Chicago and London: University of Chicago Press, 1982.

———. *Victorian Anthropology.* New York: Free Press; London: Collier, 1987.

Taylor, W. Cooke. *The Natural History of Society in the Barbarous and Civilized State: An Essay Towards Discovering the Origin and Course of Human Improvement.* 2 vols. London: Longman, 1840.

Thompson, E. P. *The Making of the English Working Class.* New York: Vintage, 1966.

Thomson, Basil. *The Fijians: A Study of the Decay of Custom.* London: Dawsons, 1968.

Trollope, Anthony. *An Autobiography.* London, New York, Toronto: Oxford University Press, 1950.

———. *Doctor Thorne.* London: Dent; New York: Dutton, 1967.

———. *The Eustace Diamonds.* New York: Modern Library, 1947.

341

Turner, George. *Nineteen Years in Polynesia: Missionary Life, Travels, and Researches in the Islands of the Pacific.* London: Snow, 1861.

Turner, Victor. *The Ritual Process: Structure and Anti-Structure.* Chicago: Aldine, 1969.

Tyler, Stephen A. "Post-Modern Ethnography: From Document of the Occult to Occult Document." In *Writing Culture: The Poetics and Politics of Ethnography*, ed. James Clifford and George E. Marcus, 122–40. Berkeley, Los Angeles, London: University of California Press, 1986.

Tylor, Edward B. "Anthropology." *Encyclopaedia Britannica.* 11th ed. London and New York: 1910–11.

———. *Anthropology: An Introduction to the Study of Man and Civilization.* New York and London: Appleton, 1923.

———. *Primitive Culture: Researches into the Development of Mythology, Philosophy, Religion, Language, Art, and Custom.* 2 vols. London: Murray; New York: Putnam, 1920.

———. *Researches into the Early History of Mankind and the Development of Civilization.* Ed. Paul Bohannan. Chicago and London: University of Chicago Press, 1964.

———. "Wild Men and Beast-Children." *The Anthropological Review* 1 (1863): 21–32.

Voget, Fred W. *A History of Ethnology.* New York: Holt, Rinehart and Winston, 1975.

Wagner, Roy. *The Invention of Culture.* Englewood Cliffs, N. J.: Prentice-Hall, 1975.

Watt, Ian. *The Rise of the Novel: Studies in Defoe, Richardson and Fielding.* Berkeley and Los Angeles: University of California Press, 1964.

Wax, Rosalie H. *Doing Fieldwork: Warnings and Advice.* Chicago and London: University of Chicago Press, 1971.

Webb, Beatrice. *My Apprenticeship.* Harmondsworth: Penguin, 1971.

Weber, Max. *The Protestant Ethic and the Spirit of Capitalism.* Trans. Talcott Parsons. London: Unwin, 1985.

Welch, Claude. *Protestant Thought in the Nineteenth Century.* 2 vols. New Haven and London: Yale University Press, 1972.

Wesley, John. *Wesley's Standard Sermons.* Ed. Edward H. Sugden. 5th ed. 2 vols. London: Epworth, 1964.

———. *Works.* 3d ed. 14 vols. London: Mason, 1829–31.

Whatley, Richard. "On the Origin of Civilisation." In *Lectures Delivered before the Young Men's Christian Association from November 1854 to February 1855*, 3–36. London: Nisbet, 1879.

Wightman, W. P. D. "Introduction." In *Essays on Philosophical Subjects*, by Adam Smith, 5–27. Oxford: Clarendon, 1980.

WORKS CITED

Williams, John. *A Narrative of Missionary Enterprises in the South Sea Islands: With Remarks Upon the Natural History of the Islands, Origin, Languages, Traditions, and Usages of the Inhabitants.* London: Snow, 1837.

Williams, Raymond. *Culture and Society, 1780–1950.* New York: Columbia University Press, 1983.

———. *Marxism and Literature.* Oxford: Oxford University Press, 1977.

Williams, T. R. *Field Methods in the Study of Culture.* New York: Holt, 1967.

Williams, Thomas. *Fiji and the Fijians.* Ed. George Stringer Rowe. 4th ed. London: Kelly, [1884].

Winch, Donald. *Malthus.* Oxford and New York: Oxford University Press, 1987.

Wittgenstein, Ludwig. *Remarks on Frazer's "Golden Bough."* Ed. Rush Rhees. Trans. A. C. Miles and Rush Rhees. Retford: Brynmill, 1979.

Wordsworth, William. "Ode to Duty." In *The Poetical Works of Wordsworth.* Ed. Thomas Hutchinson and Ernest de Selincourt. London: Oxford University Press, 1961.

Yeo, Eileen. "Mayhew as a Social Investigator." In *The Unknown Mayhew: Selections from the "Morning Chronicle," 1849–1850,* ed. E. P. Thompson and Eileen Yeo, 51–95. New York: Schocken, 1972.

Zingg, Robert M. "Feral Man and Cases of Extreme Isolation of Individuals." In *Wolf-Children and Feral Man,* by J. A. L. Singh and Robert M. Zingg. New York and London: Harper, n.d.

INDEX

Durkheim, Emile *(continued)*
144; on liberty, 54; on psychology, 132; relativism of, 324 n.
35; and Adam Smith, 104; society divinized by, 56–57; and
Spencer, 13, 328 n. 7; on totemic marking, 316 n. 12; and
Trollope, 266, 267–68, 274,
277; and Wesley, 55, 255, 300;
The Division of Labor in Society,
54, 69; *The Elementary Forms of
the Religious Life*, 6, 263–64,
296, 312 n. 6; *Moral Education*,
60, 71–73, 104, 241, 292; *The
Rules of Sociological Method*, 5,
13, 16–17, 40, 69, 258–59, 282,
324 n. 35; *Socialism*, 71; *Suicide*,
70, 101, 317 n. 19

Earnestness: Victorian cult of, 30
Economic man. See *Homo economicus*
Economics, 69–70, 90, 91, 105, 123,
223. *See also* Political economy
Economic Studies. See Bagehot, Walter
Einstein, Albert, 11
*Elementary Forms of the Religious Life,
The. See* Durkheim, Emile
Eliot, George (Marian Evans): *Middlemarch*, 257, 258; *The Mill on
the Floss*, 33; *The Spanish Gypsy*,
33, 325 n. 9
Eliot, T. S., 22
Ellis, William, 156, 158, 283, 313 n.
17, 320 n. 10, 327 n. 23; on
Areoi societies, 210, 213; on disciplining primitive people, 44;
on Christian new birth, 173;
ethnographic ambivalence of,
166–69; on fieldwork, 174; and
Frazer, 135–36; on learning
Tahitian, 186; on Polynesian depravity, 159–61, 179–80, 208–9;
on Polynesian superstition,
171–72, 199–201, 233; on the

system of Tahitian culture, 187–
91, 197, 201–2
Empathy. *See* Sympathy
Empirical observation, 35, 57, 65,
156, 257, 311 n. 19; Bagehot
on, 142, 144; and "depth," 255,
256, 299; in ethnography, 8, 14,
53, 150, 160–61, 163, 227; Fleck
on, 4; Geertz's belief in, 17–18;
Lévi-Strauss on, 14, 17; and
Mayhew, 209, 231; problematic
status of, 10, 12, 27, 73, 133,
143; and Adam Smith, 82; in
early sociology, 13; in Thomas
Williams, 177–78. *See also* Fact
Empson, William, 26
Encyclopaedia Britannica, 51
Engels, Friedrich, 326 n.18
English Constitution, The. See
Bagehot, Walter
Enlightenment, the: and theory of
culture, 61, 74
Episteme, 38, 41, 137; Foucault on,
30, 31, 310–11 n. 19
Equilibrium: in classical economics,
126; natural, 105; social, 100–
101; unstable, 139
Eros, 83, 315 n. 9
*Essay on the Principle of Population,
An. See* Malthus, Thomas Robert
Ethnocentrism, 2, 3
Ethnographic subjectivity, 170, 177,
192, 193–94; defined, 158; and
modernist self-alienation, 232
Ethnography, 43, 87, 108, 151, 255;
and exploitation, 155; as interpretation of symbolism, 197;
Martineau's recipe for, 191;
Mayhew's new mode of, 221–
32; and original sin, 53; origin
myth of, 151; participant observation in, 67–68; problem of
data glut in, 193–94; and psychic change, 172–84; value-neu-

352

INDEX

Individuality *(continued)*
  capitalism, 71; Malinowski on,
  43; Mill on, 54; novelistic principle of, 258–59, 266; in science,
  73; Trollope on, 284, 285, 292–97
Infanticide: Malthus on, 108, 109–
  10; in Mayhew, 211, 212; in
  Polynesia, 160, 175, 176, 213
Infinite regress. *See* Regress, infinite
Influence, 25, 26, 27
Instinct, 36, 40, 58, 62, 194; aggressive, 84; of exchange, 94; of imitativeness, Bagehot on, 140–43,
  145, 147; Malthus on, 114, 122;
  Mayhew on, 209, 234; in nineteenth-century moral ideology,
  298; in social theory, 35–36, 39,
  184; Trollope on, 269, 288
Institution, 129, 130–31, 228, 259
Intellectual history. *See* History, in-
  tellectual
Internalization, 40
Interpretation, 25, 88, 232; in eth-
  nography, 153–54, 163, 189–91,
  200–201, 204; in Mayhew, 230,
  251; in social science, 38, 261.
  See also Meaning; Symbolism
Interpretation of Cultures, The. See
  Geertz, Clifford
Intimacy, cultural, 163–65, 173, 175–
  76, 181, 198. *See also* Fieldwork;
  Participant observation; Sympa-
  thy: in ethnographic fieldwork
*Introduction to the Work of Marcel
  Mauss. See* Lévi-Strauss, Claude
Invention of Culture, The. See Wagner,
  Roy
Invisibility, 14, 16, 255–56, 308 n.
  11; Foucault on, 10, 264; Spen-
  cer on, 11, 12
Itard, Jean, 48–51, 52, 55, 59, 112;
  on desire, 71, 101, 127; on
  human nature, 61, 251, 296. *See
  also* Victor of Aveyron

Jack Sheppard (Ainsworth), 240
Jamaican rebellion (1865), 32–33
James, Patricia, 113, 118
Jarvie, I. C., 320 n. 8, 321 n. 20
Jay, Elisabeth, 311 n. 1
Joyce, James, 298
Jude the Obscure (Hardy), 213
Junker, Buford H., 172, 186, 319 n. 5

Kluckhohn, Clyde, 2, 21
Kroeber, A. L., 2, 21
Kuhn, Thomas S., 4, 30, 65, 224
Kuper, Adam, 311 n. 20
Kurtz, Mr. (in *Heart of Darkness*), 154

Labor, division of, 100, 103, 107
Labor theory of value. *See* Value
Lamarck, Chevalier de, 143
Land: in Mill's political economy, 76
Language: and ethnography, 164,
  165, 185–88, 301; Mayhew on,
  242–43; Polynesian,168, 203.
  See also Linguistics
Law, Jules D., 327–28 n. 1
Law, 48, 85, 139, 282–83; divine, 41;
  economic, 101, 116, 233; in
  primitive society, 64–65, 67;
  and social theory, 42, 68, 253
Leach, E. R., 150, 174, 320 n. 7
*Lectures on Justice, Police, Revenue and
  Arms. See* Smith, Adam
Leibniz, Baron Gottfried von, 315
  n. 6
Lemert, Edwin W., 2
Lepenies, Wolf, 257, 308 n. 10
Leviathan. See Hobbes, Thomas
Lévi-Strauss, Claude, 17, 229, 296,
  322 n. 27, 328 n. 8; and the culture concept, 17, 161, 201, 205;
  on fieldwork, 14, 172, 184; on
  human evolution, 314 n. 21,
  319 n. 38; on modern cultural
  analysis, 17, 43; on relativism,
  178, 184; *Introduction to the Work*